POCKET GUIDE TO INTERPERSONAL NEUROBIOLOGY
POCKET GUIDE TO INTERPERSONAL NEUROBIOLOGY

THE NORTON SERIES ON INTERPERSONAL NEUROBIOLOGY

Allan N. Schore, PhD, Series Editor
Daniel J. Siegel, MD, Founding Editor

The field of mental health is in a tremendously exciting period of growth and conceptual reorganization. Independent findings from a variety of scientific endeavors are converging in an interdisciplinary view of the mind and mental well-being. An interpersonal neurobiology of human development enables us to understand that the structure and function of the mind and brain are shaped by experiences, especially those involving emotional relationships.

The Norton Series on Interpersonal Neurobiology provides cutting-edge, multidisciplinary views that further our understanding of the complex neurobiology of the human mind. By drawing on a wide range of traditionally independent fields of research—such as neurobiology, genetics, memory, attachment, complex systems, anthropology, and evolutionary psychology—these texts offer mental health professionals a review and synthesis of scientific findings often inaccessible to clinicians. These books aim to advance our understanding of human experience by finding the unity of knowledge, or consilience, that emerges with the translation of findings from numerous domains of study into a common language and conceptual framework. The series integrates the best of modern science with the healing art of psychotherapy.

A NORTON PROFESSIONAL BOOK

DANIEL J. SIEGEL, MD

POCKET GUIDE TO INTERPERSONAL NEUROBIOLOGY

An Integrative Handbook of the Mind

W. W. NORTON & COMPANY

New York • London

For information about permission to reproduce selections from this book, write to Permissions, W. W. Norton & Company, Inc., 500 Fifth Avenue, New York, NY 10110

For information about special discounts for bulk purchases, please contact W. W. Norton Special Sales at specialsales@wwnorton.com or 800-233-4830

Manufacturing by Quad Graphics Fairfield
Digital production: Joe Lops
Production manager: Leeann Graham

Library of Congress Cataloging-in-Publication Data

Siegel, Daniel J., 1957–
Pocket guide to interpersonal neurobiology :
an integrative handbook of the mind / Daniel J. Siegel. — 1st ed.
p. cm. — (The Norton series on interpersonal neurobiology)
Includes bibliographical references and index.
ISBN 978-0-393-70713-7 (pbk.)
1. Neuropsychology. 2. Thought and thinking—Physiological aspects.
3. Interpersonal relations. 4. Brain—Localization of functions. I. Title.
QP360.S4853 2012
612.8—dc23

2011044216

ISBN: 978-0-393-70713-7 (pbk.)

W. W. Norton & Company, Inc.,
500 Fifth Avenue, New York, N.Y. 10110

www.wwnorton.com

W. W. Norton & Company Ltd., 15 Carlisle Street, London W1D 3BS

6 7 8 9 0

FOR ALEX

CONTENTS
CONTENTS

REFLECTIONS AND ACKNOWLEDGMENTS

REFLECTIONS AND ACKNOWLEDGMENTS

Thank you for joining me on this journey into the nature of the mind! Weaving the entries of the *Pocket Guide* together to reveal the sphere of knowledge underlying Interpersonal Neurobiology has been an exciting challenge, and I hope you will find that this exploration of mind, brain, and relationships is of value in your professional as well as personal life. Building and being a part of a community of people who nurture integration and well-being in our world is one of the most rewarding endeavors in which I've been fortunate to participate. Whether we are together in person at our monthly seminars and the annual IPNB conference at UCLA, or online in our global mindsight community, sharing this journey to bring more compassion and kindness into the world is a profound privilege.

Creating a common ground in which to bring science and subjectivity into a deep and respectful discussion with each other has been a wonderful conversation to facilitate over these last two decades. Our interdisciplinary community continues to grow, and I am deeply grateful to the many people who have been a part of this emerging new approach to understanding the mind and promoting mental health in the world.

The Mindsight Institute is a wonderful home for Interpersonal Neurobiology, a place where it has been nurtured to grow and develop. Caroline Welch has been a powerful presence in our work and organizing the Institute and moving it to a new level of outreach in the world. Eric Bergemann, Tina Bryson, Erica Ellis, and Aubrey Siegel are mental health professionals who were a part of the institute from the beginning. Stephanie Hamilton and Whitney Stambler offer regular support for our many programs, nearby and around the planet. The many members of the Global Association for Interpersonal Neurobiology Studies (MindGAINS.org) are a continual source of stimulation and encouragement. Bonnie Goldstein and Marion Solomon of the Lifespan Institute have been of invaluable support in the creation of the annual Interpersonal Neurobiology Conference held in collaboration with UCLA. Deborah Malmud, Vice President and Director of Norton Professional Books, has been of great support in working with me to create the Norton Series on Interpersonal Neurobiology. She has great insights into what the field of mental health has needed. Working together to develop the series over this past decade has been an honor and a pleasure. Vani Kannan, the Associate Managing Editor of Norton Professional Books, has also been of great assistance. I would also like to thank Allan Schore for serving as the Series Editor in recent years.

In the creation of this book, Lee Freedman, Laura Hubber, Lynn Kutler, Sally Maslansky, Adit Shah, Aubrey Siegel, and Caroline Welch offered invaluable comments regarding the whole manuscript. The Norton Interpersonal Neurobiology authors Bonnie Badenoch, Lou Cozolino, Pat Ogden, Steve Porges, and Ed Tronick were so generous with their time in reviewing the annotated index and nodal network and offering helpful suggestions. I thank each of these individuals for their devotion to this work, and their support of this unusual approach to presenting knowledge in our field. And our wonderful drawings are the result of the combined artistic work of David G. Moore (the drawings of the hand model and of the brain in figures D-1, 2, and 3), and Madeleine W. Siegel, aka MAWS, and company.

The approach of the *Pocket Guide* has been to weave an integrated handbook of the mind in a non-linear way so that the reader, you, could make this sphere of knowledge your own. The discussions in this book of the concepts and scientific principles, the research findings, and the facts, have been possible only because of the hard, painstaking work of a wide range of researchers from over a dozen different disciplines of science. As described in the introduction, the references to those thousands of studies can be found in the many other Norton Interpersonal Neurobiology texts, as well as the second edition of *The Developing Mind*. Here, I would like to acknowledge the gifts of those scientists whose shoulders we stand upon in Interpersonal Neurobiology. It is their work that creates the foundation for us to build this interdisciplinary view of mind, brain, and relationships, and to attempt to create new ways to define the mind and to bring more well-being into the world. Finding the universal principles across many academic fields, discovering the consilience that emerges when usually independent research endeavors are explored together, has been an exciting challenge at the heart of creating this integrative approach. I hope you'll find that this effort has born fruit, and that you and all of the people in the many parts of your life will be the beneficiaries of our collective efforts.

INTRODUCTION

"We are all outsiders when we travel. Whether we go abroad or roam about our own city or country, we often enter territory so unfamiliar that our frames of reference become inadequate. We need advice not just to avoid offense and danger, but to make our experiences richer, deeper, and more fun." So begins the preface of *Travelers' Tales*, resting in my hands in this old bookshop on the edge of a river. I am in Paris, scouting out a location in France for a think-tank we'll have for an international group of scientists from Asia to Europe to the United States, studying the mind and mental health. In this shop, the oldest of English bookstores in this vibrant capital city, I am ready to write for you a pocket guide for the field of Interpersonal Neurobiology (a field that we sometimes abbreviate as IPNB).

I've been on a four-week journey eastward from California—teaching in Colorado and New York along the way, meeting with a philosopher/physicist/physician here, seeking out a geographically central place for people to convene. And then, off the shelf, I found *Travelers' Tales* by O'Reilly, Habegger, and O'Reilly, which articulates a perspective we need, including having more "fun" along our journey:

There may be no city more uplifting [than Paris] to the human spirit. It is a place to explore the dimensions of yourself or those of someone you love—to walk and talk, to argue about life, to sit and contemplate the events of human history which have played themselves out here on these streets, on the banks of this river.

And yet as heavy with tradition and culture as it is, the City of Light has bestowed on countless millions the gift of the incandescent present, an image, an experience or moment into which all life is condensed, to be reflected upon for years to come. Paris is a place to feel especially alive, and it's here now, waiting for you to come, sample its treasures, and make it yours.*

And so we begin our journey into interpersonal neurobiology together from this city . . . to travel in a way that I hope will be uplifting to your spirit as it invites you to explore yourself and others. While we will highlight the profound insights of many human endeavors to understand the nature of our inner and outer realities, we will also be diving deeply into the insights of the present moment.

A BRIEF HISTORICAL AND CONCEPTUAL BACKGROUND

Many fields have explored the nature of mental life—from psychology to philosophy, literature to linguistics. Yet no common home where each of these important perspectives can be honored and integrated with one another has been created in

---

* O'Reilly, J., Habegger, L., O'Reilly, S. (2002). *Travelers' tales paris*. Berkeley, CA: Publisher's Group West. (p. xx)

which people seeking their collective wisdom can find answers to some basic questions. These inquiries have puzzled our species for centuries. What is the purpose of life? Why are we here? How do we know things, how are we conscious of ourselves? What is a thought or a feeling? What is the mind? What makes a mind healthy or unwell? And in modern times, we can even ask: What is the connection among the mind, the brain, and our relationships with one another and with this planet which we all share?

As a student in high school and college, I was fascinated by these basic questions. After studying biochemistry, researching fish metabolism during the day, and working at night on a suicide prevention help line, I longed to find a way to connect the power of objective science with the centrality of our subjective mental lives. Could the molecules I had been studying in the lab that allowed salmon to transition safely from fresh to saltwater be in some way related to the equally important reality that the way we communicate with another person in crisis can mean life or death? I entered medical school eager to explore the interconnections between science and subjectivity—our different ways of knowing about the realities of life. I found that the various divisions of the field of medicine, each studying a different system of the body, did not communicate well with one another. An internist would know the organs of the body but would not communicate well with the surgeon about to perform a procedure on her patient. A pediatrician would be helpful to a child but would not have been taught about how the psychiatric illness of the parent might be negatively impacting the child's development. When I was in school, too, many of the fine teachers we had approached their patients, and their students, as if they had no center of inner experience—no sub-

jective internal core we might call our mental life. It was as if
we were just bags of chemicals and bodily organs without a self,
without a mind. After leaving medical school for what ended
up being a year of travel and internal exploration, I returned
to my medical training thinking for the first time that I might
enter the field of psychiatry.

Back in the early 1980s, the specialty of medicine that focused
on mental illnesses was at war with itself. Fractured by historical rifts among the community-based physicians, the pharmaco-
logically-oriented psychiatrists, and the psychoanalysts, the field
was filled by tension. As a student, I was exposed to these various camps and was struck by how little collaboration, or respect,
seemed to exist among them. I decided to enter pediatrics as a
specialty instead, but I soon found that my passion for things
related to the life of the mind drew me to enter psychiatric
training despite these tensions and rifts. By the end of my clinical education in adult, and then child and adolescent, psychiatry,
I felt uneasy about what I was learning—or, more specifically,
not learning. I felt that we were trained well in the diagnosis
and treatment of disorders, but we had little focus in our studies on what created or even defined health. This was the general
state of education not only in psychiatry but in the many fields
of mental health as well.

To learn more about healthy development, I pursued a
National Institute of Mental Health research training fellowship
and studied the nature of narrative, memory, and family communication. I was eager to see if there was a way to create collaboration and synthesis across a wide range of ways of knowing
about our human condition, of what this being human was all
about.

Then, in the early 1990s, back at the beginning of the

Decade of the Brain, the field of psychiatry could further its focus on the "biological basis" of psychiatric disturbances such as schizophrenia and manic-depressive illness by exploring the correlations of atypical brain functioning with mental dysfunction. These were important efforts to relieve real illnesses with effective treatments such as medications. Yet while the colorful brain scans from new technological advances including positron emission tomography (PET) and functional magnetic resonance imaging (fMRI) scans were quite exciting to behold, it was important then, as it still is now, to realize that these are powerful insights that need to be understood in their fuller context. Brain-flow changes—or metabolic alterations associated with such changes—can be measured. As scientists, we depend on numerical measures to study our areas of interest. But statements that these scans were enabling us to "see the mind in action" seemed like enthusiastic overstatements of the truth. After all, is blood-flow change a measure of the mind? And what exactly is the mind? Is the mind merely the activity of the brain?

I've had many a scientist follow me after a talk saying that the answer is a simple "yes" and anything short of that is "reversing science." But, I've said to them as I'll offer to you, the answer is more complex than stating "mind is simply brain activity." As we'll see, the open-minded approach to answering this fundamental question yields some powerful insights into the inner nature of subjective experience. These are the fundamental questions at the beginning of our inquiry in this "integrative handbook of the mind." The responses to this single question—what is the mind?—have generated more heated discussions than any other query I've encountered. And the "integrative" part of this book's subtitle refers to many layers of differentiated elements linking together. We'll be combining a range of sciences into one framework; we'll be linking nonscientific explorations of reality that come from direct experience into our discussions with science; and we'll even be exploring ways in which you, the reader, can create a more "integrated," internal mental life for yourself and those around you. Hence, the multiple meanings of the notion of an "integrative handbook."

What this all means is that I am inviting you to be fully present as you dive into this book. I'll be here, too, and so this is meant to be a journey together. We may end up raising more questions than providing concrete, final answers, but perhaps this is exactly what the mind is about: the creation of possibility rather than the constriction of limitation, as we may, in openminded fact, actually come to see.

Now, back to our background story. When I was asked to run the training program in child and adolescent psychiatry at UCLA, at the start of the Decade of the Brain, I invited about 40 scientists from over a dozen different academic departments to participate in a study group in which we would address one "simple" question: What is the connection between the mind and the brain? The composition of the group included individuals from anthropology, molecular biology, cognitive science, education, genetics, linguistics, neuroscience, neurosurgery, physics, psychology, psychiatry, mathematics, computer science, and sociology. We were a gathering of professors and graduate students, clinicians and researchers. As the facilitator of the group, I found the initial meetings fascinating but of concern because the group could come to no consensus as to what the mind was. The brain was the easy part of our question: It was an organ of the body that was intricately connected to the whole of the body proper through the extended nervous system, which was distributed from head to toe. In fact, whenever we speak of the "brain" in this book, we'll be using that term to signify this extensively distributed set of neurons we call the "nervous system" and its many components that are interwoven with the body as a whole.

But what was the mind? Each of the various disciplines had a range of descriptions that it would use to articulate this important aspect of human life. An anthropologist stated that the mind is what is shared across the generations. A neuroscientist said the mind is simply the activity of the brain. A psychologist stated that the mind is composed of thoughts and feelings and includes our consciousness and the subjective nature of our internal lives as well as the output of the mind, which are our behaviors. While such descriptions enabled these devoted and thoughtful researchers to pursue their own disciplines' work, it did not help us find common ground in our interdisciplinary group. Many a book even with "mind" in the title, it turns out, describes the mind (thoughts and feelings, a "self-concept," a "vague term," and the like) but does not define what the mind, or even a part of the mind, actually "is." In our group, this lack of a definition led to tension among the various members that became quite destructively intense, and I was concerned the group would disband after just a few meetings.

Bodies of water can be a soothing source of insight at times of such distress. So I took myself for a long walk along the beach (just as I strolled along Paris's river, the Seine, when I was preparing to begin to write this pocket guide) and it occurred to me then that these various *descriptions* of the nature of the mind might find a common home if a working *definition* of the mind could be offered. I am not obsessed with definitions, but sometimes being specific about a term, like "mind," can inspire us to find deeper and shared universal meanings hidden within the different descriptions. Along the Pacific back then, watching the waves move in and out from the sandy shore, it seemed to me that what each of the different disciplines was speaking about in their separate descriptions was the flow of something across time. The aspect of reality that changes across time is a flow of a fundamental part of our lives, *energy*.

Though physicists themselves often struggle with exactly what energy is, there seems to be a consensus that "energy is the capacity to do stuff." Energy comes in various forms, including the energy of light, electricity, motion, heat, and, in the case of neural firing, electrochemical forces. When we try to picture energy flow, it might be most helpful to begin with the image of electricity as electrons flow down a wire. But energy flow also happens as heat is transferred from one object to another, or as sound waves move through the air and one voice spoken here is received by the ears of someone over there. Energy happens as the photons bounce from these written symbols called words into your eyes. Energy is a real aspect of the physical world in which we live.

But while our mental lives are filled with the flow of energy, the mind is more than a conveyor of energy flow like the electrical wire. Naturally the subjective internal life we call our "mental world" is filled with all sorts of wonderful as well as terrifying things: We can have feelings of ecstasy, pleasure, joy, satisfaction, pride, happiness, and clarity. We can also feel the *subjective experience* of sadness, loss, anxiety, anger, fear, dread, and terror. Images can fill our "mind's eye" with recollections of joyful moments or terrifying past events. And we can create newly formed images from imagination. As we know, our mental life is filled with inner experiences such as feelings, thoughts, images, memories, hopes, attitudes, intentions, beliefs, and dreams. These and many other *processes* are the *activities of the mind*. We also have the experience of knowing, the subjective sense of being aware of these various activities of the mind, from sensation to concept. But what are these processes, really? What is the experience of knowing within awareness? Beyond simply describing the nature of subjective experience and consciousness, is there a way to define what the "mind" actually is?

A common philosophical and scientific stance to take is that we just don't really know. There is a lot to be learned, academicians appropriately state, and it is better to not limit ourselves with the constraints of a definition. We could take a similar position—as many in these helpful fields do—that the mind should not be defined at all. The mind, as a word, is used as a placeholder for the unknown—a term denoting something we just don't yet know clearly, and perhaps never will. Maybe this is why so many fields that deal with the "mind" do not define it. Taking the step of defining the mind, some philosophers have told me, would limit our understanding of this important dimension of what it means to be human. "Don't do it," they've said to me. And defining the mind, some scientists say, is not yet possible because we don't know exactly what it is. That's why they are studying the mind.

Yet as educators interested in developing a strong and resilient mind in our students, not defining the term "mind" leaves us in the dark. As parents focusing our efforts on helping our children develop healthy and flexible minds, not having even a working definition of the mind as a starting place limits us. And for those of us who work as *mental* health professionals—as psychotherapists we are therapists of the mind—is it really fair for us to say that we work in a field of the *healthy mind* when in fact we haven't even tried to make a working definition of what that actually means? That does not seems quite right. And here we'll explore what might be done to provide the fields of clinical work, organizational consultation, reflective practice, education, parenting, and any other efforts to cultivate a healthy mind, with a starting point.

Along the beach back in the beginning of the 1990s, I felt that this absence of a clear (at least working) definition of one aspect of the mind was threatening our interdisciplinary group cohesion and success. And so wrestling with a place to start, coming up with a "working definition" that seemed to fit with what everyone was describing as his or her focus on mental functions, seemed important in order to facilitate our discussions.

In reflecting on what each of the various disciplines was describing as mental life, it seemed that the mind had something to do with *regulating* the flow of not only energy, but specific patterns of energy flow that we call "information." *Information* is something that stands for something other than itself. Information is a symbolic energy flow pattern, a pattern that *means* something. For example, if I write "Eiffel Tower," you may see an image of that gridiron structure in Paris within your mind's eye (whatever that is). These squiggles of the written word or the sounds of the spoken word are not the tower itself—they *stand for* the tower. The tower, on the other hand, is itself. Symbols of the tower may exist as information in your, well, your mind, in your subjective experience in this moment—representing not only the architectural structure but also perhaps a first trip to Paris where you began to feel romantic, or independent, or homesick. For me it was a moment in a relationship when a friend and I had to iron out some differences in how we were to travel together on our journey through Europe. Still, the tower itself is the tower. I look down the river and I can see it now, but my perception of it is not it. And the information of the tower for each of us may be quite different. Our minds are filled with information—with symbolic meanings emerging from energy flow patterns that stand for many associated things. In fact, information itself, as we'll see, initiates a flow of further information as we have cascades of meaning that emerge, making each of us unique, each moment a one-of-a-kind experience.

And yet there is another important element of the mind beyond its being the movement of information within us. Your experience of seeing the Eiffel Tower right now was not coming from just "you." I wrote the name of the tower, and your mental life created the image. How did that happen? As any parent, anthropologist, or sociologist knows, we don't live in isolation from one another. Our mental lives are profoundly relational. The interactions we have with each other shape our mental world. Yet as any neuroscientist will tell you, the mind is shaped by the firing patterns in the brain. And so how can we reconcile this apparent paradox—that the mind is *both* embodied and relational? Shouldn't something like "a mind" be located in one place, come from one source, be owned by one person? That's the question we'll address in illuminating the nature of mind. If you like words that begin with "em" you're in luck, because you can state that the mind is both embodied in an internal physiological context and embedded in an external relational context. *Embodied and embedded is the fundamental nature of mind.*

What emerged from those deep conversations in our interdisciplinary group was a respect for the unique ways in which separate academic pursuits explored the nature of reality. The idea for the field of interpersonal neurobiology was born from that process as a way of linking a wide array of scientific disciplines in thinking about the nature of the mind and mental well-being. I felt then, as I still feel today, that finding a way to weave one view of reality based on the findings of all the branches of science could provide a solid foundation for understanding the nature of our lives. When I offered the following definition, each of the members of the group found this compatible with their individual perspectives:

"A core aspect of the mind can be defined as an embodied and relational process that regulates the flow of energy and information."

With this definition we found a shared conceptual space in which to dive deeply into our fundamental topic: What is the connection between mind and brain? Working with this definition, the group could find common ground with which to communicate and we went on to meet for four and a half years. Since that time, much new science has emerged and interpersonal neurobiology as a way of knowing about the mind, well-being, and our human lives has grown in many ways. In 1999, the first edition of my book *The Developing Mind* was published; it proposed this approach as an interdisciplinary way of understanding the mind and mental health. Not only could we try on a working definition of the mind, but we could also propose what a "healthy mind" might be. Twelve years later, in the second edition of that book, over 2,000 new scientific references were gathered to support or refute this fundamental approach. I had the privilege of working with 15 research interns this past year who were given the assignment to "prove that interper-

sonal neurobiology and *The Developing Mind* are wrong." With
that challenge, they updated the references and we revised
whatever needed to be changed. Mostly what was found was
that the statements that read "Science has not yet shown this
to be true" could now be changed to reveal the new support
for many of those initial hypotheses. And so the writing of this
pocket guide is fueled by this exciting moment of validating
the essential conceptual structure and proposals of interpersonal
neurobiology from over a dozen years ago with established scientific empirical research.

In this last decade, we also moved the field forward with the
Norton Professional Series in Interpersonal Neurobiology, of
which this book is a part. After initially serving as the series editor and putting out 15 books in the series, I am happy to have
passed that role on to the current series editor, Allan Schore,
who has been assembling many more exciting new books
for this professional library. The nonprofit group GAINS (the
Global Association for Interpersonal Neurobiology Studies at
MindGAINS.org) has also emerged in the last 5 years to support the work of professionals in various fields drawing upon
this approach for their work, including the domains of psychotherapy, education, organizational functioning, contemplative
practice, parenting, and religion. Through the teachings of the
various authors of titles in the series, professionals in a range of
fields have received direct teaching related to this new interdisciplinary way of thinking about our lives and the nature of
well-being.

It seemed in those early years, as it still does today, that a
home is needed in which a wide variety of ways of knowing can be respectfully represented. For this reason, it has been
important to keep interpersonal neurobiology "discipline neu-

tral" and to nurture this field to embrace the broad approaches we human beings have created to attempt to understand the nature of reality. Science is our starting point, but it is not where we end our endeavors. Carefully constructed research is a wonderful tool, when examined with the perspective that it is not the be-all and end-all of knowledge. Many aspects of life are not measurable in quantitative terms, and these real facets of being human may be difficult to assess in the necessary statistical analyses of peer-reviewed academic journals. When it comes to the mind, other ways of knowing about our subjective realities through inner reflection and contemplation, poetic explorations, musical expressions, and artistic creations are profoundly important even though they may not be reducible to numbers on a chart or displayed neatly on a graph. Perhaps at some time in the future they will be measurable, perhaps not. The issue is this: Something can be real even though it is not now, or ever, capable of being numerically analyzed. Yet science, though it often depends on careful measurement, remains an essential foundation for this interdisciplinary work.

One reason that a scientifically grounded approach such as interpersonal neurobiology is helpful is that we can make predictions about what future studies might come to demonstrate. The updating of *The Developing Mind* lends support to this approach in that many of our predictions—based on the synthesis of scientific findings from a range of fields and projecting these implications forward as hypotheses—have now been confirmed by independent scientific labs with their new research. In science we need preexisting hypotheses to predict outcomes and not merely explain, in retrospect, why something may have been discovered. In a number of areas now, interpersonal neurobiology has served as a source of prediction to validate later discoveries. These findings support the validity of many general principles and processes such as integration, regulation, and the importance of social experiences in the development of a healthy mind.

If during your reading you become interested in accessing reviews and syntheses of the extensive scientific studies themselves, please see the latest edition of *The Developing Mind* (Siegel, 2012) and the many Norton books in this series, which collectively contain thousands of references. If you want to read how interpersonal neurobiology can be applied to parenting, please see *Parenting from the Inside Out* (Siegel & Hartzell, 2003) and *The Whole-Brain Child* (Siegel & Bryson, 2011). In the world of mindfulness, *The Mindful Brain* (Siegel, 2007) offers you an in-depth and up-close examination of how interpersonal neurobiology principles can illuminate ancient contemplative practices and their modern educational and therapeutic effects. If you are seeking an application of interpersonal neurobiology to yourself as a psychotherapist, or as a general citizen in the world, *The Mindful Therapist* (Siegel, 2010) will be of interest and explores a number of hands-on, practical applications such as the Wheel of Awareness and the Plane of Possibility, which can help in understanding and developing your own mind. And if you are looking to be immersed in the actual stories of people who have applied these ideas in their own lives, diving deeply into a number of "domains of integration" within therapy or in daily life, *Mindsight* (Siegel, 2010) will be helpful in providing step-by-step descriptions. These are among the many published available resources that allow you to see the supportive science and the ways to apply these concepts in the day-to-day process of living and awakening the mind of yourself and others. First and foremost, enjoy the journey!

THE POCKET GUIDE

Why a pocket guide? In each of the books mentioned above, and many of the books in the series, you will find a wealth of information, stories, and science that could fill a professional training program or a clinician's library with an abundance of reading. So isn't this enough? Why a guide? Many readers and students of interpersonal neurobiology have requested that there be some form of "summary" or "outline" or "glossary" that they could have at their fingertips. They've requested something without many or any references, a book filled with just helpful ways of learning about the material. The referenced works are all in publication—so why not have a direct exploration of these intricate ideas themselves? This guide is designed to be of use as a companion to assist you in seeing the intricate foundations of interpersonal neurobiology as you actively read the other related texts. Teachers, therapists, consultants, parents, and others who have studied this field have suggested that such a guide would be of great value. The common element of their suggestions was that the contents of such a guide be both accessible and practical. Now that this interdisciplinary way of knowing is well into its second decade of life, it seems fitting that such an accessible and practical guide to the field be created to help with the application of interpersonal neurobiology out in the world. We are not just about exploring a way of knowing—we are devoted to trying to help the world become a healthier place in which we all can live.

To make this book concise, I have naturally needed to summarize large bodies of science and cull the essence of each concept and what the topic is about, and then explore its practical implications and what this understanding of the mind means in our life, our work, and our world. To keep this book truly a pocket guide, something you can literally put in your (perhaps big) pocket, and to honor the request for a streamlined overview, as mentioned earlier we'll need to forgo many scientific references that you can find in the numerous previously mentioned texts. Science expands exponentially and it is fascinating, but this is not the book to explore the primary empirical sources of this knowledge. This guide is intended to help you create the internal and integrated framework of this broad interdisciplinary field so that you can easily make this knowledge your own in a productive and enjoyable manner, from the inside out. In other books you'll find more extensive reviews and references of the science and more detailed discussions of the applications of the material for various disciplines such as clinical work, parenting, education, and reflective practice. This book, in contrast, can truly focus directly on integrating a network of knowledge that fits with our basic stance in science that "chance favors the prepared mind." It is my hope that this book will prepare your mind for all the wonderful ways we can cultivate healthier minds in our personal and professional lives.

And so this pocket guide's goal is to provide a different sort of learning experience than the other books mentioned above. The goal is to offer a direct experience of the sphere of knowledge that comprises interpersonal neurobiology. If you are looking for an extensive set of identified and previously published scientific references that support the ideas and statements of interpersonal neurobiology outlined here, please see the abovementioned texts, as you will not, by design and by request, find them in this guide. Instead, this is a way of immersing yourself in the intricate foundation of the field. The entries of this guide serve as the scaffold of the overarching framework and

also provide an exploration of the interwoven ideas and processes. While the entries are conceptually interconnected to one
another, each entry also can stand on its own so that you can,
literally, enter into this guide at any "entryway." These entries
can be read in a linear sequence if that is your preference, but
they do not need to be read in that way in order for them to be
fully grasped individually or as a whole. In other words, you can
dive in anywhere and go anywhere and the sphere of knowledge will be created by your own exploration of this material.
In this way, the pocket guide is not a linear book. The mind
doesn't work only in a simple linear sequence, and so my aim is
to create a new approach to reading and learning in the essential structure and process of this book that reflects more directly
the many ways the mind itself absorbs and integrates information. In this way, the process of reading this book mirrors the
book's content regarding the mind itself.

How you read this pocket guide is up to you. You may have
a particular preferred style of learning and you can determine
the sequence of entries you choose to read. You may begin with
any entry and then move to another, depending on your needs
at that moment, following your spontaneous inclination and
where it takes you at that point in time. Each entry has several terms that are "nodes" in a larger interconnected network,
a weblike set of interrelated facts, ideas, and processes. "Node"
is a term commonly used in discussions of how networks of
interrelated elements function. A network consists of nodes that
have mutual ties or linkages that connect them to other nodes
in the system. A node can be a person in a social network or it
can be an idea or fact in a knowledge network. In this guide my
aim is to create for you a process in the reading that allows you
to explore the exciting interconnected network of ideas and

facts that form the knowledge network underlying interpersonal neurobiology.

The nodes and other important general terms are all *italicized* for ease of reference throughout the text, indicating to you that the word or phrase can be found with its brief definition in the annotated index, which is really an extensive glossary with page numbers. In this way, the annotated index may become a helpful resource to which to refer repeatedly as you explore these ideas. At the very end of this annotated index you'll find the listing of all of the nodal terms by themselves, without definitions, in the nodal network section. Following the nodes as a bridge to read different entries enables you to interweave the conceptual framework as you move in and out of various entries in your own personalized manner.

The process of exploring this network of knowledge enables you to read through a given entry with ease, diving in to an entry topic that seems relevant to you right then, finding what is meaningful for you, what has value and interest. Each entry is written to be accessible regardless of whether or not you have read any prior entries. In this way, each entry can be a starting point, or a passageway to enter the network of knowledge. The topic revealed in the title of each entry serves itself as a node in that it has extensive linkages to other ideas found in a wide range of other entries. For example, if you are interested in the topic of "memory," you may turn to the entry with that title. There you will find a discussion of how we learn and the impact of experience on our lives. In the course of reading, you will encounter other nodes that are highlighted within the text. Let's say you find the brain structure, the hippocampus, of interest. You can then turn to the annotated index and find a definition of the term and the other page numbers throughout the book where "hippocampus" is also discussed. You'll find all of these nodal terms also listed in the nodal network section (where they are simply listed with their entry numbers and no definitions) so that you can readily see the network of interconnected ideas, become familiar with this network, and be able to find them in the entries with ease. Now you can read an entry that happens to discuss the hippocampus and the impact of trauma on this brain structure. You may then find that you are interested in pursuing "trauma" as a node, and you turn to the annotated index and nodal network to get oriented with definitions and to find other entries, this time related to trauma. As you can see, you can then explore the entry devoted to trauma where you may encounter other nodes related to "narrative" or "prefrontal function" or "attachment" and then pursue, at your own pace and discretion, those various interrelated processes. You create your own learning path! This is a network of knowledge and this way of presenting the material is designed to encourage you to explore this material in a way that has meaning and interest to you.

I know that at first this all may sound daunting but that's the challenge I have faced as the person with the typing fingers, not one you should have to deal with as a reader. If this has been done well, any place you enter, any entry, will be a beginning that will naturally and comfortably lead to any other place in the guide that will be readily accessible no matter where you've been before in the book. I've had to hold on to this perspective throughout the writing, and I hope you'll find that the flow works for you. You will create the linkages among the many nodal terms by following your own interests and weaving the whole of the network of knowledge in the very process of reading in your own unique interest-driven manner. Our emotions and our interests harness our attention and reinforce learning. In this way, you will shape your own learning and weave the network of knowledge into your own self-directed approach to understanding. You will determine for yourself how to explore the intricately interwoven nature of the mind. I hope the efforts to create such an integrative process within this book will work well for you and that you'll enjoy this personalized process as it deepens the learning that unfolds!

Because this guide is not structured as your typical book might be, let me just describe in a bit more detail its structure and process so that diving into it may be done more effectively and with more ease. The entries of the book have been kept to a minimum in their number and in their length. Though the sequence of the entries in the book is natural and in an unfolding nature, as you'll experience for yourself if you choose to read this guide in that way, they are also intricately interwoven like a tapestry, so that diving in at any entry and choosing your next entry could lead you in all directions. To achieve this integrating and personalized effect, I have portrayed the network of interconnected information as a set of entryways into the framework. This table of entries—not a succession of chapters to be read in a specific sequence, but rather a collection of entries to be read in any order—reveals numbered sections only for the benefit of finding them spatially in the book, not for the intention of being read in this order. Page numbers in this book reflect the entry number and then the page of that entry (7–5 is the fifth page of the entry numbered 7). Within each entry in addition to the entry topic (which is also in bold type), there are several other *nodes**, the core concepts or terms that are used within an entry. Any node is denoted in *italics with an* ★ following it only the first time it appears in that entry so that you know this is a nodal point in the interconnected network of ideas (listed in the nodal network). If you encounter an *italicized* term (with or without an asterisk), you can turn to the annotated index at any time and find a brief definition as well as the page numbers in which that term is used. After you encounter the highlighted term for the first time as you read, your mind will be primed to watch for it in the remainder of the entry, actively engaging you with the material. If you are interested in pursuing that node further, you can turn to the nodal network section and find other entry page numbers where that nodal idea or term is discussed. Also, within the text you will find shaded passages that serve as easy visual reminders of key ideas that can be reviewed as desired to further integrate the scaffold of knowledge. I have also included a few selected drawings and figures at the end of the book to help support this whole-view approach.

In trying to describe the nature of this guide to others, what came to mind was the image of a "sphere of knowledge" that was the foundation of the book. A sphere is a three-dimensional structure that has an inner space (think of the inside of a ball) and an outer surface. I envision the entries of this book as the curved regions of the sphere's surface (see Figure A in the figures section at the back of the book). We can enter the sphere through one of these surface entryways, these surface regions, which invite us to explore the sphere of knowledge. Once in an entry, we'll encounter italicized and asterisked *nodes** that we can follow inward, into the inner space of the sphere. We can imagine these nodes as being points of intersections that are linked by various lines that, from within the inner space and the surface of the sphere, send radiating links to a wide array of other nodes inside the sphere and on the surface (see Figure B).

For example, if you encounter the term *empathy** in an entry you are reading, you can go to the nodal network and find the page numbers within seven other entries in which the term, empathy, is explored. One of those may be an entry that is specifically about relationships, such as *attachment**. As you turn to that entry and dive into its text, you may encounter the term *integration**, read about it there, and then feel inclined to refer back to the nodal network where you'll find other entries from which you can choose to pursue further reading. Now as you read this next entry, you encounter another perhaps unexpected term, *awareness**, and your interest is piqued and you then go to the nodal network to take in the web of nodal connections that allow you to explore other entries. Once you are in an entry, you are back to the familiar and useful complementary linear discussions of the information. This is how you can move from entering a node as the topic of an entry at the sphere's surface, to nodal linkages within the inner space of the sphere, back to the entries at the surface, to create a network of this sphere of knowledge (see Figures A and B). This is three-dimensional learning! But don't worry: you wont need 3-D glasses! This approach may be something new, but I hope you'll find it deeply rewarding, helpful to your learning, and even enjoyable.

To support the accessibility of this approach, I've elected to define every term in the index—so the annotated index forms the book's extensive glossary. The 43 entry titles are listed there along with approximately 115 other terms that together form the nodal network. There are an additional 240 or so index items that are important terms, also listed and defined in the annotated index, but they do not have extensive interconnections throughout the book. I've included these *italicized* (but without an asterisk) terms in the index for your ease of access and reference. We can consider these index items as foundational terms that perhaps get us inside the sphere but that only link to a small number of entries on the surface; so for this reason they are not considered "nodes" and are not labeled with asterisks.

In the annotated index and in the nodal network you'll also find that some terms are designated as academic terminology with the letters "Res" following the phrase, signifying that it is a "research-derived term." This means that the term is generally accepted and used in research branches of academia. In contrast, other terms will have the designation of "App" following it, meaning that it is an important interpersonal neurobiology idea and term that is fundamental to practical applications in the broad fields of clinical work, education, organizational consultation, reflective practice, and parenting within this perspective—but the terms are not necessarily utilized by individuals in purely academic areas of pursuit. Being informed of this distinction can be quite helpful in knowing the perspective from which these terms originate and where they can be used with common understanding and acceptance. Often these practical terms emerge from the layers of subjective experience that are at the very heart of the practice and engagement of medicine, psychotherapy, education, consultation, parenting, reflection, and other ways that we help people grow and heal in our professional and our personal lives. In this pocket guide—with its entries and nodal interconnections—you'll find a foundation that blends the best of academically rigorous research-based science with the useful, practical approaches that you can then apply in creative ways to promote growth and well-being in a range of relevant settings. This weaving, through the process and content of the book, is how you become the active and unique organizer of this experience about, among many other things, integration and the mind.

I have tried to make the medium the message by having the process and content interwoven in this opportunity for active learning. Overall, the guide is an attempt to be integrative in its many layers of interconnected ideas. Some of these ideas can be found within highlighted areas throughout the various entries. The integrating attempt here, with its many entryways of access and *nodal** points of interconnection, attempts to blend both modes of nonlinear and linear learning into what I hope will be an empowering experience of synthesis for you. When we differentiate concepts from each other and then link them, we integrate knowledge. And integration—of sequential and holistic learning, of personally subjective and scientifically objective learning—as we'll soon see, is our central theme for the whole of interpersonal neurobiology.

The pocket guide is designed to be helpful in your personal and professional application of the interpersonal neurobiology approach to developing a healthy mind, an integrated brain, and empathic relationships. This guide strives to make the experiences of growth and awakening that are at the core of our journeys "richer, deeper, and even more fun," as my Parisian travel guide suggests. I hope this small companion will likewise help you to feel especially alive and to sample interpersonal neurobiology's fascinating treasures and make them yours. Bon voyage.

Italicized terms = key idea or process

Italicized terms with star★ = nodal idea or process

shaded text = key concepts

***bold, italicized, asterisked terms*★** = entry title; serves also as
a node in the network of knowledge

1
1

MIND

CONCEPT: WHAT IS IT?

"Mind★" relates to our inner *subjective experience★* and the *process★* of being conscious or *aware★*. In addition, mind can also be defined as a process that regulates the flow of *energy and information★* within our bodies and within our *relationships,★* an *emergent★* and *self-organizing★* process that gives rise to our *mental activities★* such as *emotion★*, thinking, and memory. Subjective experience, *awareness★*, and an *embodied★* and *relational★* process that *regulates★* the flow of energy and information are fundamental and *interdependent★* facets of mind.

Our mental lives are filled with the personal subjective experiences of thoughts, feelings, *memories★*, and other mental activities that directly influence our behavior—our external actions in the world including our interactions with other people. While such *mental processes★* texture our inner lives and fill our awareness, they also can be seen as how the mind regulates energy and information flow. These mental activities also include our beliefs, attitudes, *intentions★*, hopes, dreams, *percep-*

tions★, reasoning, *intuition*★, and images. We can have a feeling inside of ourselves that has a sense of the truth about something, an *implicit knowing;* and we can also have a more explicit sense of the specific details and facts of our knowledge. Both implicit and explicit processes influence our thinking, feelings, and behaviors. Mental experience also includes our *states of mind*★ and our *mood*★. Each of these mental processes has a subjective texture, a "qualia" or essence of its personally experienced nature, a subjective quality that is real but often cannot be fully described or easily quantified. We may not be able to say exactly what subjective experience "is," but we "know" when we see or hear something, have a feeling, see an image in our mind's eye, *remember*★ an event, and intuit a gut feeling or heartfelt sense about something. Because the nature of our personally experienced inner mental lives is not quantifiable or directly observable, it is challenging to measure in the numerically precise way so often needed in science. Self-reports of subjective experience are useful and can be quantified in many ways, but these descriptions are not the same as the inner experience itself. Despite this feature of mental life and the reality that it is difficult to study in an objective and quantifiable manner, subjective experience is quite real.

Another aspect of mind that is difficult to study in a controlled or measured way is *consciousness*★, our experience of being aware. You know when you are aware: You have a sense of knowing, and you know about something in particular—the "known." I can know that right now I am remembering swimming at the lake. This experience of being conscious of memory has two facets: The knowing (I know I am remembering the lake swim) and the known (I was in the water yesterday). While we cannot say exactly "what" awareness "is," the experience of knowing and of the known is a fundamental aspect of our mental lives. In many ways, we know about our subjective experience by way of consciousness, as it is the inner experience of knowing and the texture, the qualia, of the known. Awareness is also a crucial aspect of how we use the mind to alter the course of our lives, to learn new skills and even change the structure of the *brain** itself, and to reflect on what has *meaning**. Awareness makes choice and change possible.

But what does it really mean to be aware, say, of our thinking? And what is thinking? We can ask a seemingly simple question such as, what is a thought? And every person who is asked will provide a different answer. We actually don't truly "know" what a thought—or a feeling—really is. No kidding! We know when we have one, naturally, but to pin down an actual shared definition of a thought is quite challenging. As we dive deeply into the basic proposal that the mind is a process that arises from energy and information flow—in our bodies and in our relationships—we'll be able to see more clearly and more deeply into what a thought, or an emotion, actually "is." We'll soon see that some systems give rise to an emergent process called self-organization that both arises from the system, and then in turn regulates that system. In this case, we'll be looking deeply at the proposal that the system we are talking about is the flow of energy and information through our relationships and through our bodies. And when we ask what the connection between these mental processes and the brain is, we can enter another world of fascinating and heated discussions. In one group of 40 scientists from a dozen different disciplines who assembled to address this very question of how the brain and mind relate to one another two decades ago, there was no consensus on how to address this issue. Defining the brain was "easy" compared to finding a shared meaning, or even a shared description, of what "mind" is.

Beyond the important dimensions of subjective experience and awareness, beyond our mental activities of emotions, thoughts, and memories, the mind has another important feature. This aspect of mind relates to how our mental life regulates our lives and our interactions with the world.

This core aspect of the mind can be defined as "an embodied and relational process that regulates the flow of energy and information." This is the self-organizing, emergent process that is fundamental to our working definition of mind.

IMPLICATIONS: WHAT DOES THE MIND MEAN FOR OUR LIVES?

After directly surveying over 100,000 *mental health** professionals from around the globe, I found the following results. When asked if they had ever had even a single lecture defining what the mind is, 2 to 5% responded "yes." This means that more than 95% of the psychiatrists, psychologists, social workers, psychiatric nurses, masters-level therapists, occupational therapists, educational therapists, movement therapists, dance therapists, art therapists, music therapists, and others had never been given a lecture defining the mind. I myself had none. (A similar result was found for the question about defining "mental health.") About 4,500 teachers of kindergarten through 12th grade were also asked these questions, with similar results.

Various fields of science and of philosophy take the position that the mind is an unknown and should not or cannot be defined. I know this may sound surprising to you, as it certainly did to me, but after repeated discussions with various leaders in these fields and reviewing the scientific literature, this is the state of our current situation regarding the lack of a definition of mind. From the point of view of *consilience**, this working definition of a core aspect of mind as being a regulatory process is consistent with what a wide range of scientists seems to infer about their studies of the mind, even if they don't explicitly offer a definition. The stance of *interpersonal neurobiology** is that this is a working definition, a place to start. For the last two decades, the use of this conceptualization has had several important implications.

Once we say that the mind is both embodied and relational, it means that to know our minds we need to know about the body, including the *nervous system** that is distributed throughout, and interacts with, the entire body. This we'll call, for short, "the brain." Noting that the mind is also a relational process makes some people feel as if they don't then "own" their own minds. The mind is influenced by, indeed fundamentally created in part by, our social interactions as well as our relationships with entities beyond our bodily selves, with experiences we have with the environment surrounding us. In this way we can say that the mind is both embodied and it is embedded in our relational worlds.

Process implies that the mind is a verb, not a noun. In science we call this an emergent process that arises from the interaction of elements of the *system** in question. Here the "system" comprises both the body and the world of interactions, especially the social signals we share with others in our interpersonal relationships. In this book, we'll focus primarily on this social relatedness of the human mind, but our relationship with nature, and indeed with the planet as a whole, is a vitally important way our mental—and ecological—lives are shaped.

This is our proposal: The mind is an emergent, self-organizing process that shapes how energy and information move across time. This aspect of mind is a natural, emerging, and self-organizing dynamic process that arises as a fundamental property of the system of energy and information flow that is created in both the body and in interactions with others and our environment. This emergent process arises from energy and information flow and then also shapes energy and information flow across time. This is the *recursive** property of mind that is typical of *complex systems**. A complex system is a cluster of interacting entities that is open to influences from outside of itself and capable of entering chaotic states. Does that sound like it fits your own experience of mental life? The way we are thinking here is that the complex system in question is not merely our head-based brain, but the system of energy and information flow that is distributed throughout the body and that is exchanged in our relationships. Mental life is an emergent, self-organizing process of this embodied and relational flow of energy and information. The mind is not separate from our bodies or from our relationships—it both arises from them and it regulates them.

"Regulates" is an important aspect of this working definition of a core feature of the mind. Regulation entails two parts: monitoring and modulating. We see how something moves and then we shape it. We regulate that something by our ability to *track* and then transform the "stuff" that is moving. If you are driving a car, for example, you need to have your eyes open to monitor where you are going and your hands and feet working the steering wheel and the accelerator and brakes to modify the car's movement. With this regulatory aspect of mind elucidated with this definition, a teacher, parent, or clinician can focus on how monitoring and modifying can be strengthened. We can teach ourselves and others to monitor with more stability so that we can see with increased depth, clarity and detail. Once we have this view of energy and information flow in body and in relationships now in sharper focus, it becomes possible to modify that flow in a more specific way that moves the system—body and relationships—toward well-being. As we'll see, when we move energy and information flow toward something called *integration**, we move toward *health**. This way of developing the skills of monitoring and modifying makes a stronger, healthier, more flexible, and resilient mind.

But what exactly is being regulated? And where does this regulation actually take place? We are saying that mind arises in both our bodies and our relationships. This is hard for many people to accept at first glance, so bear with me. Mental processes are not just in the body—they are in our personal relationships, and they are embedded in our culture. This perspective on mind embraces both the science of the brain and the science of families, groups, communities, *cultures**, and societies. We are saying that the mind is not "just the activity of the brain" but instead can be seen as an emergent, self-organizing process that arises from bodily processes as a whole as well as from our relationships. So mind is a process that emerges from both the body and our relationships: Mind is both embodied and relational. Okay. Let's stay with that possibility for a moment. But then what is the "thing" that is actually being regulated, the something that is shared by the body and by our relational communication? The answer is energy.

*Energy** is described by physicists as the "capacity to do something." I once spent a week with dozens of physicists and this is the bottom-line of what they said we understand about the real, scientific, and important process called energy. Sometimes energy can enable "work" to be done but at other times it is just an "ability to do stuff": a potential to create, to induce movement, change, or action. *Information*★ can be seen from this perspective as a swirl of energy with meaning, a pattern of energy that symbolizes something other than itself. The phrase "Eiffel Tower" is a form of energy pattern that is symbolic for the tower, but it is not the tower itself. The energy of the tower can be carried as sound waves via kinetic energy (when we hear the words) or light waves via the energy of photons (when we see the words written out). This is how we communicate with each other in a relationship—through the sharing of energy and information flow. In the brain, electrochemical energy is carried among *neurons*★. Each of these forms of energy can have a pattern with meaning, an energy flow that stands for something other than the energy swirl itself. This is what we mean by information being carried by energy—but not all energy flow has information. Loud sounds may have features, aspects, textures, and measurable dimensions, but these data are not the same as information as we are defining the term here. Meaning and symbolic value are the essence of information. Information is one particular pattern in the movement of energy across time—something we call *flow*★.

Taken as a whole, this core aspect of the mind as an embodied and relational process that regulates the flow of energy and information places this facet of the mind within both our social interactions and our *neural firing*★ patterns. We do not need to separate the two—each is a fundamental part of what the mind is and where the mind resides. The system we are focusing on is not brain *or* relationships—it is a system that entails the flow of energy and information within the brain and between one another. Just as a coin has a heads, tails, and edge, the one reality of energy and information flow has at least three facets: sharing in "relationships," embodied mechanism in "brain," and regulation in "mind."

The self-organizing processes emerging from energy and information flow in our bodies and in our relationships certainly give rise to our mental activities, which channel that flow and function as important regulatory aspects of our mental lives. It may also be that the other two facets of mind, our subjective experience and our experience of awareness, ultimately can be seen as emergent processes that arise from this flow as well. Seeing the mind, in part, as a regulatory process that shapes the energy and information flow from which it arises reveals the self-organizing and the recursive properties of complex systems—in this case of energy and information flow in our bodies and in our relationships. Subjective experience and awareness may be natural emergent processes arising from this flow, but are these aspects of mental life "self-organizing" or are they some other emergent property of this system? What "exactly" subjective experience and awareness actually "are" is a fascinating question that requires us to truly have an open mind in our journey to understand them more fully.

Applying this working definition of the regulatory aspect of mind to the wide range of efforts to support the growth of a healthy mind empowers the professional, the parent, and anyone interested in strengthening their own mind to embrace the exciting new findings about how relationships and the brain each contribute to the healthy growth of individuals. As we'll see, by defining a "healthy mind," its growth can be cultivated in ways that make these endeavors easier to outline, readily accessible, and more effective.

While we are not explaining the deep nature of consciousness or of "what" exactly subjective experience is, we are highlighting a very important aspect of the mind as a regulatory process. The direct application of this definition of the self-organizing function of mind is that we can teach others, and ourselves, to regulate in a more robust manner. By learning to monitor with more stability, the details of energy and information flow in the body and in relationships can be seen with more clarity, depth, and detail. Then we are in a position to learn to use those newly perceived dimensions of energy and information flow to modify them toward health. A healthy mind is one that can regulate energy and information flow toward integration, the linkage★ of differentiated★ aspects of a system.

We can learn to integrate our brains and bodies, linking differentiated areas of neural function to one another. And we can learn to promote integrative communication★ in our relationships as we honor each other's differences and promote compassionate★ communication. The ultimate outcome of such embodied and relational integration is kindness★ and well-being.

In essence, when we teach others and ourselves to monitor with more depth and clarity, we enable the flow of energy and information to become more vivid and the details more stable and in focus. With this stabilized lens to sense the mind's activities—the flow of energy and information—the capacity to modify this flow of energy and information then becomes possible. This can be envisioned as creating a virtual tripod of the lens with which we sense energy and information flow (see Figure C). As we teach others to monitor with more depth and modify with more specificity toward integration, the mind becomes stronger. Yes, feelings and thoughts and memories and our awareness of the subjective inner experience of them are all real. Mind may not be visible under a microscope or weighable on a scale, but our mental lives are not only part of reality, they are the essence of our humanity. And here we also see how defining one aspect of the mind as regulatory empowers us to approach mental *development* by being much more specific in how we can facilitate the growth of a healthier, stronger, and more resilient mind.

2
2

RELATIONSHIPS

CONCEPT: WHAT ARE THEY?

*Relationships** involve the sharing of *energy and information flow**. When we communicate with one another, we are exchanging *energy** in the form of various signals that often contain informational value. A smile "means" something when we communicate it to another person, connoting a sense of a pleasant internal *state** of joy or contentment. A smile may also "mean" that the other person is anxious, masking that unpleasant state with a forced smile that itself has informational value pointing to a very different *meaning** of the facial expression. Sometimes we are simply just present, our energy is felt, and we share this energy flow with or without symbolic value. In this case, there may be no particular *informational** meaning communicated in the other's *presence**, though it may be "meaningful." It all depends on the meaning of the term "meaning"! When there is no specific *representational** symbolism—word or nonword—to an energy pattern, we simply call this "energy." This is the reason we use the phrase "energy *and* information,"

though it is true that all information is created with the *flow**
of energy across time. Not all energy has information. I men-
tion all of this here as relationships are filled with all sorts of
ways we communicate—or share—energy and information
flow with one another. And because relationships are about
the emerging patterns of this exchange over time, we need to
use the concept of flow. This is how the "flow" term, though it
seems vague to some people, actually is essential. Relationships
involve the sharing of the change in energy across time, the patterns of energy flow, that at times contain informational value.
Imagine the various relationships you have with other people:
Sometimes we feel understood and our inner meanings of the
mind* are seen and respected. Other relationships may be more
challenging, and the inner reality of our feelings and thoughts
are unseen and disrespected. We send out communication to
another person through the energy of our words and by way
of our *nonverbal** expressions that can be heard and seen, but
the other person does not create informational meaning from
these energy signals. We feel disconnected, misunderstood, and
alone. The nature of our relationships is directly shaped by how
energy is exchanged and information is created in this sharing
of energy and information flow.

IMPLICATIONS: WHAT DO RELATIONSHIPS MEAN FOR OUR LIVES?

When we define relationships in this way, it becomes possible to note how energy and information exchange patterns
establish their own habitual ways of existing in the interactions
between people—or even with groups of people or nonhu-
man entities, such as the living planet Earth. Within one-to-one

interpersonal relationships, called *dyads,* we can find that these patterns continually reinforce themselves in—at times—unhelpful ways. The mind we experience in our own subjective world can become filled with frustration if the other person does not see and acknowledge with positive regard our own inner world. *Mindsight** is a term that refers to this ability to see and respect the inner world of another—and even of ourselves. Mindsight is how we create the information, the meaning, embedded in the energy patterns sent from one person to another. *Empathy**, *compassion**, mind-mindedness, psychological mindedness, *reflective function, mentalization**, and *theory of mind* are useful scientific terms that also refer to this important concept of how one person sees the informational value—the significance and meaning—of the internal subjective mental world of another.

In relationships within families, one can see the *intergenerational transfer* of patterns of communication that are reinforced by the repeated experiences of energy and information flow exchange patterns. Recent discoveries in the field of *epigenetics** have also revealed that alterations in the control molecules *regulating** gene expression** may also be important in this intergenerational passage of patterns of communication. For example, the experience of extreme *stress** in one generation may be passed on through gametes, the egg and sperm, such that the ability to regulate stress may be compromised in future generations. These epigenetic changes can directly affect the parts of the *central nervous system* that control the *hypothalamic-pituitary-adrenal (HPA) axis* so that the release of the stress hormone *cortisol** cannot be properly modulated. When this occurs, the accumulated effect of stressors on the individual, called the *allostatic load*, is significantly increased. Without neural control that is balanced, the *system** of the family can further perpetuate the *dysregulation** of *emotional*★ response and experientially this pattern can further disturb the *development* of *healthy*★ regulation within the family system. If one generation has experienced overwhelming events, like a famine or genocide, it is possible that the children and even grandchildren may have inherited regulatory epigenetic factors that compromise the ability to soothe stress. We are affected not only by behavior and the stories we hear, but also by the regulatory molecules that control gene expression in areas of the *brain*★ that control such important functions as our stress response.

From a more macro-perspective on larger systems, our society can be viewed as functioning by way of the sharing of energy and information flow. We call this *culture*★ and can understand this through the *interpersonal neurobiology*★ lens as how energy and information patterns are shared within our larger society in the form of communication between and among people and the symbolic elements of media and the methods of interaction within various groupings. The *context*★ of culture directly shapes our mind as culture is a form of *relational*★ *process*★ fundamental to how the mind functions and how the brain develops.

Seeing the mind as a relational process enables us to view interactions of shared communication within dyads, families, schools, communities, and our larger societies as essential aspects of how the mind develops across time and functions in the present moment. This view makes mind, relationships, and the brain part of one reality: energy and information flow. Who you are is not independent of your relationships or your *embodied brain*, but it emerges from them. Culture is not an "add-on" for professionals to understand, but it is the relational matrix in which the mind emerges. Teachers, clinicians, and parents—indeed, each of us in the world—can harness the power of relationships to nurture the healthy growth of others. We can also move to be active *"cultural evolutionists"* as we attempt to create the conditions for healthy relationships within our modern societies. A healthy relationship, we can propose, involves the honoring of differences between people and cultivation of their *linkage** through compassionate, respectful communication. As we'll see in virtually all the dimensions of interpersonal neurobiology, this finding—that health emerges from the linkage of *differentiated** parts of a system—reveals how *integration** is the foundation of good health.

When a relationship is integrated, it moves over time with harmony. That sounds right, but what exactly is an integrated relationship? In a relationship, integration entails the cultivation of compassionate communication bringing the inner worlds of two individuals into close contact. Integration is the linkage of differentiated parts, and so an integrated relationship involves honoring differences and promoting compassionate connections. This is a relationship characterized by *integrative communication** in which each person's inner world—the subjective aspect of mind—is honored for its unique features and is interconnected in caring communication.

Integration is not the same as blending. Integration requires that we maintain elements of our differentiated selves while also promoting our linkage. Becoming a part of a "we" does not mean losing a "me." Integration as a focus of intervention among a range of *domains of integration** becomes the fundamental basis for how we apply interpersonal neurobiology principles to the nurturing of healthy relationships.

3
3

BRAIN AND BODY

CONCEPT: WHAT ARE THEY?

The **brain**★ is a term that is usually used to refer to a part of the body that rests in the skull and contains billions of cells clustered in various groupings. The skull-based cluster of cells, the top of the *central nervous system* we commonly call the brain, is inextricably interconnected with the whole of the body through the peripheral nervous system and all the signals from the body's physiological *processes*★. Input from the extended *nervous system*★ directly impacts how the skull-based cells, or "head brain," functions. Hormonal input from the bloodstream shapes brain processes, as does the influence of the immune system. To consider that "the brain" is independent of this extensive input from throughout the body makes little sense. For this reason, in *interpersonal neurobiology*★ we use the simple term "brain" as a shorthand reference for the neural mechanism of the whole of the *energy and information flow*★ that moves throughout the extensive interconnections of the body proper and the skull-based collection of cells in the head. In short, "brain" is our way of referring to the *embodied*★ mechanism of the energy and information flow in the body.

IMPLICATIONS: WHAT DO THE BRAIN AND BODY MEAN FOR OUR LIVES?

Knowing about the brain empowers you to transform confusion into *insight*★, self-blame into self-*compassion*★. When we teach others and ourselves about the brain's mechanisms of energy and information flow, the *mind*★ is strengthened as we move from blaming the *self*★ for automatic behaviors and instead transform our experience into self-understanding and self-responsibility. "This may not be my fault because my brain did this, but this is my responsibility to make a change" is a common response from those who are taught about the brain. Even young children can learn how the energy and information flow moves through the mechanism of the brain. This is the "embodied" aspect of the *relational*★ and embodied nature of the mind.

When the various components of the brain are learned, we become empowered to move from being passive historians of what our brain has cooked up for our lives to being the active authors of our own unfolding brain-influenced stories. For example, when we learn that the *linkage*★ of *differentiated*★ parts of the nervous system is an important way that we integrate the brain and enable it to function harmoniously, we can learn to create this *integration*★ intentionally in our lives. How we focus *attention*★ specifically activates certain regions of the skull-based brain, enabling us to selectively turn on certain regions. When areas are selectively activated, this creates the possibility of inducing structural changes in the brain. This is a huge implication of learning about brain function and harnessing the power of attention to create important changes in both function and structure. We do not have to be passive about what we do with the neural side of our lives. For example, there are certain brain regions that are particularly integrative in that they actively link different areas to one another. Knowing about this can help us search for these areas in brain research, and to even consider how focusing the mind can activate and strengthen these integrative regions. Integration in the brain creates a balanced and coordinated nervous system. In turn, an integrated brain permits *empathic★ relationships★*. An integrated brain is important for a resilient and *healthy★* mind.

One area of the brain that is particularly integrative is the *prefrontal cortex★*, which rests behind the forehead. In a *hand model of the brain★* that we use in interpersonal neurobiology, this integrative region is located at the area where your middle two fingernails rest when the fingers are folded over the thumb in a fist. The hand model reveals the three major areas of the *triune brain* (see Figure D-3). The fingers overall represent the outer *neocortex* or *cortex★* that enables us to perceive the outside world and to think (see Figure D-1). Below the frontal part of this cortical region rests the *limbic★* area—represented by the thumb—which processes a number of fundamental experiences such as our *emotions★*, motivations, various forms of *memory★*, the *appraisal* of *meaning★*, and our *attachment★* relationships (see Figure D-2). Below this thumb-limbic area is the palm-*brainstem★* region, an area that serves as the mechanism of basic *arousal★* of the body and brain, and the *fight-flight-or-freeze reaction* to threat. Input to the brainstem and limbic areas also comes from the spinal cord (represented by the wrist) and ultimately rises up to our midline prefrontal regions in the cortex.

The prefrontal cortex links these differentiated areas to one another. This regulatory area exerts a dominant influence on modulating input from the lower areas, a process sometimes called *descending inhibition*. A *"cortical override"* process can occur in which *subcortical*★ activations are overridden by the inhibitory input from the cortex, especially the prefrontal regions. The prefrontal areas coordinate and balance input from the cortex, limbic, brainstem, and bodily regions as these are connected even to the input from other brains (that is, other people). In this way, the prefrontal cortex integrates social, somatic, brainstem, limbic, and cortical systems all into one functional whole. This integrative mechanism enables us to function in harmony in our bodies and in our social worlds. But the prefrontal cortex can go "offline" as we "flip our lids" as represented by the sudden raising of the fingers above the limbic thumb (see Figure D-3). Now you can see how we go down the *low road* and lose many of the *middle prefrontal functions*★ such as *emotional balance*, empathy, and *morality*★. We can no longer be flexible in our responses, can lose insight into ourselves, and can act from irrational impulses that we feel justified in the moment to turn into sometimes harsh and harmful behaviors. This is a temporary *state*★ of a *frontal release* in which the *regulating*★ prefrontal regions no longer balance the subcortical processes from below. Such a *rupture*★ in our relationships with others breaks the interconnected sense of a "we" that comes from *integrative communication*★. Here we see how impediments to *neural integration*★ create impairments in interpersonal integration.

When people learn about how the brain functions, examples such as the "low road" can turn a crisis into an opportunity for growth. Without such an understanding of how the brain goes offline at times, many individuals are harshly self-critical and are so *ashamed*⋆ of their behaviors that they do not return to their child, friend, spouse, or colleague to make a *repair*⋆. Self-recrimination becomes persistent as self-hatred, a pattern of lack of self-compassion combined with hostility and self-derogation. This increases the likelihood of future "low road" behaviors that will occur with more intensity and frequency and will continue to remain unrepaired.

Even very young children can be taught about brain basics in school. When we know about the embodied aspect of the mind, we can alter the mechanisms through which energy and information can flow. The key to this approach is that *aware-ness*⋆ can be *"awakened*⋆*"* through knowledge and skill building to change the way energy and information flow through the brain itself. We know now what we only had an *intuition*⋆ about from clinical experience earlier in our scientific knowledge: The mind can change the activity and the structure of the brain. By harnessing the power of awareness to intentionally focus energy and information in a new way, *neural firing*⋆ can be altered. Attention is the process by which energy and information are focused through the *circuits*⋆ of the brain. When we focus attention in integrative ways, for example, we can cultivate differentiation and then link these differentiated regions to one another. The neuroscientific saying *"neurons that fire together, wire together*⋆*"* reveals how the associated activation of *neurons*⋆ changes their linkages to one another. The process of using attention to change the activity of the brain—and therefore ultimately its very architecture—is a part of the larger process by which experience changes neural structure. This process is called *neuroplasticity*⋆.

The applications of interpersonal neurobiology are based on the neuroplasticity finding that how we focus our attention directly shapes the activity and the structure of the brain. This focus of attention can be within our internal world and in our relationships with one another. Because of this now-established fact that the brain changes in response to our focus of attention, we can realize that mind, brain, and relationships are profoundly interwoven with each other. Recurring patterns can alter the way we connect with each other, how we experience our subjective inner lives, and even how we come to shape the architecture of our own brains. This perspective fuels the interpersonal neurobiology view of interventions in schools and in *psychotherapy*. We are in a position to empower individuals to take charge of their lives and learn the skills that can help them begin to change the neural proclivities that, without awareness, could remain on *automatic pilot*★ and leave an individual passive. We can embrace the now-proven truth that how we focus our attention can transform the brain's structure. The key is to inspire people to rewire their brains toward integration and therefore health and resilence.

4
4

TRIANGLE OF WELL-BEING

CONCEPT: WHAT IS IT?

The ***triangle of well-being***★ is a three-pointed figure that is
a metaphor for the idea that *mind*★, *brain*★, and *relationships*★
are each one part of one whole (see Figure E). But how are
they connected with one another? Are they just three separate domains of reality—or do they compose one reality with
at least three aspects? We can envision the triangle as being a
metaphoric map, a visual image that signifies one reality with
three *interdependent*★ facets. The triangle represents the *process*★
by which *energy and information flow*★ and how the flow changes
across time. Relationships are the *sharing* of that *flow*★. The
brain is the term for the extended *nervous system*★ distributed
throughout the whole body and that serves as the *embodied*★
mechanism of that flow. And what is the mind? We are proposing
that the mind is an *emergent process*★ that arises from the *system*★
of energy and information flow within and between people.
One aspect of mind is something called *self-organization*★, an
emergent process that *regulates*★ that from which it arises. And

so we see mind as arising from the movement of *energy** in the system composed of the body and of relationships. What arises is the emergent self-organizing process that regulates the energy and information flow. Mind, among other attributes, is in part the regulatory process that shapes energy and information flow within and between people.

And so here is our triangle in brief: Regulation (mind) entails the monitoring and modifying of the flow of energy and information. Sharing (relationships) is the exchange of energy and information between two or more people. The mechanism (brain) is the structural means through which the energy and information flow occurs within the body. The triangle depicts one system, the system of energy and information flow, as it passes through the mechanism of the body (brain), is shared (relationships), and is regulated (mind). This is not splitting the three aspects. Instead, mind, brain, and relationships are three aspects of one reality—the system of energy and information flow.

At times, some scientists have expressed concern that this model is dividing these elements in an unhelpful way. In response to these statements, it is important to note that the triangle metaphor actually implies the opposite. With this view, we have one reality with three facets—not three distinct domains of separate realities. A coin has two sides and an edge, but we see the whole of the coin by accepting its *differentiated** parts. When the whole is seen as energy and information flow—a view new to many in a wide range of fields—then the interconnected nature of brain, relationships, and mind emerges into a coherent framework.

And so this is a triangle about energy and information flow. The arrows of influence that one can draw on this triangle point in all directions so that the mind is influenced by both relationships and the brain; relationships are influenced by both the mind and brain; the brain is influenced by both mind and relationships. The arrows connecting each of these three elements point in all directions. Please note that from the *interpersonal neurobiology*★ perspective, this triangle embraces our ground of reality, our starting point for diving deeply into the nature of subjective and objective aspects of our lives. We see the emergent process of mind as being embedded in the triangle. We cannot separate these three elements of energy and information flow from each other: They are three facets of one reality. This is not a *dualism* (or a trioism); rather, this is a "monism" in that we see the one reality as being energy and information flow patterns. The three *primes*★ of experience—the irreducible aspects of the system—are mind, brain, and relationships. There is no need to find a way to simplify this triangle, to reduce one element into the other. We don't need to reduce the two sides of one coin into one side; there are just two sides and one edge of one coin. Here we also have three aspects of one coin, of one reality: embodied mechanism, interpersonal sharing, and regulation.

When we move from a basic triangle of human experience to a triangle of well-being, we have entered the realm of addressing the question of what are a *healthy*★ mind, a healthy brain, and healthy relationships. From an interpersonal neurobiology perspective, *integration*★ is the definition of good health. Integration is the *linkage*★ of differentiated elements. A healthy mind, a healthy brain, and healthy relationships emerge from integration. The structural connections of differentiated areas to one another in the body enable flexible and adaptive regulation. A well-regulated brain coordinates and balances its functioning through being integrated. The functional connection of differentiated individuals to one another permits *compassionate** and *empathic** communication and rewarding relationships to be created. Healthy relationships thrive with *integrative communication** in which differences are honored and compassionate connection is cultivated. A *coherent** inner mental life arises from such embodied and *relational** integration. An integrated mind is a resilient and healthy mind. And so we could state that health emerges with integration in the triangle. We could also reframe this as health emerges from a balanced and coordinated brain, empathic and connected relationships, and a coherent and resilient mind.

IMPLICATIONS: WHAT DOES THE TRIANGLE OF WELL-BEING MEAN FOR OUR LIVES?

The triangle of well-being transforms how we approach our interpretation of scientific findings. Though this is not how mainstream science views things, in interpersonal neurobiology we can use this lens of integration to recast how we understand energy and information flow through the brain as revealed in various brain-scan findings. We can reinterpret the field of mental disorders (usually called the field of *"mental health**"* though neither the mental nor the health is usually defined). We can also reframe how we approach understanding relational experiences within families, couples, classrooms, or companies. Integration becomes our framework, and energy and information flow becomes our focus.

Integration creates harmony. Impaired integration results in *chaos** and/or *rigidity**. Brains or relationships that are not integrated move outside of this *river of integration★* and onto its banks of chaos and rigidity (see Figure K). The river is a visual depiction of the central flow of harmony bounded by the banks of chaos on one side and rigidity on the other. One profound implication of this finding is the reframing of the *Diagnostic and Statistical Manual of Mental Disorders* (the *DSM*), used as a "bible" of psychiatric nomenclature. An interpersonal neurobiology view of this important manual sees each symptom of each syndrome in that text as an example of chaos or rigidity that results from impaired integration. This proposal has been supported by an emerging set of scientific findings discovering that major psychiatric disorders, such as manic-depressive illness, schizophrenia, autism, and developmental *trauma★* and *neglect★*, appear to be associated with impairments to *neural integration★*.

With this perspective on integration and health combined with the exciting new findings about the power of *neuroplasticity★* to change the structural interconnections in the brain across the life span, we are in an exciting and new position to design *creative★* ways of promoting health in our lives. The natural implication of this interpersonal neurobiology view of integration at the heart of health is that we can empower each other to discover novel and effective approaches to promoting wellness in our relationships, our brains, and our minds.

The triangle of well-being places the mind, brain, and relationships into a framework that illuminates their interdependent qualities. This empowers us to weave a range of academic pursuits and practical applications that makes these three facets of our human lives fully integrated. The triangle reveals three mutually influencing facets of one reality.

In interpersonal neurobiology we have an approach to clinical assessment in the therapeutic setting that evaluates chaos and rigidity and views these as windows into impaired integration in brain and relationships. Integration requires the linkage of differentiated elements of a system—and so impairments to integration may involve either or both of these facets as not being well developed. Various *domains of integration*★ can then be assessed to see if linkage and differentiation in that area of life are not well developed, and clinical interventions can be created to target the *development* of those functions in the individual's or family's life.

An interpersonal neurobiology view begins with a foundation in health: We each have a natural push toward integration. The nature of the impediment to integration may be some combination of genetic, experiential, or chance factors. Without pathologizing, this strategy then recognizes each individual's innate potential to "heal" and become "whole" by releasing the blocked capacity of that person to integrate the brain and relationships. The role of the clinician, teacher, or parent, then, is to facilitate the discovery of this potential for integration inherent in each of us. This is the way we awaken the mind to create health in the person's life.

Applying the triangle in everyday life enables us to see how our minds emerge not only from neural mechanisms but also from relationships we have with other people and with our planet. This means that we don't "own" our minds, but rather we have an expanded sense of identity that goes beyond the boundary of our skin, beyond a definition of *"self"*★ that is limited to just our bodily encasement. When studies of happiness, health, longevity, and even *wisdom*★ are reviewed, the key feature shared by each of these attributes is relationships. We can see how the triangle makes relationships equally as important as the embodied mechanisms of brain in shaping the mind. When relationships are integrated, a person's mind thrives and the individual is healthier, happier, wiser, and lives longer. Not bad for one point of a triangle!

At the heart of the triangle of well-being is a fully integrated view of energy and information flow: the way it is shared in relationships, passes through the embodied mechanism of the brain, and is regulated by the self-organizing emergent embodied and relational process of mind. All of this can be found in one diagram: We can hang our scientific hats on the integrated nature of the triangle's interconnected points.

5
5

AWARENESS

CONCEPT: WHAT IS IT?

Awareness★ is a fundamental aspect of mental experience with which we have the subjective sense of knowing or being conscious of something. There are several facets of awareness, including the subjective quality of that of which we are aware, sometimes called the "qualia" of something such as the scent of a rose or the redness of its petals. We also have the experience of knowing, the subjective sense of being aware that something is in the "spotlight" of our *attention*★. You know right now that you are reading THIS word, THIS. And then there is the object that we are aware of, the subject of our attention, the "thing" that we are now having a sense of knowing, of seeing, of, well, of being aware of—our sense of the "known." This is when we know we are smelling the rose, know we are touching its leaves, holding its stem, placing it in someone's loving hands; we know, from that person's smile, that the resultant tears, embrace, and connection are real. Awareness is a *process*★ that involves at least three aspects: a subjective felt sense, a knowing, and a known.

The term awareness and the term *consciousness*★ are seen by many as synonyms. Though sometimes people extend the personal use of consciousness to refer to a wider, shared process, even this broader use of the term consciousness can still be seen as a form of shared awareness, of something being in the front of many persons' *minds*★, of a cultural awareness, of a "collective consciousness." When we come to see that consciousness permits choice and change, then this shared awareness can be at the heart of creating large-scale shifts in human *culture*★. Rather than being some mysterious metaphysical influence, instead the direct experience of shared awareness may have concrete effects on *relationships*★ and on *brains*★. In this way, *cultural evolution* may occur by a shift in shared awareness that is transmitted in the profoundly important but often subtle patterns of interpersonal communication that are a fundamental part of our socially embedded and interconnected mental lives.

Awareness and consciousness are of great interest to a range of academicians, from neuroscientists to philosophers, and they are the subjects of literature and poetry. The experience of music and dance bring the rhythmic motion of the body in tune with our inner subjective awareness. The fundamental nature of our relationships is shaped by awareness: When we share something in awareness with another person, it changes the nature of that experience, alters the *flow*★ of *information processing*★, and creates the closeness we feel with another person.

IMPLICATIONS: WHAT DOES AWARENESS MEAN FOR OUR LIVES?

Awareness is empowering in that it allows a person to have choice and the ability to change from an automatic *mode*★ of being to one of active engagement with the world. From a *relational** point of view, awareness permits people to transform the way interactions are unfolding as new modes of sharing energy and information can be introduced to alter old, engrained patterns. Inside the brain, the experience of awareness permits the *energy and information flow** through the *nervous system** to move in new ways—enabling, for example, nonintegrated *states** to move toward *integration**. For these reasons, then, it may not be a surprise that every form of *psychotherapy* seems to involve awareness at its core.

The *neural correlates* of consciousness reveal which areas of the brain are activated during the *subjective experience** of awareness. This notion of correlation, of temporal association, is an important concept in that we don't really know the connection between brain firing and mental awareness—or any mental phenomenon, for that matter. Neural correlation is a scientific way of describing how brain activity seems to co-occur in time with the subjective mental experience of thinking, perceiving, or being aware of something. In this way we can say that a range of neural regions seems to become active when consciousness arises. The *brainstem** helps to *regulate** states of alertness. The *limbic** region and related *anterior cingulate** help to assess events and orient attention with a signal that, if it could speak, might go something like this: "Pay Attention Now!" The *cortex** serves as a source of the mechanism of *perceptual** filtering, shaping the nature of what we are aware of as it compares prior experiences of similar events or objects with ongoing, here-and-now sensory input. This is how *top-down** flow from the past encounters the *bottom-up** flow of ongoing sensory streams of energy and information. The result of the crashing of top-down with bottom-up can directly shape what we are aware of in the present moment (See figure G). The *prefrontal cortex★*, especially the *dorsolateral prefrontal* region on the sides, plays an important role in how we put something on the chalkboard of the mind within *working memory* for short-term, temporary *memory★ storage★*. This is how we seem to keep something in the front of our minds so that within awareness, within this working memory, we can reflect on something, manipulate it, and then *encode★* the outcome of such processing of this more elaborated form into storage for access at a future time.

We can teach people to develop forms of awareness that empower them to create integration in their lives. What this means is that awareness is the gateway to fostering and respecting the *differentiation★* of others and the cultivation of *linkages★* through *compassionate★* and *empathic★* communication that are at the heart of vibrant relationships. An *interpersonal neurobiology★* approach sees awareness as the gateway to change by how it affords the opportunity to channel energy and information flow in new and more integrative ways. Awareness and knowledge of the structure of the brain can also be powerful components necessary to promote the linkage of differentiated elements of the nervous system. In these ways, the mind can regulate energy and information flow within its two residences—the brain and relationships—through the empowering process of awareness.

While we do not know exactly what awareness "is," we do know that awareness is an active ingredient in every form of education and psychotherapy. With awareness, *explicit memory★* is engaged as a more flexible and adaptive form of top-down learning. With awareness, *narratives★* can emerge that *make sense★* of otherwise bewildering experiences. When parents bring

awareness to their children in the *co-construction* of their life stories, they allow children to make sense of their experiences
and open the gates of lasting change. Awareness may be essential for well-being, and it is a tool of the mind that empowers the movement of our relationships and our brains toward
integration.

6
6

MINDFUL AWARENESS

CONCEPT: WHAT IS IT?

Mindful awareness★ can be described as a form of *aware-ness*★ in which we are alert and open to present experience without being swept up by judgments and prior expectations. While there is still ongoing discussion about how to define being mindful, the overall sense of the term is revealed in the notion of being fully present for an inner or outer moment of experience, of being accepting and open. In contrast, the term "awareness" by itself can infer a way of knowing that might be nonmindful in that we can be aware of a prejudicial belief, for example, and act hostilely toward others because of these pre-existing *mental models* of hostility. In this case we may be fully aware, but we are not mindfully aware in that we are not being open and accepting; rather we are filled with preexisting judgments. Some interpretations of mindful awareness, then, and the way we are using it in *interpersonal neurobiology*★, imply discernment or a moral stance. This stance is one of positive regard for others, a *nonjudgmental awareness* that is imbued with acceptance at its core, of *compassion*★ toward *self*★ and others. Some views of mindful awareness restrict the idea of being mindful more to the aspect of the focus of *attention*★, of stating that the spotlight of one's focus is on the here-and-now in an open manner and that we should leave the characteristics of compassion and kind regard to other constructs such as self-compassion, *empathy*★, and *morality*★.

Mindful awareness can be an innate part of an individual's life, or it can be intentionally created by practices such as *meditation*, yoga, tai' chi', qigong, or centering prayer. To highlight this distinction, we can describe a mindful *state*★ and a mindful *trait*. A state is a temporary activation of mental or neural *processes*★, such as a *state of mind*★, that comes and goes moment by moment. A trait is a repeating way of being, something that can be a habitual pattern or a natural way of interacting with the world. The terms "mindfulness" and "mindful traits" are used in various ways in the scientific literature and may refer to a way of being and to measurable enduring aspects of a person's personality, respectively. Studies of mindful traits, for example, reveal elements of being nonjudgmental, nonreactive, aware of moment-to-moment experience, being able to label and describe the internal world, and, independently for those who practice mindfulness techniques such as meditation or yoga, being self-observant.

Whether a state or a trait, the exact meaning of the term "mindful" as applied to these conditions is actually in the process of being clarified. Whatever the precise definitions and terminology that are ultimately agreed upon, it is clear from a wide range of studies that the ability to be aware of moment-to-moment experience and to be able to disengage from distracting automatic thoughts, feelings, memories, and behaviors and return to being in the present is good for your *health*★ and even good for the health of others. Studies of those with mindful awareness using a broad application of these features reveal that it is of benefit to the health of the *mind*★ in terms of balanced *emotional regulation*★, flexibility, and approaching rather than withdrawing from challenging events. Being mindful makes you more empathic and improves the health of *relationships*★. And being mindful improves the health of the body in terms of enhanced immune function and increased telomerase—the enzyme that maintains the telomeres at the ends of chromosomes and thus enhances cellular longevity. Mindfulness also helps you have more *resilience*★ in the face of chronic pain. Mindful awareness helps minds, relationships, and our *embodied*★ lives.

IMPLICATIONS: WHAT DOES MINDFUL AWARENESS MEAN FOR OUR LIVES?

The health benefits of mindful awareness suggest that it is a good, essential, and important thing to have in our lives however we ultimately arrive at a specific definition of this way of being. Having the ability to be present for our lives is good for us. Given that *mindful awareness practices*★ are available for children, adolescents, and adults, it makes sense that such mind-training practices have a powerful potential to promote well-being and resilience across the life span. Helping to intentionally create mindful states over time may be at the heart of creating mindful traits in a person's life that promote resilience and well-being.

From an interpersonal neurobiology perspective, mindfulness is a profoundly integrative process in the mind, *brain*★, and relationships. This is our view of why being mindfully aware is associated with well-being. This also means that teaching mind-fulness-promoting skills can be seen as a way of cultivating *integration**. Given that integration is at the heart of health, *kindness**and compassion, developing a regular skill-building program for people across the life span makes a lot of integrative sense.

*Neuroplasticity** is the way the brain changes in response to experience, learning to focus attention in a way that promotes mindful awareness can change the structure of the brain. Studies have repeatedly revealed that the parts of the brain most implicated in these studies vary but generally include integrative regions that *link* cortex*, limbic** area, *brainstem**, body proper, and social inputs from other brains. These integrative areas influence *executive functions**, including emotional regulation and the focus of attention, as well as *emotional and social intelligence*, such as the capacity for empathy and self-understanding. These regions include the *anterior and posterior cingulate**, the *orbitofrontal* cortex, and both the medial and *ventral* aspects of the *prefrontal** region, including the *insula** and the limbic *hippocampus**.

One way of conceptually assembling some of these integrative areas of the brain that are activated in mindful awareness is to view them as part of a *middle prefrontal** group of regions of the frontal cortex (see Figure D-1) that serves to connect the body proper, brainstem, limbic area, cortex, and input from other people, (or other brains if you will). The nine functions that arise from the integrative processing of the middle prefrontal area are body *regulation**, *attuned communication**, *emotional balance, fear modulation, flexibility of response*, insight**, empathy, *morality**, and *intuition**.

Here is a fascinating finding. The functions of the middle prefrontal cortex are found as outcome measures for both mindfulness practice and for (the first eight of the nine) secure parent-child *attachment*. This overlap between mindfulness and attachment hints at the notion that some shared process may exist between these two seemingly distinct aspects of human life. One proposal is that the inner *reflection** of mindfulness practice involves a form of *internal attunement** in which an observing self attunes to an experiencing self in an open and kind way. Likewise, secure parent-child attachment is characterized by *interpersonal attunement**, a form of communication that involves a parent attuning to a child in an open and kind way. Attunement, internal in mindfulness and interpersonal in attachment, can therefore be seen as a manifestation of integration. In fact, one important outcome of integration is kindness—toward others, and toward ourselves.

These nine prefrontal functions are also shared in other ways. A survey of a broad range of psychotherapists suggests that these nine middle prefrontal functions are a comprehensive description of *mental health**. A number of individuals from diverse backgrounds have shared the view that this list depicts a way of living a wise and kind life, as taught by way of the oral or written teachings of a broad range of *wisdom** traditions throughout the world—including the Inuit and Lakota traditions of North America, the Polynesian *culture** in the Pacific, the Hindu and Buddhist traditions of Asia, the Islamic and Jewish traditions originating in the Mideast, and the Christian religions that developed in Europe. These nine middle prefrontal functions are a result of *neural integration**—and so these findings suggest that mindfulness, *secure attachment**, mental health, and living a wise and kind life may each be the result of and also cultivate neural integration.

The concept of integration being at the heart of health and

resilience enables us to see that mindful awareness training is a profoundly integrative practice. With the intentional creation of mindful awareness, the brain can be stimulated through the focus of attention to link *differentiated* areas to one another and relationships can be made to be more empathic. As the mind is both embodied and relational, the use of this form of awareness to promote integration reveals how we can intentionally promote health across the many aspects of our lives.

From an interpersonal neurobiology perspective, any intentional creation of integration is a part of the overall approach toward health. In this direct way, we see mindful awareness practices as a fundamental part of not only clinical interventions, but also educational experiences. Often such a practice requires that we "take *time-in**" to *reflect** on the inner nature of our subjective mental lives. This time-in practice enables an individual to become internally attuned, to have an observing-self focus attention in the here-and-now on the experiencing-self in the present moment. With this increased capacity for internal attunement, we can propose that the individual is actually harnessing the same neural mechanisms at the heart of interpersonal attunement. In this way, mindful awareness from time-in actually cultivates the neural machinery needed for empathy and compassion toward others. Attunement is the shared mechanism found in healthy relationships with others and in the relationship we have with ourselves. In this way, mindfulness can be seen as a way of becoming your own best friend. As a wide range of studies suggests that the most potent positive factor promoting health, longevity, and "happiness" is our interpersonal relationships, perhaps we can include mindfulness as a way of not only enhancing those social connections but also enriching the relationship we have with ourselves? Imagine sharing your home, the body, with your best friend instead of a neutral observer or even a hostile opponent. This is the power of mindfulness to create well-being throughout the *triangle*★ of human experience. Why not provide such integrative training to people, encouraging regular time-in for young and old, so that their brains can become more integrated, their relationships with the self and others can become kinder and more *meaningful*★ and compassionate, and their minds can become more flexible and resilient?

7

ATTENTION

CONCEPT: WHAT IS IT?

*Attention** is the *process** that shapes the direction of the flow of *energy and information**. Attention can be within *consciousness**, so that we are aware of the object of our attention. Attention can also be *nonconscious**, in that the energy and information flow is being directed but we are not aware of that *flow**. The formal terms for these are focal (conscious) and nonfocal (nonconscious) attention.

IMPLICATIONS: WHAT DOES ATTENTION MEAN FOR OUR LIVES?

When we use *awareness** to intentionally shape the direction of the flow of energy and information, we are strengthening the ability of *focal attention* to function by creating the possibility of choice and flexibility. We can select what to pay attention to, sustain that attention, and then switch attention as needed. Children, adolescents, and even adults can be taught to strengthen focal attention. In many ways, focal attention enables us to turn *intention** into action with a sense of purpose and volition. Also, when focal attention is used in the moment, our *explicit memory** for that event can be more effectively created. Long-term *encoding** of memory involves solidifying the synaptic *linkages** among *neurons** through *long-term potentiation*. If these forms of stored memory are explicitly encoded, they are accessible as factual and autobiographical *representations** that can be sorted through as needed. Explicit memory is more flexible and fluid than its implicit counterpart.

Nonfocal attention also shapes our memory, but it primarily influences *implicit memory** that *encodes** and *stores** our *emotions**, *perceptions**, sense of familiarity, and our bodily response. When focal attention is blocked, as may occur during a *traumatic** experience, the explicit memory created by the *hippocampus** in the *limbic** region cannot be created. In this situation, the increased connectivity among neurons—the basis of memory itself—is formed but involves areas of the *brain** not linked together by the hippocampus. These implicit neural associations influence our feelings, thoughts, decision making, and behavioral reactions often without our knowing the origins of these implicit influences. For example, the *basal ganglia* beneath the *cortex** may be responsible for rule-guided behavior that can be learned implicitly and enacted automatically. The *amygdala** may also implicitly encode emotional responses of fear, for example, that can be *primed* to respond without an awareness of its derivation from past experience.

One explanation for this finding is that nonfocal attention shapes what is formed in implicit memory, and this neural assembly does not require the hippocampus for encoding or *retrieval**. In other words, when *information** is being *regulated** (attention) without awareness (nonfocal) we have neural *circuits*★ activated that encode and then store the experience as implicit memory. The hippocampus is not engaged, because this integrative structure requires awareness (present with focal attention) to guide information *integration*★. And so the elements that are laid down when only nonfocal attention is being used to process an experience are only in an implicit form.

Divided attention is the process by which focal attention is placed on one aspect of an experience, such as a nontraumatizing element of the environment during an attack. Nonfocal attention is directed at another element of an experience, such as the traumatizing aspect of the event. The experience of divided attention is that we are only aware of that which was in the spotlight of focal attention; we are not aware of the nonfocally attended elements, but they are encoded and stored in implicit forms. Divided attention in this way can lead to a blockage of explicit encoding for the traumatic aspect of an experience because that was not in the spotlight of attention during the experience. Only implicit elements are encoded and stored. In addition to this mechanism of divided attention, the release of large amounts of *cortisol* may further inhibit hippocampal activation and block the explicit encoding of an overwhelming experience. The simultaneous release of the *catecholamine* norepinephrine (or adrenaline) may increase implicit memory encoding for the nonfocally attended, emotionally distressing, physically painful aspects of a trauma. Unfortunately, nonfocal attention and the subsequent creation of implicit memories of a traumatic experience are not inhibited by the division of attention and may even be intensified by this release of norepinephrine.

This profile of increased implicit memory and blocked

explicit memory encoding for a traumatic experience may be an important mechanism for the creation of posttraumatic stress disorder. From an *interpersonal neurobiology*★ perspective, trauma is a painful example of impaired integration.

An understanding of the roles of nonfocal attention and focal attention in the differential encoding of implicit and explicit memory can not only help to understand the impact of trauma on the *mind*★, but also can lead to new strategies of clinical intervention. Impaired integration is at the core of how physiological responses and divided attention may have negatively impacted an individual. Integrative interventions then are the natural application of this perspective on how to treat trauma. Teaching traumatized individuals the skills of *mindful awareness*★, internal imagery, and resource building can enable them to use the focus of attention in order to intentionally alter their internal *state*★ of *dysregulation*★. Attention can play a major role in the movement of posttraumatic memory configurations toward a more integrated state that accompanies the process of healing.

From an interpersonal neurobiology perspective, attention is the "scalpel" that helps us remold *neural pathways*: Attention is to a clinician or teacher what a scalpel is to a surgeon. Individuals can be empowered with focal attention to move the neural proclivities of trauma into new states of integrative firing. Children whose teachers capture their imagination and inspire them to pay attention will be able to learn and build a scaffold of knowledge about the world and themselves. Attention is the driving force of change and growth.

Attention is the process that regulates energy and information flow—and in this way it is not what the mind "does," but it is what the mind "is." Attention, for example, in individuals who have experienced trauma is at the heart of how suffering manifests itself. Hypervigilance to pay attention to subtle forms of stimuli that remind the individual of a painful past event reveals how attention has been enslaved by trauma. Numbing is a way that focal attention, attention within awareness, has been blocked from taking in signals from the body. Attention becomes usurped by trauma.

How does this relate to integration? When *chaos★* or *rigidity★* is found, the areas of a person's life where integration is impaired can become the focus of clinical intervention. Intervention involves the focusing of attention on underdeveloped areas to enable them to become *differentiated★*. Next, separate regions are then linked by the simultaneous focusing of attention on the processes that emerge from these differentiated areas. The result of the aphorism *"neurons that fire together, wire together★"* is that the *neural firing★* patterns will change because of the focus of attention. Where we focus attention stimulates neural activation among interconnected neurons. This coupling of neuronal firing leads to changes in protein synthesis and the enhancement of synaptic connections. This is how we use the focus of attention to SNAG★ the brain: stimulate neuronal activation and growth. As these patterns of firing change, neural connections rewire.

At our interpersonal neurobiology home, the Mindsight Institute, we use the saying that we want to "inspire to rewire." This means that our *relationships★* with others can serve as the motivator to enable us to focus our attention in new and integrative ways that create a resilient mind and a healthy brain.

NEUROPLASTICITY

CONCEPT: WHAT IS IT?

Neuroplasticity* is the ability of the *brain** to change its structure in response to experience. Experience activates *neurons**, which then can turn on genes that enable structural changes to be made that strengthen the connections among activated neurons. Even the focus of *attention** is a form of experience that activates neurons, turns on genes, and makes structural changes to the connections among neurons. In this way, the *mental process** of focusing attention can change the physical structure of the brain. This is neuroplasticity. How does this happen? Understanding some of the details of the science behind these processes can help answer that important question.

Neural firing* entails the movement of charged particles called ions in and out of the *cell membrane* of the neuron's long length, called an *axon*. This electrical process is called an *action potential* and is similar to the notion of the *flow** of electricity down the neuron. When that movement of charged particles, the ions of the action potential, ultimately reaches the end of the neuron it leads to the release of *neurotransmitters*. These are chemicals that can excite or inhibit the downstream neuron by how they diffuse across the *synapse*★ that is *linking*★ two neurons to each other and by how they engage the receiving *receptors* of the downstream neuron's membrane. The space between the two communicating neurons in which the transmitter is released, the synapse, is basically the way that neurons link to one another. The long axonal length connects either to the downstream neuron's cell body or the receiving *dendrites*. It is through these linkages that electrochemical *energy*★ flow involving the action potential and neurotransmitter/receptor engagement takes place. When neurons fire, action potentials flow down the membrane of the presynaptic neuron and transmitters either activate or inhibit the postsynaptic neuron. If activated, that downstream neuron in turn initiates an action potential—the equivalent of a current—that flows down its long length to the synaptic end and the sequence then continues. All of this is what neural firing means.

What this reveals is that one aspect of neural function can be seen as the movement across time of electrical (ions moving in and out of the membrane of the neuron) and chemical (neurotransmitter release and receptor engagement, like a key interacting with a lock) forms of energy. Electrochemical energy flow is the *embodied*★ mechanism represented as the brain in our *triangle*★ of human experience.

In some situations, this neural firing turns on the genetic machinery in the neurons' nucleus to lead to the production of proteins and the creation and strengthening of the connectivity among neurons. Electrochemical energy flow initiates the activation of genes and the alteration of the structure of the brain.

There are two described ways in which synapse formation

occurs early in life. One is by an *experience-expectant* mechanism whereby genes encode the nature of connections to be made in the fetus and young infant that "anticipate" that the child will experience basic, species-generalized events, such as exposure to light and sound, to maintain the previously established synaptic connections of the *perceptual* * systems* * of sight and hearing. In contrast, an *experience-dependent* mechanism also exists by which individualized experiences, such as seeing your mother at the park or hearing your father's voice while swimming in the pool, uniquely activate the genetic machinery to create synapses that depend on that particular set of experiences in order to be created.

These basic neural connections set up early in life by either mechanism create the foundation for how the brain will participate in *information processing* * as the child grows. The focus of attention and the ongoing stimulation of neural firing continue to mold the interconnected architecture of the individual throughout the life span.

IMPLICATIONS: WHAT DOES NEURO-PLASTICITY MEAN FOR OUR LIVES?

Neural firing is associated with mental experience, such as perceiving or thinking or feeling or *remembering* *. When we remember, the firing of neurons occurs in a pattern that is being shaped by a past experience. This way that the past influences present functioning is how we learn, how we remember, and it is created by changes in neural connections. The way that experience shapes neural structure is called neuroplasticity. The simple mechanism is this: The firing of neurons can lead to alterations in the strength of connections among those neurons that are firing together. How does this occur?

When neurons actively fire, they release transmitters and become a part of a wave of neuronal activations in that moment, and this activity sometimes leads to the *genetic expression* of *information** from the cell's nucleus. Within each nucleus of our cells rests the deoxyribonucleic acid, or *DNA*, that contains the building blocks, the alphabet, of our genes. The sequence of nucleotides that makes up our chromosomes, the clustering of our genetic letters that form the words of our genes that we've inherited from our ancestors, carries the necessary information to build our bodies—and shape our neural architecture. The *expression of genes* leads to the production of proteins that then can alter the structure of our bodies and brains.

Genes are like books in a library—they must be read in order to have an impact on the world. When genes are expressed, the double helix DNA that is coiled around itself in the nucleus of the cell is unraveled and single-stranded RNA (ribonucleic acid) is transcribed. This RNA then moves to the cell's main areas outside the nucleus, the cytoplasm, where a ribosome translates the RNA sequence of nucleotide molecules into sequences of amino acids that make up the proteins that are now produced. These proteins become a fundamental part of how the body changes its structure—in this case, how neurons make new or stronger synaptic connections with one another.

The key issue is that we have an average of ten thousand connections linking an average neuron to other neurons. With one hundred billion neurons, this makes for hundreds of trillions of synaptic linkages. When we also realize that the brain's neurons are surrounded and supported by trillions of *glial* cells—including those called oligodendrocytes and astrocytes—we become humbled by our ignorance about "how the brain works."

We do know that when we develop skills after many hours (some postulate at least ten thousand) of practice, the oligodendrocytes produce *myelin*. Myelin is a fatty sheath that coils around the axon. When myelin is present, the speed of the action potential passage down the axon is 100 times faster. With myelin, too, the time for recovery before the next firing occurs—the refractory period—is 30 times shorter. The amount of enhanced functioning that a myelinated *circuit** has is 3,000 (30 multiplied by 100) times that of a non-myelinated circuit. It is no wonder that Olympic athletes can perform feats we can only marvel at, because we haven't taken the disciplined time to coil myelin around those same neural circuits of skill.

And so neuroplasticity involves a number of ways in which the brain's structure changes in response to experience. We've already covered two: *synaptogenesis,* in which synapses are created or strengthened, and myelinogenesis, in which circuits are made more efficient and quicker by the laying down of an insulating sheath along the interconnected axons. There may even be changes in the way our glial cells enable the blood flow to supply the needed oxygen and nutrients to activated regions as well. And two other ways neuroplasticity impacts neural structure are *neurogenesis* and *epigenesis**. Neurogenesis occurs across the life span and involves the *differentiation** of neural stem cells into fully mature neurons in the brain. This process may take about two to three months to enable a stem cell to create a fully developed neuron in the interconnected web of the brain. This is in contrast to the more rapid establishment of alterations in synaptic linkages, which may occur within minutes to hours and become *consolidated* over a period of days to weeks.

Studies have identified this more slowly occurring neurogenesis in the *hippocampal*★ region, but future research may reveal neural stem cell differentiation in other areas as well. For neuroplasticity, the issue is that structural changes in the brain may involve synaptic growth from preexisting neurons that are now connecting to one another for the first time or are strengthening existing connections, or they may involve the more time-consuming growth of new neurons that then are able to grow their synaptic linkages to a wide array of other neurons. If we then add myelin into this growth, we increase the effective functional coupling of these synaptically interconnected neurons by 3,000 times and make quite an efficient neural machinery of *energy and information flow*★. It is the marvel of human achievement, whether we watch the Olympics, listen to a concert pianist, soak in the gorgeous art of a painter, or simply gaze at the amazing way we can function as social creatures deeply invested in the *compassionate*★ care and understanding of others that we appreciate the mystery and majesty of our human capacities to develop complex skills. Our possibilities are wide open—if we use our *minds*★ wisely!

Beyond synaptogenesis and neurogenesis, on top of the growth of myelin and whatever other important but yet undiscovered experience-shaped functions of our supportive glial cells, we also have the finding that experiences alter the way genes are expressed. These epigenetic changes suggest that how energy and information flow through the *nervous system*★—how neurons are activated—directly alters the control molecules that *regulate*★ the expression of genes.

Epigenesis is the process by which experiences impact the regulation of gene expression. This alteration in the expression of genes then influences how structural changes will be created in the brain itself. It is important to note that these studies do not suggest that experience alters the sequence of nucleotides in the genome—that is, genes themselves are not being changed. We must be very careful not to overstate the situation, as this is a point of serious historical significance in science. Instead, the regulatory molecules that are a part of the chromosome's architecture are altered. Again, experience does not alter the sequence of nucleotides that makes up the genetic letters and words of the books of our chromosomes, but experience does influence the librarians that regulate the release of those books. Genes are not changed by experience; the expression of genes is changed. It is these regulatory molecules (histones and methyl groups along the chromosomes) that directly shape how and when genes are expressed and therefore how and when brain structure will be changed in response to experience.

The implications of epigenetic findings are huge when we appreciate that recent research has found that severe *trauma*★ and *neglect*★ in childhood can alter the expression of genes responsible for the circuits that control our response to *stress*★. In other words, not only are the integrative circuits of the brain not growing well in cases of neglect or *abuse*★, but the very hormonal equilibrium that would support being resilient in response to stress is compromised because of the long-lasting epigenetic regulatory changes. Furthermore, preliminary studies suggest that these epigenetic changes may be passed along through our grandparents' gametes—the sperm and the egg—so that we literally "inherit" epigenetic compromises to our ability to *self-regulate*★ based on the stresses our grandparents may have experienced. These are the passages of epigenetic changes—not genetic changes! Knowing about these possibilities may help us focus more attention on the nonintegrated circuitry that is involved in such compromised self-regulation that may persist across generations. Future research will need to support the notion that we may be able to alter our own internal states and reverse these epigenetic challenges with therapeutic interventions.

One interesting finding relevant to this issue is that *mindfulness** practice increases the level of an enzyme that supports the longevity of our cells. Preliminary findings about the positive impact of mindfulness *meditation* on the enhancement of telomerase, the enzyme necessary to maintain the molecules called telomeres at the end of each chromosome that maintain cell longevity, support the hopeful view of the power of the mind to alter even epigenetic regulation of gene expression.

Neuroplasticity has an upside and a downside. The challenge is that negative experiences can alter brain structure in long-lasting ways that make life difficult. The positive opportunity that neuroplasticity affords is that it is never too late to use the focus of attention to alter the brain's architecture. What we need to know is how we can optimize the brain's integrative functioning by learning to focus our attention in integrative ways. The basics of neuroplasticity also point to several elements that support how experience—including the focus of attention—can alter neural connections in lasting ways.

Seven—or possibly eight—aspects of our life support neuroplasticity. These include the following:

1. Aerobic exercise—when medically possible, voluntary exercise can support continued brain growth.
2. Good sleep—we consolidate our learning from the day when we get a good period of sleep with plenty of REM (rapid eye movement) *states** for dreaming.

3. Good nutrition—the "soil" of the brain's structure requires good food and water, including safe sources of omega-3's, in order to function properly and allow the "seed" of good attentional focus to work well.

4. *Relationships**—our connections with others support a vibrant and plastic brain.

5. Novelty—when we get out of a rut and expose the brain to new stimuli, when we are playful and spontaneous, we keep the brain growing and young.

6. The close paying of attention—when we avoid multitasking and distractions and care about what we are focusing on, we can actually stimulate the release of chemicals locally and widely that support neuroplasticity.

7. *Time-in**: When we focus on our inner sensations, images, feelings, and thoughts, reflecting inwardly, we encourage the growth of regulatory, integrative neural circuits.

8. And, possibly, humor—some preliminary studies suggest that when we laugh we promote the *healthy** growth of the brain. Neuroplasticity, it seems, is in fact a laughing matter.

In *interpersonal neurobiology** we seek to find direct applications of science for practical use in the world. One way of applying the basic principles of neuroplasticity is to suggest a "daily diet" of *mental activities** that promote the healthy growth of the mind, brain, and relationships. A colleague, David Rock, and I created a *healthy mind platter** to parallel a suggestion for a daily intake of food (see Figure J). Our suggestion is that people find a way to embed the activities from the platter within a regular routine. Regularity appears to be the key in habit creation and maintenance, as well as in the promotion of neuroplastic changes. The seven suggested mental activities include sleep time, physical time, connecting time, down time, play time, focus time, and time–in.

In terms of growing integrative fibers to support a healthy brain, mind, and set of social relationships, the specific ways we focus attention drives the specific firing of neurons. Attention activates the specific pathways of neuronal activation in the brain. Those neurons that are activated together will strengthen their connections with one another. When such couplings are integrative in nature, we can see how the focus of attention might promote the growth of integrative structural changes in the brain that would support the integrative functioning at the heart of health.

9
9

SNAG: "NEURONS THAT FIRE TOGETHER, WIRE TOGETHER"

CONCEPT: WHAT IS THIS?

SNAG★ is an acronym that stands for "stimulate neuronal activation and growth." When we SNAG the *brain*★, we are intentionally trying to promote *neural firing*★ and the subsequent *gene expression* that enables *neurons*★ to grow their connections with one another.

This simple acronym is based on the work of a number of ingenious thinkers. While this whole approach of *interpersonal neurobiology*★ enables us to "stand on the shoulders of giants" as we find the *consilient*★ findings across a wide range of disciplines, here we'll name just a selected few of those whose work in the field of *memory*★ and neural functioning have enabled this SNAG concept to even exist. Many more researchers could be cited here, but that is not the purpose of this guide. Instead, this brief review will just give a flavor for the kind of research that supports this acronym. A number of clinical and academic writers have written that when associated neurons fire, the probability of their firing together in the future is enhanced. Sigmund Freud called this property the *Law of Association* and Donald Hebb discussed this same notion in his own writings and so neuroscientists speak of *"Hebb's Law"* or the "Hebbian synapse" created by this associational firing. Carla Shatz, a neuroscientist paraphrasing Hebb, used the easily remembered phrase ***"neurons that fire together, wire together."**** And Robert Post and colleagues extended that phrase with the added "and survive together," connoting the way that we need to "use it or lose it" in brain terms—if neurons are activated together, they will not be pruned away. This loss of neural connections with disuse is called neural pruning, *parcellation*, or *apoptosis*. Fred Gage has revealed how novelty stimulates the growth of new neurons in the *hippocampal** region of the brain. And Eric Kandel won the Nobel Prize for his work revealing how neural firing actually activates gene expression and supports these associational patterns of synaptic growth. Michael Meaney and others have also contributed to our understanding of how experience and subsequent neural firing influence brain growth by revealing how early experience shapes not only neural connections in areas regulating the *stress** response, but also the ways in which the *epigenetic** control of gene expression in those neural areas is altered.

IMPLICATIONS: WHAT DOES FIRING TOGETHER AND WIRING TOGETHER MEAN FOR OUR LIVES?

We are our *attention**. The more intense and perhaps specific our neural firing (which we create with the focus of our attention), the more long-lasting synaptic changes we'll likely initiate in our brain. As one aspect of *mind*★ is the *process*★ that *regulates*★ the *flow of energy and information*★, the mind is attention. What you do with your mind can change the structure of your brain. Attention is that process that regulates *informational*★ flow. We can see through the studies of *neuroplasticity*★, then, that one aspect of the mind—a process that regulates energy and information flow—can alter the structure of the brain. In parenting, teaching, and *psychotherapy*, we use the *relational*★ aspect of mind to focus the attention of our child, student, or client/patient to activate neural firing in a way that can potentially change the brain's structure. This is the fundamental basis of learning. This is SNAGing the brain.

Once the brain's synaptic wiring is altered, pathways that serve as the mechanisms of energy and information flow in the *nervous system*★ will make it more likely for these patterns to continue. This is the enhancement of learning. Whether experience was involuntary, as in *abuse*★ or *neglect*★, or voluntary, as in choosing what to pay attention to in daily life or in school, we become changed by where our attention is placed. This is the way learning can be both negative and positive. Humans are profoundly and lastingly influenced by experience.

Energy and information flow drives neural firing. When neurons fire together, they strengthen their synaptic connections and make it more likely that the associated firing patterns will recur over time. For a teacher, this is good news if educational experiences can shape the brain of the students in a positive way—supporting their preparation for a future we cannot know. As the saying goes, if we use how we were taught yesterday to teach our children today, we are not preparing them well for tomorrow. In this way, education can intentionally SNAG the brain of the students toward *resilience*★ by focusing on the important *R's* of *reflection*★ and *relationships*★ that develop resilience. We no longer need to be limited by educational programs that leave our integrative *prefrontal circuitry*★ behind. In fact, we can have a program of "no prefrontal cortex left behind" as we cultivate *time-in*★ practices that honor the importance of both reflection and relationships at the heart of the resilience created by a well-developed prefrontal integrative region.

In psychotherapy terms, we need to realize that our job is to see in "four dimensions" as we perceive across time, noting that the person in front of us lives within *synaptic shadows*★ from a long lived life in the form of *narratives*★, memories, ways of focusing attention, and the interactions this individual has with us. Part of the art of being a therapist is to learn to see across time, including looking into the potential future possibilities so that we can intentionally support the movement of those we are helping toward a more integrated way of living.

Parents can become awakened to the opportunity—and the challenge—to create more integrative experiences for their children that SNAG their brain toward *integration*★. Being aware of this potential can make parenting truly the way to harness the power of neuroplasticity to change future generations beginning at home.

For anyone helping others or themselves grow toward integration, it is helpful to know the circuits of the brain that are in need of neuroplastic growth. A parent should know about how the particular regions of a child's brain need support and stimulation to grow in an integrated way—for example, *linking*★ the left and right *hemispheres*★ or connecting the body's responses with cortical *awareness*★. A teacher can implement a curriculum that has neuroplasticity as a central tenet, creating an entire program that supports whole-brain integration. Therapists, knowing about the power of attention to alter the structure of the brain, can reframe the nature of the therapeutic relationship and enhance their ability to implement experiences that SNAG the brain toward integration.

The brain does not change in a vacuum. Interpersonal neurobiology reminds us that the brain is profoundly social. With this view, we can turn to our *triangle*★ of mind, brain, and relationships and keep in the front of our minds the reality that even neuroplastic changes are facilitated by supportive relationships. Studies of teaching young children language, for example, reveal that computer-based teaching, which often lacks a relationship to another person in the experience, does not work nearly as well as relationship-based approaches. The *limbic*★ area of the brain that involves our motivational *states*★ and memory formation is linked directly to our need for *attachment*★ relationships.

Applying all the seven (or eight!) factors of neuroplasticity, including relationships and the reflection of time-in, can support the *healthy*★ growth of the brain. When we SNAG toward integration, we get neurons to fire together and wire together in profoundly transformative ways.

THE BRAIN IN THE
PALM OF YOUR HAND

CONCEPT: WHAT IS IT?

***The brain in the palm of your hand**★* is a phrase referring to the *hand model of the brain*★ that we use in *interpersonal neurobiology*★ to have a, well, handy model at a moment's notice when we need to refer to the anatomy of the major regions of the *brain*★ (see Figure D-3). By envisioning the brain, people become empowered to make changes in their lives with more efficacy and self-*compassion*★. For this reason, the hand model has become useful in a wide range of settings, from parenting and education to organizational functioning and *psychotherapy*.

With the thumb folded over the palm and the fingers encircling the thumb as you make a fist, your knuckles facing you represent that area behind your face, and the back of the hand symbolizes the neural area beneath the back of the skull. The wrist represents the spinal cord that sends *energy and information flow*★ to and from the neural structures in the skull itself. Lifting up your fingers and now your thumb, you can see the palm, or-

*brainstem**, as the deepest (and oldest) part of the skull-encased part of the brain. Put your thumb back down and you have the *limbic** area, at least on one side (the limbic region, and the *cortex** above it, are divided into a left and right side). Put your fingers back over the thumb and you'll see how the cortex, the highest (and newest) part of the brain, enfolds the lower *subcortical** limbic and brainstem regions.

It is helpful to learn about brain anatomy and function because when we can "see" how these structures and *processes** are *differentiated**, we can then *link** them with more specificity (see Figures D-1 and D-2). How can this be done, you might ask? The focus of *attention** is the route to specifically activating regions of the brain and then linking them together. There is nothing like experiencing something from the inside out to see if a claim of something being useful has validity. The hand model of the brain and its applications is a case in point. Some initially resist—or outright dismiss—the usefulness of anyone knowing about the brain. But when an openness ensues following a realization of its personal capacity to empower people in a range of settings, generally enthusiasm and curiosity replace initial hesitancy to take on something as odd and new as thinking about how the brain influences your subjective and interpersonal life. This approach simply becomes a handy way of learning more about yourself and others.

IMPLICATIONS: WHAT DOES THE BRAIN IN THE PALM OF YOUR HAND MEAN FOR OUR LIVES?

Knowing about the parts of the brain enables us to use attention to focus on the functions of specific regions, differentiate their functioning, and then promote their linkage. The hand model makes the major areas visibly clear and demonstrates how, for example, the *prefrontal** region links the cortex, limbic area, brainstem, body proper, and even the neural signals from other people.

The body proper sends a set of signals from the muscles and bones and from the internal organs, such as the intestines and the heart, upward through the spinal cord (represented by your wrist) and the *vagal nerve* (the tenth cranial nerve that goes directly from the body into the brainstem), and then ultimately into the prefrontal region (represented by your fingertips). These nonrational sources of *information** influence our reasoning in important ways. This can be called the "*wisdom** of the body" and serves a vital role in decision making of all sorts. As the heart and gut are part of this process, we can understand statements such as "a heartfelt sense" or "my gut feeling" as prefrontal *integration** of bodily data into an integrated approach to living. These are our "heart-brain" and our "gut-brain." These inputs from the body are registered in the integrative *middle prefrontal** region and in this way they interact with other cortical processes including those of *empathy**, *insight**, and *morality**.

The brainstem (represented by the palm) is an ancient region that includes clusters of cells called nuclei that are involved in *regulating** basic bodily functions such as respiration and heart rate. The brainstem also houses the nuclei that mediate the survival responses of the *fight-flight-or-freeze* reactions that become activated when we feel threatened. As basic and ancient *circuits**, the brainstem is sometimes called the reptilian brain that is (evolutionarily) over three hundred million years old.

The limbic area (symbolized by the thumb) is a more modern—two hundred-million-year-old—region that evolved when we became mammals. This area includes the *amygdala*★ and the *hippocampus*★. It helps mediate at least five important functions: it works with the brainstem and body proper in creating *emotion*★; it works with the brainstem to create our motivational *states*★ that drive us to explore, affiliate with others, reproduce, and regulate our resources; it appraises the value and *meaning*★ of experience and orients our attention to things that matter in our lives; it differentiates various aspects of *memory*★ *encoding*★; and it is a part of creating our drive for *attachment*★ *relationships*★—seeking comfort from others who take care of us.

The cortex (represented by the folded fingers over the palm and thumb), known also as the *neocortex* or cerebral cortex, evolved in more modern times in our mammalian history, and it generally is six layers thick and makes *neural maps*★ that represent a wide range of things. A map is the way a cluster of *neurons*★ fires in a pattern that symbolizes something we call a neural *representation*★. This is a neural re-presentation, or symbol, for something other than the *neural firing*★ itself. This is how the electrochemical *energy*★ *flow*★ of neural firing becomes information—something that symbolizes something other than itself.

One initial way of understanding these cortical maps is to think of the cortex in the following overly simplified way (but this, of course, is just a way to get oriented). The back of the brain—at the back of your hand model—generally makes maps of the outside world. As we move forward in the cortex, toward the front knuckles facing you, we make maps of the body's skin (registering touch), then when we reach the *frontal lobe* we make maps of behavioral action with the outside world (our motor and premotor/planning frontal area). When we reach the front-most part of the frontal lobe, called the "prefrontal cortex," we've now come to the area that makes maps of entities far from the concrete physical world, the general focus of the more posterior portions of the cortex.

The frontal lobe is where your second knuckles start and move toward your fingernail region. Your last knuckles down to your fingernails represent the prefrontal cortex. Here in the prefrontal area we can make maps of time, connecting the past, present, and future. This is called *mental time travel*. This capacity enables us to plan . . . and to worry. *Prospective memory* is the way we carve out maps of the future based on what has happened in the past. These maps shape how we perceive here-and-now ongoing experience. We can also make maps of our own *mind*★ and maps of others' minds. These can be called *mindsight maps*★ in that they enable us to see the mind itself as a mind, not just thoughts, feelings, and memories. We see these *mental activities*★ as mental activities, realizing that these are an inner subjective source of personal experience, for ourselves and for others. This is the power of *mindsight*★. This region is also involved in making maps of morality—enabling us to have moral imagination, to have moral reasoning, and to engage in moral action. This can be seen as how we make a mindsight map of "we" on top of our capacities to make a mindsight map of "you" (for empathy) and of "me" (for insight). These are all prefrontally mediated processes, especially coordinated by the cortex.

On your hand model, the middle portion of the prefrontal cortex is located at the area of the middle two fingers, between the last knuckle and the fingernail area. Notice how when your fingers enfold your thumb, this middle prefrontal region touches the limbic and brainstem areas, just as it is directly linked to these regions in the brain itself. If you lift your fingers up and put them back down, you may be able to see how this region is integrative—it links widely separated areas to each other. The middle prefrontal cortex receives direct input from the body proper, through a layer of the spinal cord called *Lamina I** and the vagal nerve. This integrative prefrontal region processes the signals, especially *nonverbal** input, from other people to create a neural map of their mental states—and even our own internal image of our mental life.

When we "flip our lid" at times when we are out of control, we become "dis-integrated" as the middle prefrontal region stops coordinating and balancing the neural firing patterns of the subcortical regions. Raise your fingers up suddenly and you'll have a visual image of how this *low road* behavior can occur. Without the modification of the integrative functioning of the prefrontal cortex, the lower and more impulsive limbic and brainstem areas can run amok. This is sometimes called an "emotional" or "amygdala" *hijacking*. We've temporarily lost our *descending inhibition* in which the higher cortical areas downregulate the activity of the lower subcortical regions. There is no coordination and balance of the *system**, and we have "lost our minds."

Even kindergarten children can be taught about how their prefrontal regions keep the lower areas functioning well by use of the hand model of the brain. Using words such as "upstairs brain" or "downstairs brain" can make these cortical and subcortical areas more easily remembered. Schools that teach this model empower their pupils to know how their own internal mechanisms work so that they can be more aware of their impulses and become more flexible in their responses. Parents can teach children about the brain, and using these basic areas of brainstem and limbic regions as the "downstairs brain" can make the model even simpler. With an upstairs brain coordinating the functioning of the downstairs brain but needing the impact of these important lower subcortical regions to feel things, children can grasp how the basic systems of the brain function. Add to this model the asymmetry between the left and right sides of the brain (called *laterality*), and many of the important mechanisms shaping our daily lives can begin to be understood at a basic level by even very young children. With understanding we have the chance to change the way the brain can sometimes make people behave on *automatic pilot**. With such internal *awareness**, the opportunity to modify behaviors in a *healthy** direction is made available.

It is a fascinating finding that when people have a visual model of the brain, they become more compassionate with others and with themselves. In this approach of interpersonal neurobiology, we distinguish mind from brain from relationships and then see them as part of an integrated whole. Visualizing the brain invites people to realize that while the brain may have been activated in a certain way, it was "out of their control." This ability to visualize how this happens lets people come to understand that a negative behavior may "not be their fault" but it is their responsibility to learn, if possible, how to use their mind to change the way their brain functions. By letting go of the self-blame and the ensuing self-derogation, people can move from internal hostility to self-compassion. Being kind to oneself is a crucial starting place for lasting change. And being kind to oneself also opens the doors to being kind to others. After a *rupture** in communication down the low road, making a *repair** is essential. Realizing "it is not my fault but it is my responsibility" allows us to move with strength and openness to making the crucial repair after such ruptures.

11
11

SPINAL CORD AND LAMINA I

CONCEPT: WHAT ARE THEY?

The **spinal cord**★ (represented by your wrist in the *hand model of the brain*★) carries *energy and information*★ between the body and the skull-based *brain*★. One layer of the spinal cord is called **Lamina I**★, and it is important in bringing the *energy*★ *flow*★ from the interior of the body upward to the brain. We become aware of our body's *states*★ by the input from Lamina I (and the *vagal nerve*) into our skull-based brain. First, this energy flow moves to the *brainstem*★, which helps to *regulate*★ bodily functions and states of *arousal*★. Fight, flight, and freeze are reactions the brainstem creates in response to any threat if present or even if imagined. As data move upward in the *system*★, this neural flow from the body moves to an area just below (or what some consider a part of) the *limbic*★ region— the *hypothalamus*—that helps regulate hormonal release from the brain to adjust bodily functions. And now flow moves to areas of the *cortex*★—in the *middle prefrontal region*★. In particular, some flow goes to the area called the *anterior cingulate*★, which coordinates bodily input with *attention*★ and the generation of *emotion*★. Another flow from Lamina I moves up into the cortex by way of a middle prefrontal area called the *insula*★, especially the right anterior insula. When we become aware of our bodily state—something called *interoception*★— the *anterior insula*★ is activated.

IMPLICATIONS: WHAT DO THE SPINAL CORD AND LAMINA I MEAN FOR OUR LIVES?

The body is an essential part of how the *mind*★ functions. As we've seen, we can define a core aspect of the mind as an *embodied*★ and *relational*★ *process*★ that regulates the flow of energy and information. As regulation involves the monitoring and modifying of something, we need to be well versed in how we monitor the embodied part of energy and information flow. Internal *awareness*★ is a vital part of *emotional and social intelligence*. Interoception has fascinating implications. One is that *neurons*★ called von Economo neurons, or neural spindle cells, create *links*★ between the two middle prefrontal areas—the anterior cingulate and the anterior insula. Developmental and cross-species studies of *self-awareness*★ suggest that the existence of these spindle cells is related to our ability to recognize ourselves in a mirror. It may be, too, that these findings reveal how self-awareness is mediated by input from the body (insula) and its direct and indirect linkages (via the cingulate) to this part of the brain that coordinates bodily input with emotion and its regulation, the control of attention, and the way we are embedded in social *relationships*★. For example, studies have revealed in a number of laboratories how the mediation of bodily pain and the neural response to social rejection involve overlapping pathways. Social isolation hurts, literally. But even more, the capacity to be aware of our bodily state in a balanced way is important for both self-understanding and for the ability to be *empathic** and *compassionate**.

The finding that *mirror neurons* seem to activate the insula in both the sending of *information** downward from cortical *perception** and back upward from bodily responses to what we see in others suggests that this spinal cord/Lamina I/insula flow may serve a crucial social function. Mirror neurons enable us to soak in the internal state of another person, providing a neural mechanism with which we both simulate another's internal state and imitate that person's behavior. Mirror neurons link what we see from others with what we feel and what we do. In other words, our body serves as a kind of antenna enabling us to pick up the sometimes subtle signals from others, shift our bodily state, and then sense these changes in our own body to then imagine what another person might be feeling. This proposed route, involving mirror neurons, insula, and *subcortical** responses, is then sent back up to the middle prefrontal region; the route may be the foundation for compassion and empathy.

If experiences in modern life do not support children being open to their own bodily states, we may be setting up a *cultural** situation that does not nurture either self- or other-understanding. When we turn to the asymmetry of the cortex, we find that the right *hemisphere** has an especially rich input of bodily data compared to that of the left cortex. The right side of the brain also has a specialization in *nonverbal** signal reception and expression. With these findings, we can see that an overly dominant focus on the left hemisphere's tendency to dominate in logical analysis, *linguistic representations*, and decoding of the world in literal ways that are often quite distant from the *wisdom*★ of the body in families or in schools or in some aspects of digital communication may create a set of learning experiences that does not nurture the basics of interpersonal relationships or self-awareness.   Interestingly, the left hemisphere seems dominant for our social *display rules* that govern how we are supposed to act in social situations. Yet our understanding of the inner life of the mind and of the signals of one's own body seems to have a right hemisphere dominance in function. Impoverished emotional and social intelligence may result from insufficient growth of these important and asymmetric mechanisms of interoception.

In school, in therapy, and at home, we can encourage others (and ourselves) to honor the input of the body. When we realize that the body is an important source of *intuition*★ and wisdom, we can see that our limbs and our torso have deep sources of knowledge for our lives. There are extensive *neural networks* around the heart and the intestines, for example, which may serve as complex *information processors*★. We get a heartfelt sense and a gut feeling literally from the spider-web-like information processors around these organs of the body: our "heart-brain" and our "gut-brain."

When we use a *time-in*★ process and reflect inward, we create a neural set of firings that may be at the heart of the interoceptive states that are necessary for emotional and social intelligence. In the various reflective processes of *mindful awareness*★ practices, a body scan may serve to activate the flow of Lamina I and vagal nerve data into the insula and link this input to the functioning of the anterior cingulate to facilitate interoception. The resultant middle prefrontal activation may serve as an important form of vertical *integration** enabling the energy and information flow from the body to reach the cortex where it can be coordinated, balanced, and explored with conscious awareness.

12
12

BRAINSTEM

CONCEPT: WHAT IS IT?

Sometimes called the "old reptilian brain," the **brainstem***
rests at the bottom of the skull, and it includes collections of
neurons* that help monitor and modify basic bodily functions
such as heart rate and respiration. The brainstem also influences our *states** of *arousal**—such as if we are awake, sleepy,
or asleep. The brainstem's *reticular activating system* plays a crucial role in this shaping of our arousal states. Some associate
a related area, the *cerebellum*, as part of our "old brain" that
helps to coordinate not only physical motion and balance, but
our higher functions as well. Located within this area, too, are
cells responsible for mediating the reactions to threat. These
are the "*fight-flight-or-freeze*" responses that get triggered when
we sense danger looming. The brainstem works with the *limbic** area just above it to influence our motivational drives and
our *emotional** states.

IMPLICATIONS: WHAT DOES THE BRAINSTEM MEAN FOR OUR LIVES?

Knowing about the brainstem can greatly enhance our *insights** into "what drives us" in our behaviors. People may often be taken over by basic brainstem states: fighting with others, fleeing from challenges, or freezing in a state of helplessness. Sometimes the feeling of helplessness in the face of overwhelming threat is so great that instead of these activating *reactive states* of fight, flight, or freeze, we may automatically engage an ancient *immobilization defense reaction* that causes us to shut down, faint, or even feign death. This can be called a *"dorsal dive"* in which the *dorsal branch of the vagal nerve*, a part of this more ancient reactive *system** discussed in the *polyvagal theory* of Stephen Porges, is activated and our blood pressure drops, our heart rate lowers, and we can pass out. This may be of evolutionary survival advantage as predators generally do not eat dead animals (and fainting makes us appear dead so we won't be eaten), and if we are bleeding after an attack, going flat after we faint is an important way to maintain blood flow to the head after a serious injury. This ancient and powerful immobilizing freeze response can become initiated when we feel helpless, when there is a sense that there is nowhere to go, no escape, and we feel literally helpless and frozen.

Without knowledge of this area of the *brain**, some people are extremely hard on themselves. After freezing, running away, or fighting back as a quick impulse in response to something perceived as a threat, we can feel mystified as to what just unfolded in our behavior or our internal reactions. "Why did I do that—what is wrong with me?" By knowing about these internal *embodied** mechanisms of *energy and information flow**, we can be kinder to ourselves and gain deep insights into the origins of our responses and reactions. This is how we can be *compassionate*★ toward ourselves instead of being harsh and critical. That is one of the most amazing and powerful implications of *interpersonal neurobiology*★: Knowing about the brain enhances self-compassion.

When we use the *hand model of the brain*★ to literally see the brainstem in the palm of the hand, we can appreciate how this deep and old region "underlies" everything our brain does. Living with a reptilian brain buried deep in the modern human brain helps us understand many of our otherwise inexplicable inner experiences and external behaviors. Fighting back when we are on *automatic pilot*★ can be understood as the brainstem breaking free from cortical control. Having the impulse to flee when confronted with a challenge may be merely our ancient survival instinct expressing itself, and this reaction does not mean that we should necessarily leave a situation—though maybe we should. We can analyze from an open and curious place what is happening and what we should do. This is the opposite of being on automatic pilot, of being "mindless" and a slave to our brain's reactivity. And for those who experience the feeling of sheer helplessness, even at the sight of blood in a film, knowing about the immobilization reaction of the brainstem can help turn confusion into clarity. The *cortex*★ can help us reflect on these *subcortical*★ *processes*★ and offer us the opportunity, with *awareness*★, to create choice and change. We do not have to do whatever the brain is signaling us to do at the moment. We can use a *cortical override* mechanism to let subcortical processes arise and fall in their activations as we allow them to simply come in and out of awareness but do not follow through with their directives. This is the power of the *mind*★ to shift how the brain may be ruling our lives.

In interpersonal neurobiology we embrace both the embodied and the social essence of the mind. Because *integration*★ is at the heart of *health*★ in our approach, we then need to know about these *differentiated*★ areas in order to *link*★ them to each other. Awareness permits us to have choices in how we behave. By coming to accept internal firing patterns, we can actually see them more clearly and then move the flow of energy and information via *intention*★ and focused *attention*★ to actively change them. This is how we use awareness to pull ourselves out of automatic pilot. This can be called having an *awakened mind*★. The framework of the brain's various regions enables us to monitor more clearly, and then to move toward, a more balanced and coordinated way of being—a more integrated state—so that we can feel at home in our own brains.

LIMBIC AREA

CONCEPT: WHAT IS IT?

When we evolved as mammals, the **limbic area**★ of the *brain*★ developed and enabled us to build more complex functions than the lower *brainstem*★ region by itself could create. Represented as the thumb in the *hand model of the brain*★, the limbic area includes the specific regions of the *hippocampus*★ and the *amygdala*★ that reside in the medial temporal lobe on both sides of the brain. Some views suggest that the right limbic region takes in data from the body more fully than the left. Interestingly, the left hippocampus helps to *process*★ a kind of *explicit memory*★ called factual or *semantic memory*★, while the right hippocampus has been reported to mediate the *episodic* and *autobiographical*★ forms of explicit memory. In other words, the right can be seen as the processor of bodily input and memory *encoding*★ about the *self*★ whereas the left seems more directly involved in assessing and *remembering*★ aspects of the outer world. The limbic amygdala is important in face *perception*★, especially on the right side of the brain, as well as in mediating certain *emotional*★ responses, especially that of fear and anger.

Limbic circuits blend emotions, bodily functions, and social interactions in many ways. Some scientists place the master regulator of endocrine function, the *hypothalamus*, as a part of this limbic region as it controls the impact of hormones on the body and the brain itself. A region called the *anterior cingulate*★ is also considered limbic and has a direct role in governing *attention*★, registering bodily states, influencing *emotion regulation*★, and participating in *social cognition*. Emotions and social *context*★ influence our experiences and the ways we encode memories as exemplified by the *flashbulb memory*, in which a shared emotionally charged event, like a presidential assassination or the crashing of a space shuttle, becomes stored in our brains with intense associations.

IMPLICATIONS: WHAT DOES THE LIMBIC AREA MEAN FOR OUR LIVES?

There are five important functions mediated by the limbic area.

1. Working with the brainstem, the limbic area helps to create motivational drives such as the inclination to reproduce, monitor resources, or to explore. These are the *subcortical*★ origins of motivation as the limbic area and brainstem are below the *cortex*★.

2. Combining input from the body proper with signals from the brainstem, the limbic areas help to create emotional *states*★ such as anger, fear, sadness, and joy. This subcortical input of "emotion" to our higher reasoning of the cortex

suggests that our cortical processes are directly impacted by these nonrational but important subcortical ways of knowing.

3. The limbic areas serve to appraise the *meaning*★ of incoming perceptions of events. This evaluative process shapes how we feel, determining if something is important and worth paying *attention*★ to—and so this limbic *appraisal* shapes how we orient our attention to something and then further direct attention. It is in this process that some authors place the anterior cingulate, and sometimes even the *orbitofrontal* region, as part of the limbic area. Others see these as regions of the *prefrontal cortex*★ that bridge cortical and limbic functions. These are just human-defined anatomic names and distinctions; the important issue is that these bridging *circuits*★ establish the *integration*★ of subcortical input with cortical processing. This is how the *middle prefrontal cortex*★ plays a crucial role in integrating the *differentiated*★ subcortical input with the cortical processing.

4. Various differentiated forms of memory are encoded via the limbic area, including the important *implicit memory*★ process of emotion, such as fear via the amygdala, and the explicit memory process involving the hippocampus, which is activated with *focal attention* to an experience. Explicit memory can be thought of as the integration of implicit elements of encoded experience into the factual and *autobiographical*★ forms of memory.

5. During our mammalian evolution, the limbic area created *attachment*★ to a *caregiver*★. For two hundred million years, mammalian young have depended on their caregivers for survival. This is considered one of several *behavioral systems* or *emotional operating systems* that evolved over millions of years

and that mediate other functions such as resource allocation and affiliation. The hormone oxytocin may help facilitate the intensity of this attachment capacity, but all mammals regardless of oxytocin levels depend on their caregivers for sustenance.

One implication of the limbic area is that it is an interface between the more impulsive and "primitive" brainstem and the higher, often more rational cortex. Integration in the brain would therefore honor the differences in these regions and promote their *linkage** through collaboration, not internal warfare. An *interpersonal neurobiology** approach enables the activity stemming from these regions to be known and then linked with other areas.

When we become aware of the *nonverbal** input from the subcortical regions, including the limbic areas, we open the *mind** to subtle but important signals that shape our internal worlds. These are not word-based thoughts, but rather are felt sensations that arise in *awareness** and may be difficult to articulate. Knowing about these five limbic functions can bring clarity to a previously befuddling set of feelings and impulses. As the limbic area forms only partially in the womb, this region of the brain is shaped by our early experiences with caregivers after birth. Knowing how these basic processes then interact with both prior experience and with ongoing interactions with others can help move a person out of *automatic pilot** in which the feelings from below have held sway over their daily lives.

Given that the limbic area shapes how we appraise the meaning of events, knowing the hand model and seeing the limbic area's distinct location from the higher areas of the cortex can help us realize that sometimes a "feeling" is indeed not a fact.

We can feel compelled about something or someone, and this feeling may be influenced by survival reactions from the brainstem's input and the evaluative activities of the limbic area as much as it is a fair assessment of a present situation. Awareness of the comings and goings of limbically induced states can help create an internal *mental space* of awareness in which to observe and not react to limbic lava or limbic withdrawals when they occur. This mental space enables us to pause and reflect, giving time for the wash of feelings to move on and for new states to be created. This is akin to *time-in*★ practice that develops the hub in the *wheel of awareness*★.

Acknowledging that the mind is an *embodied*★ and social process helps us to create this important mental space that is a part of *mindful awareness*★. From the hand-model perspective, we can see this as the way the cortex holds limbic input in awareness but creates a buffer that delays impulsive response. When we "rest in awareness" we can sense that the lower area's input is honored, and so it can be differentiated but it is not enslaving us. *Top-down*★ no longer needs to imprison *bottom-up*★, nor does bottom-up need to threaten top-down. This is how an *awakened mind*★ moves toward being more spacious and stable. It is this acceptance of our ongoing moment-to-moment experience that sets the stage for us to be present with what is and then move our internal state to a more integrated way of being.

14
14

CORTEX

CONCEPT: WHAT IS IT?

As the *brain*★ evolved, the intricate interconnections within the higher regions became more elaborate. The **cortex**★ is the part of the "outer bark" of the brain that evolved when we emerged as mammals, and it is sometimes called the "neo-mammalian brain" or, simply, the "*neocortex*" or cerebral cortex. The cortex has enabled us to have neural *processes*★ that *repre-sent*★ things such as the outside world by way of creating *neural maps.*★ As primates, we elaborated the frontal regions; as human beings, we evolved more intricate prefrontal areas that symbol-ize aspects of the world beyond the physical domain. We can think, imagine, and create concepts that are ideas freed from the *constraints* of the outer world. For example, the frontal portions of the cortex enable us to imagine what freedom is, to think of ways to change the future and make a better world, to plan a more effective way of teaching, and to write poetry that evokes images in others. Sitting atop the *subcortical*★ *limbic*★ and *brain-stem*★ regions, the *prefrontal cortex*★ serves to help *regulate*★ these older and less conceptual but equally important neural areas. In this way, the integrative aspects of our prefrontal cortex may carry out the *linkage** of these different neural regions.

IMPLICATIONS: WHAT DOES THE CORTEX MEAN FOR OUR LIVES?

Just as evolution has moved from lower to higher brain regions over time, so, too, does *development* reflect this trajectory. In the womb, genes play a dominant role in expressing the instructions for how and when *neurons** will grow from the neural tube that will become the *spinal cord** and the cluster of neurons that will become the *brain** encased in the skull. The first to grow, based on this genetic information, is the brainstem that is well formed at the time of birth. Partially formed are the limbic areas that continue to grow in the first years of life based on information from genes and from the influence of experience.

The cortical areas are very undeveloped at the time of birth. While genes continue to play an important role in how *synapses** will later form even in the cortex, this lack of development in utero makes experience especially important in shaping how the cortex will mature. *Neuroplasticity** likely is present throughout the brain, but the cortex is the area most well studied, revealing how open it is to changing in response to experience throughout the life span. Cortical change is based on the growth and strengthening of neural connections through *synaptogenesis** and the maturation of neurons, and their subsequent interconnections via the *differentiation** of neural stem cells by way of a process called *neurogenesis.* In addition, *myelinogenesis* leads to the laying down of the insulating fatty *myelin* sheath along interconnected neurons to make a *neural pathway* or *circuit*★ that is 3,000 times more effective in the transmission of neural signals than an unmyelinated pathway. Myelin deposition may be the outcome of skill training.

Yet a fourth way in which cortical architecture is shaped by experience is the alteration of the regulation of *gene expression* in the process of *epigenesis*★. In each of these ways, the cortex is highly molded by experience across the life span. We are continually shaping our cortical architecture—not only in childhood and *adolescence*, but throughout our lives. Family experience influences our cortical development and may play a part in how *attachment*★ relationships shape many aspects of our functioning, including *emotion regulation*★ or *affect regulation*★ and our *narrative*★ self-understanding. *Culture*★ impacts cortical development as well, with *energy and information*★ passed along through *relationships*★ and communication streams that directly influence our cortical activity.

The realization that the cortex is a neural *system*★ with emerging functions throughout the life span has changed how we view "localization" of specific functions to specific regions in this area of the brain. We now know that neural processes emerge from an ever-changing set of interactions within the connections among various distributed regions. Yes, the cortex has distinct lobes that generally serve to create certain functions. The posterior lobes help process information about the external environment with the occipital lobe creating maps of three-dimensional space including vision, the temporal lobes processing sound, and the parietal lobes mapping out touch and the *perception*★ of the external movement of the body. The *frontal lobe* contains the areas that mediate our voluntary movements, plan our actions, and enable us to think, imagine, and focus our *attention*★. But there are intricate processes that rely on widely distributed areas to help create the complex capacities we have. As just one example, the region where the temporal and parietal areas meet plays an important role in making maps of *mental processes*★. And so the fuller picture of the cortex must embrace a few realities: The widely distributed processes of the whole brain enable complex processes, such as *mindsight maps*★, *executive functions*★, and *consciousness*★ itself to emerge; also, the brain is constantly shaping and reshaping itself as we move through life. The brain, and the cortex in particular, is not a static organ but an ever-changing interacting system of subsystems that respond rapidly and fluidly, in *health*★ at least, to changes in the environment. Experience continually stimulates neuronal firing and the brain responds with a *flow*★ of changes in response. This is how our cortex can be considered a *complex adaptive system*★.

We have also now learned that the ability of the *mind's*★ attention to direct *neural firing*★ can actually alter brain structure. In this way, *awareness*★ itself becomes an "experience" that molds the physical architecture of the brain. This response of the ever-changing cortex to ongoing experience seems to be a lifelong capacity. While important regulatory structures are shaped in early development, later years may still have potential, under the right conditions, to create significant, lasting, and helpful changes in the cortex's architecture.

We should not be overly simplistic and expect that anyone can change in any way. But at the same time these new studies open the doors for intervention and education to imagine, in *creative*★ and previously unheard-of ways, strategies to help create change throughout our lives. Simply examining the power of relationships and one's own mind-set, *intention*★, and focus of attention to shape health in our later years reveals how we should keep an open mind about keeping the brain actively growing and changing. The implication of these findings is that we can train the mind to harness the power of attention to move the brain toward *integration*★ and health across the life span.

The cortex affords us opportunities and challenges. Knowing about the profound plasticity of this region of the brain means that we can empower others and ourselves to use attention as a tool to intentionally shape our own neural architecture. From an *interpersonal neurobiology*★ point of view, integration is the fundamental neural process that can be created to enhance our functioning. One form of attention training that is highly integrative is *mindful awareness practice*★. By intentionally creating a curious, open, accepting, and loving (*COAL*★) *state*★ during a practice period, by taking *time-in*★ and reflecting on the inner nature of mental life, the individual can create an integrated state of neural firing. Areas of the *middle prefrontal cortex*★ that link widely separated regions to each other have been shown to be activated during mindfulness practice and to change in their structure following extended training.

Learning to sense the *synaptic shadows*★ that early experience casts upon neural architecture is a powerful application of cortical understanding. These are the ways in which the past has shaped the web of synaptically interconnected neural circuits including the integrative middle prefrontal area. We can view these shadows, for example, in how the autobiographical narrative of an individual reflects how early experiences have shaped cortical function and structure.

Knowing about the interactions among the more ancient subcortical areas and the more recent cortical evolution also can influence how we approach our own internal lives. From the interpersonal neurobiology perspective, the application of this knowledge is aimed at helping people be "more at home in their own *nervous system**" so that their understanding leads to a deeper sense of comfort and well-being. The body proper (muscles, bones, heart, lungs, intestines), the brainstem (*fight-flight-or-freeze* response) and limbic area (emotion, motivation, *appraisal of meaning**, attachment, *memory**) are the subcortical regions that are profoundly important for everything the cortex "does."

These subcortical inputs appear to have a more direct impact on right *hemisphere** functioning, and so knowing the differences between ways of being that emerge from the left and those that emerge from the right can help guide us in being more open to these subcortical factors. The two sides of the cortex, left and right, perform not only differentiated functions but also enable distinct ways of "being" for the individual. This *laterality* or asymmetry is an important element in our evolution, revealed in studies that demonstrate how we've had differences in the left and right sides of the brain for hundreds of millions of years. Ultimately this awareness can help us to integrate our functioning and avoid the ways in which we adaptively shut off input from one region or another to survive. Interpersonal neurobiology's aim toward integration is to move from just surviving to thriving.

15
15

THE BRAIN AS A SYSTEM

CONCEPT: WHAT IS THIS?

The brain as a system★ functions as a whole in which the
differentiated★ areas *link*★ their signals to one another in the creation of the system's overall functioning. From a linear point of
view, we would see one region being "responsible" for a particular function and then "producing" some output that is then
handled by another region. While some linear aspects of *brain*★
function certainly exist—such as at the level of single *neurons*★
and their signaling through *neurotransmitter* release and downstream *neuronal firing*★—the overall output of the brain is more
like a spider web of interconnected *processes*★ than a linear chain
of events. Even with this simple linear synaptic view, we quickly
find that the average neuron in the *cortex*★ is connected directly
via a *synapse*★ to 10,000 other neurons. This means that there
are literally trillions of synaptic connections in the skull portion of the brain and the number of variations of on-off firing
patterns of this organ has been estimated to be 10 times 10 one
million times. The various possibilities of activation, amazingly,

are thought to be greater than the amount of known atoms in the universe. And so it is natural, given that immensity of variation, to have the feeling of wanting to give up and forget about the brain—or certainly think of it in more linear, simplistic, or what some might say "reductionist terms." This area "does this" and that area "inhibits that." Who could blame someone for trying to simplify such complexity to get a grasp on such a *complex system**? And we are making such simple initial statements from this more linear perspective as a starting place here in this guide all the time. The importance, though, is to know when we are simplifying things. Our linear thinking loves to have a concrete, accessible explanation that *makes sense**, some way of looking at things that we can grasp. We soon learn that no matter what we do, it is always possible for someone to make the comment "it is more complicated than that." This is *always* true! Words can never capture the complexity of our *nervous system's** functioning.

And so we are humbly trying to move away from our longing for simplicity and move into a more realistic view of the brain not as a linear processor, but as a massively interconnected system. This system within the skull is complex enough. And then when we realize that the system we are calling "brain" is also intimately and inextricably interconnected with all bodily processes—from immune function and hormones to the peripheral neural input from the senses and the *autonomic** nervous system with its *sympathetic* and *parasympathetic* branches—we can take a deep breath and just open ourselves to the immensity of these extended intricacies. Now let's take the necessary next step and imagine that our "brain" is also profoundly social in addition to being *embodied**. We then come to see that the electrochemical *flow** of *energy**—the embodied mechanism we've been discussing—is influenced by both internal somatic and external relational processes. We are embedded in a web of interconnected energy flow patterns with the world around us. We are both embodied and embedded. And so an attempt to see clearly and fully into the nature of the brain as a system means that we need to look for the transduction of energy flow through the body and through at least the interpersonal world of shared communication, of the exchange of energy and information. Exciting new studies of the impact of *relationships*★ on brain function— such as how holding the hand of someone with whom you have a wonderfully supportive relationship rather than one of hostile vigilance—can alter the way the brain in the skull responds to an impending shock. Science reveals clearly that our social world directly shapes how our *neural firing* unfolds. These studies illuminate how we help one another *regulate*★ our *internal states*★ through attuning to the internal states of the other person as part of what is called *mutual regulation, co-regulation,* or *dyadic regulation.* Ed Tronick's "*Still-Face Experiment*" (see Figure F) demonstrates how a young infant's own equilibrium depends on the *attuned, contingent communication*★ with a *caregiver*★ who is attending to signals that communicate his or her internal, subjective state. From an *interpersonal neurobiology*★ perspective of the *mind*★ as an embodied and embedded process, we can understand how relationship connections and neural connections both contribute fully to the creation of our physiological equilibrium and our mental reality.

The brain's spider-web architecture lends itself to this *parallel distributed processing,* or PDP view. Though any perspective is naturally filled with controversy, it seems generally agreed upon that much of the brain's input and output pass through intricate layers of simultaneous, distributed, and highly interconnected neural firing patterns. Our view of the brain as a system invites us to consider that what is composing that system is more than what is in the skull itself. We are beckoned to not have a "single skull" view of our lives. We are embodied, not just "enskulled," and we are embedded in a social matrix of interconnected relationships. Indeed, the *self**★* is much more than our skin-encased bodies, let alone what simply happens between our ears. The brain is a fundamental part of these embodied and embedded patterns of *energy and information flow**★* that create an interconnected system.

IMPLICATIONS: WHAT DOES THE BRAIN AS A SYSTEM MEAN FOR OUR LIVES?

When we speak about certain areas of the brain "doing" this or that type of function—such as the *hippocampus**★* integrating *implicit memory**★* into an *explicit**★* form—we need to be mindful that while areas have a dominant role in a certain function, ultimately the inputs and outputs to that function involve a wide range of areas and processes. Yet we need to begin with some statements like this to get us oriented and anchored in an initial foundation, or an initial view. Then we need to keep the mind wide open—avoiding premature closure of categories and the narrowing of how we conceptualize what is going on. If we keep an open mind, we can build a map of the territory of mind, brain, and relationships that is open to continual expansion and revision.

A case in point is this. Research on individuals with lesions—such as tumors, damage from strokes, or injuries to specific limited areas—has repeatedly shown that explicit memory will be blocked, for example, with damage to the hippocampal region.

After an accident an individual may not be able to encode new elements into explicit memory (called *anterograde amnesia*) or be able to recall the period of time for a few months before the injury, a condition known as *retrograde amnesia*. This reveals how the hippocampus is necessary for both the encoding of explicit memory and, for a few months, the *retrieval** of that memory. While we can say that this suggests that the hippocampus is essential for explicit memory processing, it does not mean that other areas don't also contribute in some way to these functions of *encoding** and initial retrieval. Even when one area is necessary for a certain function to occur, as demonstrated by lesion experiments, for example, we must keep in mind that that area may be performing a linking function and many other regions may likely contribute to that function as a part of a larger system.

When we focus in interpersonal neurobiology on *integration**—the linkage of differentiated parts of a system—we need to highlight the unique contributions of the physically separated areas and their functional specializations. Integration lets us embrace the reality of our lives as part of massively interconnected systems of processes, ones that include the brain in the skull, the whole of the body, many bodies and how they communicate with each other, and the larger world in which all of these enfolded levels of subsystems and functions arise. This approach has both scientific validity and practical utility. Let's take the hippocampus as one neuroanatomic region for an example. The hippocampus is important for explicit processing and the *brainstem** does not have that role, for example. The anatomy of the hippocampus reveals that it is composed of neural interconnections to widely separated areas that *encode** implicit memory. And so we can say that the hippocampus is an integrator of implicit memory. Yet implicit memory may involve firing patterns related to the brainstem nuclei's history of being activated in response to threat. Implicit elements of fear or freeze reactions, for example, may become part of what the hippocampus integrates into a larger sense of the self over time in the creation of *autobiographical memory**. In this way, we can make the statement "the hippocampus integrates explicit memory from its implicit components" but we need to keep in mind that this doesn't exclude the participation of the brainstem— or the input from other neural regions, or from other people. How we construct a *narrative** of lived events with others can directly shape the way that memory is processed throughout our lives. The hippocampus—along with the integrative *prefrontal** region—takes input from a wide range of sources and links them together to form both explicit memory and our life stories.

Likewise, when we examine the architectural distinctions between the left and right cortical regions and the *subcortical** asymmetries that feed those sides differently during early *development*, we can understand that the system of the right *hemisphere** and the system of the left are in fact distinct from each other. This is a developmental, anatomic, and functional specialization of each side. And so our basic notion of differentiation reveals that areas of the nervous system do indeed find quite unique configurations and functions. Such asymmetries, in fact, have existed for hundreds of millions of years. When we then examine how certain neurons connect widely separated areas to each other, we can see how that linkage is carried out by these neural fibers and this anatomic connection gives rise to the integration of separate areas into a functional whole. This is how integration is fundamental to the notion of the brain as a functional, interconnected system. It also points to the evolutionary finding that integration builds on ancient *circuits*★ to create new and more complex capacities by linking differentiated areas to each other. We can intentionally move systems toward integration in the effort to catalyze an individual's development of new capacities. When we design strategies of intervention to harness the power, for example, of the hippocampus to integrate *memory*★ with *focal attention* or the *corpus callosum* to link processes from the left and right hemispheres, we can see the positive outcome of such integrative therapeutic efforts.

What exactly are the origins of this "system" we are speaking about when we refer to "the brain"? A sperm and egg unite with their partial complements of genetic material to form a whole, the conceptus. This single cell divides, becoming two cells, then four, eight, sixteen, thirty-two, sixty-four and on and on until the growing embryo is differentiated such that some cells are on the outside and some are on the inside. A portion of the outer layer of cells, the ectodermal layer that is bound to become our skin, folds inward and forms the neural tube. In other words, all of our neurons have the same origin as skin cells! The skin itself is at the interface of the outside and inside world, and so, too, is the nervous system that always links the outer and the inner. The system of the brain not only links the widely distributed nervous system that extends throughout the body proper, but it also continuously scans the environment and responds to what it perceives. We are all about connecting our inner and our outer realities.

The brain's *default mode,* its state of activity when not given a task to perform, is a case in point. There is a set of interconnected regions, a default mode circuit, that becomes activated when the brain is "at rest." These areas are social circuits that are also involved in self-*reflection*★. These circuits of our social surveying brain seem to be on continual "on" mode even when we have nothing we are told "to do." The individual is now alone, so it may in fact be that we are searching with our social circuits to find some support or assurance in this strange scanner situation in which we are now alone inside a noisy machine! Or it may be that we are naturally with a "chattering brain" that is continually surveying our environment, seeking out social sources of support and connection. Whatever the *meaning*★ of this finding, we have the activation of a circuit of "selfing" that seems to be turned on without a formal task being given. This emerging creation of a self, this selfing, may reveal in fact how the *self is a plural verb* rather than a singular noun. We are always unfolding (verb, not noun) and we are finding our sense of self in connections to others whether these connections are real-time, remembered, or imagined. This default mode or "resting state" reveals that we have a set of circuitry surveying the inner world and social surroundings, trying to understand what is going on, in others and in ourselves. We have a busy brain that creates a "monkey mind" that is often on the go in the creation of an ever-changing narrating and socially interdependent self.

The *triangle of well-being*★ (see Figure E) and the *brain in the palm of your hand*★ are visual depictions of how the brain functions as a system. In the triangle we see the energy and information flow throughout our human lives: that flow is regulated by the mind, shared in relationships, and passed through the embodied mechanisms of the nervous system and whole body that we are simply calling the "brain." Here we see that applying the triangle in everyday life enables us to place the brain in its full *context*★ as a system—it is one part of a larger energy and information flow, not some separate collection of cells doing "its own thing."

The system to which we are referring has everything to do with the flow of energy and information, internally and externally. The person and his or her brain do not live in isolation from the surrounding social environment, or from the present bodily demands or synaptic connections shaped by past experiences. Each of these elements of the environment, the body, and past experience shapes our present activations in the brain.

The *hand model of the brain** also offers a way to apply this systems thinking from the inside out. Highlighting the importance of integration, we can see how knowing the differentiated areas of this bodily system called "brain" enables us to honor the unique contributions of the various areas and then cultivate their linkages. You might wonder that if the brain is indeed a system, doesn't this just happen automatically? Wouldn't a system just move toward integration on its own? The answer is that, yes, often people do just find well-being on their own so to speak. But for many of us, something in life—our genetics, our *temperament**, our experiences, or perhaps just being human in a complex and often unhelpful modern world—makes us adapt by shutting off such integrative functioning. We shut off integration by not differentiating areas or by not linking them. The result of such impaired integration is *chaos**, *rigidity**, or both.

And so an interpersonal neurobiology application of this systems view is to nurture differentiation and cultivate linkage. Fortunately, complex systems have an innate drive to maximize complexity and to integrate and create harmony. This lets us see that our job is to *join* with systems and release impediments to integration. This puts us in an aligning stance of joining with and assisting, rather than dominating and taking over all control. The way we join is to detect perturbations to the *FACES*★ flow of integration, sensing when a system is moving away from being flexible, adaptive, *coherent*★, energized, and stable. Chaos and rigidity are the outcomes of such impairments to integration. Now we look for aspects of the system—of the brain, of relationships—where differentiation is not present and linkage is blocked. Without the knowledge of these various neural regions that compose the system, it would be difficult to know how to focus *attention*★ in order to support differentiation and then facilitate linkage within the brain as a complex system. For this reason, educators, clinicians, parents, and anyone interested in helping to nurture the developing mind should know about the triangle, examining the ways in which mind, brain, and relationships interact. For the brain as a system—but one component of the larger system depicted by the triangle of human experience—we can then dive deeply and effectively into various *domains of integration*★ and promote well-being in a systematic way. We can link various neural functions, aiming a focus of attention to stimulate the neuronal activation and growth of differentiated regions with one another. With this applied knowledge we become empowered to free ourselves—using our mind to develop integration in our brains, in our relationships with others, and with ourselves.

16
16

INTEGRATION

CONCEPT: WHAT IS IT?

The basic proposal of *interpersonal neurobiology*★ is that **integration**★ is the fundamental mechanism of *health*★ and well-being. Integration is the *linkage*★ of *differentiated*★ parts of a *system*★. Differentiation means that subsets of a collection of elements— water molecules in a cloud, functions of the *mind*★, regions of the *brain*★, people in a family—are able to become unique or specialized in their individuality. Linkage means that subsets interact with one another. For a cloud, this means that areas of the cloud mix and mingle and influence the other areas. For a mind, this means that various *mental activities*★ such as thinking or feeling or *remembering*★, the various aspects of a *state of mind*★, have an impact on other activities or *states*★ and can interact and collaborate with one another. In the brain, *energy and information*★ flowing from one region has access to and influences the other areas of the brain in a reciprocally impactful way. For *relationships*★ in a family, linkage would mean that the unique (differentiated) members of a family shared time together and that their communications reflected a *compassionate*★ and respectful interest in the internal experiences of the others. Integration is the linkage of differentiated parts in whatever system we focus upon.

Systems that are open to influences from outside of themselves and that are capable of chaotic behavior are formally called *complex systems*★. A cloud, a mind, a brain, and a family are each an examples of open, chaos-capable systems—each is a complex system. The division of mathematics that deals with probability focuses on complex systems and reveals that these systems are *nonlinear dynamical systems*. Nonlinearity means that small inputs have large and unpredictable long-term outcomes. Dynamical means that there are *emergent processes*★ that arise from the interactions of elements of the system. One of these characteristics of complex systems is that the system has a *self-organizational*★ *process*★ that arises as an emergent property of the interactions of the elements of the system. There is no programmer and no preexisting set of plans or instructions that shape how self-organization unfolds. Self-organization emerges from the interactions of elements of the system—and then in turn influences the functions of those elements from which the process of self-organization emerges.

Self-organization reveals that the most probable pathway of a complex system is to move toward "maximizing complexity." As this is not necessarily intuitive for most people, the feeling of maximizing complexity is often best revealed by hearing members of a choir sing a song in harmony. With the differentiation of the voices of each singer, singing in harmonic intervals, along with the linkage of their voices through verse and chorus, the listener can feel the vitality and thrill of the harmonious emergence of the song. Harmony is the outcome of integration. The harmony, in turn, influences the flow of the song and creates even more harmony. This is the nature of a self-organizing system that is freely able to move toward maximizing complexity by linking its differentiated elements.

IMPLICATIONS: WHAT DOES INTEGRATION MEAN FOR OUR LIVES?

At a very basic level, integration enables the coordination and balance of a system to unfold over time. A complex, nonlinear system has a natural push toward integration. In interpersonal neurobiology, we see integration as yielding the flexible, adaptive, *coherent**, energized, and stable (*FACES**) *flow** that is bounded on one side by *chaos** and on the other side by *rigidity**. This *river of integration** is a visual metaphor for how harmony runs down the center of the river, and each bank of the river represents deviations from integration into chaos or rigidity (see Figure K). When we examine various mental disorders, what is revealed is that virtually all of them can be described as clusters of chaotic and/or rigid symptoms that we would say are examples of impaired integration. When this view is combined with recent technological advances in studying brain structure and function, such as research on the *default mode* or children with histories of *abuse** or *neglect**, we can see that the integrative fibers of the brain are either structurally or functionally impaired. Hence, we see integration as the heart of health; impaired integration results in the chaos and rigidity that are the hallmarks of dysfunction.

One important implication is that complex systems have a natural drive toward integration. In this way, educators, parents, or clinicians can see their jobs as liberating the natural inclina-

tion of each individual to move toward well-being and health—
to move toward integration. This stance of the innate property
of integration can be translated as a natural push toward health.

Complexity theory reveals that when a system differentiates its
parts and then links them, it has a self-organizational flow that
maximizes complexity. Because mathematicians define their
technical use of the term "integration" as addition, you will not
see the use of the formal term integration in their descriptions
of the self-organization of complex systems. (For someone in
mathematics, the integration of 3 and 5 is 8, and the unique features of 3 and 5 disappear; so integration, for a mathematician,
is the sum of the parts. In this sense, whether 8 was achieved by
combining 7 and 1, 6 and 2, 5 and 3, or 4 and 4 does not matter:
The whole in this case *is* the sum of its parts.) In common language, however, we can use the term integration to signify the
linkage of differentiated parts in which those unique aspects of
the individual elements do not disappear, and the whole in fact
is *greater* than the sum of the parts. This is the nature of the term
"integration" as we are using it in common language terms in
interpersonal neurobiology. To use another analogy, integration
is more like a fruit salad with heterogeneous elements rather
than a smoothie that has been blended into a homogeneous
mixture. This maintenance of the differentiated qualities of the
individual components of the system even while linking them
together is an essential aspect of integration. Linkage does not
mean addition or making the same. Integration is not homog-
enization. Both differentiation and linkage compose integration.

Complexity theory reveals that when a system is not linking
its differentiated parts, when it is not moving to maximize complexity, it moves either toward chaos or rigidity. The movement
of an integrated system, in contrast, moves in harmony with

a sense of *coherence**. In mathematical terms, coherence means that the processes by which the system moves across time are *emergent** and incorporate the various elements from outside of themselves (they are *open systems*) as they encounter them in a way that allows the system to grow and change across time. A fun acronym to embrace one interpretation of this mathematical view of coherence is the word itself, *COHERENCE**: connected, open, harmonious, engaged, *receptive*, emergent (something arising in new and ever-changing ways), *noetic* (a sense of knowing), compassionate, and *empathic**.

The implications for this view of integration as the heart of self-organizational movement toward well-being are vast and ever-emerging themselves. One such implication is in reframing a view of *psychopathology*. From the integration perspective, we can see that people develop with impaired *self-regulation** stemming from impediments to integration. A new look at the *DSM-IV* (the *Diagnostic and Statistical Manual of Mental Disorders*), reveals how each of the symptoms of each of the syndromes fits this suggestion that chaos and rigidity are the signs of impaired integration. When we combine this new perspective with the emerging findings mentioned above that are arising with new forms of technology now available, we can see expanding forms of support for the proposal that integration is the fundamental mechanism of health. These studies demonstrate that impediments to integrative functioning exist in those individuals with schizophrenia, manic-depressive illness, and autism possibly due to genetic vulnerabilities and environmental exposure to toxins or infections. Other studies have demonstrated that experiences can also impair integration, as they reveal how childhood abuse and neglect are associated with impaired growth or damage to integrative brain fibers. Given that integration is the underlying mechanism of self-regulation, these research findings support the general view of mental disorders as involving challenges to the capacity for *regulation*★ in a coordinated and balanced manner.

Another important implication of this interpersonal neurobiology view is that we can define both the mind and healthy minds as emerging from integrated relationships and integrated *nervous systems*★. Instead of simply labeling disorders and listing symptoms, we can now have an overarching framework in which impairments to integration are seen as the cause of this movement away from harmony. We can reframe the field of *mental health*★ to actually focus on mental *health*★—on integration—and then have a natural view of how impediments to integration—whatever their cause—result in various forms of difficulties. Interventions can then be designed to promote integration, regardless of the cause of the impairment.

A wide range of etiologies including the spectrum of genetic and experiential origins serves as underlying mechanisms of impairments to integration. There is no need to fight over the contributions of genetics versus experience, as if they were at odds with each other instead of continually being engaged in a reinforcing loop of mutual interactions. A new approach to clinical assessment involves the examination of an individual's present and past life experiences for chaos and rigidity as manifestations of impaired integration, whatever their primary cause. At the heart of this framework is health. We can reformulate the *DSM* by offering first a definition of health as integration, and we can then see the wide array of disorders that have been articulated as examples of impairments to health because they are impairments to integration. Health emerges with integration, and clinical assessment and intervention can use this foundation in the effort to help move individuals' lives from chaos and rigidity to more harmonious functioning. The goal in this view is not simply to attempt to reduce or remove symptoms and lift someone out of a diagnostic classification grouping, but rather to provide the tools to create a more integrated life of health, internally and interpersonally. Well-being and thriving are the goals, not merely the eradication of symptoms.

New approaches to clinical evaluation can be created in which chaos and rigidity are the primary signs of impaired integration and states of harmony are revealed in the FACES flow of a life of health. The exploration for *domains of integration** serves to organize the search for where differentiation or linkage is not well developed. Once a domain is identified, clinical interventions can be designed to help promote integration in that area.

Differentiation is facilitated by focusing *attention** in ways that specify the nature of the *circuits** to be activated. This is how we *SNAG** the brain: that is, stimulate neuronal activation and growth. With the *close paying of attention**, the local release of substances (such as brain-derived neurotrophic factor, or BDNF) and the general release of transmitters (acetylcholine by the nucleus basalis just above the *brainstem**) facilitate the *neuroplastic** process by which *gene expression* can catalyze the creation of new synaptic growth.

With differentiation in progress, linkage can be initiated. Just as we use the left and right legs to walk or the left and right hands to play piano, the simultaneous or alternating activation of differentiated areas cultivates their linkage. "*Neurons that fire together, wire together**" is the general mechanism that SNAGs the brain toward linkage. With the linkage of differentiated areas, often the integration that emerges creates its own properties of more harmonious and adaptive functioning. In many ways, positive *emotion** can be seen as a shift that enhances integration and promotes a sense of vitality, expanding our sense of connection to ourselves and to others. In this way, the natural outcome of releasing the blockages to differentiation and linkage is often to harness the innate push toward integration that is a birthright of the individual and creates a positive sense of harmony and vitality. Sensing the empowerment that comes with such an emergent unfolding is often a wonder to behold.

17
17

CREATIVITY, HEALTH, AND THE RIVER OF INTEGRATION

CONCEPTS: WHAT ARE THEY?

Integration★ is the central concept in *interpersonal neurobiology*★ that illuminates the fundamental mechanism underlying well-being. This view offers a window into the nature of **health, creativity, and the river of integration**★ that reveals the dynamics of living a full and free life. Health is the optimal functioning of the organism that enables it to live in a flexible, adaptive, *coherent*★, energized, and stable (*FACES*★) flow across time. Creativity is a way of being in which life emerges in new and fresh combinations of inner experience and outer explorations. The river of integration is a metaphor for our *flow*★ through life in which the central flow of the river is in the FACES movement of harmony, and the banks of the river represent the *states*★ of *chaos*★ and *rigidity*★ when we are not in an integrated flow (see Figure K).

IMPLICATIONS: WHAT DO CREATIVITY, HEALTH, AND THE RIVER OF INTEGRA- TION MEAN FOR OUR LIVES?

In interpersonal neurobiology we view health and creativity as emerging from the same integrated flow of life. Deviations from this flow move us into chaos, rigidity, or both. Yet this flow is not in a straight line. For life to truly be *emergent**, we need to move toward both banks of the river of integration: Sometimes we feel stuck, rigid, flat, or living a too-predictable existence. At other times we feel flooded with *emotions**, images, or memo- ries—chaotic, explosive, or out of control. Creativity emerges as we move in a serpentine fashion through the river of life, moving toward—but not becoming stuck for long periods of time—on the bank of rigidity or the bank of chaos.

Another implication is that integration is a lifelong *process**, not a final product. As integration is a verb, not a noun, we can continually move toward an integrative flow. As a river continu- ously flows, our life unfolds in the direction of continual emer- gence. Integration is the *intention** and the direction of life, not a final product or fixed endpoint of a journey. Integration truly is the journey, not the destination.

The romantic notion of an artist's life needing to be filled with turmoil and personal pain has been dispelled by careful studies of artistic inclination and output. But artistic expression is only one form of creativity. The notion of creativity as we are using it here is a larger concept that refers as much to outward expression as it does to inward experience. We are defining the breadth of living a creative life as involving an immersion in a way of being that is filled with a deep sense of emergence and *presence**. Emergence is the experience of an *energy and informa-*

tion flow★ arising anew as a fresh *perception*★, a new perspective, a spontaneous gesture. Presence is an emergent property of our existence in which we are open and *receptive* to ourselves and to others, ready to receive and ready to connect. Presence emerges with an *awareness*★ that lets go of preexisting judgments and expectations—what some might call a *mindful awareness*★.

In the study of the *brain*★, we humans have discovered some secrets of our inner neural space. These discoveries enable us to create visual images of the brain, but this is just a schematic; obviously the brain is much more complicated than such a schematic image can portray. But the gist of how one aspect of the brain's structure and function interact is as follows. This is one view among many that may help us get the sense of how prior experience and ongoing sensation may interact in the brain and shape our experience of being aware. Even if the details are not exact or yet fully clarified, the broad strokes of this schematic view have great relevance for understanding aspects of our subjective experience and what we can do to improve our lives. The *cortical columns* that make up our cortical architecture are essentially six layers thick, the width of six playing cards stacked one on top of the other (see Figure G). Incoming flows of energy from sensation move from layer 6 to 5 to 4. At the same time, the cortical layers at the top respond to this incoming *bottom-up*★ stream from layer 6 by activating related *neural firing*★ patterns from *memory*★. We see a rose and while our bottom-up experience senses it as if it were the first time, our *top-down*★ flow knows this is a flower, names it as "r-o-s-e" and creates summaries of this and all other prior roses, flowers, or walks along this same old path. This top-down flow from layers 1 and 2 and 3 sends streams of prior knowledge, judgment, and expectation hurling downward to crash into the bottom-up stream. The crashing of this top-down with the bottom-up flow of sensation between layers 4 and 3 from an array of columns— we can propose—shapes how we become aware of what is happening in the present moment. (Interestingly, we have more neural synaptic interconnections in this very specific area than our primate cousins, the great apes.)

The ways in which clusters of *neurons*★ within columns in the *cortex*★ are *linked*★ within a given region is called *intraregional integration*. When related but distinct areas of the brain are linked, we call this *interregional integration*. One of the many differences between the left and the right *hemispheres*★ of the cortex may be that the left specializes in intraregional integration, producing detail-oriented analysis of certain forms *of information*★; in contrast, the right may have more interregional integration permitting a cross-modality form of *information processing*★ and enabling that hemisphere to decode the "gist" of a situation, perceiving *context*★ rather than text.

The art of living in a creative way may involve the art of being mindfully aware and open to experience as it arises without being swept up by judgments or automatic processes that dominate our perceptions of the whole. This presence of mind may be created by the *differentiation*★ of these various forms of processing, right and left. *Mindful awareness practices*★ may permit a differentiation of these various ways of knowing and may also enable the bottom-up streams to flourish so that they are not swallowed up or dominated by the top-down flow of summarized life memory from our busy, knowledgeable, and future and past-minded top-down-oriented cortices. We may even have anatomically separated, large clusters of neural circuits that are distinct for our observing, narrating *self*★ and for our ongoing streams of sensory experience that might support what we can call our sensing or experiencing self. In other words, freeing ourselves from the potential tyranny of top-down domination (such as the sometimes continual chatter of our narrative self) that obliterates, or at least obscures, the freshness of bottom-up (as in our experiencing self) may be a lifelong challenge for many human beings. Living creatively, allowing new, spontaneous combinations of experiences to emerge as we live our lives, may be all about freeing our bottom-up processes and allowing their emergence to blossom.

And so mindful awareness becomes not just a practice one can do to promote health (which it has been demonstrated to do in so many domains of our lives), it also becomes a way of being that catalyzes creative living by integrating top-down with bottom-up. Emergence arises naturally if we can relax the unfortunate tendency of our cortical architecture to filter everything we see through the dulling lens of prior experience. We have a proclivity to observe and narrate, perhaps to gain a sense of control and certainty, instead of sensing and experiencing with a fresh and open mind. What we need to embrace is uncertainty. Learning to thrive with uncertainty is the root of creativity. With such a stance, we come to live not only with health, but also with the fresh emergence of creative living as we float down the FACES flow of the river of integration.

Embracing the power of how we focus awareness to transform our brain and our *relationships*★ with others, and our very selves, opens the door to a broad range of applications of integration in our everyday lives. With awareness comes the possibility of choice and change. If our attention is drawn to external factors, enslaved only by the abundance of stimuli from the outside world, we run the risk of becoming a passive participant as externally compelling energy and information drive our lives.

Instead, there is room to escape this prison, to find a starting place of inner awareness, to create a sanctuary that provides us with the first step toward an inner driven clarity. This is especially challenging in these ever more digitally connected times. But finding a sense of *coherence** begins with taking *time-in**, drawing from an inner well of possibility shaped by more than what is on a visual screen or carved out by other external input to an already overwhelming set of bombardments.

One view is that *cohesive** ways of being exist in which we become stuck in repetitive states that reinforce their very existence. Habits become entrained in the flow of digital media and can become one such imprisonment. But we also have *narratives** that are cohesive, logically stating who we are and why we are here but not being open to further change. Sometimes we can have familiar but chaotic states that recurrently overwhelm our experiences and flood us with emotions and impulsive reactions to others. We might call ourselves "hot under the collar" or we might be prone to meltdowns or rages. Even in this chaos there is a kind of repetitive nature to such *low road* behaviors that reveal the way they, ironically, create a rigid pattern to our personality. Overall, these cohesive states keep us stuck in rigidity and chaos: They are far from the harmonious and emergent flow of the river of integration.

Getting *lost in these familiar places** of chaos and rigidity is part of the allure that holds people in these recurrent states. There is certainty in familiarity, and a great fear of the unknown can embed people in these *recursive** and often-destructive patterns in the attempt to avoid uncertainty. This is how patterns of *mind** can create impediments to health.

Integration invites emergence. But emergence and presence are not predictable. They are not controllable, not certain, often not familiar. These states of health require the courage to face the unknown and not withdraw into the familiar but constraining dominance of excessively relying on a top-down predictive frame of mind. And so living a life of health and creativity is an act of courage. We invite the vulnerability of uncertainty into our lives when we move toward integration. Yet we do not need to go to these places alone; we can be present to support one another in this emergence.

Applying this approach to integration is a creative act from the inside out. Living creatively is not about creating a product, but living a life fully present and open to things as they are. Living creatively is also filled with the thrill of possibility and the *gratitude* for this miracle of being alive. As the self emerges in these new ways with integration, being generous and kind is a natural outcome—toward others, and with ourselves. Beginning with ourselves and extending our open mind to others, integration becomes a way of being present that opens the doors to healthy and creative ways of being in the world.

18
18

RELATIONSHIPS AND INTEGRATIVE COMMUNICATION

CONCEPT: WHAT ARE THEY?

Relationships* are the sharing of *energy and information flow**. **Integrative communication*** involves the sharing of energy and information in which each individual's internal world is respected and allowed to be *differentiated** and then *compassionate** connection is cultivated. Integrative communication promotes the *development* of *healthy** relationships as it honors differentiation and *linkage**. When we support a child's discovery of her own passions and cultivate these interests as she grows, she will be able to differentiate her growing sense of *self** from her parents. By being interested in these passions, having discussions about them and being appropriately involved in how they develop, we promote the linkages of the differentiated elements of a parent-child relationship. When we connect with others in compassionate forms of *emotional communication*, we are connecting our internal worlds with others. When children look to their parents to know how to feel and how to respond, we call this *social referencing*, and it is a fundamental *process*★ with which children come to *regulate*★ themselves and learn about the world. We come to learn from these interactions that connecting is good, an experience that is driven forward by our *social reward system*. In many ways, these synaptic linkages within our neural circuitry are reinforced within this communicative linkage, which Louis Cozolino has termed our *social synapse*. This integrative communication can take place in all healthy connections between people and may help explain how longevity, health, and even happiness are each correlated with the presence of social relationships in people's lives. We continue to grow and develop across the life span; supportive relationships nurture lifelong development. Within healthy relationships there is a sharing of a focus of *attention*★ on something other than the individuals in the relationship. Often there may be a sharing of attention on a third object, a process called *joint attention*. As attention is the regulation of *information*★ *flow*★, the sharing of attention in this way is truly the *joining* of *minds*★. These relationships can be between friends, relatives, lovers, colleagues, parent and child, teacher and student, clinician and client/patient, and employer and employee. When relationships are truly integrative, we not only care for others in their distress, but we also take joy in others' joy and pride in their accomplishments in an important process called *empathic joy*. Relationships that are integrative thrive and promote a *creative*★ expression and vitality.

IMPLICATIONS: WHAT DO RELATIONSHIPS AND INTEGRATIVE COMMUNICATION MEAN FOR OUR LIVES?

Integrative communication infuses the relationship with a sense of openness, possibility, and respect. Each member of this form of connected relationship benefits, and a sense of *emergence** (with its feeling of novelty and freshness) imbues the relationship with life. Vulnerability is respected, and truth honored. Problem solving is enhanced when people work collaboratively. While achieving this form of communication for some comes naturally, for others, it may be necessary to first develop an internal *state** of *presence** in order for such communication to unfold. If an individual is filled with doubt and uncertainty, envy or hatred, integrative communication will be quite challenging to achieve. In such situations, the work toward achieving the capacity for integrative communication may need to come from the inside out.

The period of *adolescent* development offers a helpful window into the importance of integrative communication in maintaining healthy parent–child relationships. The *brain** undergoes developmental phases from conception onward that generally move from the bottom up, and from the back forward. What this means is that the last area of the brain to actively reorganize itself in our development is the very front of the frontal area of the brain, the *prefrontal cortex**. While much research is actively exploring the ways in which these neural changes influence the adolescent mind, there is much support for the notion that *adolescence* is a period in which this region of the brain is in an active stage of remodeling. The process of weighing cost-benefit ratios, for example, appears to excessively favor the positive, enjoyable outcomes of an action. Adolescents may choose behaviors very well aware of the risks, but over-emphasizing the benefits during this age such that their behavior puts them in unnecessary danger. Educational programs that simply try to educate teens about risks may not be successful as their brains are in fact not blind to the endangering aspects of a behavioral choice; instead, their brains' *limbic** and prefrontal regions appraise the excitement, fun, social benefits, and novelty as highly attractive and rewarding. Risk is built into an adolescent's neural calculations. To maintain integrative communication, it is important to honor these differences, but also provide a differentiated point of view so that insights can be offered in a respectful manner that does not induce a *reactive state* (in which adolescents intensify their endangering choices and parents' understandable fear and frustration shuts off open channels of communication). Becoming aware of how we maintain receptivity in a relationship is crucial for any stage of development, and can be especially challenging in the parent–adolescent relationship during these years of significant neural reconstruction.

For adults and teens, knowing the difference between being in an integrative, receptive versus a nonintegrative, *reactive* state can be an important part of the way we create and sustain integrative communication. The *no-yes procedure* reveals how when we hear each word said repeatedly we experience a reactive state of *fight-flight-or-freeze*. "No" evokes these reactions to threat; "yes" often relaxes this reactivity and enables us to enter a state of receptivity. As our muscles relax and our mind becomes open to others, and to our own internal experiences, we have the possibility of becoming fully present in our interactions. This is the "*yes state*," the *receptive state* necessary for engaging in integrative communication. This is how we activate a *social engagement system* and can likely build on an open self-engagement system* as well.

Learning to be aware of when we are in the "*no states*" of fight, flight, or freeze can help us to pause and take *time-in** so that we can move our internal state toward receptivity. We become ready to engage with others, opening ourselves to the emergence of integrative connections.

We can teach ourselves to become aware of our internal state of receptivity by experiencing the *no-yes procedure*. We then can learn how to use simple *mindful awareness practices** to bring ourselves out of reactivity and into receptivity. This is the necessary place to begin inwardly, to take time-in, in order to become receptive outwardly. This is how we can say that integrative communication is initiated from the inside out.

Next, we can reflect on our own history of integrative communication. Our own *Adult Attachment Interview** findings can be a useful source of *reflection** on what we ourselves have experienced in the past. These possibly frustrating times of disappointment or rejection, confusion or despair, can leave a mark on *memory** such that we are implicitly reluctant to engage in an open way with others now. Memory affects our mind, shaping our sense of possibility, curtailing our sense of freedom. Experience directly shapes the *synaptic shadows** that cast their effects on our openness to new experiences. Applying these ideas of integrative communication moves us beyond just knowing our own *nervous system**—an important and necessary place to begin the journey to connect. Now we can also enter the uncontrollable and uncertain world of connecting to others, and we can take the steps to fully engage with the unfolding experience of being with another person. This engagement takes time, and patience, especially if we have been wounded in the past.

Knowing ourselves brings us the strength to be open to knowing someone else. In the *wheel of awareness*★ practice, for example, we can develop the inner strength of becoming aware of all our senses, bringing in the outer world, the inner world of the body, our mental life, and even our sense of connection to others. This "eighth sense," our *relational sense*★, enables us to see how we are fundamentally connected to other people. Our sense of identity is not limited to the body that we inhabit during this lifetime, but it can be felt to extend out to our connections to others now, and to those who have lived before us, and to generations to come. This is how we extend a skin boundary definition of "me" to become fully a part of a "we." Integrative communication links us with others in new and life-affirming ways as it opens our lives to experience a deepening expansion of our sense of who we are in the world.

19
19

THE NEUROBIOLOGY OF WE

CONCEPT: WHAT IS IT?

Becoming a part of a "we" does not mean that you lose a "me." **The neurobiology of we**★ reveals how this blending of me and we emerges within our *relationships*★ and the functions of the *brain*★ itself. Patterns of *energy*★ pass through our neural *circuits*★ and are shared in our relationships with one another. These swirls of energy at times contain symbolic *meaning*★, *information*★ that stands for something other than itself. When our experiences in the past were filled with connections with others that were unreliable, we may approach communication with others in a way that shuts off the risk of our being hurt yet again. We may live a life of isolation, creating a sense of independence that allows us to survive but limits the sense of vitality we can feel. We may also find that our inner sense of *self*★ has been made tumultuous with inconsistent and intrusive experiences with others on whom we depended for comfort and connection. In this case, we may depend on the connections with others for a sense of well-being, with disabling doubt, *anxiety,* and fear. We are highly *reactive* to the ambiguous communications that may fill our daily lives with dread and uncertainty. Understanding the neurobiology of we can help illuminate the nature of these echoes of the past and early but now-outdated survival strategies. These *synaptic shadows*★ of the past constrain our present experience as well as how we can construct a more helpful future. Such *insights*★ can help us grow beyond these challenging foundations toward the integrated *state*★ of thriving as both a strong "me" and a vitalizing "we."

IMPLICATIONS: WHAT DOES THE NEURO-BIOLOGY OF WE MEAN FOR OUR LIVES?

Both genes and experience shape the brain's structure. The experiences we have with others can alter our openness to being fully present and allowing *integrative communication*★ to arise in our relationships with others. One way of understanding the implications of this finding is to learn from the recent insights into one set of social circuits in the brain, the *mirror neuron* system.

Discovered at the end of the last millennium, a set of *neurons*★ was found that is active when a purposeful action is taken or when that same type of action is perceived. "Mirror" properties indicate that there is a mirroring of action and *perception*★. The key to these neurons is that they only respond to acts with *intention*★—revealing that the brain is capable of making *neural maps*★ of others' actions that symbolize their intentions. As intention is a *mental process*★, this finding powerfully illustrates how the brain makes an image of the *mind*★ of another—even before it can form words or intellectual understanding.

The basic perceptual steps involved in mapping intention are to first detect predictable sequences of behavior in others. Once predictive sequences are perceived by way of the interaction of mirror neurons and the related area of the superior temporal sulcus, a map is thought to be created that represents this predictable sequence in the form of a neural *representation*★ of the other's intentional state. This is how the brain anticipates the immediate next action of a perceived sequence and derives information from that detection.

Next, this *neural map*★ *primes* the brain to enact that same behavior: Mirror neurons map out intentional states in others and they also prepare us to imitate intentional acts. These neurons also have been found to enable us to simulate the internal states of others. We take in what we see expressed in the often *nonverbal*★ signals of others and then drive that perception down into the *subcortical*★ regions where we change our bodily state, our *brainstem's*★ activation, and our *limbic*★ firing. These subcortical shifts are then sent back upward, through the *insula*★ in the *middle prefrontal cortex*★ with which we can become aware of our internal state through a representation of the body's state called a *somatic map* (see Figure D-1). When we see someone with tears on his face, our own *resonance*★ with those tears brings a heavy feeling in our chest and perhaps tears to our own face. Sensing these shifts in our own bodily state are used by the middle prefrontal area to ascertain first "how am I feeling in my body" and then "what do I feel *emotionally*★?" The next step in this interoceptive path is to attribute what I am feeling now to what I imagine might be going on inside of the other person. "These tears on my face are about his sadness. I wonder if he is sad." *Interoceptive*★ *awareness*★ is the gateway for how we make a map of what we empathically imagine the other person might be feeling. These are the possible steps and neurobiological mechanisms for both *empathy*★ and *compassion*★.

As the middle prefrontal region is also a general location mediating *self-awareness*★, it becomes an important issue that we come to feel another person's feelings with related sets of circuits with which we come to feel our own feelings. How do we then know who is who? Are these feelings I am aware of now "from" me, or are they from my perception of you? A related example of this type of overlap is in the findings that social rejection activates the same parts of the brain involved in physical pain—aspects of the *anterior cingulate*★ portion of our middle prefrontal area. Our socially embedded self and our *embodied*★ self have overlapping neural circuitry. These findings remind us what the *triangle*★ of human experience depicts: The "self" as experienced as the "mind" is in fact both embodied and *relational*★. These brain-scan findings offer supportive empirical evidence that the mind is, in fact, emerging from both the bodily and the social *contexts*★ in which we live. The "self" is both embodied and embedded. These are not two separate domains of experience, but instead are the essence of how the mind emerges from the *energy and information flow*★ within and between us.

The neurobiology of we focuses on these issues and reminds us that "we" is a part of "me." But at times experiences with family or peers, or within the larger *culture*★ in which we live can lead us to withdraw from being open to the "me emerging from we." Various mind states can be *defensively* created to attempt to avoid reminders of what may have been a potentially painful and confusing way in which the "self" was obliterated in these various settings in the past. Parental intrusions or unavailability in insecure *attachment*★, a history of being bullied at school by peers, or feeling a lack of place and identity within a bustling and anonymous culture can each be the soil from which inner turmoil grows. In these situations, the "self" is not clearly formed as both a *differentiated*★ entity and, at the same time, an entity *linked*★ intimately with supportive others. *Integration*★ entails this tension between differentiation, on the one hand, and linkage on the other. Impairments to integration can push a "self" toward either the extreme of excessively differentiated ways of being without linkage or toward fusion with a loss of a differentiated identity. Whether forced to live in isolation or intruded upon in derogation, extreme forms of impairments to integration make the self take refuge in excessive withdrawal and differentiation or to become lost in intense anxiety-driven longings for connection. And in the future, the self can inadvertently and *nonconsciously*★ participate in the creation of a self-fulfilling prophecy in which we get *lost in familiar places*. Part of this *recursive*★ *process*★ is imbued with a protective aim: Why take a chance of being confused about who is who and just withdraw in isolation? There are two often nonideal extremes: one of being autonomous and unaffected by others (like a rock, without access to feelings or readily seen influences of others upon itself) and one of being internally confused and fused with others (like a vulnerable infant, but now perpetually dependent for its very existence on the continual interactions with a parent). Finding a path toward being a solid me and being able to *join* in the vitality of a living, breathing, supportive we is the overall and ever-emerging goal.

The synaptic shadows from the past directly influence how we experience our present. Such echoes of direct experience and the ways we have attempted to adapt to them each constrain how we are able to engage others in a *healthy*★ we. An application of this perspective invites us to reflect on the nature of these past experiences that necessarily pushed *devel-*

opment toward a restricted way of being. Excessive intrusion and subsequent overreliance or painful dismissal and defensive and precocious autonomy limit the capacity for the integrative communication at the heart of being a vibrant we. The mirror neurons discussed above are a part of a larger *resonance circuit*★ that enables us to feel another's feelings and not get lost in their internal states. We can resonate and not become fused with another person. This resonance allows us to *"feel felt"* by the other person, and that person can feel felt by us. This is quite different from becoming the other person—of excessive linkage without differentiation. Integration requires that we maintain both linkage and differentiation. Knowing the neural steps that may be involved can help illuminate how this can be achieved.

Interoception★ is the key to empathy and to self-awareness. Applying various *mindful awareness practices*★ to support the activation and growth of the insula as part of the resonance circuit can be a direct way to increase the capacity to become a part of a we without becoming lost as a me. Self-understanding is more than an intellectual capacity to know what we've experienced in the past. This *self-knowing awareness*, or *autonoetic consciousness*, involves learning to be open to whatever arises in our sensory world. We take in the incoming stream of signals from the outer world—through sight, hearing, taste, smell, and touch—while also receiving input from the inner world of the body. This interoceptive capacity to be open to the signals of our muscles and bones in the limbs, and those from the inner organs of the torso (our genitals, intestines, lungs, heart), give us a deep sense of connection to ourselves, our bodily sense of being alive.

When we take in nonverbal signals from others—their facial expressions, eye contact, tone of voice or *prosody*, gestures, posture, and the timing and intensity of their responses—their inner world is being transmitted to our senses. These signals are perceived by our *nervous system*★, assessed by our mirror neuron regions, and relayed downward from these cortical areas through our insula to the limbic, brainstem, and bodily regions below. These areas and these processes are each a part of what has been called the *social brain*. The subcortical shifts that literally *resonate*★ with what we see in another are then transmitted back upward, through the insula, to the middle prefrontal area. We call this process resonance, and the circuits that make all of this possible are the resonance circuits. These interoceptive abilities are at the apex of the resonance circuit and we use our own sense of a bodily self to become open to the sense of the other.

In studies of empathy, individuals who are shown a photograph of a gruesome accident can be overwhelmed in their response and shut down their capacity to help if they ask the question: What if that were *me*? How would *I* feel? Instead, if they ask the question, "how does *that* person feel?" they are more likely to have the internal resources to extend themselves and help others. The gist of these findings is that if we fuse together you and me, "I" will become lost and overwhelmed. We will become confused, fused-with. Joining is not the same as fusion. Mirror neurons might be better thought of as "sponge neurons" because they help us to sponge up the feelings of others—not to literally mirror them and become an identical reflection back of what we see in others. Sponging up the other allows us to feel part of what he or she feels, not to become them. Resonance involves connection, not confusion.

With time, the integrative push of the resonance circuits can help people overcome the synaptic shadows that keep them in the dark and prevent them from connecting with other people. It is possible to focus on both differentiation and linkage as we see the central role of integration in the neurobiology of we. From an *interpersonal neurobiology** perspective, we work at promoting such inner and interpersonal integration through the fundamental process of attuning to the internal subjective states of both self and other that fill our lives with meaning and connection.

20
20

ATTACHMENT

CONCEPT: WHAT IS IT?

The term **attachment**★ in the field of psychology refers to the *relationship*★ between the child and a caregiver. Attachment research is the scientific investigation of this important relationship that begins at the very start of life and has continuing effects throughout the life span. *Attachment theory*★ is the overarching conceptual framework through which attachment research is conducted. While it may seem that attachment studies would be generally accepted, there are actually quite a number of alternative views expressed by a range of researchers in the field. Some suggest that the interactions between child and *caregiver*★ are mostly determined by genetics, often expressed within the inborn *temperament*★ of the child. Others point to the terminology used by attachment researchers as not openly embracing the wide cultural variations in how, by whom, and in what social *context*★ children are raised. Still others are concerned about how attachment is measured and the reliability of these procedures for trying to categorize and classify patterns of behavior. Keeping these many points of view in mind, we can then openly examine the powerful findings from attachment research, understanding their implications and applications. We need to appreciate the limitations of any branch of research, especially when it comes to understanding a specific individual, the complex ways in which neural *systems*★ interact within relationships, and the pervasive and important influences of *culture*★.

Attachment research began with the work of John Bowlby and Mary Ainsworth, who formulated the basic concepts and strategies of study for attachment theory. At its heart this approach proposes that the patterns of communication between a caregiver (often but not always a parent) and an infant lead to a pattern of attachment relationship that will create an *internal working model* of security if that parent offers sensitive caregiving. Parental *sensitivity* is defined as a way in which a parent perceives the child's communication signals, *makes sense*★ of those signals by understanding their *meaning*★ for the child's internal mental world, and then responds in a timely and effective manner to meet the child's needs. This sensitivity permits the parent to engage in a *responsive* way with the child by utilizing *contingent communication*, where a signal sent by the child is responded to by the adult with a signal sent back that matches, or is contingent, with what was initially sent. Such contingency, from an *interpersonal neurobiology*★ point of view, is an example of interpersonal *integration*★. Each person is honored for being a unique individual but is then *linked*★ through contingent, compassionate, caring communication.

Over time, attachment theory suggests, these repeated patterns of interaction form the experiential crucible in which an internal working model is formed. When the patterns of communication are consistent, predictable, and filled with *repairs*★

when the inevitable *ruptures** in attunement occur, there is the creation of a working model of security, a mental *representation** of the relationship as reliably contingent. This *mental model* enables the child to use the attachment figure as a *secure base* so that he or she can go out and explore the world. Just seeing the attachment figure activates the model that can then serve as an internal source of soothing and comfort. Here we see, from an integration perspective, how built into attachment thinking is the notion of *proximity seeking* for connection (linkage) and the cultivation of exploration (*differentiation**). In this way, attachment research illuminates how integration is at the heart of early forming relationships. The pattern of *secure attachment** enables the child to go out into the world and reach her full potential, engage with others in meaningful ways, and be able to *regulate** her *emotions** well so that life is full and in equilibrium.

When a child experiences a break in the attuned, contingent communication—as will inevitably happen—the sensitive caregiver *mindfully** takes note of that rupture and then engages in the crucial *process** of *interactive repair* to reestablish the attuned connection. No parent is perfect, and no relationship is without challenging moments. The key to security is not perfect *attunement**, but the *intention** for connection and the repair when our human lives encounter the unavoidable miscommunications. When a rupture occurs, an intensification of emotion ensues that interrupts closely aligned connections even further. The result is a tumbling out of *alignment*, a feeling of disconnection and despair, and a longing for reconnection. This is powerfully illustrated in the *Still-Face Experiment* (see Figure F). After a disconnection, equilibrium is established through dyadic realignment at the heart of repair. This is the cycle of connection, disconnection, *dysregulation**, reconnection, and repair.

IMPLICATIONS: WHAT DOES ATTACHMENT MEAN FOR OUR LIVES?

The formal study of attachment, for almost 50 years, has resulted in some profoundly helpful basic ideas that form a useful foundation for understanding the ways in which *mind**, *brain**, and relationships are inextricably interwoven within the *triangle of well-being**. For this reason, understanding the research basis for some of the implications of attachment theory and research is important in order to not overstate the findings.

Books abound that review the hundreds of research projects affirming much of what we know today about the importance of the early child-parent relationship. Sometimes the primary caregiver is not a parent but another relative, a nanny or other caregiver, or an older sibling. We will use the term "parent" here just for simplicity—but bear in mind that various individuals can serve as *attachment figures** for the growing child. An attachment figure is generally thought to be the older, stronger, and wiser figure in a child's life. The availability of each of these qualities isn't always the situation with a child's parents.

Attachment theory suggests that we humans, as mammals, need to be close to our caregivers for survival. Our 200-million-year evolutionary history built in this mammalian need for attachment within our genetically determined core of neural structures, which motivates our behavior and helps us develop well. In rodents, for example, the physical closeness and touch of the parent (the mother) directly shapes the regulation of the baby's physiology, alters the *expression of genes* via *epigenetic** changes, and directly affects how the brain can harness a response to *stress**. These early interactions with the mother directly shape the architecture of the growing brain and have lasting effects, empirical research has demonstrated, across the life span. In our monkey cousins, the importance of the *presence** of the mother has also been established, revealing that prolonged separation can lead to lifelong detrimental effects on behavior and the brain.

The study of human infants is limited by the longer period of dependence on their parents for support; the fact that they have large peer, educational, and cultural influences on their *development**; and the reality that we cannot control but can only observe the genetic connections between a parent and child. Furthermore, some views of evolution point to the central importance of "alloparenting," in which human communities achieved great developmental strides and even a much larger individual brain capacity because of cooperative child-rearing practices. Unlike in other primates or most mammals, in hunter-gatherer groups and in many traditional human societies, infants are raised under the watchful eyes of a small set of collaborative caregivers who share the role of attachment figure. These varied relationships enable a young child to develop a wide array of strategies for survival, but make research more difficult for scientists interested in the impact of caregiver–infant relationships on an individual's development. However, even with these challenges, attachment researchers have created rigorous studies that have attempted to control some of these variables and find significant patterns of outcome. In this entry, we'll highlight some of these basic discoveries to illuminate the nature of this point of view.

The early experiences children have with their caregivers shape the long-term development of a number of *mental processes**. The ability to balance one's emotions, to reduce fear, to be attuned to others, to have *insight** and self-understanding, to have *empathic*★ understanding of others, and to have well-developed moral reasoning have all been found to be associated with what is called secure attachment. Security of attachment is essentially a way of summarizing a classification or grouping of a type of relationship. Security is not a feature of the child, but rather it describes the nature of an interpersonal connection—a repeated pattern of sharing *energy and information*★. A given child can have a secure attachment with one parent, and yet an insecure form of attachment with another parent.

This finding contrasts with the notion of temperament, which is a feature of the child that is felt to be present at birth and to have significant influences from the genes of the child. Temperament is extremely important in helping us understand the ways in which the *nervous system*★ has certain proclivities for responding—such as how *reactive* a child is or how sensitive he or she is to novelty. A child has one temperamental profile of neural propensities, yet can have distinct forms of attachment to various caregiving figures. The idea that temperament and attachment describe two very different but each important factors influencing development is further verified by researchers' attempts to find a correlation between temperament and attachment but finding no statistically meaningful association. In other words, temperament is something we are born with; *attachment classifications*★ are something we acquire through experience that are specific to each of our relationships with particular attachment figures in our life.

Genes play an important role in how we respond to stress, and a number of studies reveal that having variations in the genes controlling the metabolism of various *neurotransmitters* influences how we deal with suboptimal attachment experiences, such as *trauma*★. For example, children who have parents who are the source of terror, as revealed in studies of *disorga-nized**** attachment, have a more challenging time dealing with this form of trauma with certain genetic variants than other children. But these studies do not support the notion that genes create the attachment pattern in the child's relationship to the caregiver, but rather that the genetic variation in transmitter control shapes how that child will be able to respond to the stress of what the parent has provided in his or her experiences. Again, even with this disorganized attachment finding, child-hood attachment is seen as an outcome of experience with caregivers, not as a product of inherited genetic information.

Naturally there is tension between researchers in various fields dealing with development, such as attachment and its emphasis on experience within relationships in contrast to genetics, with its focus on inherited features influencing behavior. Another source of distinct perspectives is in the area of developmental attachment in the study of parent-child relationships and the study of romantic attachment, or attachment between adults. While both forms of attachment research are inspired by the work of John Bowlby and Mary Ainsworth and their original formulation of the ways in which one person draws comfort from another in a self-regulating, secure relationship, their spe-cific procedures and focus of study are quite distinct.

There are two ways in which attachment in adulthood has been studied. The original approach was through the work of researchers, like Mary Main and Alan Sroufe, who studied how the *Adult Attachment Interview******,* or AAI, could be useful in pre-dicting how a child would become attached to a parent. This semistructured interview consists of about 20 questions inquir-ing into how the adult recalls and makes sense of his or her childhood history. The AAI interview is audio-recorded and then transcribed, and the transcription is coded into about 20 scales that are rated from 1 to 9. The profile obtained then is used to classify the adult in one or two broadly defined categories of attachment. These categories for the parent are then correlated with the finding from the assessment of the child's relationship with the caregiver—the child's attachment with that adult being administered the AAI—starting at around 1 year old. Broadly speaking, the child's relationship can be seen as secure or insecure, and this then correlates with the parent's AAI finding of security or insecurity with a high degree of statistical power—even if the AAI is given to a pregnant couple and the child is not yet born. Here we see that the AAI view of "adult attachment" is depicted in what is called a "*state of mind with respect to attachment*," a *state*★ that reflects how an adult has made sense of his or her own life history revealed in a *coherent narrative*★. In many ways, this assessment shows how the adult is open in a mindful way to how the past has influenced him or her in the present.

A second approach to "adult attachment" has been used in the exploration of romantic attachment and extended further into adult relationships more broadly. Phil Shaver and Mario Mikulincer have led a robust set of research studies, initially driven by short self-report measures of how adults approach romantic attachment experiences, which have basically demonstrated that these explicit self-report measures of security or insecurity correspond to a number of ingenious explorations of implicit responses, including differences in brain-scan findings and physiological reactivity. In this approach, studies have revealed how security in adults is associated with the capacity to be helpful as a leader at both a direct practical level and in the area of emotional support, even in the setting of a military group's functioning. In contrast, insecure leaders can intensify the group members' underlying avoidance or *anxiety* to the detriment of both the individual and the group as a whole. Overall, this approach to adult attachment suggests that a person carries within her, within the functioning of her mind, a mental representation of attachment security that has allegedly been derived from early experience. This mental representation creates a sense that problems can be faced and resources will be available to find solutions. This is security, and it has a positive impact on how people interact with others, including how they lead in a group. With insecurity in contrast, patterns have been established, mediated by the mental models of avoidance or of anxiety, that lead to a decrease in reliance on others (in *avoidance*★) or an intensification of seeking others for support (in *ambivalent or resistant*★ attachment) in sometimes unhelpful ways.

These characteristics are seen as values along a spectrum, not categories within which people are rigidly defined. When these values reach a certain level, however, researchers can summarize this spectrum finding with statements referring to a "secure" or "avoidant" or "anxious" adult, knowing that individual variation is large. This is just the way research is carried out—by statistically detecting significant patterns from grouping large numbers of individuals together and seeing what could not be seen with single case examples. Because of this, individual interpretation of these findings needs to keep in mind the vast variety of characteristics and developmental experiences each of us may have had and not be restricted by an overly simplistic view that the whole of a person is locked into one category or another.

The challenging state of the science is that some studies reveal how this self-report way of defining your own adult attachment status, validated with many forms of statistical analyses, does *not* correlate well with the AAI classification of adult attachment. Clearly, both measures (the AAI of developmental adult attachment, and the self-report measures of romantic adult attachment) have validity and statistical power to predict a number of findings of how a person relates to his child (AAI) or to his partner (self-report). Further work needs to be done to clarify what these research protocols are measuring, how their valid conceptual constructs overlap and differ, and how the field of adult attachment can benefit by a synthetic view of these two different but important measures of attachment in adult life. Much remains to be learned, and we can be grateful for both explorations of the nature of attachment in our lives.

Knowing that our mammalian heritage makes the attachment between child and parent an important aspect of how the mind and brain develop empowers us to work with families and communities to support how infants are treated. Knowing about alloparenting empowers us to understand that as humans, we need the support of a network of caregivers to provide the collaborative nurturance that appears to be our human legacy, a cooperative way of living all too often forgotten in the isolation of modern urban cultures. Interpersonal neurobiology embraces the power of relationships to shape the brain, as well as the power of the brain to shape relationships. Given that the brain develops much of its regulatory *circuits** during the first 5 years of life, these early years are of vital importance for helping the next generation develop such outcomes as *emotional and social intelligence* and *executive functions**. One approach to viewing these outcomes is that the first eight of the nine *middle prefrontal functions** are created by attuned, *integrative communication** between parent and child. Here is our basic proposal: Integrative communication between caregiver and child stimulates the activation and growth of integrative fibers in the brain. Integrative fibers in the brain are those that enable the coordination and balance of the nervous system at the heart of self-regulation. In other words, interpersonal integration cultivates *neural integration**.

Teaching parents how to create a mindful, reflective stance in their lives is an effective strategy that is supported by the research that suggests that parents who can see their own and their child's mind clearly are those that provide a secure attachment relationship. The "inside out" approach to parenting teaches caregivers about the brain, relationships, and the mind in such a way that helps them make sense of their lives and create integrative communication with their children. The "whole-brain" parenting approach takes this application one step further in teaching parents about the nature of integration and how they can promote the development of an integrated brain in their own children. Keep in mind that integration in the brain is the basis for *self-regulation**—how we regulate our *attention**, behavior, emotion, and thinking.

Even with security serving as a source of *resilience**, either in childhood or if achieved in adulthood, we are not guaranteed a life without difficulties. Genetics and temperament, chance, peers, education, socioeconomic status, culture, and other important influences on development each contribute to the challenges that we face as we grow and move out into the world. At least if we offer security of attachment in our relationships with children from the beginning of life, we'll be providing an important starting place of connection in which the brain and the mind can have a source of resilience from which to start the journey of life.

Overall, attachment research validates the notion that parents matter. Interventions to help parents provide the kind of secure attachment that serves as a source of resilience will be of great benefit to the next generation. Whether we look at adult attachment through the lens of developmental studies with the AAI or with the self-report approach, it is clear from all of this research that people can and do change with changing circumstances. We can "*prime*" the brain to lean toward security. We can make sense of our lives and earn security. The brain is continually changing, and creating a new interpersonal set of experiences can help bring us as adults from insecurity to security. Everyone, including ourselves, will benefit from such a movement toward integration.

CATEGORIES OF
ATTACHMENT

CONCEPT: WHAT ARE THEY?

Research on the *relationship*★ between child and *caregiver*★ has resulted in the finding that several **categories of attachment**★ can be assessed and then studied over time. For a researcher, measurement is crucial in order to perform statistical analyses on the data collected to determine whether predictions of the studies have been confirmed or disproven. In the natural course of *development*, however, each individual has a unique assembly of internal and external factors that shape how they grow and change across time. Clinicians can be sensitive to the spectrum of features each individual brings to his or her life. But scientists have the task of finding patterns that are often best assessed by gathering many individuals, measuring specific aspects of their lives, and then performing statistical analyses that determine if these patterns have any causal relationship to one another. The research-established *attachment*★ categories have met these criteria and have been important in both predicting future outcomes of longitudinal studies and for establishing the foundation of attachment as a developmental framework for understanding the specifics of how our early relationships shape who we become. However, these "categories" more likely represent a broad spectrum of relationally related features so that each of us may have, more or less, various elements of each of these clusters. It may be best to consider these as descriptions of aspects of how we adapt to relationships, not a fixed or discrete box in which we are forced to fit.

The broadest characteristic of a categorical view of attachment, at its most basic level, is to determine whether an individual shows elements of security or insecurity. Keep in mind that these elements can change over the lifetime with *reflection*★ and with further development in new kinds of relationships. These are not fixed categories! In adult attachment, these are called "*states of mind with respect to attachment*" in order to honor the open and changing dimension of these groupings. Security broadly refers to the notion that an internal sense of being able to rely on others for a *healthy*★ form of *interdependence*★ exists. This is sometimes called an *internal working model* which is a mental *representation*★, or a *neural firing*★ pattern, that creates in the person a felt sense that others are dependable and can and should be relied upon as needed. The sense of *self*★ is open and interactions with others are rewarding. Developmentally, sensitive caregiving from the parent is thought to create this *mental model* of security such that the child can go out into the world and explore, feel good about himself or herself, and find close, rewarding connections with others.

With insecurity, the child is faced with a different kind of parenting behavior. In the broadest terms, the research suggests that we can move in one or two ways. We can become anxious and fret that the caregiving we need will not be enough. Generally this is thought to arise from interactions with caregivers that are inconsistent and intrusive. A child may need the caregiver but had learned that she cannot rely consistently on that *attachment fig-ure*★ to soothe and protect her. This is called an *ambivalent or resis-tant attachment*★. The other dimension is that of *avoidance*★. Here the child is not seen and not attuned to in a reliable way, and the child then uses the adaptive response of avoiding the need for the caregiver. Behaviorally avoiding the parent following sepa-ration is the classic finding for these relationships. Notice how we don't say the "child is avoidant" but rather that the relation-ship is avoidant. This same child can have a secure, or an ambiva-lent, attachment with another caregiver. Studies reveal, however, that even with this avoidance as a survival strategy, the child still "knows," beneath the higher parts of the thinking *brain*★, that relationships do indeed matter. Adults with this stance also show implicit, inward, neural signs of needing others. But this learned approach of avoidance is generally characterized by an exter-nal set of behaviors that avoid, or minimize, the expression of the need for others in their outward actions. Naturally if you are the romantic partner of such an individual it can be frustrat-ing, if not outright isolating. In contrast, ambivalently attached persons maximize the attachment *system*★, heightening the need for others to the point of being excessively and anxiously cling-ing to others for support that they might otherwise get from themselves. In other words, self-soothing is often in short sup-ply for the ambivalently attached person. For his or her partner, a sense of being unable to fill the "bottomless pit of neediness" and "nothing being quite good enough" can be extreme reactions to this *anxious sense of self*. There is no reliable internal work-ing model of attachment within the individual that would serve such a self-soothing function. In this case, all soothing is being sought from external sources. This places a huge burden on the romantic partner of such an individual. The avoidantly attached person, in contrast, has shut off the external need for others and in this way has become isolated and filled with a *disconnected sense of self* in his or her avoidance strategy. While we can understand the adaptive origins of such ambivalent and avoidant strategies, we can also see why these forms of insecurity can lead to impediments to *integration*★ and to how the *mind*★ flexibly functions within relationships.

A final form of insecurity can be seen to arise when there is both excessive approach (anxious) and excessive avoidance (withdrawal). This is sometimes called *disorganized*★ attachment in the developmental literature and fearful avoidance in the self-report adult research. When a child is threatened, there are two *circuits*★ in the brain that are activated simultaneously and that are incompatible. One is the *brainstem*★-mediated, 300-million-year-old survival-based *reactive* circuit to get away—to flee—from the source of threat. The other is the 200-million-year-old attachment circuit that activates a need to "go toward the attachment figure to be soothed and protected." One message—a feeling of terror induced from the parent's behavior—activates two circuits that create opposite actions: to go away from and go toward the same person. The problem is that the attachment figure is both the source of the terror and the child's source of protection and so there is no solution for this "biological paradox." And so this combination of the two general strategies of avoidance (minimize attachment) and *anxiety*/ambivalence (maximize attachment) may be due to terrifying experiences in the child's life with the caregiver such that the biological imperative of the attachment system—to go toward an attachment figure for safety and soothing—is in direct conflict with the circuits of survival that drive the child to pull away from a source of threat. When the attachment figure as the biological source of safety is also the origin of terror, the adaptive strategy of the child collapses and there is no solution. This is a biological paradox and generates fear without resolution. The internal world of this individual fractures, and then there is a *fragmented sense of self*, and the child is prone to develop clinical *dissociation*★. It is for this reason that this combination of approach and withdrawal is a disorganized form of insecure attachment, one that has the most negative outcomes for the child.

IMPLICATIONS: WHAT DO CATEGORIES OF ATTACHMENT MEAN FOR OUR LIVES?

The categories of attachment, these clusters of developmental patterns that have been determined by researchers over hundreds of investigations, reveal that children's relationships with their caregivers can generally fall into four groupings within the broadest characteristics of secure versus insecure (this latter being composed of avoidant, ambivalent, disorganized), as described above. In the majority of children in the general U.S. population, a *secure attachment*★ is found. The basic developmental research paradigm is called the *Infant Strange Situation*. This instrument evaluates the relational attachment status at around a year of age by assessing how infants seek *proximity* to their parent after a brief separation, and examines how quickly they return to explore and play with the toys in the room. During the first year of life, children whose relationships were evaluated as secure showed that, in direct observation of parent-child interactions, the parents were generally *attuned*★ to the internal needs and feelings of the children. Later studies would find that an even stronger factor for predicting the child–parent attachment classification than the direct observations of parent–child interactions was the finding of the *coherent*★ *Adult Attachment Interview*★ *narrative.*★ This finding reveals how parents can flexibly reflect on their own childhood experiences and *make sense*★ of how these have shaped their development into adulthood.

Further studies elaborated this general finding in proposing that the important mechanism of secure attachment was the parental capacity to reflect on the mind, a skill called *mentalization*★. This ability would enable parents to sense the inner mental life of their children and of themselves. This *reflective function* found in parents with children securely attached to them reveals that seeing the mind of the child, which in *interpersonal neurobiology*★ we call *mindsight*★, plays an important role in the child's development. Mindsight refers to both the ability to sense the mind of oneself and others and to move that interaction toward integration.

These mindsight abilities, enabling us to sense and shape the mind, also overlap with the concept of *mindful awareness*★. A number of initial studies across a range of measures have correlated the tendency to be mindful with adult security of attachment. From the viewpoint of interpersonal neurobiology, we consider this finding as a possible example of the shared manifestation of integration in internal *awareness*★ (a form of *internal attunement*★ for mindfulness) and within interpersonal relationships (a form of *interpersonal attunement*★ with secure attachment). That both mindfulness and secure attachment are associated with the integrative functions (at least eight of the nine) of the *middle prefrontal cortex*★ further lends support, not proof, for the *consilient*★ view that integration is at the heart of well-being, internally and interpersonally.

Children with secure attachments with their primary care-givers generally meet their intellectual potential, are able to *regulate*★ their *emotions*★ well, have *empathic*★ connections with others, and are able to be flexible and resilient. Like their parents, these children generally grow up to have "made sense of their lives," having *insight*★ and being able to articulate how the past has impacted their present life, as revealed in their having a *coherent narrative*★ as measured by the AAI. If significant negative experiences have unfolded in their lives in the interim and they have not been able to "work through such experiences," even a securely attached infant can develop various forms of insecurity later in childhood. Security is a source of *resilience*★ and is not a guarantee of well-being or even of continued security. This finding from attachment research reveals the general view of the mind: Life is an unfolding *process*★, not a final product, and attachment is not a permanent, unchanging fixture in an individual's life. Security sets a solid initial foundation, a kind of psychological immunization, but is not a certainty determining a particular outcome. Likewise, insecurity may create challenges, but these challenges can be generally overcome with new and integrating experiences later in life. These experiences can involve reflection and immersion in new personal or therapeutic relationships.

About a fifth of the general population in the United States has been reported to have *avoidant attachment*★ in which the infant acts as if the parent never left the room even after this attachment figure returns during the Infant Strange Situation study. In the first year of life, observations of the relationship between child and parent revealed parental discounting of the child's needs and feelings, a kind of emotional distancing. The parents in this relationship have a *dismissing*★ narrative finding in the Adult Attachment Interview in which the parents state that they do not recall their childhoods and that relationships during their childhoods had little impact on their development. This insistence on a lack of recall is not the same as *childhood amnesia*, the normal developmental finding that most people do not have a continuous *memory*★ for their lived experiences before 5 or 6 years of age. Instead, there appears to be a lack of recollection, and perhaps even *encoding*★, of relational experiences throughout childhood and *adolescence*. These adults also insist that relationships have not been and are not important in their lives. When their own children grow into young adulthood, the children, too, are generally more likely to have a similar narrative stance of minimizing the importance of relationships in life. Overall, the avoidant attachment and the dismissing adult *state of mind with respect to attachment* are each thought to reflect an adaptive strategy that minimizes the innate, inborn, genetically created attachment system's activity. These strategies of survival to a cold relationship have *synaptic shadows*★ that persist in the child's life. It is a self-fulfilling prophecy: The very relational qualities that were a part of an attachment relationship are then inadvertently recreated by the child/teen/adult. Here we see that experience, in this case in relationships early in life, shapes the way people adapt and that these adaptive strategies persist into adulthood.

A long-term, longitudinal study revealed that when children with a primary attachment that was deemed to be avoidant grew into their school years, they were experienced as controlling by their peers. A teacher, without knowing these family findings, would respond to such a child in a distant, uninvolved manner much like how the parent treated the child at home. *Temperament*★ does not correlate with attachment categories, but it is understandable that one could view this self-fulfilling prophecy as a manifestation of an innate quality of the child, rather than the learned response that research has clearly demonstrated it to be. Clinical impressions of the avoidant grouping and the adult dismissing counterpart suggest that part of this synaptic adaptation may be revealed as an internal disconnection, perhaps reflecting impaired integration across the *hemispheres*★, which "shuts down" the full range of emotional experience in the internal and interpersonal lives of these individuals.

Less than an eighth of the population in earlier studies of children have an *ambivalent or resistant attachment*★ with their primary caregivers in which the child fusses and is not easily soothed even when seeking proximity to the caregiver after his or her return in the Infant Strange Situation. The parents of this ambivalently or resistantly attached child during the first year of life are thought to have been inconsistent in their *attunement*★ and at other times to be intrusive. This intermittent reinforcement heightens the drive for attachment but does *not* yield an internal mental model that "all will eventually be okay" in the child's life. Hence the term "insecure" attachment refers in this case to a relationship that is anxious and ambivalent. This child's anxious *state*★ is also reflected in the parent's state of mind with respect to attachment. The parent's own Adult Attachment Interview narrative reveals a *preoccupied*★ state of mind with respect to attachment in which issues from the past intrude upon reflections in the present. This form of an incoherent narrative may reflect an impediment in the integrative functioning of the brain. In other words, impaired *integrative communication*★ in interactive experiences may be the root of impaired growth of integrative neural fibers. These would be the synaptic shadows of suboptimal attachment. The result of this insecure preoccupied attachment state of mind would be a lack of coordination and balance in the *nervous system**, with ensuing manifestations as narrative discourse with memory intrusions and emotional disequilibrium during interactions with a child.

Historically, a fourth category of attachment was added after the initial finding of these first three broad groupings of secure, avoidant, and ambivalent/resistant. Relationships were categorized as disorganized and disoriented if the child's response in the Infant Strange Situation was filled with "approach-avoid" behaviors in which he first moves toward and then away from the caregiver in the room. Sometimes the child might fall on the floor or turn in a circle. The impression is that there is no organized approach to how to deal with the return of this caregiver. Observational studies in the home suggest that the parent is offering frightened or frightening behaviors to the child. The "biological paradox" is that two circuits in the child's brain are simultaneously activated. One circuit is that of the over 300-million-year-old survival reflex: "I am being terrified by X, so I should get away from X." Yet the attachment circuit, shaped by 200 million years of evolution, is activated under this threat and motivates the infant to move toward the caregiver to be protected from harm. Inside the child is an unresolvable war between two impulses, and the internal world of the child collapses. Unlike the other forms of attachment, this one has no strategy, and hence the notion of disorganized relationship. This move-away/move-toward dilemma has no solution—and thus this has been called "fear without solution." Because of this, disorganized attachment has the most negative outcome of all the other groupings. Children with disorganized attachment have significant challenges with *emotion regulation**, maintaining *attention** and clear reasoning under stressful conditions, and having rewarding and recipro-cal relationships with others. In addition, these children have a high probability of developing clinical dissociation in which the internal sense of self, the continuity of *consciousness**, and the access to memory are all fragmented.

The Adult Attachment Interview of parents with children who are disorganizedly attached to them reveals the finding of adult *unresolved** *trauma** or grief. This is a serious and fortu-nately treatable condition. Within this semistructured interview and the transcription of its 90-minute interchange between researcher and parent, one can see a disorientation or disorgani-zation in the linguistic output in response to queries about loss or trauma. This disorganized narrative reveals an intrusion of unintegrated memory into the linear telling of the adult's auto-biographical story to the researcher. It should be noted that this disorientation in the adult's narrative is parallel in quality to the child's internal fragmentation described above, and in the dis-organized behavioral response upon that parent's return to the room during the Infant Strange Situation. These are examples of what interpersonal neurobiology would view as *chaotic** pat-terns in the flow of *energy and information**, within and between people.

The Adult Attachment Interview appears to be the only research-based and empirically validated instrument that makes an assessment of and distinction between unresolved and resolved forms of trauma and loss. Research shows that hav-ing been traumatized or having suffered a serious loss is not predictive of one's offspring having a disorganized attachment.

However, having *un*resolved trauma or loss is predictive. This is a vitally important finding and a clinical note of profound significance. Parents who can resolve their traumas and losses can extinguish a transfer of disorganized attachment experience on to the next generation.

Offering professionals their own opportunity to take the Adult Attachment Interview provides an important window into the synaptic shadows that their own childhood experiences may have created in their lives. The great news is that attachment categories can change over time. We can resolve trauma and loss, and we can move from insecurity to security. Attachment is not fixed. Relationships of various sorts—with a changed parent, with other relatives, with a teacher, a friend, a clinician, a spouse—can each help to move an individual from insecurity to security. From an interpersonal neurobiology perspective, we envision that insecure forms of attachment are reflections of how nonintegrative communication yielded impediments to the growth of integrative fibers in the brain. Because the brain can continue to change across the life span, the key is to find a way to "inspire to rewire" people's brains so that they can move toward integration.

The research on attachment offers a powerful tool to detect patterns by which early relationships shape how children develop. While these patterns have been essential for placing individuals into categories for statistical study, each of us is unique. When performing the Adult Attachment Interview on yourself or others, please bear in mind that you are a one-of-a-kind person. And, at the same time, you are a human being who shares the long history of our species on this planet. We do have general tendencies that can lead to a sense of disconnection (avoidant and dismissing categories), a sense of

confusion and uncertainty (ambivalent/resistant and preoccupied categories), or a sense of internal fragmentation of the
self (the fearful avoidance, approach/withdrawal of disorga-
nized/disoriented and unresolved trauma or loss categories).
The reason to know about how to assess these patterns is that
often when we can *"name it we can tame it."* Knowledge, often
expressed with words we can share with one another, illuminates the inner darkness with a clarity that just groping around
in a nameless dark may not be able to yield. While words help
us to clarify reality, they are not to be mistaken for reality.
Integration then involves holding the tension of using maps
such as words to get somewhere and name that place, but then
we must let such maps go to see the true nature of what is
actually there in front of our eyes. Each of our attachment histories is our own, and honoring that uniqueness is essential,
too, in respecting our journey to integrate our lives. In other
words, while there may be a name of a category (ambivalent,
avoidant, disorganized) that helps illuminate some patterns in
your life, there are many unique details that need to be honored beyond these categorizations and memberships in particular classifications. This tension is the essence of integration
while it encourages us to be both *differentiated*★ (unique) and
linked★ (a member of a grouping).

Programs that apply the fundamental principles of attachment to helping families nurture security can build on these
important findings. Teaching reflective skills that enable mindsight to flourish can help an adult develop a coherent narrative
and can provide the attuned, mentalizing experiences children
need to thrive. Such mindsight skills, based on seeing the life
of the mind and moving its *flow*★ toward integration, are at the
heart of resolving trauma and moving from the nonintegration

of insecurity to the integrative functions of security. From an interpersonal neurobiology approach, teaching about the interconnection of mind, brain, and relationships moves us beyond just focusing on attachment and into the larger issue of internal and interpersonal integration at the heart of healthy development across the life span.

22
22

MINDSIGHT

CONCEPT: WHAT IS IT?

The term **mindsight**★ emerged years ago in my own *mind*★ when I experienced the lack of *awareness*★ of the inner world by a number of my professors in medical school. This inability to "see the mind" had serious negative effects on the patients, and on us, their students. But how could someone not see the mind? It turns out that we use very different neural *circuitry*★ to sense mental life than we do to see physical objects or think about the *systems*★ and mechanical aspects of the world, such as the anatomy and physiology of the body. Mindsight at its most basic definition is the ability to see the mental world of the *self*★ and others. Since that initial use of the term back in the early 1980s, mindsight as a concept has broadened to embrace the larger *context*★ in which the "mind" exists. Mindsight is the ability to sense the *energy and information flow*★ of the *triangle of well-being*★: to sense the flow of energy and information as it is shared between people in *relationships*★, as it *flows*★ through the neural circuits of the body, and as it is *regulated*★ by the mind. When we develop mindsight skills, we not only monitor this flow within the mind, *brain**, and relationships, but we are afforded the capacity to modify and shape that flow toward *integration**.

IMPLICATIONS: WHAT DOES MINDSIGHT MEAN FOR OUR LIVES?

Seeing the larger picture of mindsight as a way of skillfully sensing and shaping energy and information flow in the mind, in our relationships, and in the brain yields broad implications for how mindsight can be taught in schools, in families, and in *psychotherapy*. As the brain is a term used in this perspective to mean the body and its distributed *nervous system**, this is a fully *embodied** and *relational** conceptualization of our mental lives. Essentially what this *interpersonal neurobiology** view suggests is that we can empower students and teachers, children and parents, patients and clinicians, to work collaboratively to create more *empathic** relationships, more integrated brains, and more resilient and *creative** minds.

The basic curriculum for a mindsight approach is centered on the triangle of well-being (see Figure E). When relationships, brain, and mind are placed on "equal footing," we can see that we are not alone in the world and that we can understand how the brain works with relationships in shaping our mental lives. We can learn that the focus of *attention** is a powerful tool to transform lives toward *health**. This empowerment extends the impact of mindsight training beyond the benefit of the individual person or family; mindsight skills produce an integration in relationships and the brain that has the potential to alter how our larger communities function and how our *cultures** can support a more empathic and *compassionate** society.

Mindsight is the mechanism beneath *social and emotional intelligence*. Cultivating these forms of intelligence has been associated with improvements in academic performance, *emotional*** well-being, and decreases in school bullying. For educational administrators, these findings can be seen as a call to action and a win-win-win situation in which the major domains of *development* are each improved.

Making sense* of one's life as a parent and having the *mentalizing** skills to see the mind of oneself and others are the research-proven features of the sensitive *caregiver** that are associated with *secure attachment**. Though security is not a guarantee of a trouble-free life, secure attachment does provide a source of *resilience** in the face of stressors in the future. We give people driving lessons before they take the car out on the road (and even require a driving test to boot)—so why aren't we offering parenting lessons based on science before people raise their children? Mindsight is a teachable skill with benefits for all involved.

Another implication of these mindsight findings is in the field of mindful education and *mindful awareness** training. Becoming aware of the present moment without being swept up by judgments, learning to be mindfully aware, has research-proven benefits for mind, brain, and body. We enter a *"left shift"* in which we are able to approach, rather than withdraw, from life's challenges. Mindfulness training may increase immune function and support healthy *epigenetic** regulation. Mindfulness also increases empathy and *insight**. One way of interpreting these findings is that when people are given the tools to see the mind clearly, to stabilize attention long enough that the details of energy and information flow become vivid and in focus, then we are offering a mindsight-skill training that has all the benefits of integrating mind, brain, and relationships.

A mindsight-skill training approach is really all about an *internal education**** in which the inner side of our mental lives, our relationships, and even our *embodied brains* is made the central focus of the curriculum. The basis of such an approach is to cultivate a way to regularly take *time-in**** in order to develop the skills of internal *reflection**** and interpersonal connection. Social and emotional intelligence, based on the mechanism of mindsight, are outcomes of an internal education. Time-in practices offer a form of internal education, teaching about the nature of *mental activities****, the impact of relationships on our well-being, and how the brain serves as a source of internal *processing****. As the brain changes in response to experience—including the ways we pay attention—this view is an empowering vision that provides a way to use the mind to improve the brain and relationships.

Some of these findings are drawn from the work of social and emotional intelligence programs, while others are from mindful awareness studies. The mentalization found in secure attachment also reveals how a *reflective function* that is a form of internal understanding is important in our parent-child relationships. Yet the internal world is rarely the focus of our traditional educational programs. While reading, writing, and arithmetic (the classic *"3-R's" of education*) are naturally vitally important, these ideas about mindsight suggest that three more R's might be added to our list to greatly enhance modern education: reflection, relationships, and resilience.

The application of these ideas in a variety of settings— from schools and organizations to family programs and clinical work—can base the approach on the science of such an internal education. Yet programs in education and in *mental health****— over 95% of them—do not offer a definition of the mind. The mind is composed of at least three dimensions: subjective, inner, personal experience; *consciousness*★ or the sense of knowing within awareness; and the *self-organizing*★ emergent, embodied, and relational process that regulates energy and information flow. When we take the step of defining one aspect of the mind as this self-organizing regulatory process, and identify regulation as entailing both monitoring and modifying, then we can organize this internal education to include skill training in these two regulatory components. Taking time-in can be the regular practice that develops and strengthens the mindsight skills of monitoring with more stability and depth and modifying toward integration. We can teach people how to regulate toward health by enabling them to develop the capacities of monitoring more clearly and modifying with more specificity and strength. These are teachable skills and rarely the focus of our didactic, family-based, or clinical strategies of application. The goals of such internal education would be to promote health with more empathic relationships, an integrated and more regulated brain, and a creative, resilient, and vital mind.

23

23

ATTUNEMENT

CONCEPT: WHAT IS IT?

When we use *mindsight★* and its capacity to maintain an open stance to the internal world of ourselves and of others, we are able to achieve **attunement★**. Attunement is the way we focus on the flow of *energy and information★* in an open and *receptive* manner. The *circuitry★* of our own *nervous system★* is such that if we attune, we come to create *resonance★* in which our observing *self★* takes on some of the features of that which we are observing. If we are attuned to another, this creates an *interpersonal resonance* in which each person *feels felt★* by the other. The experience of *joining* two subjective inner worlds with each other is sometimes called *intersubjectivity*. When this joining is with respect and care, this *interpersonal attunement★* is the basis of *secure attachment★*. If we attune to ourselves, this creates an internal resonance in which our observing circuitry aligns with our experiencing self and we have an open, mindful *state★* of *awareness★*. When we take *time-in★* to pause and reflect on our inner experience, we create the possibility of such *internal attunement★*.

Mindful awareness★, in this view, is a form of internal attunement that creates a deep state of internal *integration*★. When we are *compassionately*★ communicating with others, we attune to their internal state in an open and receptive way that engages two *minds*★ into a sense of a "we." This is the heart of secure *relationships*★. Attunement builds on itself, and practicing internal attunement makes us more likely to be *empathically*★ attuned to others. This is why taking time to focus *attention*★ on the inner experience in the moment actually also makes us more sensitive to the inner life of others. Internal attunement and interpersonal attunement can mutually reinforce one another.

IMPLICATIONS: WHAT DOES ATTUNEMENT MEAN FOR OUR LIVES?

Attunement and integration go hand in hand. Practices that promote internal or interpersonal attunement likely involve similar circuitry. What this suggests is that knowing ourselves deeply supports our knowing others' internal worlds as well. How do we come to connect in such a way? We likely harness a core aspect of our social circuitry that supports the process of attunement. The *resonance circuits*★ involve a pathway from the *perceptual*★ *systems*★ of sensory intake (sight, hearing, touch) that pass through the *thalamus* and then through the *thalamocortical circuit* on the way to the *cortex*★. Within the cortex rest the *mirror neurons* which initiate a set of neural cascades in firing that produce the flow of signals (energy and information) downward through the *insula*★ and into the *subcortical*★ regions. These areas below the cortex include the *limbic*★ and *brainstem*★ regions along with the body proper, with its many responses including those of our muscles, intestines, lungs, and heart. Changes in our subcortical states are then passed upward along *Lamina I** and through internal sensory input via the *vagus* nerve to the brain-stem and then on to the insula and its portions in the *middle prefrontal region** (see Figure D-1). In other words, we drive *information** down from our cortical perception into the body, and then these bodily changes come back up into our cortex. The various parts of this middle prefrontal cortex enable us to have *interoception** so that we perceive the internal state of the body (and likely the state of the brainstem/limbic areas). As we come to know ourselves, being in touch with our subcortical states, we open the gateway through this mirror neuron-insula-body-insula-middle prefrontal *flow** that then enables us to also know someone else. We come to resonate in ourselves with what we sense in others, enabling separate selves to become a part of a functional whole.

While resonance can occur automatically, coming to appreciate this emerging sense of connection involves awareness. Awareness is the key to creating not only appreciation, but also *flexibility in our responses**. Awareness of our internal state is a key skill necessary to facilitate self-knowing and other-knowing. Even distinguishing others' *emotions** from one's own emotional response can make the difference between becoming over-whelmed by empathic contact or being able to stay in equilib-rium and extend a hand to help others in distress. Resonance does not mean becoming a copy of the other person; rather, it means joining while maintaining one's own *differentiated** iden-tity. It is through this *self-knowing awareness* that empathy and compassion are created and able to be maintained. Attunement, both internal and interpersonal, shares the same fundamental resonance circuitry and mutually reinforces itself.

The flow of energy and information in our lives manifests

through various forms. To understand attunement fully, we need to see the direct application of energy and information flow in our ways of seeing the world. As the "object" of attunement is at this level of *energy*★ flow patterns, it is helpful to keep in mind that the signals—internal or interpersonal—that are the focus of attention in attunement will vary according to the nature of the attunement in that moment. In schools we emphasize words and logical *processes*★, rewarding the *syllogistic reasoning* that searches for concrete cause-effect relationships in the world. But emotional and social skills are often more subtle and intricate than that, built upon a nonlinguistic, nonlogical way of knowing about the interior of our own and others' subjective lives. Applying these notions of attunement requires that we embrace the importance of these other forms of knowing about reality. Students must certainly focus on the concepts a teacher is relating, but education has the potential to go much farther than the important reading, writing, and arithmetic of present programs and into the *R's* of *reflection*★, relationships, and the cultivation of *resilience*★. Attunement is a dance of connection, from the inside out, that ultimately can be expressed with words to some extent but its creation blossoms in a nonworded world of *primary experience*. When students can be taught this way of integrating their lives, resilience can be created as they learn the skills of *healthy*★ reflection and relationships that can set up the foundation for a lifetime.

Applying these ideas requires that teachers, parents, and clinicians immerse themselves in this nonworded world first. There is nothing like direct primary experience to create a deep sense of knowing in the realm of attunement. Yet this way of experiencing the world is often far from the day-to-day curricular menu. The programs that work to support internal and interpersonal attunement can honor this by acknowledging the scientific reality of the importance of first-person inner *subjective experience**. Time-in practices such as the *wheel of awareness** or breath-awareness offer direct ways in which primary experience can be honored.

After this important beginning, the details may vary but the intention is to share the same fundamental stance of respecting the inner world of all involved. Being open to sensory experience beneath prior expectation naturally invites us to embrace uncertainty. There is no "right or wrong," no "answer key" to this approach. Instead, internal education that begins with a focus on lived experience highlights our need to honor the many ways that energy and information are experienced in our lives. With this beginning of internal attunement, the stage is set for interpersonal attunement to flourish. From an *interpersonal neurobiology** view, these forms of attunement are examples of integration—beginning within ourselves and then *linking** our own inner world of primary experience to that of others. This is truly joining from the inside out.

FOLLOWING RUPTURE
WITH REPAIR

CONCEPT: WHAT IS IT?

We can create ideals for how to live: We can attempt to be attuned and open to whatever is going on inside of others, to be kind whenever possible, to be attentive and open. We can even have a notion to have self-compassion and be *receptive* to the many layers of our inner *self*★ that need nurturing across a lifetime, or a day, or a given moment or *mood*★. But life is full of breaks in these ideals, challenges to whatever we feel is a proper, correct way of being that we have not been able to achieve. Instead of beating ourselves up for the imagined or actual failures to meet these high standards, what we need is to **follow ruptures with repair**★. A rupture is a break in an optimal way of relating to others, or to our own inner selves. A repair is an active effort to acknowledge the rupture and establish anew the *attuned*★ connection that serves to create *compassion*★ toward ourselves and toward others.

IMPLICATIONS: WHAT DOES FOLLOWING RUPTURE WITH REPAIR MEAN FOR OUR LIVES?

Some of the most insidious internal *processes*★ that impair *healthy*★ living are the feelings of self-hatred and self-blame. If interactions with another person have not gone well and such *states*★ of hostility toward the self emerge, it is unlikely that an open and genuine effort at repair will be able to occur. Attempts to discount that a rupture occurred, or to rationalize it away, minimizing its significance, can ironically and sadly intensify the negative impact of a rupture. Such minimization can occur in both the internal *awareness*★ and the interpersonal acknowledgment, creating a further distancing between two people. When such ruptures without repair happen repeatedly, wariness may grow inside a person that the other is not to be trusted. This loss of trust itself is a form of chronic and often hidden rupture, a state of distancing mistrust, which further distances two people from one another. A sense of distance and deadened connection emerge in such painful states of disrepair in a *relationship*★.

Shame★ is a *state of mind*★ in which the neural *circuitry*★ of being *emotionally*★ in need of connection may have been repeatedly frustrated. The ensuing response may be to turn the eye gaze away, and to have a heavy feeling in the chest and a nauseous feeling in the belly. A thought may chronically emerge that the self is defective—not wrong in its actions (as in guilt), but bad at its core. The toxic feeling of shame is so intense at times that this state may "go underground" and become part of the large inner world of the *nonconscious*★ mental life we all have. This shame state, though, can continue to influence our responses and drive our behavior. For some, external and publicly visible achievements may become an intense focus of work but when actually accomplished they may give little sense of success. The self believes it is defective no matter what the external world may say and the internal pain continues, whether beneath or within conscious knowing.

Close relationships, too, may be ultimately unrewarding as shame-imprisoned individuals come to believe that anyone who loves them must either (a) not yet be seeing the true badness of who they are and rejection is just around the corner, or (b) be so "dumb" or "worthless" for wanting to connect with someone like them. Shame traps the individual in isolation despite a desperate longing for connection. The Groucho Marx line of "why would I be a member of a group that would have me as a member" can be the theme of the shame-dominated person.

From an *interpersonal neurobiology*★ point of view, shame is an adaptive response to a negative life situation. By maintaining the important attachment figure as "good" and "competent," the dependent young infant or child maintains an inner sense that someone in the world is able to protect them. If a child can create an internal mental stance through shame that sees the self as defective, it can create at a deep, *primary experience* level a way to feel as if the *caregiver*★ is fine—perfectly capable of seeing them, soothing them, and keeping them safe. The sacrifice of a positive attitude toward the self is adaptively made in order to maintain sanity and a semblance of some sense of security in the world. How painful a solution! Better to be filled with shame than to lose all hope of being safe and secure. In these ways, then, shame protects the young child. As the child grows, however, the pain of such negative attitudes toward the self, and the deeper reality embedded in *memory*★ of rejection and despair, all are too much to hold within awareness. To "know" within *consciousness** is different than to have a mechanism at play that one simply keeps away from the *subjective experience** of knowing within awareness.

This is an important example that reveals how the *mind** is more than consciousness, and more than subjective experience. These are indeed important aspects of our mental life. Yet here we see how also viewing the mind as a *self-organizing**, *emergent** process that *regulates** the flow of *energy and information** enables us to delineate a core aspect of mind. *Mental processes**, like shame, can exist outside of consciousness and outside of subjective experience. Mind organizes the experience of the self within the world.

And so for many individuals for whom shame was a *developmental* adaptation, the pain is just too much and the workings of this state of mind are out of awareness. Yet the impact on relationships—with the self and with others—continues to play out throughout life unless something is done to illuminate these hidden sources of pain and distress. One way shame impacts us is in limiting how free we feel to acknowledge our own suboptimal behaviors. If a rupture has occurred in our close relationships, being open to our role in that break in connection and then taking responsibility and authentically apologizing for our misdoings may be quite difficult. It is a part of being human to contribute to disruptions in connections with others. Yet processes like shame can keep us from freely acknowledging our role and making a repair to reconnect with the other person. These impediments to repair can severely constrain the health of a relationship.

Repairing a rupture requires that we acknowledge what happened and make an effort to reconnect. While shame states are one form of impediment to such repair, sometimes stubbornness, pride, ignorance, or just plain selfishness may make an individual contribute to a rupture but not be able to acknowledge his or her role in the disconnection. Narcissism, for example, may pervade a person's view of the world and prevent him or her from taking responsibility for a role in a disruption. *Defensive* statements that it was only the other person's fault or an unwillingness to take at least part of the responsibility for the rupture can rapidly shut down efforts at repair. This is clearly a limitation to *integration★*.

When the *triangle of well-being★* is at the front of our minds, we can stop the self-blame or the denial and own the fact that, as human beings, no one is perfect. And if we have the ability to work on the way shame has contributed to this difficulty with repair, then we can move forward openly in finding new ways of being with others and with ourselves after a rupture. The key is to embrace the humility of our humanity, connect with ourselves in a compassionate way, and then make an effort to reconnect with the other person. The triangle reminds us that integration is the key to health, and a rupture to that integrated state needs repair to make the triangle whole again. No one is an island; no one is perfect. We are the outcomes of a dance of connection of where we've been in that triangle, who we are now, and how we empower ourselves to create a future that we can actively shape. We do not need to simply repeat patterns of adaptation from the past. In this view, it may not be our fault but it is our responsibility to use our awareness and *intention★* to follow a rupture with repair.

Often after a rupture, the intense feelings of shame or anger, frustration or guilt, are so great that we go on *automatic pilot★* and do not have the *presence★* of mind to see our *reactive* reflexes. The *Still-Face Experiment* offers a visual illustration of how reactive

and dysregulated an infant can get when a parent stops responding in a contingent way to her (see Figure F). With the parent's
face being still, the baby no longer has the attuned responses
that she needs to keep herself in equilibrium. These early relational circuits of other-dependent regulation do not disappear
as we grow. Instead, we remain forever interconnected, especially with significant others in our lives. These developmental origins of the power of rupture to disrupt our internal states
and make us feel vulnerable when an attachment figure is not
protecting us from harm enable us to see why rupture for us as
adults can sometimes be so disabling. With the activation of a
survival state of mind induced with the feeling of threat after
rupture, we ready ourselves for the behavioral responses of *fight,
flight, or freeze.* From this internal state of *reactivity**, it is quite
difficult if not impossible to make a repair. If shame is activated
during such a rupture, then the pain of disconnection may also
be associated with a feeling of humiliation and hostility. In these
states of mind, it may be quite difficult to apply the lessons of
the importance of repair. In this case, taking a "break" may be
crucial to minimize damage created with continued efforts at
that moment.

The key to initiating a reconnection is to begin with the
*mindful** state of being aware that we realize we are more than
our present thoughts, feelings, or memories. Our identity
does not need to be our reactive *fight-flight-freeze* states in that
moment. We must have the *space of mind* to sense that even these
highly compelling internal ruptures away from a *"yes state"* of
openness are but transient states of mind. Knowing that a state
of mind can be dissolved and shifted into another state is an
important *mindsight** capacity and is fundamental to *emotional
intelligence.* If ruptures are repeated and prolonged, if repair is

not easily achieved, the individual may need to do some *intra-personal* work in developing the hub of the *wheel of awareness** before being able to move forward with ease. This and other *mindful awareness practices** can be important ways of approaching challenges to repair. Mindful awareness practices include ways of *differentiating** what we are aware of—such as a feeling, thought, or memory—from the experience of awareness itself. In other words, with mindful training we learn that a feeling, a thought, and a memory are not the totality of who we are. *Mental activities** are not the whole of our identity. When years or decades have passed and accumulated mistrust, anger, isolation, and fear have enveloped a person's life, initiating a basic program that builds this space of the mind is essential. Introducing a mindful way of being into the *system**, within an individual and within a relationship such as a couple or a family, can be a life-transforming process. The great news is that the inner sanctuary from which repair can be initiated is always available to be nurtured and can bring important reconnections in our relationships.

25
25

TIME-IN AND MINDFUL AWARENESS PRACTICES

CONCEPTS: WHAT ARE THEY?

Mindful awareness practices*, or MAPs, are what the UCLA Mindful Awareness Research Center (marc.ucla.edu) uses as a term to refer to the many approaches to developing the skill of being *mindfully** aware. Yoga, t'ai chi ch'uan, qigong, centering prayer, and mindfulness *meditation* are examples of practices that focus *attention** on the present moment. One way of viewing the commonality of these strategies is that they focus *attention on intention* and also create *awareness of awareness*. In creating and maintaining the postures of yoga, for example, one needs to be aware of how *awareness** is focused or instability and imbalance will ensue. In one aspect of mindfulness meditation, the breath is the focus of attention. When the focus of the *mind** inevitably wanders and becomes distracted from this target of the breath, the intended goal is to redirect attention back, again and again. If one forgets what the *intention** of the practice is—to focus on the breath—then the exercise cannot be performed well.

Here we see how stabilizing attention involves being aware of awareness (Am I aware of what I am aware of right now?) and paying attention to intention (Am I following through on my intention to focus on the breath?). These are two key ways that mindful awareness practice strengthens the mind itself.

"Time-in*" is a term that can be used to refer to the ways in which we can take time to focus inward, to pay attention to our sensations, images, feelings, and thoughts as we *SIFT** the mind's inner experience. Taking time-in each day can promote improvements in *emotion regulation**, attention, and *empathy**.

IMPLICATIONS: WHAT DO TIME-IN AND MINDFUL AWARENESS PRACTICES MEAN FOR OUR LIVES?

William James, a founder of the field of modern psychology, proposed over 100 years ago that the exercise of returning a wandering attention to its target again and again would be the "education par excellence" for the mind. Although he also stated that people did not know how to accomplish this, we now know that for thousands of years in traditions in the West and the East, mindfulness practices have been doing just that. We also now know that the *brain** changes in response to experience throughout the life span, and we can say that a mind-training exercise that builds the capacity to be aware of awareness and pay attention to intention will strengthen the *circuits** of *executive functions**. These functions include the ability to sustain attention, to avoid distractions, to selectively change attention and then focus on the designated target, and to allocate the resources necessary to accomplish a task. In our own preliminary study of using MAPs for those with attentional challenges, the MARC group at UCLA was able to find as much executive function improvement as one does with the use of stimulant medication in adults and adolescents with attention deficit challenges. Other studies have been and are being done to explore the use of mindfulness practices in a range of conditions that may respond to increasing the stabilization of attention and the *regulation*★ of *mood*★ and *emotion*★.

Mindful awareness practices clearly do more than improve and strengthen attention. As research has demonstrated, by using the Mindfulness Based Stress Reduction (MBSR) program, created by Jon Kabat-Zinn and studied by Richie Davidson and other investigators, we can improve a wide range of functions such as the workings of the immune system, the capacity for empathy, and the ability to move toward rather than withdraw from challenges in life. This latter finding involves a shift in enhanced electrical activity in the left frontal area of the brain. Recent studies out of the University of California have found that strengthening the capacity to sustain mindful awareness can even increase telomerase, the enzyme needed to maintain the telomeres at the ends of chromosomes that sustain the life of the cell.

When we view MAPs as a way of attuning to the *self*★, we can see that these mindfulness practices promote a form of *internal attunement*★ akin to the *interpersonal attunement*★ of a *secure child-parent attachment*★. Our *interpersonal neurobiology*★ view is that *attunement*★—internal or interpersonal—promotes *integration*★ in the brain. Integration is the *linkage*★ of *differentiated*★ parts of something, and it permits the coordination and balance of a *system*★ that optimizes *self-regulation*★. This may explain why the integrative functions of the *middle prefrontal cortex*★ overlap with a wide array of findings, including mindfulness practices, secure attachment*, and many therapists' views of what would entail mental health*. These same integrative functions appear to be at the heart of wisdom* traditions that promote living a life of kindness* and connection.

The interpersonal neurobiology view of these overlapping features is that at their core they each share the process* of integration. From this vantage point we see integration as being created from within, engaging people interpersonally, and even linking the inner and outer experience of being an individual in a larger collective whole. Because the inner world of our subjective experience* and our awareness is developed in mindful awareness practices across the broad spectrum of activities, these can be seen as a way of "taking time-in." As research has also demonstrated that the regularity of practice is a key feature in developing the health*-promoting benefits of these practices, time-in becomes a fundamental part of a "daily mental diet" of essential activities to keep the mind, the brain, and our relationships* healthy. This is embedded in the healthy mind platter* as a visual reminder of the daily activities needed to attain well-being (see Figure J).

MAPs are mind-training programs that integrate the brain and our relationships—with others and with ourselves. A way to think of this integration is that an observing self-state is able to attune to a sensing/experiencing self-state. This is internal attunement. Though for thousands of years various religious traditions have promoted such practices, the fact is that these forms of focusing attention are a way of strengthening the mind by altering the integrative, regulatory circuits of the brain. Internal attunement stimulates the activity and then the growth of integrative regions in the brain—ones that link specialized areas to one another. This is the way in which the internal focus of attention in a mindful way *SNAGs*★ the brain to become more integrative as it stimulates neuronal activation and growth. A simple process like focusing on the present moment as we pay attention to attention and are aware of awareness is a way of making the brain and our relationships healthier. These practices are truly a form of mental fitness, a kind of "brain gym" and "relationship enhancer" that is a basic human health-promoting activity. While researchers are still debating the exact operational definition of mindfulness itself, the finding that taking time-in to strengthen the capacity to focus awareness on awareness and attention on intention actually helps in so many ways ought to empower us to embrace the importance of this inner practice for well-being now. There is no need to wait for some definitive agreement on what exactly mindful awareness does and does not entail before we apply this important form of mind-brain-relationship fitness in our lives.

One issue that sometimes arises in defining terms is whether being mindful is primarily a way of focusing attention on the present-moment experience or whether it also entails more of a *state*★ of positive regard for self and for others. The acronym *COAL*★ embraces this latter notion of a way of being aware that is imbued with kindness: The letters stand for curiosity, openness, acceptance, and love. This COAL state of being suggests that mindfulness naturally involves the self and other-directed *compassion*★. This finding is consistent with the view that internal attunement and interpersonal attunement go hand in hand. From an interpersonal neurobiology point of view, this perspective is natural in that we see integration as the heart of these forms of internal and interpersonal attunement, which are the essence of how we see what it means to be mindful. It is far more than a way of focusing attention but is seen through this lens as more a way of being in the world. Time-in practices cultivate this COAL state toward the self, enabling the observing self to attune in an open and attentive manner to the experiencing self. With time, intentionally created states can become natural *traits* of being that occur without effort. This is how being mindful, whether from practice or from innate traits, is viewed as a way of living in the world. In this way of being, "shoulds" are released and *primary experience* is the focus of attention: *Bottom-up** processing (I am experiencing this right now) becomes relatively freed from the possible tyranny of *top-down** processing (I should be experiencing, or thinking, or feeling this or that right now).

Here is the key: Mindful awareness and its internal attunement activates the circuitry of the brain that is also a part of being empathic with others. This is crucial to realize because some consider internal *reflection** a "selfish" act, but, in fact, when done mindfully, it actually develops the circuitry of empathy. This is how internal integration through time-in practice stimulates the very neural regions needed for interpersonal integration. The outcome of such integration is compassion and kindness. Kindness is integration made visible.

An alternate view is that "mindful awareness" is really just about focusing attention on the here and now; it is not something imbued with kind regard. In this perspective, additional qualities, such as self-compassion, other-directed compassion, a sense of being a part of a larger whole and a member of the human race, and the capacity to articulate what is going on inside of oneself are important attributes. As mentioned above, others consider these as a part of the larger idea of mindful awareness. Beyond these active debates about semantic distinctions, we can state simply that the focus of attention in an internally attuned manner is very helpful in life. Time-in practices encourage people to remove themselves, even briefly, from the external distractions of everyday life, the stimuli that often pull attention toward the outside world with the sights and sounds of digital media. Time-in enables the mind to develop the important ability for *interoception**, which enhances *self-aware-ness** and the capacity for empathy. If we learned to perform time-in practices each day, much like when we try to eat a balanced diet for bodily health or brush our teeth daily for dental hygiene, we'd have healthier minds, more integrated brains, and more compassionate relationships.

Pausing and focusing inward to escape the busyness of the day is the aim of mindful practice. Regular, daily practice is an intention, an ideal goal, not a strict pressure to create in our lives. This is where the term "time-in" originated. Making a break from the incessant demands of our busy lives, time-in can possibly become something familiar for us, something that could be done regularly like resting or sleeping each day. I've gotten a unanimous positive response to the term from many walks of life (in contrast to my earlier efforts to try out "brain-brushing"). In fact, seeing time-in as a part of a menu of daily mental nutrients embeds this important practice, fundamental to creating mental well-being, into our daily activities. This is the idea of time-in as part of the healthy mind platter. Working together, we need to make some approach, something that is easy for all ages to grasp and to be motivated by, an activity that can be readily applied in our fast-paced and digitally connected worlds. We need to be able to say something like, "Have you taken time-in today?" or "How did you take your time-in today?" as reminders to breathe, to reflect, and take time in our lives to connect with ourselves.

26
26
26

THE WHEEL OF AWARENESS

CONCEPT: WHAT IS IT?

The wheel of awareness★ is a practice I created in order to focus on the integration of *consciousness*★ as a *domain*★ of *development* in our lives. *Integration*★ is the *linkage*★ of *differentiated*★ parts, and so what would the elements be that are differentiated in the experience of consciousness? We can distinguish the many different things that can be known: senses that bring in the outside world, the felt experience of the body, and our *mental activities*★. We can even sense our connections to others. And we can distinguish the experience of *awareness*★ or knowing from that which we are aware of, the known. These are the many elements of consciousness that can be differentiated from one another. How can these then be linked to create integration?

One way of depicting this integration of consciousness is as a wheel, with a center *hub* and an outer *rim* (see Figure H). The hub represents the experience of awareness itself—knowing—while the rim contains all the points of anything we can become aware of, that which is known. We can send a *spoke* out to the rim to focus *attention** on one point or another on the rim. The rim itself can be divided into four sections, each which can be differentiated from the others. In this way, the wheel of awareness becomes a visual metaphor for the integration of consciousness as we differentiate hub awareness from the rim elements, and the four sections of the rim from one another.

IMPLICATIONS: WHAT DOES THE WHEEL OF AWARENESS MEAN FOR OUR LIVES?

By creating a practice that is based on a scientific view of integration at the heart of *health**, we can focus directly on the way in which a mind-training exercise can integrate *mind**, *brain**, and *relationships**. As the wheel of awareness exercise is not derived from religious or contemplative tradition, it is possible to use this approach in schools without a concern about mixing education with religion. Furthermore, young as well as older children can be taught this practice and it enhances their abilities to stay focused and to understand the power of their own *emotional** lives to inform, but not control, their behaviors and reactions.

The four sectors of the rim can be visualized along the rim's circumference as four slices of a pie that depict various *mental processes**. The first segment contains the points from the outside world: our sight, hearing, olfaction, taste, and touch. The second segment contains the input from the interior of the body and enables us to have *interoception** of the muscles and bones of the body (head, limbs, and torso), as well as the input from the genitals, intestines, lungs, and heart. The third section represents mental activities, such as emotions, thoughts, images, *con-*

cepts, memories, beliefs, attitudes, *moods**, *intentions**, hopes, and dreams. Finally, the fourth segment represents the sensations of our connections with others, a *relational sense**.

Putting numbers on these senses is helpful for some. The first five senses bringing in the outside world are in the first sector, the sixth sense of the body is in the second sector, a seventh sense of seeing mental activities is in the third sector, and the eighth relational sense is in the fourth sector. But notice how the numbers can get a bit confusing . . . so it is sometimes just more straightforward not to label the senses, one through eight, in this diagram. The use of an image of a spoke, sent from the hub outward to the rim, enables a visual metaphor to be created of focal, directed, concentrated attention. Sometimes one can just allow anything from the rim to enter the hub and experience open awareness. But at other times, and in doing the initial wheel practice, it is helpful to systematically do a "rim review" so that one moves the spoke, sector by sector, around the rim with intention and *regulation**. This is part of the training of the attentional *system** of the mind that links the rim to the hub.

The training of the mind through this practice refines the ability to differentiate these distinct senses from one another and also to differentiate the senses from awareness itself. This is a vital differentiation, often not present in our daily lives. The responses of those who have been long-term meditators as well as those who have never mediated before to this wheel of awareness exercise have been quite encouraging, and fascinating. When we integrate consciousness, powerful changes in life can occur. The hub represents a *spaciousness of mind* that gives us room to pause and reflect. The use of the spoke to direct attention reaffirms the person's innate capacity to choose where to place attention. Impulses may arise, and we can learn to just sense these as points on the rim within the hub of our mind, not acting on them but just noticing them come and go within awareness. We can put a space between impulse and action, choose our various options, and remain fully present even when there is a lot of busy chatter arising from the rim.

One important additional implication should be mentioned as a general point. Whenever we use a metaphor, like the wheel of awareness, we need to realize that it is just a map of a territory and not the territory itself. In other words, there is no wheel anywhere except as a drawing, a map on paper, or in our mind's eye, our imagination. This is just a visual analog of a functional reality of distinguishing knowing from the known, of separating out the many things that can be known from one another. And as with any map, it is only useful if it can be a guide to arriving somewhere. It should not, and cannot, replace actually being somewhere. It is helpful to remind people of this view with the following analogy. If you were traveling from Asia or Africa or Europe and you wanted to visit Yosemite Park in California but arrived in New York City, what would be most helpful for you? Should we say, "Go west, young person!" And then just keep our fingers crossed and hope that you'd find your way? Possibly. But how helpful would that be? Another option is to give you a map of the United States, perhaps set you on a means of transportation to the West, and ultimately you'd more rapidly arrive at the national park. Yosemite would be a lot easier to find if you had a map! Yet we'd expect you to put the map you had in your pocket so that it served as a guide and not a distraction once you were actually in Yosemite! You'd experience all the waterfalls, the rivers, the forests, the deer and bear, and the gorgeous cliffs with your direct sensory input. The map got you there and can represent a place, but it is not a replacement for the experience of being there.

The same is true for the wheel of awareness. It is simply a map to get you to the Yosemite Valley of your own mind and to do so in an integrative way. Once you are there, the mind is yours to experience directly. No one should tell you what your own subjective, inner mental sea is like. But we *can* offer a guide to get you there more rapidly. Once there it would be helpful to place the map in your pocket and soak in the sights of your inner life.

The wheel of awareness is now being used in a variety of schools, in *psychotherapy* practices, and in *meditation* programs. In one educational setting, a teacher told me that a young student said she needed a time out to "get back in her hub" when she was finding herself about to fight with another child on the yard. "Coming back to the hub" is a quick metaphor one can use as an easily accessible reminder for oneself, or others, to remain in or return to an open, *mindful** place. And indeed, the wheel of awareness, though designed as an integration of consciousness exercise, is considered to meet all the criteria for a mindfulness practice.

There are freely available recorded versions of the wheel on my website, www.drdansiegel.com, and the formal practice is published in a number of books about the applications of *interpersonal neurobiology**. The power of the practice is that each time it is experienced the rim changes, so the novelty factor is high. This keeps kids (and teens and adults!) motivated to explore the architecture of their own minds. In a basic view of the hub, the spacious sense of knowing, there is sometimes an analogy made to being beneath the surface of the ocean where it is calm and clear. For many, the hub represents a parallel analogy to this place beneath the surface, beneath all of those crashing brain waves of sensation, feeling, and thought. For those afraid of water, the idea of a wheel may be more readily embraced than a metaphor of the mind being like the ocean (especially if there is *trauma*★ associated with water).

For those not afraid of water, here is a way to explore this comparison of the mind to the ocean. In this ancient story, it is told that deep beneath the ocean it is tranquil and clear. And from this deep place of clarity, one can look upward to the surface and notice the conditions there. It may be flat, filled with choppy waves, or inundated with a full storm, but no matter what those conditions, deep beneath the surface it remains calm and clear. Then the story goes on to compare the mind to the ocean: Just sensing the breath brings you beneath the surface of the mind where it is also calm and clear. From this place you can just notice the mental activities that are the brain waves at the surface of your mental sea. Deep beneath the surface, it is calm and clear. And from this deep place, you can just notice the mental activities, the feelings and thoughts, memories, and images that rise and fall as waves on the surface of the mind.

The place beneath the surface is akin to the hub of the wheel of awareness. And the breath is used to bring the individual to this deeper place, this hub of the mind. From this inner place of open possibility, the specific thoughts or feelings can be noticed and received, but not identified with as the totality of who the person is. The rim does not define the whole of the *self*★. This is the freedom to expand a sense of self as having more than just mental activities. For many, the hub experience opens up a sense of having "come home" or finding "an inner sanctuary" with which they can move through daily life with a deep sense of ease and equilibrium. This is how differentiating hub from rim plays an important and sometimes transformative role in creating an inner sense of clarity. Anxieties, worries, and even physical pain have been repeatedly reported, amazing as it sounds to me, too, to markedly decrease and remain improved after practicing the wheel of awareness.

The systematic exploration of the four sectors also enables a broad range of sensory inputs to become differentiated from each other. The wheel practice honors the importance of the body as a source of deep *wisdom*★ and nonworded ways of knowing. Practitioners can explore the nature of how mental activities arise and fall away and what the "space in between" mental activities actually feels like. Just this aspect alone awakens people to become an expert in the functional architecture of their own minds. That, by itself, is an invitation to the power of taking *time-in*★, of exploring the sea inside. And finally, the exploration of the eighth relational sense enables the wheel practice to remind us of the reality of our coexistence and interconnectedness as living beings who share our common home, this planet we call Earth.

As the hub "strengthens" with an individual's practice, we can imagine that part of the neural correlate of the hub, the *middle prefrontal region*★, also becomes synaptically reinforced as well. A more advanced part of the application of the wheel practice is to have the person focus a spoke onto the hub itself. Bending the spoke, in the mind's eye, back toward the hub enables people to experience firsthand what direct *awareness of awareness* itself feels like. Many individuals find this part of the practice profoundly illuminating. To help explain the similar reports of many individuals in completely separate situations and differing *cultures*★, I have found the *plane of possibility*★ to be a useful attempt to map out one way of seeing how knowing is different from the known. However one interprets the exercise of the hub on hub, the *subjective experience** of that phase has fascinating implications for our health. Ultimately this general practice—rim review and hub on hub—can become a part of one's daily life routine, not just something one does during a practice period. If time is a constraint, this approximately 20-minute practice can easily be divided into four segments, yielding a practice of 5 minutes a day. Doing part of a "rim review" each day enables us to embrace the integrated nature of our own mind, honor the importance of the body, and acknowledge our interconnectedness with one another.

27
27

MIDDLE PREFRONTAL
FUNCTIONS

CONCEPTS: WHAT ARE THEY?

*Interpersonal neurobiology** seeks to find the *consilience** of knowl
edge in which we look for common principles that emerge from
independent ways of knowing. One consilient finding has been
the central role of *integration** in the creation of *health**. Looking
at the fields of *psychopathology*, emotion research, neurobiology—
including the fields of *social neuroscience* and other branches of this
broad discipline—psychology, physics, systems theory, and mathematics has led to the view that integration—the *linkage** of *differentiated** parts of a *system**—is at the heart of well-being. In
this search, a clinical challenge became an opportunity to deepen
an understanding of how to bring neuroscience findings into
the world of *subjective experience**. The clinical care of a family in
which the mother had been in a terrible car accident and injured
the region of her *brain** behind the forehead led to the search for
some understanding of how her inner mental world, interpersonal world, and neural world could all mutually influence one

another. The outcome of that search for consilience is the compilation of the **middle prefrontal functions**★. This list, now expanded from its initial grouping, basically attempted to piece together a cluster of regions in the brain that included the *anterior cingulate*★, the *orbitofrontal cortex*, and the medial and *ventral* portions of the *prefrontal*★ region (see Figure D-1). Because these "separate" areas actually work together as a functional whole and because they were all either midline horizontally or vertically, I used the simple term "middle" to denote their clustering as an integrated and integrating unit. The functions of the "middle prefrontal cortex" then are the outcome of firing of these various regions as they work together to link widely separated areas of the nervous system. The ultimate reality of their functions is that they emerge from the linkage of the *cortex*★, the *limbic*★ area, the *brainstem*★, the body proper, and even the signals from other brains (the social world). In other words, the middle prefrontal region is profoundly integrative of at least five differentiated neural inputs.

Middle Prefrontal Functions:

1. Body Regulation—keeping the organs of the body and the *autonomic nervous system*★ coordinated and balanced.

2. *Attuned Communication*★—tuning in to the internal *state*★ of another.

3. *Emotional Balance*—enabling internal states to be optimally activated: not too aroused, not too deflated.

4. *Response Flexibility*★—pausing before acting to reflect on available options of response.

5. *Fear Modulation*—reducing fear.

6. *Insight*★—*self-knowing awareness*★ that links past, present, and future. This is a *mindsight*★ map of "me."

7. *Empathy*★—imagining what it is like to be another person,

to see from another's perspective. This is a mindsight map of "you."

8. *Morality**—imagining, reasoning, and behaving from the perspective of the larger good. This is a mindsight map of "we."

9. *Intuition**—having access to the input from the body and its nonrational ways of knowing that fuel *wisdom**.

IMPLICATIONS: WHAT DO THE MIDDLE PREFRONTAL FUNCTIONS MEAN IN OUR LIVES?

Taken as a whole, these nine middle prefrontal functions serve as a useful description of what *mental health** may entail. Given that these functions emerge from extensive *neural integration**, we can see the scientific underpinnings of the view that health emerges from integration. What cultivates these nine functions?

The first eight of these nine middle prefrontal functions have been proven to be outcomes of secure parent–child *attachment**—the ninth function, intuition, has not yet been studied in attachment research. Given that this list was created from brain studies and the attachment findings were discovered independent of the research on the brain, it is natural to see this as another example of consilience with separate areas of study sharing a common finding. We can draw a possible inference that *integrative communication** between parent and child promotes the growth of the child's integrative middle prefrontal cortex. Integrative communication occurs when each person's differences are honored and their linkages are created through *compassionate** communication. *Energy and information flow** that is integrated between people stimulates the growth of integrative fibers in an individual's own brain that then permit internal integration to occur—the linking of differentiated areas of one's own *nervous system**. This is the essential idea: Integrative *relationships** cultivate integrative brains.

Keep in mind that when we speak about integration, we are not using this term as a metaphor, like the *wheel of awareness** or the *triangle of well-being**, but as a proposed core mechanism at the heart of health. With our focus in interpersonal neurobiology on energy and information flow patterns, we can look at relationships (sharing), *mind** (*regulation**), and brain (*embodied** mechanism) as all being connected directly to one another, as a functional and physical reality, not a metaphor. These are three aspects of one reality: the reality of energy and information flow. With integration, too, we have the dual aspects we can study of both the functional and the structural interconnections of differentiated elements.

When I was first introduced to the world of formal *mindfulness** practice, it was after this list had long been compiled. Yet it turns out that the results of mindfulness research revealed that each of the nine middle prefrontal functions are outcomes of mindfulness practice. And as Jon Kabat-Zinn told me at a meeting when I first brought this to his *attention**, this list is also the way of being mindful, not just the outcome of mindfulness as demonstrated in research. Here is another example of consilience. The benefit of consilient thinking, among many, is that it helps us predict the outcome of future studies. Consilience also enables us to interweave the various sciences so that we can draw on their varied and great wisdom. When we find universal principles emerging from a wide variety of research disciplines, we can also feel more confident that these are solid findings, not simply an exciting but temporary discovery or transient phase of thinking. We build on the important and difficult work of researchers from independent disciplines to make a picture of an integrated whole. And indeed this consilient finding leads to the hypothesis that mindfulness practice will likely be associated with the growth of middle prefrontal fibers and other integrative regions, a finding that was later found to be true in several independent labs. That is the power of consilience: to make hypotheses and see how future research from any of a range of disciplines may support or refute the proposals.

Finally, in teaching about these functions in various places around the world, I have been approached by a number of individuals who have told me that their cultural tradition—be it of the Inuit tribes in Alaska, the Lakota of the Midwest, the Polynesian in the Pacific, or the Hindu *culture*★ in India—has in various ways taught many of these nine functions through the oral or written traditions of their people for thousands of years. Wisdom and *kindness*★ are natural parts of these traditions, and they are natural outcomes of the middle prefrontal functions. Integration is at their core, and integration is the consilient *process*★ we are identifying in this consilient work.

Can you sense how exciting this consilient approach can be? We find consilience among attachment, brain research, clinical practice, mindfulness research, and wisdom traditions when we explore the middle prefrontal functions. Taken in isolation, each of these fields stands alone in its approach. But in seeking consilience, we intentionally try to find commonalities, constructing bridges across disciplines, and attempting to create a "whole-elephant" view of reality not easily obtained with any single perspective in isolation from the others.

When we apply the consilient principles of integration to our daily lives and work, it is helpful to keep in the front of the mind that integration is potentially present in a broad range of human activities. In the study of *complex systems*★, there is a recurrent *flow*★ in which patterns at one level of system intricacy emerge into patterns at higher-order levels. When we embrace the notion that every small change we create in ourselves becomes manifest in our interactions within the network of connections we have with others in our lives—then we can take a deep breath and be open to the intricate and often unseen linkages not available to the naked eye. Integration is expressed in the nine middle prefrontal functions, but it does not stop or start with these functions or these integrative regions of the brain. But these functions and a focus on integrating ourselves from the "inside out" are a graspable place to begin to change the world, one person, one relationship at a time.

If taking *time-in*★ to focus in a mindful way on the inner nature of experience develops these integrative middle prefrontal regions (see Figure D-1), then we can see how something as simple as a time-in practice in schools might be an inexpensive but powerful way to promote more *resilience*★ in our youth. We can now say that *reflection*★, relationships, and resilience can be the "new *R's of education*" and adopt a policy of "no prefrontal cortex left behind"! What a great way for teachers to begin to truly educate the mind directly and help to strengthen the capacity to monitor and modify energy and information flow toward integration.

The application of *mindful awareness practices*★ and the interactive experiences that promote *secure attachment*★ are both grounding places to begin to conceive of how to promote the nine middle prefrontal functions in schools, at home, and in society more broadly. This is how we take a mindsight–skill building approach to education, family life, and the larger communities in which we live in order to cultivate integration and create a kinder, more resilient and compassionate world.

28
28

ENERGY AND
INFORMATION FLOW

CONCEPT: WHAT IS IT?

How are the *mind**, *brain**, and *relationships** part of one reality? In a journey to address this question, it has been fascinating to explore various perspectives from a range of disciplines, from neuroscience to psychology, anthropology to philosophy. *Interpersonal neurobiology** is based on a *consilient** approach where we attempt to find the universal principles shared across independent disciplines of knowledge. In attempting to find a consilient view about mind, brain, and relationships, there has actually been some intense nonagreement and even rancor in contrast to other moments of collaboration. One source of concern has been the misunderstanding that seeing these three elements—mind, brain, and relationships—as not the "same" makes them somehow independent of each other. Quite to the contrary, our consilient approach sees these as three aspects of one reality as we explore the ways in which our mental life, our neural realities, and our relational worlds are parts of one whole. Another issue has been the statement that *energy** is "not a scientific term." As any physicist or chemist or biologist will tell you, energy is a scientifically validated reality. Despite these concerns, new vistas can be revealed if we push ahead and work together, across disciplines, to understand these various aspects of our human lives. Addressing the fundamental question of how mind, brain, and relationships are interrelated can bring us to a new view that opens a window onto the world of *health** and *compassion** and of healing and *kindness**. Part of the challenge has been to understand deeply the perspectives and the concerns of the various disciplines of science, embrace their *wisdom**, and find some way to *link** their perspectives. Interconnecting mind, brain, and relationships has been a journey of discovery that riles some, but it has yielded profoundly helpful *insights** of great promise in linking many fields of knowing together.

The body has a richly distributed *nervous system** that extends throughout its torso and limbs and sends signals to and from the skull-encased cluster of nervous tissue we call "brain." We could use the term "body" or, emphasizing the neural aspect to focus on **energy and information flow***, we can simply use the term "brain" and remind ourselves of its *embodied** form. We'll lean on the latter, in its simplicity and accessibility as a term, but remember that, for us, "brain" always means the whole of the body. We have a *kinesthetic* sense of the movement of the body; the *interoceptive* input from our muscles, bones, and internal organs; and a wide range of hormonal, immune, metabolic, and cardiovascular system influences on our bodily *state** that directly impact the brain's functioning. To have an accessible phrasing of these influences, we simply say that the brain is the embodied mechanism of energy and information flow. *Neurons** send electrochemical energy down their interconnected components and this energy changes over time. This change is called *flow*★. The ions flowing in and out of the activated neurons' membrane—the *action potential*—are how electrical energy in the form of polarization and depolarization moves across time in the nervous system. The release of a *neurotransmitter* at the distal end of the neuron, in the form of a chemical that passes across the *synapse*★ and then links with the *receptor* molecule in the membrane of the receiving neuron, is literally the way chemical energy is transduced. The nervous system is a way that electrochemical energy changes across time. This is energy flow. One objection to the phrase "energy and information flow" registered by some in academics is that it sounds too "soft." If physics is hard science, then energy flow is a solid scientific reality.

And what exactly is *information*★? From a *cognitive sciences* view, information is a pattern of energy flow that symbolizes something other than the pattern of energy flow. In other words, some patterns of energy flow have *meaning*★ beyond the characteristics of the flow of energy. The name "Golden Gate Bridge," for example, is more than just the sounds of the phrase or the squiggles of these clusters of letters. It "stands for" the bridge over the San Francisco Bay: It symbolizes something other than the letters themselves. The words are patterns of energy (patterns of photons moving for sight, sound waves as air molecules moving for hearing) that stand for something other than the patterns of energy. Words are information in that they carry meaning beyond the energy swirls upon which they ride! The word "pattern" suggests a form in which something occurs, and that form changes across time—it flows. In our mental lives, information itself is not static. Perhaps "information" is best considered a verblike entity, not a noun. As a form of movement itself, information leads to more *"information processing*,"* which means that the pattern of energy, the swirl we call information, is itself inducing new changes in the patterns of energy flow as they move across time. Just imagine the Golden Gate Bridge for a moment and see how information quickly transforms and moves along in your mind across time.

The entity that makes up a pattern and is changing across time is energy, or what physicists ultimately state is "the capacity to do something." That something sometimes is work, but sometimes not. This capacity to do stuff is, for many physicists I've interviewed, as close as they, as scientists, or we, as human beings trying to articulate the nature of, well, nature, can get to defining this basic stuff of the universe.

Energy is the capacity to do stuff. Energy is potential.

Of course, Albert Einstein wrestled with this issue in finding the profoundly influential connection between energy and matter with his equation, E (energy) = m (mass) times c (the speed of light) squared (multiplied by its own value). And so, literally, even mass is (highly condensed) energy. Our nuclear age knows this all too well.

On the human side, can we build on physicists' emphasis on energy and explore the possible ways our relationships, our brains, and our mental life may be understood by thinking in terms of energy? It seems like a reasonable consilient approach. Yet the intense negative reaction to this starting position by a number of individuals in fields including psychology, philosophy, and neuroscience has been fascinating. In one case, for example, a neuroscientist said that this approach was "reversing science" by not seeing mind and relationships as just "outcomes of brain activity." A psychologist said that there is "no need whatsoever to evoke energy and all its soft implications" in exploring the nature of mental life. He called on some of the popular writings in psychology in the 1970s and said that we should never be so "ill-informed." And a professor of philosophy urged that "the mind can never, and should never, be defined as it will limit our understanding." I honor all of these concerns, but if we approach the use of "energy and information flow" in a cautious and scientifically consistent manner, we can openmindedly see if indeed there is anything useful about doing so. Let's keep an open mind and see where this takes us! And, for those doubtful individuals in particular, we might just say that because these entities of mind, brain, and relationships have not been explored this way in the past does not mean we should not do so now. As my old advisor once said, "You should have the courage to be wrong." We need to have that courage, and it seems that, by building a whole-elephant consilient view of the important parts shaped by individual disciplines, using the concept of energy and information flow is actually a fruitful way to go.

When we communicate with one another, we share energy and information flow. Relationships are built from patterns of communication, which are really patterns of sharing energy and information flow. In this fundamental way, we can see how relationships and the brain are not the same. Energy and information are shared between and among people. This is a relationship. The energy and information flow inside of us passes through neural connections. This is the embodied mechanism of energy and information flow we are going to call, simply, "brain." Relationships and brain are not the same; they are two sides of one coin, the coin of energy and information flow.

And then we come to our most challenging term, the topic of this pocket guide: the mind. What are the implications of using the fundamental notion of energy and information flow in exploring the nature of mind?

IMPLICATIONS: WHAT DOES ENERGY AND INFORMATION FLOW MEAN IN OUR LIVES?

The mind has several aspects we should delineate as clearly as is possible. There seems to be a consensus that our everyday use of the term "mind" includes our feelings, thoughts, memories, images, beliefs, attitudes, hopes, dreams, and *perceptions**. If we use the broad term "*mental activities**," we'll be able to have a useful phrase that captures this list of generally agreed-upon content that makes up our mental life. These are the waves of our mental sea. We can see them, hear them, feel them, and know them.

Now the knowing experience is perhaps a bit different than a mental activity. Or is it? Let's walk through the reasoning a bit here and see where we go. We can be aware of a feeling or *emotion**, or we can sense an affective state, a *mood**. All of these—feelings, emotions, *affect*, mood—are words that attempt to articulate some sort of inner reality of what is happening in that moment. We may, of course, communicate this outwardly, to send this something out of our "inner selves" and into the world for others to see and hear and feel. But the origins, most people might agree, are in some inner essential something. Now we could place this in the body if we want, and fine, let's do that for now. Your heart is heavy, tears are flowing, and your throat is choked up. You say, "I am feeling blue. . . . I feel sad. . . . I am lonely. . . . I feel lost." Whatever these emotional states are— body states—you have your subjective sensation of those bodily signals. And so we come to a most challenging moment in our journey. Is there a difference between a physiological state of the body and the subjective sensation of that state?

Let's reflect on that for a moment. We can have a body shift in its state and not be aware of it. We don't have the conscious experience of that sad feeling or even an *awareness*★ of heaviness in the chest. But we do have the shift in the body. This line of experiential *reflection*★ (not even reasoning, really, just reflection) reveals that a body's shift in state can exist without a *subjective experience*★ of that change in state. And so, on one basic level, we need to assert that these are in fact different elements of our inner reality. Both are real, but they are different. Bodily state and the neural activities that accompany it and our subjective experience are not the same. They are related, yes—but not the same.

If you go along with me for a moment with this, then we have the next question as to what "subjective experience" actually is. We don't have a good response for that question except to share our own, well, subjective point of view. Here is one way of approaching this conundrum. Some things in life, some things in science and mathematics, are said to be *"primes*★*."* A prime is something that is not reducible to anything else. A prime number, such as 5, is not reducible to another number, whereas 6, a nonprime number, *is* reducible to 3 times 2. And so a prime cannot be made into other numbers—it is solid ground, irreducible, not transformable into something other than itself. That is what the scientific term "prime" means. Here is the proposal: A prime in our mental lives may be the nonreducible quality of subjective experience. It seems like a rationalization—which it certainly is as a way of reasoning what to do with reality of subjectivity—but let's play with this a bit more to see where we can go.

If energy flow manifests as the physical property of "the capacity to do stuff" in its many forms, we don't try to reduce, say, photons to anything further. We accept photons as energy, movement of air molecules as energy, and chemical transformations as energy. For sound, air molecules moving are the prime of the physical mechanism of energy flow. When you hear a song, the sound waves manifesting the kinetic energy of air molecules moving is not reduced into something else . . . it is just patterns of the movement of air that ultimately will activate a chain of electrochemical transformations in your brain. And so at the physics level of energy patterns, we somehow feel at ease letting that physical manifestation of energy flow—air molecules moving—just be what it is, a pattern that is a prime.

In the brain, linked neurons become active when we listen to the song. Brain studies suggest that different forms of music will evoke different activation patterns in the brain and body as a whole. And so we can see that, especially for sound, there is a direct correlation between patterns of energy as music and patterns of *neural firing** as brain activity. This is the passage of energy from air to brain.

In relationships, we can sense the physical sharing of energy patterns as they flow (move across time) between two people as an enduring exchange *process** we know from our personal experience. If I smile at you each time I see you come into a room, you'll come to expect that signal as part of our connection, as patterns that are part of our relationship. In a close relationship, the feeling of love is created by patterns of *attuned communication** between lovers, a prime we can honor as one of the wondrous experiences of our *relational** lives. We don't need to reduce the act of sharing to something else. Relationships are the way we connect with one another. In many ways, a relationship reveals how the whole is greater than the sum of its parts. This is the *emergent** quality of a prime experience: It cannot be reduced to you or me—the smile is created between us.

And now we come to mind.

Our discussion of the prime of subjective experience as a possible way to continue our discussion on mind is useful because we can start with a stated assumption that subjectivity cannot be reduced. *It is the mental experience of the felt reality of something.* "Felt reality" reminds us that subjective experience is "real" even if it cannot be quantified, even if it cannot be compared from one person to another, even if it cannot be isolated and cultured in a tube. Subjective experience is real. But what is it?

The mind has several dimensions. Ones we've discussed above are the activities of mind, such as feelings or thoughts. Another is the subjective experience of those mental activities. A related aspect of mind is *awareness**. Awareness can be seen to include a sense of knowing and the subjective experience— the felt reality—of the known. To put it more simply, awareness (and its synonym for now, *consciousness**) has the sense of knowing and the sense of the known. I can be aware of heaviness in my chest, tears in my eyes, a lump in my throat. At that moment I am conscious of the sensation of these bodily states, and I might even think as a thought that I am sad, feel the overarching sensation of "sadness," and even be aware that I am aware of being conscious that I am sad. Each of these has the two dimensions of felt reality: I am sensing within awareness the known and the knowing.

You could argue that knowing is itself the sense of the known—that there is no true sensing of knowing. And this is all fine. However we divide these notions, one arising issue is this:

There is a distinction between the experience of the known and the experience of knowing. In this way, we are wrestling with the idea, the notion, that the essence of awareness is quite distinct from a mental activity. The reason to make this distinction is that it carries some interesting and helpful implications. If perception of heaviness in the chest, what is called *interoception**, is the act of being aware of the interior of the body's state, then body state is the known and the awareness is the knowing.

If I remember a time not so long ago when a dear friend died suddenly, I can also be aware of shifts in my body, memories of our relationship, the shared grief among our friends, the memorial to honor his life. These feelings and images and thoughts and sensations are all activities of my mind. They are real, but you cannot measure them and cannot truly assign numerical values to their subjective textures. They are known as felt realities, as they are in my awareness. But awareness is not an activity of the mind; instead it is a process of mind that transcends activities. It is a process of mind, an emergent process that arises somehow in a way that no one on the planet can explain; awareness provides an important component of our mental lives that is distinct but *interdependent** with our mental activities.

Diving into the scientific view of energy as potential will help us to illuminate some of these distinctions. In a nutshell, if energy potential occurs in patterns that range from definite to open, then awareness can be seen as an openness of possibility whereas a mental activity can be seen as the realization of a potential into an actuality. Most of us are not familiar with thinking of *probability patterns**, and so this can be quite new for many. But turning to the science of energy reveals that such distributions of possibility are one way that physicists can characterize the nature of energy movement across time. Energy flow is literally the patterns in which probability changes across time. These probability patterns move in curves, changes over time that can be continuous or have abrupt transitions, and they can be altered by the very act of observing. These quantum views of energy as probability patterns are distinct from the more classical Newtonian-based views of large particles of matter, such as the properties of gravity or the acceleration of mass. Smaller than an atom, energy is governed by quantum principles that involve a number of features. One is that energy moves by alterations in probability. Another is that there are nonlocal effects as energy moves as a field, such as waves on a pond that are induced when a rock is dropped in its center: waves move in many directions at once. And quantum mechanics also describes how the act of observation has a direct impact on energy flow patterns—on the distribution of probability changes over time. This branch of physics places the act of observing directly into its principles as a factor that alters energy flow.

With this scientific set of principles in mind, we can combine studies of consciousness with first-person experiences of being aware to make some fundamental proposals about the nature of the mind. These are suggestions informed by science, ideas you can explore in your own way to establish their relevance in your own mental life.

How can we understand our mental activities and how they are related to the experience of being aware? What is a thought? What is a feeling or a mood? What is consciousness? These are challenging questions, but ones that an exploration of the nature of mind needs to address. We may ultimately come up with more questions than satisfactory answers, but that is fine. This is a helpful place for us to deepen our conversation about the mind and its connection to energy and information flow.

Awareness may be seen as arising from an open *plane of possibility**. Processes we are aware of arise from increases in degrees of possibility from probable (such as a mood or *state of mind** or *intention**) to certain (a particular thought, feeling, image, or *memory**). And so we are suggesting that energy flow—changes in probability—moves from zero (open possibility) with awareness to likely (restricted set of possibilities) for the *mental processes** of moods and intentions to one hundred percent (certainty and closed possibility) for specific thoughts, feelings or images.

A third aspect of mind beyond awareness and mental activities arises in this discussion as well. This is the proposal that one aspect of the mind is an embodied and relational emergent *self-organizing** process that *regulates** the flow of energy and information. In *complex systems**, the interactions of elements of the *system** give rise to an emergent process. This process cannot be reduced to the individual components of the system. There is no programmer and there is no program. The property of emergence in complex systems is one of self-organization. A self-organizing, emergent process regulates that from which it arises. In the case of our human lives, the system we are examining is that of energy and information flow. Here we see that energy and information flow is shared in relationships and passes through the embodied mechanism we are calling the brain. From this system of bodies interacting within and between themselves, we propose that what arises is an emergent process that regulates energy and information flow. Now we've come to our *triangle** of human experience, focusing deeply on the energy and information component and teasing out the layers of mind that are important to articulate.

Mind is the emergent, self-organizing regulatory process,

relationships are the sharing, and the brain is the embodied mechanism of energy and information flow.

When we move to this level of energy and information flow, taking the important but controversial step of diving deeply into the question of what might be truly going on in our mental lives, we can begin to see the applications of this discussion in real life.

Treating energy and information flow as the fundamental element of our lives helps in these discussions of mind, brain, and relationships. When we see that relationships are the sharing of this flow, we can honor the many ways that attuned communication links two or more people to each other. The many studies of *attachment**, for example, reveal that the way we are open and *receptive* to the internal world—the subjective aspect of mind—of another person shapes the nature of our relationship. Whether this occurs within a parent-child relationship or one of the many relationships of teacher-student, clinician-patient, leader-group member, or simply between friends, energy and information flow can be *compassionate** and attuned and can lead to a *resonance** among two or more people, which has a profound impact on the well-being of both the individuals involved and on the *cohesion** and health of the pair or group as a whole.

Energy and information flow viewed as a prime unit organizes a way of perceiving and interpreting the exciting findings from brain research. Rather than reifying the brain as the sole source of our subjective lives, we can see that the embodied mechanisms of energy and information flow have important—but not exclusive—impacts on our mental lives. I know, from sometimes painful and challenging experience, that this position is very distressing for a number of people in academic research.

And I apologize for offering something that contributes to their distress. But sometimes finding a new way of viewing something takes us into unfamiliar and uncomfortable territory. The purpose of this position is not to upset people, but to bring all disciplines into a fruitful and respectful discussion about the nature of being human. When we dive deeply into a consilient approach, drawing, for example, on the powerful findings of social psychology, anthropology, and sociology, we need to see relationships and brain as equally important though distinct influences on our mental lives. Relationships are the sharing of energy and information flow; brain is the embodied mechanism of the flow. These are just different aspects of one reality: the flow of energy and information within and among us. I do not think this view "reverses" science, but rather it opens the possibility of linking all the sciences to one another.

Now we come to the applications for the mind, taken from this interpersonal neurobiology perspective. You may not agree with this viewpoint, but please try it on, even if briefly, and see if it bears any fruit for you. Mental life, seen through this lens, has four aspects worth underscoring here. One is mental activity, including our feelings, thoughts, perceptions, images, memories, hopes, dreams, intentions, beliefs, and attitudes. This is the known of our mental life. This is how the potential spectrum of energy flow patterns has moved to increasing degrees of certainty. A second facet is awareness, or the experience of knowing. This can be seen as arising from the open possibility end of energy's spectrum—an open plane of possibility. Within the felt reality of knowing is a third aspect of mental life, that of subjective experience, the essence that is a prime, the internal quality and texture of the experience of being aware. In one sense, this is the meeting of the range of potential, from infinite to finite, from open to certain. What arises from this flow along energy's spectrum is the prime of subjective experience. It cannot be reduced any further than the reality of subjectivity. We can have a subjective felt sense of the known as we are aware of mental activities and of a subjective felt sense of the knowing experience itself. As we become aware of awareness, we can also have a subjective felt sense of it.

A fourth facet of mind is the emergent self-organizing process that arises from the embodied and relational passage of the flow of energy and information. That is, as energy and information flow within the body and between people, what arises is an emergent process that is self-organizing. This process likely gives rise to our mental activities. And these processes are *"recursive*"* in that they regulate the very elements from which they arise. This is the regulatory aspect of mind. One way that we regulate this energy and information flow is through the focus of *attention**. Attention is the process by which the information flow is channeled. This can be within awareness (*focal attention*) or without awareness (*nonfocal attention*). How we focus attention is shaped by both our brain and by our relational *context**. And the mind—as the regulatory process—is shaping this attentional process. Attention in many ways organizes our internal and interpersonal worlds.

The notion of self-organization is challenging to get a feeling for, and diving into the mathematics of it sometimes helps a bit but often leaves a new reader somewhat less clear. So let's look at a more commonly experienced example. We use the choir analogy to experience self-organization directly. If you just assemble choir singers, devoid of a plan or a conductor, they will generally find a way to sing together in a self-emergence that has vitality and a sense of life to it. Self-organization also arises in social insects, and we can see the profoundly intricate ways that members of a beehive or an ant colony have organized their interconnected lives.

Integration* can be seen as the emergent property that enables self-organization to create harmony. In a choir, each individual will find his or her own intervals, yet they will link to one another as the song unfolds. This is the creation of harmony. The vital and adaptive movement of the energy and information flow is flexible, energized, and stable. Integration enables us to see how we are profoundly linked to one another. It also enables us to sense the vitality that emerges from harmony, which is the outcome of integration. These linkages between us within communication patterns, within our relationships, help nurture the integrative connections in the brain itself. And here is the key: Integrative fibers in the brain—ones that link widely separated areas to each other— permit adaptive *self-regulation** to be created in the *executive** *circuits** of the brain.

Interconnectedness is the crucial issue. When we see that energy and information flow is the physical reality that links us as humans to one another (and to the planet), we can apply the principles of self-organization to mental life. The key, it seems to me, is to open our perspective to this level of analysis. I know this is hard for many of us who have not been trained to think in this way. It is not what we've learned in school. But the fruits of consilience are ready to benefit science, and to be of benefit for so many of us who seek to apply these ideas to help the lives of others move toward health and vitality. Integration is a natural outcome of energy and information flow among people. Our deep work can be to cultivate such integration within our own internal bodily worlds and in our relational lives. The mind—its mental activities, awareness, subjective experience, and self-organizing regulatory processes—is ready to create harmony in our lives. The key is to work together, sharing energy and information with one another, to create such intention and collaboration.

PLANE OF POSSIBILITY

CONCEPT: WHAT IS IT?

The **plane of possibility**★ is a visual graph that depicts several dimensions of our human experience. As a visual image, it has been used to expand on the first-person experience of the *wheel of awareness*★ in which the *integration*★ of *consciousness*★ is explored in *reflective practice*★. Drawing on various aspects of science, especially mathematics, physics, psychology, and *psychotherapy*, the plane graph offers a way to understand the connections between *subjective experience*★ and *neuronal*★ activity, as well as how our inner mental life can be shaped by *awareness*★.

The plane (see Figure I) is composed of two sides. One side represents subjective experience, and the other represents *neural firing*★. These are considered nonreducible aspects of reality called *primes*★. There are three axes on the figure. The x-axis represents time (moving horizontally), the y-axis reveals degrees of probability (extending vertically), and the z-axis represents diversity (moving toward and away from the viewer). At a given moment in time (x-axis), the coordinates of each of the three axes can be represented such that probability (y-axis) and diversity (z-axis) are the factors being depicted.

The element being revealed in this graphing of the plane is *energy* *flow* across time. In physics, energy is evaluated in part by the property of degrees of certainty, of patterns or curves of probability of how and where, for example, a photon will be at any given moment. If our mental lives are indeed an *emergent* *process* arising from *energy and information flow* within and between people, then this *embodied* and *relational* process may be illuminated in helpful ways by drawing on the scientific view of *probability patterns* that shift across time, rather than on pure certainties. In other words, large molecules operate by classical or Newtonian physics so that if you drop something it goes downward. This is a certainty predicted by the laws of gravity that pertain to larger-than-atom matter. With energy as an entity smaller than an atom, physics examines degrees of probability, not absolute fixed certainties. This is just the physics of energy movement across time, not a strange and bizarre application of some offbeat or fringe perspective. I say this here in a somewhat defensive stance because some scientists who've responded to presentations of this approach of applying physics to the study of *mental processes* are offended and state that the approach is unfounded. It is crucial for all of us to be skeptical, but trying on this perhaps uncommon way of thinking about the *mind* can actually be quite fruitful and practically quite useful! It is also consistent with our interdisciplinary reasoning in examining the flow of energy and information as the essence of the *system* from which the mind emerges.

If we use large-scale (sizes larger than atoms) Newtonian thinking for understanding mental life, we can come up with the alternative view that applies classical physics and linear thinking to mental phenomena. Such a Newtonian view of the mind can invite us to draw on concepts such as gravitational forces and to think in terms of certainties that lead us to view the "mind" more as a noun, an object and almost physical entity with some essential fixed dimensions, rather than a verb, an active process, that moves across time in ever-changing ways. The approach of classical physics, applied to the energy patterns we are proposing may be at the heart of our mental lives, may in fact not be appropriate or consistent with science. Some academicians state, however, that psychological phenomena are not in the "same realm" as other scientific disciplines. Mental life is somehow "different" and should not be compared to physics, or even to biology. Perhaps this is true, but why would there be a separation? Let's take the parsimonious view that mind is actually a part of one reality, a reality studied by our various sciences. If we take a *consilient*★ view, we can find the universal principles that unite the sciences, not divide them. For example, the mathematicians and the systems scientists who support the view of *nonlinear, self-organizing*★ processes that emerge from *complex systems*★ have a lot to offer our understanding of the mind, even though some mind scientists may disregard their approaches as being too, well, complex. Several times I've heard this statement from a senior academician: "I never needed to think this way in my career, so why should I start now?" He then went on to say that he was getting close to retirement and was too tired to think in new ways. I wondered what it might be like to be a faculty member in his department or one of his graduate or undergraduate students. It seems so important that we keep an open mind about these potentially helpful perspectives and the role of consilience in illuminating the nature of mind. It is possibly for this reason that virtually no academic or even clinical or educational fields, as surprising as this may sound, actually define the mind. You can sense that this is an area of heated debate—and with informed consent please be advised that there is much impassioned and sometimes opinionated argument back and forth about how to wrestle with understanding our most intimate mental experiences. But, even in the face of some understandable discomfort and disagreement, and even tiredness, let us see if this approach is useful in illuminating the nature of the mind and perhaps even the pathways to improving our mental, relational, and embodied lives.

IMPLICATIONS: WHAT DOES THE PLANE OF POSSIBILITY MEAN FOR OUR LIVES?

The plane offers us a way to see how sometimes our subjective lives are driven along by *brain** firing patterns, at times shaped by the past in *memory**, sometimes merely responding in large part to here-and-now sensory incoming experience. We can call this *automatic pilot** when we are taken over by elements of the past, a kind of *top-down** process dominated by how past *encoded** experiences entrain our present *perceptual** filtering of ongoing sensation. When this occurs, we can see this on the graph as the movement of curves below the plane that represents how neural firing patterns are "leading the mind around." This is a fairly accurate paraphrase of what many in therapy describe as how their lives feel. "I'm just a passive passenger along for the ride." With psychotherapy in mind, we actually can interpret clinical interventions that empower the individual client or patient as being a way to use subjective mental life to actually pull the brain in a different direction. Here the mind uses the brain to create itself. I know such a statement can irritate some who place the brain in the driver's seat, but there is an abundance of evidence to suggest that the arrow of influence indeed goes in both directions: Sometimes the brain drags our mental subjective experiences, but sometimes our mind drives the brain. If you say that among certain scientists, it will make you a pariah very quickly, so be careful! On the plane, mental experience can be seen as the upper curves that can "lead the way" so that the focus of *attention*⋆—what the mind is all about—actually drives neural firing in a new pattern. In the old days, this would have been a guess as to what might be going on; now we know from science that how you focus your attention can change both how a brain becomes activated and how a brain changes its structure.

"Hold on!" you may be saying, wondering where such an outrageous and "dangerous" statement may be coming from. Isn't the brain always the boss? Don't all *mental activities*⋆ simply come from neural firing patterns? This is a great question.

I know the discussion I'll invite you to join in with me here irks some from a range of scientific fields. I want you to know about this so that I, or anyone else, do not just sell you a bill of goods, or pull the wool over your eyes or lead you astray. I feel deeply committed to you being well informed and know that this approach is indeed not a mainstream view and can evoke intense negative reactions by some traditional, well-meaning, academic scholars. It would not be fair to just move along without reminding you about these potential flare-ups of emotion.

So here is the proposal. The emergent process of energy and information flow we are calling one aspect of mind has a *recursive*⋆ property—that is, it feeds back on itself—such that it can influence the elements from which it arises. This means that while mind arises from the energy and information flow in body and in *relationships*⋆ (it is embodied and it is relational), it, the emergent process itself, can re-enter (through *re-entry*⋆ loops of mutual influence) the system and influence that system directly. Yes, the emergent process affects that from which it arises! Energy and information flow through the body and its brain and through our communication patterns with one another within our relationships. So, yes, mind emerges from an embodied and relational set of emerging processes. Mind is not the same as brain, nor is it the same as relationships. Mind arises as an emergent process from these bodily and relational streams of energy and information flow. But then this emergent process we call mind can and does influence the embodied and relational sources from which it arose. Mind is self-organizing: Mind can shape the brain and mind can shape relationships. In many ways, the mind uses relationships and the brain to create itself!

This view of mind as being able to influence the very sources of its creation changes how we empower ourselves to make positive interventions in our lives. In other words, when we view mental experience as arising from an emergent process of the flow of energy and information through relationships and the body, we can then use mind to change our relationships and our neural firing patterns with *intention*⋆.

In the plane of possibility, this ability can be seen as how the mind's activity drives neural firing. Reentry is the feedback mechanism by which the flow of energy and information can then drive neural firing to take on new patterns. This is an *awakened mind*⋆, one that is no longer on automatic pilot in which choice and change now become possible. In the plane, we see this as altering the probability of a mental activity (the curves above) or a neural firing profile (the curves below).

Let's look at the graph in greater detail to see how to apply this approach in everyday life. If I am in a certain *mood**, let's say a down, hopeless *state of mind**, this *state** pervading my experience in a given moment would be represented as a *plateau** of (enhanced) probability. In this mood state, I am more likely to feel and think of things related to that state of mind: feelings of rejection, a sense of being overwhelmed, memories of times I've felt hopeless, thoughts of ending my life. What are these feelings? What are these thoughts—really? The answer is, no one actually knows what a thought or feeling truly is! Let's assume for a moment that we'll fit these basic mental activities into our *triangle** of human experience/wheel of awareness/plane of possibility visual images of mental life. Three visual depictions and one mind! What each of these corresponding images tells us is that they are depicting patterns of energy flow. This is a crucial place for us to make sure we are seeing these maps of mental life clearly. These metaphors and maps of the mind are describing energy change across time. And energy changes, it flows, as alterations in probabilities. Energy flow involves the movement along a probability curve, creating a probability pattern or change in probabilities across time. I wake up in the morning and I feel glum. I have a sense of despair, heaviness in my chest, a feeling of low energy, and a sensation of sluggishness in my body. I am down in the dumps. That is my plateau, and the specific, repetitive, and concrete thoughts I have of life being too much to bear are particular *peaks** of certainty—energy patterns that have reached a definite probability of 100% along the curve: I feel bad, life is worthless. There is nothing I can do. These thoughts are certainties along the energy spectrum; in that moment they feel like lead, heavy, unchangeable. These are particular peaks of certainty arising from the increased likeli-

hood plateau of being in a down, sad mood. Mood is the plateau; thought is a peak arising from that plateau.

When I wrote this, I was in fact feeling that way. Experiencing
this state of mind, I say to myself: What is this all about? I intentionally look for other peaks, and what arises from the plateau
of a lousy feeling or mood is an image of a close friend whose
father just died. Then the visual image of my father, ill and
incapacitated as I write these words, arises as a peak of a visual
energy flow pattern. A number of other mental activities arise—
thoughts, feelings, images—and I decide to name them. "I am
sad. Many people have recently died, or are dying. The nuclear
disaster in Japan is hurting many people there, and in the world.
This is a complicated planet; it is all so overwhelming, and I feel
helpless."

With the naming, I can feel (yes, I imagine, you may be
thinking this is bizarre, but bear with me for a bit more and see
how it works for you . . .) these incessant peaks begin to relax,
their pointiness dulling, the plateau from which they are arising lowers, and I feel myself drop down toward the open plane
of possibility. Now here, in this open plane, I feel totally different. Within moments after feeling down, helpless, in despair, I
have now shifted my internal mental state into something else.
But what is this new state? Here is the suggestion: I have now
shifted from the certainty of particular peaks and the probability of plateaus (despairing, in this situation), to a probability of
zero. Now with zero probability, possibility is infinite. Anything
becomes possible, and the unbounded variety of the open plane
has a sense of vastness and freedom.

Resting in this plane of possibility doesn't just come out of
nowhere. If I am fortunate, I may have just been born with an
ease for transitioning out of funky moods. But in my case, I

have been practicing the wheel of awareness exercise, making the hub more accessible. The hub is a metaphoric image of the proposed mechanism of the open plane: The hub is the plane. The rim points of mental processes are energy patterns with increased (mood, motivations, intention, attitude) and fixed (specific thoughts, images, feelings) certainties. A thought, an image, a perception are each an outcome of a mental activity, a point on the rim, a peak above the plane. These are all examples of energy flow with certainty. Fine. Now a mood or a general feeling . . . this may be more like an inner layer of the rim, or a plateau with enhanced probabilities, that feels a bit different from the fixed nature of a mental activity. This is the texture of a state of mind. So now we can define intentions, moods, and attitudes as plateaus with increased probability but not quite the same degree as the elevated certainty of a specific thought, feeling, memory, or image. The reality is that peaks often rise up from plateaus, so in a sense these are along a continuum. And sometimes peaks arise from the plane itself, and perhaps such mental activities (thinking, feeling, remembering, perceiving) are more flexible as they move in and out of the probability curve from 100% to 0% with more ease.

Here is the power of this approach. Just knowing that peaks, plateaus, and the plane are the architectural distributions of my mental life gives me the empowerment to move the degrees of probability downward, toward the plane of open possibility.

Let's put this in very direct terms: If I know that the mind can change the brain, then this peak/plateau/plane view helps me to see how I can shift the nature of my inner mental life. If we embrace the curves of probability, those peaks and plateaus over the plane, then we can use the mind itself to change the curve—to alter probability patterns. This ease and flexibility with which I can move my mental and neurological life from plane to plateau to peak and back again, over and over, may be the mechanisms beneath *mental health*★. We integrate peak, plateau, and plane as *differentiated*★ aspects of our probability patterns and then *link*★ them in a flexible way during our lives.

This view helps explain the many ways in which the feedback people have been providing to me about the wheel of awareness practice can be understood. For example, I met a few individuals while on tour through Australia for whom this 20-minute wheel practice led to significant and lasting decreases in the suffering they were experiencing from chronic pain and from particularly incessant worries. Emails I received many months later affirmed the continued help this practice has provided these individuals. Why would this happen right there in a single group practice? And why would continuing to practice provide continued relief? One possible explanation among many is this. If the hub represents the plane, then the wheel exercise invites people to learn directly how to bring their minds and brains from the rim (peaks/plateaus) to the hub (open plane). Practice reinforces this important skill at the heart of how the mind can change the brain. To understand the mechanism that creates this ability, it is extremely helpful to have the view of the plane of possibility. There may be other explanations, certainly, but this view is helpful as it explains the observed phenomena with the least complicated details. It does not evoke anything special, really, except to consider that mind is *regulating*★ energy flow and that energy flow takes the form of changes in degrees of probability across time. Once we see this, then the rest naturally falls into place.

So this is a working place to start, not a final answer! The potential of this overall approach in helping people become empowered to bring well-being into their lives is tremendous. When we integrate the wheel and harness the hub, we are awakening the mind! It's a great place to dive into our fundamental questions about the mind and how knowing about its embodied and relational origins can help bring mental health into our lives.

30
30

MEMORY

CONCEPT: WHAT IS IT?

Memory★ is a term signifying the way an event in the past influences a *process*★ in the future. Though we may often consider "memory" as what we can recall at will, the process of *remembering*★ actually has more layers than this. Experience involves *neural firing*★. These patterns of activation can then create temporary increases in the probability of those *neurons*★ firing together in the future. This is called *priming* and it sets an increased likelihood of future coupling of associated neural areas. From the point of view of the *plane of possibility*★, this means that, for a time, priming will be "remembered" as setting or "*instantiating*★" a certain *plateau*★ that makes more *peaks*★ likely from that altered place of probability.

Next, we can have neural firing that activates the genetic machinery of the nucleus of our neurons such that synaptic strengths are increased because of protein production and changes in the structural (not just functional, as in initial priming) connections among simultaneously active neurons. This change in neural connectivity created at one point in time will alter the way those neurons will fire in the future. So this is the way we first have *encoding*★ (activation of neurons), then *storage*★ (alteration in neural connectivity), and then *retrieval*★ (reactivation of patterns similar to, but never identical with, the initial encoding).

Early in life, this laying down of new interconnections among activated neurons yields something called *implicit memory*★. Implicit memory has a number of facets and includes our *perceptual*★, *emotional*★, behavioral, and likely our bodily sensory memory. We also have priming that can be influenced in this implicit way, and what are called *mental models*, or the generalizations of repeated experiences. Mental models are akin to schema and are sometimes called *invariant representations* in that they have a persistent stability as they generalize experiences into a summation or model of a series of events. Created by repeated past experience, mental models reinforce themselves by biasing ongoing perception to conform to expectations set by prior learning and in this way can lead to a tendency to repeatedly encode similar representations with little variation. This is a *top-down*★ process in which prior learning shapes ongoing perception and behavior. The key to understanding implicit memory in all of its facets is that we do *not* need to pay *attention*★, focal, conscious attention, to encode implicit memory. The storage of implicit memory is in various neural areas throughout the *brain*★, and it does not need to involve the *hippocampus*★, an integrative seahorse-shaped area of the *limbic*★ zone.

When the hippocampus develops in the second year of life, we begin to develop the more common form of memory called *explicit memory*★. Now we use the hippocampus to encode and store the two facets of explicit memory: factual *information*★ and *autobiographical memory★*. This latter form of memory begins as *representations★* of episodes of experience, or *episodic* memory, with which we encode and recall the *self★* at a given point in time. Autobiographical memory later includes a more organized clustering of these various episodes across our lifetime.

As we grow beyond our second year of life, we continue to encode implicit memory but it is woven together in some cases by the hippocampus, which selectively integrates these implicit forms into their more flexibly accessed explicit facets. And then, as we continue to grow, a *narrative★* form of memory emerges and builds on both implicit and explicit memory to weave together the narrated stories of our lives. Implicit mental models, the schemata that we don't even know are coming from the past, can directly shape the themes of our life stories.

IMPLICATIONS: WHAT DOES MEMORY MEAN FOR OUR LIVES?

The implications of these three layers of implicit, explicit, and narrative memory are profound. While the retrieval of any form of memory involves *consciousness★*—that is, we are aware of something in that moment—implicit memory in its nonintegrated, pure form is not tagged with the inner sensation that something is being recalled. I call this an *ecphoric sensation* in that *ecphory* is the act of retrieval. And so the important implication is that we can encode much of our earliest years of life into implicit memory, but then its retrieval into our emotional responses, our perceptual biases, our behavioral reactions (called *procedural memory*), and even our sense of the body can emerge in our experience without our knowing that it is from the past. The retrieval of implicit memory is in consciousness, but we are not aware that what is arising in *awareness** is something derived from a past event. And so implicit memory is not to be misconstrued as unconscious or *nonconscious** memory; this is implicit memory entering awareness but without an ecphoric sensation. We can be aware with retrieval of any form of memory, but we are not aware of the origins of these feelings, thoughts, notions, ideas, images, habits, or priming when they are from the implicit layer of memory retrieval. Knowing this distinction can be profoundly helpful at gaining *insight** into one's own mental life and patterns of reactivity.

Another implication is that the hippocampus's role in mediating explicit processing can be impaired during and following overwhelming experiences including *trauma**. By dividing attention so that one is focusing on a nontraumatic aspect of the environment while an attack is underway on the body, for example, the *mind** will encode implicit memory but block the encoding of explicit memory for the overall event. *Divided attention* achieves such an outcome because the hippocampus requires focal or conscious attention to create explicit encoding but implicit memory is encoded even without *focal attention*! This situation of blocked hippocampal processing of explicit memory may also be created with the effects of *cortisol*: Excessive levels of this *stress** hormone impede hippocampal functioning. When this is combined with the chemical impact of *catecholamines* (adrenaline/norepinephrine) that increase the implicit encoding of fear by way of the *amygdala**, we see that trauma can lead, unfortunately, to the profile of blocked explicit processing and enhanced implicit processing. Given that implicit memory is encoded for bodily sensations and emotion, and that implicit memory is not blocked by turning focal attention away from an event, we can see how this situation of memory processing could explain much of posttraumatic stress disorder.

Flashbacks, intrusive bodily sensations, emotions out of balance, and images of traumatic events that "seem to come out of nowhere" are all elements of this blocked explicit/enhanced implicit processing. Sometimes these intrusions can be so intense they are coupled with a *state** of *speechless terror.* These elements enter awareness with implicit retrieval, but their origins as memories are not present in awareness. This can explain flashbacks in that the feelings arising in subjective experience are in the here and now, being lived anew and not tagged as coming from the past. Some studies also suggest that chronic trauma can impair hippocampal growth, thus worsening the posttraumatic processing of explicit memory in the long run. Future research will need to explore how *psychotherapy* might reverse some of these posttraumatic outcomes.

An application of these findings for the healing of trauma is that one needs to have an *embodied** and *relational** approach to how these implicitly encoded events are ultimately integrated into a person's life. As we've defined the mind as both embodied and relational, this does not mean a person should be sitting in isolation and "working it out"; rather he or she should be working through the body and within *relationships** to make efforts to heal the mind. The regulatory aspect of mind is located in at least two places: our bodies and our relationships. Healing the mind involves going where the mind is.

Knowing how memory works is empowering for all of us. From the point of view of the plane of possibility, we can see that patterns of plateaus and of peaks are potentially manifestations of the implicit effects of past events on current processing. Certainly a peak can also be an explicit recollection, and we have the ecphoric sensation that this fact or that autobiographical detail is coming from the past. That is a fluid and flexible aspect of explicit memory retrieval. But at other times a peak (thought or image) or a plateau (*mood*★ or *intention*★) is an implicit retrieval lacking an ecphoric sensation and also is not so flexible in how it comes and goes in our lives. Often internal *contexts*★ such as emotions, or external factors such as sounds or sights or smells, can directly influence how a memory is both encoded and retrieved. This is how memory is a *state-dependent* process. When this is on automatic, implicit memory can become activated without an awareness of the context that is giving rise to this recollection or of the origins of this implicit retrieval from some time in the past. This is a way of depicting how implicit memory retrieval is not as flexible and adaptive, when not integrated, as explicit memory retrieval is. Nonintegrated implicit memory simply means that the encoding of implicit *engrams* enters storage without being interconnected by the integrative fibers of the hippocampus in the creation of the additional layers of factual and episodic/autobiographical explicit memory.

Practicing the *wheel of awareness*★ exercise strengthens the ability to sit within the hub of awareness and simply note what arises on the rim. The parallel depiction of the plane of possiblity is that from the open plane/hub, we can be open to whatever plateaus or peaks arise on the (inner or outer) rim. In other words, healing trauma may involve strengthening the capacity to flexibly move memory configurations from incessant peaks and raised plateaus of probability, to a more open, flexible movement of these *probability patterns*★ down toward the open plane of possibility. In the course of treating trauma, this flexibility is a hallmark of healing.

The spectrum of *flow*★ of degrees of probability is a reasonable way to begin to address the question of how we move from awareness (the open plane/hub of zero probability or open possibility) to the actual known element of *mental activity*★ (the plateau of mood/the peak of an image or thought). This perspective places memory solidly in the field of shifts in probability. And indeed, research on memory affirms this notion that *storage*★ of an encoded set of neural activations is the alteration in the probability of firing in a somewhat similar pattern in the future at the time of retrieval. Memory processes are all about alterations in probability. And so this view fits very well, in a *consilient*★ way, with the basic concept of the flow of *energy and information*★ and how it moves through the body and between people. We have an experience now that "makes it more likely to behave in a certain way in the future." Memory is all about probabilities, not certainties. When we view memory as being along a probability distribution, we can apply these ideas in everyday life by weaving together our view of the mind as a *regulatory*★ process and moving the pattern of probability along the spectrum from openness to certainty and back again. This is the fluidity of recall. The key to this application is to develop the capacity to move in and out of the plane and make a more fluid pattern available in our lives. Without this skill, people may become locked into particular patterns of peaks and plateaus, and become prisoners of the past.

31
31

NARRATIVE

CONCEPT: WHAT IS IT?

Narrative★ can be defined as the linear telling of a sequence of events. In our human family, telling stories is the universal way that we both communicate with one another and the way we make sense of our internal and external worlds. *Making sense★* is a *process★* of sorting through *memory★*, here-and-now experience, and imagination such that we create a *coherent★* picture of the essence of what is occurring in our lives. Making sense can be seen as an *integrative★* process, *linking★* past, present, and potential future in a way that enables these elements of thought, feeling, memory, and imagination to situate us in a social world of experience. Narrative is integrative from the inside out, bringing an inner sense of clarity and linking us to other people now, and even across time, through the recorded stories that shape our collections of books and videos and that fill our libraries and theaters with the continual unfolding of human drama.

Implications: What does narrative mean for our lives?

We are storytelling creatures, and stories are the social glue that binds us to one another. Understanding the structure and function of narrative is therefore a part of understanding what it means to be human. The *mind**, as a fundamental part of our humanity, is shaped by story. In many ways, the implication of this finding is that we have evolved over the millennia to see the world through narrative eyes. Stories not only shape our inner *subjective experience**, but they are at the heart of *culture** that links minds to minds in an expanded *self** across the boundaries of bodies and of generations. Stories capture the imagination of youth and enable young people to take on the *wisdom** of the older generation while they carve out the future to create their own unfolding stories. As far as we can tell, no other animal has this narrative ability. And because of this, our youth are open to the influence of story in family, school, and community. They take on the *meanings** embedded in the narrative telling, and then, during *adolescence*, they find a way to shift and re-shape these meanings to make them their own. The transformation of stories is the way that *culture evolves**.

On the interpersonal level, the *Adult Attachment Interview** offers an important window into the science of narrative and how the way that we make sense of our lives will influence how we raise the next generation. The AAI is a semi-structured interview that asks an individual, often a parent, how she *remembers** her experience of growing up. Her responses to these questions reveal a variety of patterns of discourse, of communicating with the interviewer, that illuminate how a narrative in many ways is an interpersonal process. About 100 years ago, Lev Vygotsky stated that thought could be considered internal dialogue. In this way, the AAI itself is a dialogue between two people, demonstrating how the communication between this adult when she was a child with her own *caregivers*★ shaped her way of thinking then and how she has come to *make sense*★ of her life now.

The patterns of communication in the AAI fall into a spectrum revealed as the transcribed audiotapes of the interview are coded using 20 variables. Though this is a spectrum of values, the clustering of data generally yields a pattern that corresponds to the four *attachment classifications*★ of (child—Adult): secure— Free; *avoidant*★—*Dismissing*★; *ambivalent*★—*Preoccupied*★; and *disorganized*★—*Unresolved*★ *Trauma*★ or Grief/Disoriented. The AAI can be given even during pregnancy with very significant correlations between the yet-to-be born child's ultimate *attachment*★ *relationship*★ at one year of age and each parent's narrative.

The implications of this work are many. The first is that what is most important is how one makes sense of one's life history rather than the common but unfounded notion that one's history leads inevitably to an unchangeable fate. In other words, if you make sense of your life, you can change the likelihood that you will pass on to your child the negative patterns of attachment that were given to you. This is fabulous news! It is never too late to make sense of your childhood experiences.

A second implication is that the mind not only remembers what happened, but also takes memory to the next step and involves a narrative process that makes sense of experience. Though we know that the act of memory *retrieval*★ can modify the form in which memory is re-*encoded*★, the narrative process may build on that fundamental retrieval/re-encoding mechanism to alter memory in a useful way. As narrative involves an observing, narrating aspect of the mind—an observing self that narrates what an experiencing self has experienced in the past—it is possible that this observing self functions to actively retrieve and then remold the meaning of recalled events. This is not a process of fantasy or distortion, but rather can be a healing form of resolution of trauma, a sorting through and finding meaning in madness, a way of making coherent what was, at the time, a disturbingly painful and incoherent reality. In this way, an ongoing narrative process brings the individual fully into the present even with the same past events. This is how finding meaning now, especially with a history of meaningless/purposeless/destructive experiences from the past, can be profoundly liberating in the present. We can move from being a passive recipient of painful events to becoming the empowered authors of our own life stories. This is the power of narrative to integrate our lives and free us from the prisons of the past.

When we come to see the internal and external universality of narrative in shaping how we live, we can open our eyes to the many ways in which stories influence our lives, for better or for worse. The fundamental application of narrative, then, is to see how one's current life view can sometimes constrain one's life even without *awareness**. For example, if I believe I cannot swim, I may avoid a pool or lake or ocean. But that belief may be part of a larger narrative of my incompetence, driven by my fear, perhaps shaped by an *implicit memory** of a past distressing event. In this way, the hidden impact of implicit memory may infuse my narrative theme without my knowing that it is coming from the past. I "simply know" that I cannot swim. Sometimes such beliefs are held steadfast, without questioning, and will limit my life in the moment as a reality not to be assessed and challenged. Narrative enables me to explore, if I take on the task of making sense, if that belief—the conscious manifestation of that *mental model* or schema—is in fact a fixed belief, not a fact.

Self-concepts shape and are shaped by the narratives we tell ourselves everyday. I avoid bodies of water, I "know" I cannot swim, and I find myself simply living on land. No problem. But our adaptations can be more distorting than simply becoming landlocked; sometimes they can make us miserable. "I am not lovable" is one such self-concept that gets woven into the enactment of my narrative of who I am by way of making me isolated and avoiding connection, intimate connection, with others. I come to believe, in a self-reinforcing feedback loop, that indeed I am not lovable because look how disconnected I am, how isolated I have been, how unlovable I must truly be. I have been alone, I am alone, and I will always be alone. My beliefs create my own worst nightmare, over and over. On and on I go, with my self-concept, belief, narrative, and enactment reinforcing the cycle for a lifetime of loneliness.

To break out of such a narrative rut is to pull out any one of those linking processes and to open the whole cycle for *reflection*★ and open examination. In the course of a chance relationship, or the course of intentional *psychotherapy*, the individual comes to learn that he or she can be in connection, that the story of being unlovable was just a defense against unfulfilled longing or a rationalization for mistreatment, and the associated beliefs about lovability and the self are buried convictions without merit. It takes courage to look straight on at these often hidden narrative themes that shape our lives. Letting them go is not always easy, as we so often get *lost in familiar places*. Learning a new reality, that the self is in fact lovable, often involves a painful immersion in the implicit memories of not actually having been loved at crucial periods in the past. This disaffirming of a conviction—that if I was mistreated, if I was unloved, that I deserved this because I am unlovable—is the essential undoing of the narrative core. In this case, the feeling of *shame*★ may be the glue that links the narrative theme with interpersonal patterns of behavior. Shame is a *state of mind*★ that can arise and become a part of a person's *developmental* pathway originating from being mistreated and misunderstood early in life.

And so we can see that applying the power of narrative in healing can liberate a life. Narrative is the overarching *integration*★ of our life's past experiences with our ongoing awareness and the way we create our future life of possibilities. In this way, restrictive narratives can be *cohesive*★ (I was unloved; therefore, I am unlovable and thus will never be loved) and logically stick together. But cohesive is not equivalent to coherent. A scientific view of coherence, in contrast, can be summarized as having qualities of connection, openness, harmony, engagement, receptivity, *emergence*★ (fresh unfolding), *noesis* (deep conceptual and nonconceptual knowing), *compassion*★ (for self and other) and *empathy*★. Coherence is open and fluid, not restrictive and imprisoning. The process of making sense of our lives integrates memory with our sense of self as it creates a *coherent narrative*★. This making-sense process is not just some intellectual exercise dealing with concepts and words. Making sense, literally, brings in all the senses, including the *interoceptive*★ sense of the body, such that we feel the embodied reality of what the past was and what it has meant and does mean in our lives. With this sensory awareness fully engaged, we can also weave the more language-centered process of understanding, in a logical way, the conceptual details of what happened, the impact of how we adapted to the experiences we've been through, and how we can learn from the past. While we cannot change what happened, we can change how we make sense of what we've experienced in our lives. This is how we integrate a coherent sense of self through the making-sense process of creating our life-stories. In this way, coherent narratives are ever-emerging with a sense of freedom and vitality. It makes a lot of sense to make narrative sense of our lives.

32
32

EMOTION

CONCEPT: WHAT IS IT?

Emotion★ is a commonly used word in everyday language yet it surprisingly does not have a commonly accepted definition. Even in science, the term "emotion" has no accepted, clear technical definition. Emotion is seen in research as a *process*★ that involves the pathway of a response to a stimulus, including its *appraisal* or evaluation and a subsequent *elaboration of arousal*★ levels in the *nervous system*★ that evoke particular reactions in thought, feeling, and behavior. Yet "emotion," even in this important and useful description, is not itself defined. What is the "emotion," really, that arises within this appraisal process? One can say that emotion shapes our overall *state of mind*★, that it is the valence of our present experience, is at the heart of our subjective and our interpersonal lives, and that its *regulation*★ determines who we are and how we behave in the world. Yes, these are all wonderful descriptions focusing on the qualities associated with what we call "emotion." Related emotion words are quite commonly used, such as feeling (the *aware-ness*★ of an emotional *state*★), *mood*★ (the overall tone of one's emotional state of mind) or *affect* (the external expression of an internal emotional state). Emotion directly relates to what we consider our state of mind to be, but what emotion actually is, is not yet clearly articulated.

Although each of us "knows" when we are "being emotional," it is actually quite challenging to state exactly what this means. In psychology, emotion is thought to be a fundamental part of an intricate cycle of stimulus evaluation and elaboration of response to that stimulus. In biology, emotion is considered a process that reflects how the physiology of the body influences the *brain*★ to shape how we "feel." In anthropology, emotion is an important way in which people connect with each other in groups and across generations. We can describe culturally how there are categories of emotion—such as sadness, fear, anger, *shame*★, surprise, disgust, and joy—that members of every *culture*★ seem to have a name for and are able to recognize universally within facial expressions. These are sometimes called universal or *categorical emotions*. We have designated *circuits*★ in the brain that are involved in "emotional systems," clusters of evolutionarily helpful *neurons*★ that embed some to these responses and others, such as play and resource allocation, that serve to organize our basic motivational drives. And we also have more subtle and varied internal states, which can be called "*primary emotions*" and are expressed as *vitality affects* in our often subtle, *nonverbal*★ expressions revealing the internal fluidity of our ever-changing states. These primary emotions precede the categorical ones and are ubiquitous in our *subjective experience*★—gentle feelings of longing, of concern, of confusion, of love, of pride. Our present state of mind, its internal texture, can be described as our emotional state, the essence of our here-and-now experience.

But what exactly is "emotion"? Why do we so readily use the term, know what we mean, but have such a hard time pinning down a definition of this part of our mental experience that seems so central to everything we do, everything that matters in our lives? Should we simply say that it is an irreducible part of our subjective experience, a *prime** of mental life, just so we don't worry about it anymore? Perhaps. But if we try to be a bit more illuminating of how subjective experience is in fact shaped by emotion, then we may reveal the underlying aspects of this thing called "emotion" in a more specific way. Let's be clear. The answer to the everyday and the scientific question about the true nature of emotion is that we know, and we don't know. Yet when we take a step back and look across all the many seemingly conflictual statements, we may be able to get a new view of what emotion is. From the many perspectives that emerge, a common thread can be extracted from these views that emotion is not a "thing" but a process—an active, dynamic, changing *flow** of something. So emotion can be considered a verb rather than simply a noun. That's a start. But what is this verb that seems to be so important in human life and for the life of the mind?

In *interpersonal neurobiology** we look for a *consilient** way of defining emotion by seeking a universal principle shared by each of the many disciplines studying the nature of human reality. Whether we look at the biological, psychological, sociological, or anthropological literature, one aspect is mentioned, often as a noncentral feature, that describes how that particular field of study approaches emotion. When one accumulates all of these various perspectives, a surprising commonality from their disparate approaches and descriptions emerges. That consilient finding is that emotion can be viewed as a process involving the *linkage*★ of separate things to one another. In anthropology, for example, emotion can be viewed as that which links people in a culture across generations. In sociology, emotion links people in groups. In psychology, emotion links a child across *developmental*★ stages and links a stimulus to a response. In biology, emotion is the way the body's physiology impacts brain function. In each of these descriptions, we see the linkage of one *differentiated*★ aspect of a *system*★ with another. From a consilient way of viewing this finding in interpersonal neurobiology, we see that in this way each of these disciplines has a focus on the linkage of differentiated parts—a process called *integration*★.

I know this may sound unusual and abstract, but from this consilient approach it is possible to view emotion as a shift in integration.

Now, not many people would see something as subjective, tender, important, and, well, *meaningful*★ as emotion as something that should be defined in terms of integration. So if you are having a moment of disbelief, you are not alone! Let me share with you how this at-first-quite-odd way of seeing emotion as shifts in degrees of integration is actually quite empowering both scientifically and personally. And in the end, I hope you'll come to see how this subjectivity-honoring approach actually broadens our understanding of the crucial role of emotion and the subjective texture of our mental lives in everything we do.

In our view of the *mind*★ as being an *embodied*★ and *relational*★, *emergent*★, *self-organizing*★ process, we can see that what is being regulated by the mind is *energy and information flow*★. Self-organization of a *complex system*★ differentiates elements and then links them to shape the movement of the system toward harmony. Without such a flexible, adaptive, *coherent**, energized, and stable (*FACES**) movement of integration, the system is prone to *chaos**, *rigidity**, or both. Now I share this with you here, because as we'll see, when we use the terms "emotional well-being" or "emotionally disturbed" we are actually referring to either a FACES flow of harmony or to the chaotic and rigid states of disorder. Likewise, when we use the term "emotionally close" we mean that we are integrated with another person—we honor our differences and have *compassionate**, caring linkages. That's an integrated *relationship**—and one that is emotionally close, rewarding, and meaningful. If I say to you that "something happened to me this morning that was emotionally confusing," one way of understanding that is that I could not *make sense** of the experience—that is, I could not integrate it into my larger *memory** and *narrative** systems of who I am. If I felt "emotionally excluded" from a group of people, does this mean that they shunned my emotions? Or could it mean that they did not integrate me into their discussion? Try it out for yourself: Each time you use the word "emotion" or its derivatives (emotional, emotionally, etc.) see if you can replace it with the idea, if not the term, integration.

Higher degrees of integration are associated with positive emotions, and they open up and strengthen the foundation of our connections to others and even within ourselves. When we feel delight, joy, love, and *gratitude*, we build integration in our lives. Positive states are pleasant because they are constructive; they build integrative connections in the brain and in our relationships with others. In contrast, we can propose that negative emotions, such as intense anger, fear, or sadness, are examples of *cohesive** states that actually decrease integration—they narrow and limit our connections. Keep in mind that the organization of a cohesive state is not the same as the integration of a coherent state that is flexible and adaptive. When we feel the tension and discomfort of these negative states, we need to realize that this does not mean that these are "bad" but rather that they are states that are decreasing our degrees of integration, and hence they need to be dealt with to alter our state back toward increasing integration. As mentioned above, self-organization moves the system toward a FACES flow by way of increasing states of integration, by linking differentiated areas to each other.

Emotion seen as "shifts in integration" enables us to bridge the exciting findings from a range of sciences, interweaving the social with the neurobiological. And what is it that is shifting in its integration? Energy and information flow is the essence of the system that we are examining. If I meet you on the street after a decade has passed from our last encounter, we may have an exchange of energy and information that is filled with all sorts of intense feelings, or not. If our past relationship was important, we may have an integrative experience, and the reunion on the street will be felt as "emotional." On the other hand, if you only knew me superficially, this encounter might have little meaning and not be emotional at all. There would be little shift in the degrees of your integrative state, little change in your sense of *self*★ from the meeting, and we each might experience this encounter as not an emotional or an emotionally meaningful meeting.

By focusing on energy and information flow patterns, we can place emotion at the center of the *triangle*★ of human experience. Emotion is not separate from our relationships, our brains and bodies, or our minds. As the state of integration in these aspects of our lives shifts, emotion arises and life has meaning. Emotion is an active verb reflecting the ever-changing states of integration within and between people.

IMPLICATIONS: WHAT DOES EMOTION MEAN FOR OUR LIVES?

I know this may all sound a bit abstract at first, but let's see how it helps to tie all the different views of emotion together and then enables us to build on their rigorous and disciplined study of this profoundly important aspect of our experience. In many ways, emotion is the subjective texture of the mind. As integration shapes the unfolding of the flow of energy and information, we have various forms of emotional experience possible at any given moment, with any given encounter. And if we take the consilient step to define emotion as shifts in integration, we can see how one can never remove emotion from *information** processing—or what is sometimes called "*cognition*" or "thinking." There is no separation of thought and cognition from feeling and emotion. Shifts in integration—alterations in the linkage of differentiated parts of a system—happen to various degrees all the time and are a fundamental part of the energy and information flow within our embodied and relational minds. Here we see how defining emotion in this way solves the "problem" of how some emotion scientists can study relationships while others study physiology. Emotion, like the mind, happens both within and between individuals. We see emotion as integrative shifts that happen in both body and relationships. Emotion is central to all that is the mind.

Let's dive a bit deeper into the classic psychological view that emotion is at the heart of the following sequence of phenomena. First, there is a process by which events—internal or external—are appraised. *Appraisal* initially orients *attention*★ as it determines that this event is worthy of paying attention to, that it is important. Next, the event that is now being the focus of attention is evaluated. Evaluation first determines if this is "good" or if it is "bad." This hedonic evaluation then initiates "emotion" (which can take the familiar categorical forms of sadness, anger, fear, disgust, surprise, shame, or joy as well as many others, such as elation, pride, or love). This emotion also gives rise to further downstream elaborations of arousal. This cascade then involves physiological shifts in the body, some of which may have occurred earlier in this sequence, that then reinforce the appraisal/evaluative process, intensifying or shifting the emotional state, and further amplifying the physiological response. This sequence can be seen as a loop rather than as a linear cause-and-effect single-direction arrow; it becomes more like a reinforcing cycle, strengthening the emotional state of mind, and intensifying the way we seek to be closer to positively evaluated events and withdraw more from negatively evaluated events.

This is a powerfully useful view of emotion from the field of psychology, but it doesn't really state what "emotion" actually is. For some scientists, it is enough. But if we are to see how the use of the term "emotion" in this way relates to, say, what a sociologist and anthropologist mean when they use the same term, we may be left without a deeper understanding. For me, the use of the notion of emotion as shifts in integration helps to link the neurological, physiological, psychological, social, and cultural dimensions of "emotion" into a coherent whole.

Consider again, for example, how we've been exploring ways of interpreting the use of the term "emotion" or any of its derivatives, such as emotional or emotionally. When you are emotionally close to someone, what does that really mean? Are you physically close so that your physiology is, literally, just centimeters away in space? Or does it mean something else? Could it mean that your mental lives (energy and information flow patterns) are aligned? Isn't being emotionally close actually a way of describing how two minds are integrated—how they are honored for their differences and then linked in their compassionate, respectful, connecting communication?

How about the phrase "emotional well-being"? What does that really mean? Are we just filled with joy all the time and avoiding distressful emotional states? Or does it mean that we honor the differences across many ways of being so we can fluidly and flexibly enter a range of differentiated states and link them together? Can we build a fluid and flexible life that is adaptive and, as we move through our lives, can we follow an open path toward new growth and development? That would make "emotionally *healthy**" mean something far more than merely having the absence of a diagnosable mental disorder! Could emotional well-being mean we are well integrated?

In contrast, what if someone *is* emotionally ill? Do their emotions then, do, well, what? Is the person filled with sick emotions? What does this commonly used term for a person with a mental disorder, the phrase "emotionally ill," really mean? I actually wouldn't know what to do with this term, and I am a board-certified clinician, but all the psychiatric disorders I've memorized don't really have a framework for tying these disorders together under one heading. That was not the goal or aim of the design of the diagnostician's encyclopedia of mental disorders, the *DSM*. And so the general phrase "emotionally ill" has, for me at least, not much meaning until we take on this consilient view. With emotion defined as shifts in integration, we can then see that emotional illness signifies conditions with impediments to integration. The result is chaos and/ or rigidity. And then when we take a closer look we come to see that every symptom of every syndrome of the *DSM* reveals chaos and rigidity! And so we can propose that this manual of mental disorders, even though created intentionally to not have a framework linking the disorders to one another or any definition of *mental health*★, actually can be reframed as a book of examples of impaired integration. With this new consilient perspective, we can propose that mental health emerges from integration. This is "emotional well-being." In this way the field of "emotional disorders" can be seen through a lens of an overarching framework of health that places disorders as impediments to health, links them to each other through the concept of integration, and even offers pathways for growth that help people integrate their lives.

Health is integration. Emotional health is integrative health. Emotional illness is integrative illness, or integrative impairment. Integration relies on both differentiation and linkage. The ways we don't have differentiation and then linkage are many and varied. They can have their origins in genes, infections, toxins, or other internally generated challenges, and they result in such disorders as autism, schizophrenia, and bipolar disorder. The lack of differentiation seen in the brain of someone with autism helps us understand the profound impairments to social communication—to interpersonal integration. In schizophrenia there are impaired linkages within the *default mode* associated with a loss of linkage to reality. And with individuals with bipolar disorder, there is a lack of linkage of the regulating ventrolateral aspects of the *prefrontal cortex*★ with the lower *limbic*★ *amygdala*★, leading to the "emotionally dysregulated" (read: integratively impaired) states of mania (chaos) and depression (rigidity).

And so in interpersonal neurobiology we can view regulation as emerging from integration. Each description of regulation in the brain or in our relationships is an example of integration. Integration—the linkage of differentiated parts of a system—enables the coordination and balance of that system. Within our bodies, this means that physiological homeostasis can be achieved. Within our relationships, this means that meaningful and compassionate connections can be created. When we are moving toward integration in our lives, we are emotionally thriving. One useful aspect of defining emotion as shifts in integration is that it enables us to study both the functional components and the actual structural aspects of integration—within the nervous system and within our patterns of communication. Regulation is the functional outcome of integration, and then a well-regulated (i.e., coordinated and balanced) system in turn promotes more integration. Integration reinforces integration.

Using the concept of "emotion as shifts in integration" empowers us to apply the vast array of emotion-focused research studies, treatment interventions, and conceptual frameworks in one coherent manner. Whether we look at the fabulous research studies of affective neuroscience and the study of the role of emotion in *dyads*, families, communities, and our broader culture, or look at the wonderful work of body-based, emotion-centered, attachment-oriented approaches to intervention, we can assemble all the *wisdom*★ of these efforts into one framework. Try it out for yourself! See how it works to consider the many ways to understand and improve our emotional lives that these approaches offer as seen through the lens of emotion as shifts in integration.

*Attachment** research, for example, can be reframed as revealing ways in which *secure attachment** relationships promote integration as the child's unique essence is honored and differentiated from the parent while linkages are established through caring, *attuned communication**. Secure attachment emerges from an integrated relationship. *Avoidant attachment** is where a linkage is not established though differentiation—excessive autonomy, in fact—is encouraged. The result is not harmony but rigidity. And with *ambivalent attachment** one sees the inconsistent and at times intrusive aspect of relatedness that reveals excessive linkage and impaired differentiation. The outcome of this pattern is chaos and an overly activated attachment drive with overarousal and distress. *Disorganized** attachment has both chaos and rigidity, as an organized strategy of response is not possible and the internal state of the child collapses in *dissociation**. Dissociation is a profound example of impaired integration.

The ultimate application of this consilient view of emotion as shifts in integration is to assess a situation through the lens of chaos and rigidity as markers of impairments to integration. Next, one looks for the *domain of integration** that is impaired in which differentiation and/or linkage are not cultivated. This assessment is then followed by intervention that places attention on the areas of a system (person, dyad, family, classroom, school, organization, community, society) that are not integrative to enhance differentiation and then linkage. With intervention, chaos and rigidity subside and ideally what emerges is an emotionally vibrant system: an emotionally healthy person, pair, family, classroom, school, organization, community, or society.

33
33
33

WINDOWS OF TOLERANCE AND RESPONSE FLEXIBILITY

CONCEPTS: WHAT ARE THEY?

A **window of tolerance**★ is the span of *arousal*★ within which a *system*★ can maintain the harmonious and adaptive *flow*★ of *integration*★. At one end of the window the system moves toward *rigidity*★; at the other end, the system moves toward *chaos*★ (see Figure M). The width of the window can be shifted, such that we can speak of "widening the window of tolerance," which means broadening the span of arousal within which the person, pair, or group of individuals can function adaptively. Windows can also be narrowed under certain situations when the *state*★ being created is less tolerated, and the system of the person or pair or group is more likely to "burst through the window" into chaos or rigidity and become nonfunctional.

IMPLICATIONS: WHAT DO WINDOWS OF TOLERANCE AND RESPONSE FLEXIBILITY MEAN FOR OUR LIVES?

Life moves through us as we move through life. As *energy and information*★ continually flow and our mental lives are riding the waves of this movement, we can move within windows of tolerance that bring us in ever-changing ways toward the edges of rigidity or of chaos. As we move through time, this shifting flow is much like a *river of integration*★ with its harmonious flow bounded by the two banks of chaos and rigidity (see Figure K). A window of tolerance is like the river, but in one slice of time. And the notion of a window, too, is that it is specific in width to the *state of mind*★ we are in at that moment of time. The implication of this is that our ability to tolerate a given state—such as sadness or fear, connection or isolation—will depend on the internal and external *contexts*★ in which we find ourselves.

***Response flexibility*★**, along with the other important *middle prefrontal functions*★, remains engaged within the window. Response flexibility enables us to pause before responding as we put a temporal and *mental space* between stimulus and response and between impulse and action. From a neurobiological perspective, this *space of the mind* enables the range of possibilities to be considered, to just "be" with an experience, to be reflected upon, before engaging the "do" *circuitry*★ of action. Response flexibility offers the individual a way of choosing to be the "wisest self" possible in that moment.

For example, if I have had a past history of being isolated and alone, filled with fear and loneliness, I may have a very narrow window for fear. With this state, I easily burst into chaos or rigidity; I cannot tolerate much fear or isolation without becoming dysfunctional. This is my familiar pattern, not my *wise** self that I might imagine if I had the flexibility to reflect on how I might want to be. Here, my past experience has been recorded in my synaptic connections. These *synaptic shadows** have shaped my internal context. An external context might be that I am presently at a party filled with neuroscientists who reject *interpersonal neurobiology**, or a group of real estate agents who find the field, and me, uninteresting, or with some high school friends who are still mad that I didn't play on the football team with them (I was a very fast runner but very slight and I chose, instead, to dance). With these external social contexts, my (*embodied** and *relational**) *mind** is *primed* to have a narrowed window. I get *lost in familiar places.* The setting is created for me to feel lousy, to act poorly, and to enter chaos, rigidity, or some combination of the two.

The mind arises in context, and here I am on edge with a narrow window. Without some *reflective** skills, my *brain** could drag me around so that I move far from the *plane of possibility** and upward into some elevated and narrow *plateaus** of feeling badly and some rigid *peaks** of thinking life is terrible. This would be one way of mapping onto the plane perspective what rigidity might look like. Chaos, on the other hand, might be an extremely wide peak such that there is a diversity of energy and information flowing all at once. In this way, chaos indeed has a rigid quality to it. We become fixed in our chaos. I am now overwhelmed, and I enter chaotic functioning such as enraged outbursts or being internally bombarded by sensations and memories of the past. This is how we can say "chaos/rigidity" is the movement away from the flexible flow of an integrated state. Prolonged rigidity and chaos are dysfunctional. It indeed turned out to be an *"emotionally** bad" experience in that I have shifted my degrees of integration downward at the high school reunion. Emotion, seen as shifts in integration, is the compass that lets us know if our chaotic and rigid states of impaired integration have dominated our states of mind as we've burst through the window.

To pull back into the window of tolerance, I need to lower my narrow (rigid) or broad (chaotic) peaks down to the more flexible plateaus, and hopefully down to the plane of wide open possibility. Integration can be seen as the free and flexible movement from plane to plateau to peak and back again. That's flexible responding! We move from an open possibility (plane) to probabilities of *priming* or readying ourselves for engagement (plateau) to focused and functional action (peak) and then back down again to openness and flexibility. This is integration.

Each of us has a window for a different state of mind, and each window may vary depending on the internal and external context at the moment. For example, I may have a narrow window for the experience of anger because this emotional state in my family was used as an entrée to being destructively enraged. For you, however, anger may have been used merely as a constructive way of protecting yourself in heated arguments that ultimately were resolved well and resulted in increased understanding. Experience has made your window of tolerance quite wide for anger. If you and I are in a close *relationship*★ and anger arises, *I* may shut down (rigidity) or explode (chaos) readily even though *you* are quite comfortable to just "sit with the anger" that is being expressed. Here you are able to stay comfortably within your window of tolerance even though I, in the same discussion, am overwhelmed by it.

Finding a way to meet each other "halfway" and maintain and recreate an integrated connection between us would require that we honor the differences between us and then promote *linkages*★. However, because my window in this situation is narrow, I may become dysfunctional more readily than you. My *middle prefrontal region*★ no longer coordinates and balances disparate neural inputs and response flexibility is lost. So I am not in an "emotional position" (an integrated position) to remain adaptive and connecting and *receptive*. In chaos or rigidity, I am no longer able to maintain a respectful, *compassionate*★ connection with you.

Now if you have a very low tolerance for isolation, my bursting through the window for anger and leaving you in a state of being rejected because I have become dysfunctional in that moment may make you enter an enraged, chaotic state or withdraw in a state of rigid isolation. Within moments, we each have burst through our respective windows and our relationship communication at that moment has been *ruptured*★.

With an understanding of windows of tolerance, we can wisely agree (ahead of time) to give ourselves space to re-enter a window, resolve chaotic or rigid states as we regain integrative function, and then make attempts to *follow this rupture with repair*★. Knowing about the windows of our minds can help us regain important interpersonal connections and internal *coherence*★, which bring well-being into our lives.

34
34

INTERPERSONAL ATTUNEMENT SHAPES SELF-REGULATION

CONCEPT: WHAT IS THIS?

Integrative communication★ emerges when one person's *attunement*★ to another person's internal *state*★ is filled with a *compassionate*★ and caring stance. When a child is young, integrative *relationships*★ with *caregivers*★ reveal how such **interpersonal attunement shapes self-regulation**★ (see Figure F). A kcy to understanding this important way in which interpersonal patterns of communication yield self-regulation in each of the interacting individuals rests in the fundamental mechanism of *integration*★. Integration interpersonally involves the *linkage*★ of *differentiated*★ elements of a social *system*★ and produces the flexibility, adaptability, *coherence*★, *energy*★, and stability (or the *FACES*★ *flow*★) of an integrative state in that moment. When the interpersonal flow of *energy and information*★ with attuned relationships is integrative, then neural *processes*★ within the individual become integrative. Within the *nervous system*★, integration is the way in which various *circuits*★ become coordinated and balanced—

the essence of self-regulation. In other words, the integration of energy and information flow between people creates patterns of flow that permit the *self-organizational** processes of the nervous system to establish a flexible form of self-regulation.

Interpersonal integration stimulates internal integration. This is how interpersonal attunement catalyzes the interpersonal regulation that then becomes more autonomous self-regulation. In *developmental* terms we can state that interpersonal patterns of communication that are integrative stimulate the activity and growth of integrative fibers in the *brain**. And it is the integrative fibers in the brain that enable self-regulation because they are the circuits responsible for coordinating and balancing the internal and interpersonal elements of the individual.

From the point of view of *complexity* or *chaos theory*, self-organization emerges out of integration and it is this process that, from an *interpersonal neurobiology** point of view, can be seen to underlie the self-regulation that is the focus of the work in psychology, *psychopathology*, and *psychotherapy*. When interpersonal and neural aspects of systems are integrated, the energy and information flow moves toward the harmonious states of "maximizing complexity." In other words, the most adaptive flow is created within integrated systems that are shaped by interpersonal patterns of shared communication *and* by the balanced and coordinated *neural firing** patterns of the brain.

The *middle aspects of the prefrontal cortex** serve as a prime example of how bodily neural processes of an individual are coordinated and linked with the input from other individuals, from others' nervous systems. Here we see, in anatomic reality, the direct ways in which the energy and information flow of the body of one person is woven directly with the interpersonal input from others.

IMPLICATIONS: WHAT DOES INTERPERSONAL ATTUNEMENT SHAPING SELF-REGULATION MEAN FOR OUR LIVES?

In interpersonal neurobiology we view energy and information flow patterns as the fundamental entity that is shared in relationships, moves through the mechanism of the *embodied brain*, and is *regulated** by the *emergent** self-organizing process of *mind**. Within our *triangle** of mind, brain, and relationships we can see how integration in one area induces integration in another. Integration catalyzes further integration. Here, for example, we are examining how the patterns of communication between two individuals can directly shape the function and growth of neural connections in the brain to create the neural conditions of self-regulation. When we look through the lens of energy and information flow patterns, then it becomes clear how interpersonal connections shape neural connections. When these are integrative patterns interpersonally, evidence supports the idea that they directly stimulate *neural integration** internally. We could also examine how neural connections can shape *relational** processes as well, so that when a brain is not integrated, for example, it leads to impediments to the creation of harmonious interpersonal relationships. Within the triangle of human experience the arrows of causal influence point in all directions: The brain influences mind and relationships; relationships influence brain and mind; the mind influences relationships and brain.

Integration within relationships means that each person honors personal differences and then cultivates compassionate connections in the form of caring, respectful communication. If this were regarding a relationship between you and me, it would involve something like this: I do not force you to be similar to me, but I respect how we are different from each other and I am interested in who you actually are. You would likewise honor our differences and together we would cultivate compassionate communication between us.

For two adults, our sense of inner harmony blossoms when we are in integrated relationships with others. For a young child and a parent, the nature of the growing neural connections will move toward integration if the communication is integrative. In the field of *attachment** research, the term of *mentalization** is used to identify the important capacity of the parent to see the mind beneath the behavior of both the child and the parent. Mentalization can be measured in the *Adult Attachment Interview** and other research instruments by assessing the capacity of the parent to use a *reflective function* in which the parent reflects on the mental life with the use of terms such as "thinks," "feels," or "knows" as indicators that she or he is considering the mental world of the child or the *self**. This is the essence of parental *sensitivity* and permits the parent to be *responsive* to the child's inner needs, not just to react to behavior, that is a key ingredient of secure attachment relationships.

In an interpersonal neurobiology perspective, mentalization is a powerful construct that enables us to operationalize an important way in which relationships become integrated. The differentiation of an individual requires that the inner world be seen and respected. Linkage is created as *contingent communication* enables the attuned response of one person to align with the signals sent from the other. The result of such attunement is the *resonance** of two individuals as they become part of an integrated "we."

We use the term *mindsight** to refer to the ways we see the inner mental world of ourselves and of others and then move those worlds toward integration. Mindsight builds on attachment, neurobiology, *complex systems**, and the framework of integration and of mentalization to empower us to create a *consilient** view that links the interpersonal and the neurobiological into one coherent perspective.

When we embrace the notion that interpersonal patterns of communication shape the activity of the *circuits** of self-regulation then we can begin to appreciate why research has repeatedly revealed the power of relationships to promote *health**. Relationships early in life stimulate the growth of the integrative regions of the brain that regulate bodily function, *emotions**, *attention**, and thought. Across the life span, relationships are an important source of vitality and they promote health in mind and body. *Empathic** relationships help the immune system function well. When applied in clinical communication, an empathic physician can even help you get over a common cold faster! With this understanding, we can now envision the mechanism with which integrated relationships promote the linkage of differentiated aspects of our mental lives and create patterns of energy and information flow internally and interpersonally as fundamental routes to well-being.

The key to applying these ideas is to become familiar with these internal and interpersonal patterns of integration. These are all about energy and information flow. Without that concept, we wouldn't be able to easily identify what exactly is being integrated. We can help others to see the inner world—to develop mindsight and the skills to reflect on the inner nature of their own and others' mental worlds. With the triangle of well-being in the front of our minds, we can help others to develop the mindsight skills that enable them to *monitor** what is happening in the body and in relationships and then to *modify** that energy and information flow toward integration. To "see the mind" with mindsight, we need to develop the skills of perceiving the triangle and to have *triception** (so that we sense energy and information flow in the body and brain, in our relationships, and in our subjective mental lives). This process takes the triangle and makes it accessible in everyday language as people learn about the brain and its differentiated regions and the importance of relationships in bringing respect, empathy, and compassion to interpersonal connections.

A simple way to remember that *attuned communication** promotes self-regulation is to recall that an essential outcome of integration is *kindness**. When we are kind to a child, she learns to be kind to herself. In turn, this internal sense of well-being enables her to go out into the world and bring kindness into her interactions with others. This is the *wisdom** of living an integrative life. Integration cultivates more integration. We naturally become *grateful** for this life we are given the privilege of living, to be *generous** toward ourselves and toward others, and to *give back* in our efforts to help those in need. Those are three "G's" worthy of committing to *explicit memory**! Even our dopamine reward circuitry becomes active when we extend ourselves to help others. We are hard-wired to be collaborative. When we are integrated interpersonally, we become integrated internally. This internal state of integration then gives rise to further integrative communication. It is a win-win feedback loop, and a way to live with the wisdom of kindness. As Mahatma Gandhi suggested, sometimes what this requires is just starting the process of "being the change we wish to see in the world."

STATES OF MIND

CONCEPTS: WHAT ARE THEY?

The phrase **states of mind**★ refers to the cluster of *mental activities*★ that is activated at a given moment of time. A state of mind may be fleeting, involving feelings, thoughts, memories, *intentions*★, attitudes, beliefs, and behavioral patterns that are activated together in a given instant. Or a state of mind may be more enduring, having repeated associated qualities that define what we might call a part of "our selves." In this case, we can use the term "*self-state*," in that this repeating pattern of associated *mental processes*★ has a recurrent presence in our lives that shapes our identity.

From the perspective of *complex systems*★ and *connectionist theory,* especially with regard to neural *systems*★ that function as *parallel distributed processors (PDP)* like the *brain*★, certain combinations of firing attain attributes that make them *attractor states,* which serve as a kind of probability basin in which activities tend to collect or coalesce. This set of firing patterns can be called a *neural net profile* in that it involves the *recruitment* of a certain pattern or profile of neural activations in a given moment of time. When the synaptic connections among these patterns of activated *neurons*★ are strengthened, these attractor states attract further *neural firing*★ patterns to them in the sense that they make them more likely to be created and then functionally connected to each other, making a state of mind a *cohesive*★ collection of firing in that moment, and potentially a recurring *state*★ in the future.

IMPLICATIONS: WHAT DO STATES OF MIND MEAN FOR OUR LIVES?

States of mind, fleeting or repeating, naturally emerge from both our *relational*★ and our neural contexts, and hence are called *context*★ dependent. Patterns of social communication within relational systems can naturally coalesce into sudden shifts of interaction in which we may find ourselves acting in certain ways without conscious, purposeful intention. This is how a group can induce changes in individual behavior, and we find ourselves "performing a role for the group."

Likewise, our neural connectivity, shaped by events from the past, can create associational patterns in our synaptic *linkages*★ that make the associations of a state of mind a recurring way of being. We can find ourselves *lost in familiar places*; we become filled with sadness, withdraw, and are plagued by recalled images of isolation within a rapid unfolding as our state shifts and we enter a new state of mind. This is simply how the brain is wired: We have the neural *processes*★ that rapidly shift their own functioning and coalesce as a set of patterned neural firing. The brain is an "associational machine" that functions by making linkages among widely distributed processes. We experience the linkages of *emotion**, thought, *memory**, behavioral tendencies, interactive patterns, and *mood** all in one rapidly assembled state of mind. The brain can shift from one state to another in rapid time, sometimes locking into a state in a *rigid** fashion, sometimes flooding us with continual shifts in states that become a *chaotic** way of being.

*Integration** entails within-state and between-state linkages of *differentiated** elements. Within a given state of mind, we can function in an adaptive manner when we are within a *window of tolerance** that enables us to respond to our inner and external worlds well—with flexibility and choice (see Figure M). We can also have inter-state integration, where we honor the differences among our internal states, fluidly moving in and out of states of mind as the situation requires. This is how states can be quite useful: We need to be able to link elements of thought, feeling, memory, and behavior to one another in order to optimize our functioning. But we also need to be able to release these associations and create new ones within unique states of mind to continually adapt to changing environmental demands. This is how we integrate across states as our contexts change throughout our days and our lives.

Knowing how our relational and *embodied** *mind** arises in context helps us to see how we need to be forever changing to meet the requirements of adaptive functioning. States of mind are rapid linkages of a range of functions that help us adapt well and function effectively and efficiently. When we apply this knowledge in our everyday lives, we can see how to use this natural associational proclivity of the mind to optimize our functioning. For example, skills emerge within a given state of mind. We can play tennis or engage in education with a specific set of associated functions: knowledge (in memory), interactive tendencies (behavioral patterns), emotions (the feeling states involved), and ways of thinking (strategies of reasoning, attitudes, and decision making). Whether we are playing tennis or teaching, we "take on a role" or invite the state of mind to fill our mental lives. A state of mind is an assembly of what can be called *implicit mental processes*★ that shape our *information processing*★ often without our knowing that these are mental actions at work. We just think or feel or behave without knowing that the biases of our thoughts, feelings, or behavior are influenced by our own mind's moods or intentions that define the texture of a state of mind—and so we call this an implicit process. A state of mind is a profoundly useful and an often-automatic assembly process that makes life work well. A state of mind is the water in which a fish swims, the air that we breathe, the inner context that shapes our experience of everyday life.

Intentionally shaping the external conditions in which we function can facilitate how we more proactively cultivate a state of mind. I can read relevant books, walk through a park reflecting on teaching, place the minds of the students in the front of my mind, and feel the generational passage of *information*★ from one person to another in my preparation for a teaching state of mind. If I am fully present for this experience, I can "get out of my own way" and just let the natural assembly take place on its own. This is how being an educator, for example, can become a way of being, of becoming fully present with the students, and is not just a limited role of being simply a conveyor of a set of facts that one is trying to impart. Teaching, for me, is engaging deeply in a conversation that connects our minds together as we explore a scaffold of unfolding knowledge. This is the extraordinary opportunity we have to *join* with each other in an open state of mind fundamental to learning, one of the miracles we have in this experience we call life. And so a state of mind becomes a profoundly useful way of living, an approach to being fully present for life.

When we know that we have many states of mind, not just one, we can also embrace the importance of integrating these states across time. I am more than a teacher, and my states of mind embrace a range that includes father and husband, son and friend. In seeing life as filled with a multiplicity of states of mind, one can apply the lesson of integration in cultivating many dimensions of our lives. We promote the differentiation of the many states of mind, the many ways of experiencing a "*self★*" across time, so that we can then link these many distinct, differentiated states to one another in the creation of an integrated life. From an *interpersonal neurobiology★* perspective, the view of a "unified self" is missing the point of the multiplicity of our normal, adaptive, ever-changing *healthy★* selves. When we apply our views of integration to this perspective, we see a direct way to integrate these many wondrous and necessary selves into our everyday lives.

MENTAL PROCESSES: MODES AND MOODS, ACTIVITIES AND REPRESENTATIONS

CONCEPTS: WHAT ARE THEY?

When we think of "the *mind*★," some often think of our thoughts. But mind, as we are viewing it here, is much more than our intellect and logical thinking. The mind in this larger view is not something that is to be contrasted to feelings or "the heart." Instead, we consider the life of the mind to be filled with our *emotions*★ and our *memories*★, to be shaped by what we believe, to be colored by our attitudes, to be molded by our "frame of mind." We see our mind as controlling our behavior as it is driven by our motivations and *intentions*★. And we can also be *aware*★ of these **mental processes of modes and moods, activities and representations*★**, knowing that we are having a feeling or a thought, sensing a belief or an attitude, seeing an image in our "mind's eye." These are all "mental processes" with differing impacts on our day-to-day experiences. In this entry we will explore some helpful distinctions across a range of mental processes and illuminate how they are a part of a spectrum of mental experiences that shape our inner lives.

Within awareness we have the *subjective experience*★ of a sense of both the knowing and of what is known. Being aware of something, knowing something, is actually not the "thing" itself. We can be aware of a *perception*★ of a flower, for example, but this perception is not the flower—it is a mental representation of the flower. A mental activity, a *mode*★ of perceiving, the mood we are in, and a representation are some of the "things" that can be known. In essense, what we know in our mental lives are our mental processes. Your subjective sense of this word, WORD, is not the word. Rather, it is the perception of the visual or auditory input of that *energy*★ that you experience, within *awareness*★, as "WORD." That subjective sense of WORD is shaped by your mood, by the mode of perception, by mental activities such as thinking, feeling, and *memory*★, and by specific representations such as a thought, an emotion, or an image. And, taking one of these mental processes as an example, if you think about WORD, what are you really doing? Let's get really basic. What, in fact, is a thought? And what does it mean to think?

Let's think about that for a moment.

Well . . . not so easy to answer, is it? Sometimes in our classes we'll spend a week on that one question: What is a thought? Something so close to home, so common in our lives, is actually quite difficult to define. In fact, our many "familiar" mental activities—like thinking, *remembering*★, feeling—are actually quite mysterious. You certainly know what these mental processes are, these mental experiences that shape our inner life. Here is a partial list of mental representations: emotions, thoughts, perceptions, memories, sensations, images, intentions, attitudes, beliefs, hopes, dreams, longings, and desires. They are created by their corresponding mental activities: emoting, thinking, perceiving, remembering, sensing, imaging, intending, biasing a stance (attituding!), believing, hoping, dreaming, motivational driving for something (creating a longing, or "longification") and desiring. In the general terminology of mental processes, we are inferring that these mental activities and even their mental representations are all verbs, action items, *processes**. In fact, as we'll see, these distinct terms are useful only so far as we realize, in the front of our minds, that they are each along a continuum of mental processes that reveal somewhat different but interrelated aspects of the *energy and information flow** through the body/brain and through our relationships. Mental processes—from moods to thoughts—can be seen as parts of the spectrum of the *emergent** process of mind. Distinguishing their unique and defining characteristics helps us *differentiate** them from one another so that we can *link** them together with intention as we create the setting to cultivate *integration** and *coherence** in our minds.

A mental activity creates the familiar sense that we are thinking or emoting/feeling, and these activites can sometimes (but certaintly not always) generate a specific thought or emotion, a representation. In many ways, as we'll see, these representations are themselves actually mental activities, not fixed entitites. And a filtering process that molds the nature of such mental activities and their associated representations is a mode. We can see things through the mode of logic, for example, or the mode of holistic perception, or social reasoning. Each are valid, but they are simply different modes that shape our ways of perceiving, of behaving, and even of being. Another filter of our mental activities and their representations that shapes our subjective mental life is mood. Mood creates an innate cluster-

ing of a number of mental activities and biases our interpretations, how we create *meaning*★, the feeling tone of our inner
life, and the way we interact with others. All of these mental
processes—our moods and modes, our activities and their representations—become a part of our *state of mind*★ in a given
moment. They are not separate "things" but interdependent
facets of the energy and information flow that shape and are
shaped by our minds.

When we get a feeling for the term, representation, at first
blush it may have the connotation—initially—of something
being fixed. Yet with some reflection we find that even a representation readily and spontaneously changes. An image of your
first bicycle from the mental activity of remembering within
memory might be considered a representation. So you might
say to me, "Dan, I have a visual representation of my first bike in
my mind's eye right now." And in that moment, we could imagine that you had an awareness of the visual subjective image of
that old bicycle. Great! Soon, you'll see (try it out now for fun)
everything associated with that image of the bike will begin to
shift, to change over time. The so-called noun of the representation actually transforms into something beyond the bike just sitting there in (mental) space. You may begin to see the first time
you rode the bike, how you fell and learned to recover from
that jolt, how someone stole the bike one day, how your parents acted when you lost it, and on and on. Nothing is fixed in
the mind: Even a representation, which may begin as a slightly
more stable "entity," turns out to be an ever-changing process.
The mind arises from and also *regulates*★ energy and information flow, and *flow*★ is a verb—as is the *information processing*★
that emerges even with representations. A representation is a
temporarily stable energy flow pattern that soon changes its

form in the forever-moving flow of energy and information in our mental lives.

In this discussion I also make a distinction between the experience of awareness and that element of which we are aware. In other words, we are proposing that there is a differentiation between the knowing and the known. But what exactly is known? And what is knowing? What does it mean to think of a memory of your bike and know you are seeing it in your mind's eye? And in the present-moment experience of taking in the input from the outside world—not just from memory—when we perceive with our senses of hearing, sight, olfaction, taste, and touch, what are we then aware of? What is perceiving and what is a perception? And if we have the *interoceptive** process of perceiving the signals sent from the interior of the body—from our muscles and bones, and from our internal organs—what are we truly sensing? What does it mean to "know how we feel"? And how about a thought? What, in fact, is a thought? And all of these activities of mind, modes, moods, and representations, all of these mental processes we can be aware of that shape our subjective mental experience, what are they? What is a visual image, a memory, or even an emotion? What are these mental activities of thinking and feeling, of perceiving and remembering, of imagining and dreaming?

The simple answer from science is that we don't really know what mental processes are. Shocking, but true. We may know something of the *neural correlates* of these processes, but what is the mental side of this experience? We do have some ideas of how to try to describe what these things are, but be informed in your thinking (whatever that is!) that while many phenomena are actively studied in science, the essence of these everyday aspects of our mental lives is truly still a profound mystery.

If awareness—also quite a mystery!—enables us to know, other mental processes are what is the known. And so mental processes are the whole of our mental lives, including awareness, subjective experience, and the various moods, modes, mental activites, and representations that shape how information and energy flow across time. Awareness is the knowing mental process that enables us to know the known. Now I know it sounds ironic to start out here stating that we don't really even know what this known is, but let's walk through this together, slowly, and see if we can come up with some shared notions that help us illuminate this fascinating situation. I know it would be simpler to just say that a thought is what you think, a memory is what you remember, and a feeling is what you feel. But I hope you'll see that staying at that level of description isn't as helpful as trying to go deeper into these questions about what, really, our mind may actually be all about. I know this is a wild ride, but let's go further and see where we end up! It may be helpful to put on your mental safety belts, so buckle up and hold on.

The first step is to state that mental life emerges from the flow of energy and information between and within us. This is the *relational**★* and the *embodied**★* aspect of the mind. Fine so far?

Next, energy and information may have a *prime**★* aspect to them, something that is not reducible to anything else. In fact, we can describe two aspects that are prime. One is the subjective mental experience of energy and information flow; the other is the objective *neural firing**★* component. The exact way neural firing and subjective experience interact with each other is fascinating, worthy of a lifetime of study. Here we'll simply say that no one really knows the exact way these two primes interact with each other. We are saying, though, that the direction of influence is at least mutual and that the *brain**★*

does not merely create subjective mental life. You may, as do certain scientists, disagree with this proposal that the mind is more than the outcome of brain activity. But let's look more deeply at some aspects of this fascinating topic to clarify some of the issues.

Mental life, which includes the intentional focus of *attention*⋆, the directing of energy and information flow, can shape neural firing as much as neural firing shapes attention. This is not a commonly accepted scientific view at this point, so please bear the controversial aspect of this perspective in mind so you are fully informed that we are going into uncommon territory. This viewpoint comes from the fascinating realizations arising from one way of interpreting modern research findings.

First of all, subjective experience is simply not the same as neural firing. They are different phenomena. If you smell a rose, as you feel the scent of a rose within awareness, this is not the olfactory nerve's *action potential* with its flow of ions in and out of the *neuron's*⋆ membrane! Subjective experience and neural firing may be correlated in time and function, but they are not the same. That is our first distinction.

Also, how you direct your intention and focus your attention changes the activity and structure of the brain as you harness the power of *neuroplasticity*⋆. We've defined the mind as an embodied and relational process (not just "enskulled") that regulates the flow of energy and *information*⋆. And so attention—the regulation of the flow of information—and intention are mental processes. What this means is that the arrow of causality at least goes in both directions between mind and brain. This is our second distinction about mind and brain being different from one another—related, but not the same.

We'd also want to reveal how this mutual influence goes in

three directions when we bring in the relational aspect of our mental lives as seen in the *triangle** of human experience. What we do with our communication between us shapes how the brain fires and what happens in our subjective experience. This is our third distinction. These are not three separate elements, but three *interdependent** aspects of one reality: Mind, brain, and *relationships** are the regulation, embodied mechanism, and sharing of the flow of energy and information.

Now if we embrace these distinctions for a moment, or several moments, we can proceed to address this central question of what the knowing and the known actually may be. This is a new proposal, a new way of diving into an old set of questions, I know. But let's see how it fits in with science and with your own subjective experience. Awareness has the sense of a *receptive* subjective *mental space* in which a quality of knowing is created. And within this open space enters that which is to be known. Here we'll try to delineate, as best we can with words that never fully do the job, what this "known" of mental activity, mode, mood, and representation might actually be.

With the *plane of possibility** and the *wheel of awareness** (see Figures H and I) we have two images that attempt to visually depict the setup: An open plane or receptive hub for the knowing of awareness; a set of *plateaus** and *peaks** and a rim for the mental moods, modes, activities, and representations that are to be known. If you haven't yet tried out the *reflective practice** of the wheel of awareness, this might be a good time to try so that you can directly experience how this immersion in your own mental processes is for you. Don't take my or anyone else's word for this!

We've said that there is one sector of the rim depicting sensory input that we can perceive; another sector of the rim represents signals from the interior of the body; a third sector has mental activities and representations in the more restrictive sense of those without a direct emergence from the physical bodily or external world-based sensation origins—such as feeling an emotion, thinking and thoughts, remembering and memories, and the like; and a fourth sector contains the sense of our interconnectedness. Along the whole of the rim, then, is represented the wide array of senses, from the outside world and the body, our various mental activities and representations, such as thoughts and feelings, and our sense of interconnectedness to other people and our planet. We can hear a sound from a bird outside, or we feel the gurgling of our stomach inside, or we can think a thought or feel an emotion, or we can sense a connection with someone a thousand miles away. The rim depicts the known of mental processes.

Even our sensations of the body or the outside world are filtered through our perceptual mental apparatus and are thus mental processes! The "known," it turns out, is a verb, a mentally constructed set of something that we'll explore more now. Let's emphasize this point. We attribute the source of a sensory input to an outside origin, but the truth is we can never really be directly sensing a flower, for example. We can only have our neural signals from the nose then translated, somehow, into a mental perception of those signals. We are not really sensing directly the molecules of the flower, as much as we might want to, but instead we somehow translate those molecules into a form of *neural net* activation that is correlated in time to our subjective mental awareness of the signaling of the flower through our olfaction and our vision. Yes, for the perception of the outside world, the mind depends upon the body to create neural firing patterns that respond to the signals from that which we are sensing in the moment. But the mental experience of that rose is not the rose, and it is not the neural firing. It is our subjective experience of the rose.

Put in other terms, your prime of becoming filled with the known of the smell of the rose (the subjective experience of the rose) is not the same as being filled with the molecular structures of the rose (the prime of neural firing in response to the rose). How do these primes really arise as functions of energy flow through our subjective and our neural lives? Let's address this question by first stating that in physics, the field of quantum mechanics suggests that energy moves by way of alterations of probability. This quantum view of energy flow lets us see that the likelihood of having a sense of the flower will be greatly heightened at the moment you are sniffing the rose than if you are, say, watching a film about the depths of the ocean. You might randomly remember the rose during the film, but the probability is that during the cinematic immersion you won't be having the subjective experience of smelling a rose. You might, but it is not as likely as when the rose is in front of you. The possibility is there, but the actuality of that possibility is unlikely to occur. These shifts in probability are what we are saying "energy and information flow" really means. This is straight from the science of energy, in the quantum mechanics view of physics, and we can then logically apply this view of the properties of energy flow to our understanding of mind once we've defined the mind as an emergent process arising from the flow of energy and information within and between us.

This shift in *probability patterns*★ in both our mental lives and in our neural functioning is directly depicted in the plane image by how we place the upward curves of probability patterns as being mental subjective experience, and the downward curves as the prime of neural firing. These are correlated but are not the same. The rose stimulates our experience, and we have the primes of neural firing and of mental experience. When we move away from the level of the plane, up or down, we are experiencing increasing probabilities from the openness of possibility in the plane itself. This movement happens in both the reality of the *embodied brain*, and the reality of subjective mental experience. These are the primes of life. These two aspects of the one reality of smelling the rose are the head and tail of one coin, or two primes of one reality. When you are aware of the scent of the rose, you are in the subjective prime of the rose. And your brain is firing in response to the molecules of the rose itself within the prime of neural firing. This distinction between neural and mental does not lessen the experience, but it helps us clarify the experience and take a step toward uncovering its essence.

And so I propose this notion. Awareness arises from the open plane of possibility. This is the experience of knowing that is central to awareness. The known arises from above the plane, experienced as a peak of certainty, say, for a thought or image or smell of the rose in that moment. These are our representational processes. The plateaus of increased probability can be seen as the filters that shape how a peak will manifest itself. This form of filtering mental process can be seen as an intention or mood, and it can also be seen as a "mode of processing." For example, we have modes shaped by the asymmetric neural firing patterns that are differentiated as *lateralized* functions on the left and right sides of the brain. Awareness arises from the plane, modes and moods reside in the plateaus, and most mental activites and representations form the peaks. This is a starting nomenclature and a place with which we can begin to visualize these mental processes and see them as all aspects of shifts in probability, interdependent aspects of our mental lives. If we are truly to embrace the suggestion that the mind is an emergent process arising from and regulating energy and information flow, then this is a natural step to see mental life as a spectrum in the shifts in probability as energy moves across time. The distinctions between modes and moods, activities and representations are actually quite blurry, as these are emergent aspects of changes in probability across a wide spectrum. We can use these terms to get oriented, but in the end they are all mental processes and the true distinctions among them are actually quite fluid and without clear boundaries. They are indeed all mental processes along a range of probability shifts as energy flows within the experience of mind. This is new for most of us, I know, but it fits with the science and with the subjective experience people often describe, as we'll see. What this suggests is that our mental lives both ride along and regulate the changes in probability patterns at the heart of what "energy flow" is all about. Mental processes transform these various degrees of probability across time. This is how we regulate energy flow and shape the formation of information. This is also the beginning of defining what thinking is: a mental activity that alters the energy probability pattern that is the essence of what energy and information flow really means. And a thought? A thought is the transformation of energy probability patterns as the actualization of possibility into the manifestation of certainty. Thinking itself is that process of transformation that makes the "possible" transition into the "probable" and then the "actual." In other words, from the plane of open possibility, mental processes arise and move us toward probability (moods and modes) and then upward toward certainty (mental activities and representations).

This way of conceptualizing the mind can be mind-boggling,

of course. We can never know something as concrete, as certain, totally predictable, fixed and containable. The mind, instead, involves waves of transformation of possibilities into probabilities and certainties, and then back again through a fluid and sometimes abrupt set of ever-emerging transitions. And for some it can also be sad, on some level, to embrace the reality that we can never really be with a rose, or with a loved one. The closest we can get is to be attuned to the neural signals that translate the intake of another person, or the flower, and let that distance be as short as possible. That neural prime is not the flower and the mental prime of our subjective experience is not the neural firing either, or the flower itself. We are, on some level, at least one step away from the thing itself. Perhaps the only "thing" we truly can be with is our own mental processes as they unfold in time. For the flower, the molecules first interact with the sensory neural *receptors*. Next, we have a mental experience that is derived from—but not the same as—neural firing. How that physical neural activity and the subjective mental experience of the flower are related, no one knows. But we can state that these mental activities are shifts in degrees of probability, exactly the way energy shifts across time. Perception is a mental process—it shifts energy probability patterns.

A "representation" is, as it suggests, a "re-presentation" or a presenting again of some initial signal. In the case of the smell of a rose, a chemical is emitted from the flower and this molecule is absorbed by the nose. The neural firing that follows the reception of the rose molecule is a neural translation of the impact of the molecule on neural firing. The same is true for sight as photons hit the retina of the eye, of hearing as sound waves (moving air molecules) displace the position of the ear drum, and of touch as contact against the skin is translated by touch receptors that send signals to the spinal cord and then to the skull-encased brain. Just try pinching yourself behind the elbow, where there are usually no touch receptors, and you'll experience firsthand how the mere act of touching the skin does not produce a sensation in your subjective awareness unless there is neural translation.

And so we use the term "representation" with regards to sensation and perception as the neural translation of signals derived from the outside world and represented (no pun intended) on the first segment of the rim of the wheel of awareness, our sensory perception of the world around us. We can also have a representation of the signals from within the body, noted on the second segment of the rim. Even though these signals originate from "inside" of us, derived from our body, they are still a neural translation of the *state** of our muscles, bones, or organs that we only know because of the passage of signals, neurological or otherwise (as in hormonal, cardiovascular, or immune), upward into the aspects of our *nervous system** that process perceptions of the interior. So even the body proper is represented in the brain. Interoception is the subjective experience of perceiving this interior set of signals.

And what do we make of our sense of connection to one another on the fourth segment of the rim of the wheel of awareness? This, too, can be seen as communication of signals (what we hear, see, smell, and sometimes taste and touch) from others who are physically close to us. But we also have a sense of this connection at a distance—from physically separate locations, from temporally distinct moments from the past or an imagined future. The *prefrontal** region of the brain appears to be able to make a *mindsight map** not only of you (*empathy**) and of me (*insight**), but also of we. It is within these integrative regions that we likely create a neurally constructed sense of our interconnectedness. Sometimes we sense our connections directly via input from others; perhaps at other times we imagine those connections and develop an internally generated sensation of our interconnected relationship. In either case, our subjective experience of interconnectedness is filled with a sense of closeness, of being a part of a we. One of the outcomes of such a mindsight map of we is *moral*★ reasoning, imagination, and behavior. These mental processes certainly arise from and also influence our integrative prefrontal fibers. Some postulate that nurturing the interconnections we have among ourselves and those we have with our planet is vital and that we should respect the need to be connected with other people and to be out in nature. This is our "connecting time" to people and planet embedded in a *healthy mind platter*★ notion of well-being. However you interpret these research findings pointing to the essential need for such relational connections for our *health*★, whatever your belief and first-person experience may be, the issue relevant to our discussion here is that we have both a relational and a neural set of energy and information flow patterns that give rise to the mind. Our relationships—the sharing of energy and information between ourselves and other people and the planet—create patterns of interconnectedness that embed us in a "we." And the neural translation of these shared signals and the creation of neural firing patterns—neural representations—establish the possibility of sensing this interconnectedness. The reality of being embedded in a larger world of other people and the planet is an important part of not only moral living, but of *mental health*★ itself.

In many ways, these three segments of the rim—our sensation of the outside world, of the body, and of our interconnectedness—can be seen initially as being formed as re-presentations of some neural process within the brain and within the mind as our subjective experience. Yes, the term representation signifies both a neural process and a mental process. From the plane of possibility perspective, these would be viewed as the mirrored peaks below (neural) and above (mental) the plane. These three rim segments are composed of various forms of *perceptual representations* that, as we've discussed, are themselves initially imbued with a sense of solidity. On the plane model, we can envision a representation as a peak with high certainty that has an experiential and neural stability. But soon even these representations reveal their verblike nature. They begin to shimmer, to transform, to transfigure into something else. Even a representation of something like, say, a rock, is in fact a dynamic unfolding process, a representation of the rock, not the rock itself. And so you think of a rock, you imagine it, and you experience it as a representation. Soon that peak moves down from such an initially fixed place to reveal how representations are indeed mental processes that are as real as the source of their initial origins but are, in fact, fluid, flowing processes.

When a representation begins to transform, we call this information processing. The verb quality of mind is illuminated when we realize that everything in the mind—even an image of a rock—is actually a verb, not a noun, and is an unfolding mental process of change and transfiguration. Representations are actually mental activities in the sense that they move and actively transform energy patterns across time. Whether we consider thinking, reasoning, calculating, analyzing, assessing, evaluating, and judging, or processes such as reflecting, feeling, sensing, remembering, mentalizing, intuiting, moralizing, or imagining, we come to the view that each and every one of these fascinating and important attributes of mind is a process of information transformation. Even the simple act of neurally translating signals from the sensory input of something as stable as a rock is in fact a process; it is a re-presentation, a verb. So representing is actually a mental process.

In terms of our vocabulary, we can see the spectrum of terminology that may be useful here to underscore. Representations are mental processes at the high peak end. Mental activities, such as those listed in the prior paragraph like thinking and feeling, are transformative processes that act on probability patterns and transform their pathways across time. For example, reasoning may manipulate various representational peaks as we compare and contrast the peak representations of a rose with peak representations of a sunflower. Even though representations are themselves processes, we can use that term to signify a mental experience with the temporary stability of a peak. It may be that having the ability to become aware of a peak representation and observe its qualities is much more readily accomplished than perceiving a mental activity—the transformative energy pattern-shifting process that happens, if you will, below a peak. We aim our attention toward such subpeak energy shifts and sometimes we can see them, sometimes not, but we certainly would have a harder time coming up with words for these "mental activities." And so a mental activity (in contrast to a representation) is a mental process—such as thinking or feeling or remembering—that "actively" transforms energy probability patterns across time. A mental activity acts on representations to change their form. I can say "I am thinking about this or that" and this description I give you will likely involve a combination of statements about peak representations and less about the more vague sense I have of subpeak mental activity.

Naturally these mental activities and mental representations have a neural correlate to them. The brain side of neural activity from the perspective of the plane of possibility is below the plane—at peak representations and subpeak manifestations of neural activities that likely are neuronal *parallel processing* functions that transform both transient neural activations and long-term synaptic couplings. This is the neural correlate below the plane of a mental activity depicted above the plane that we may become aware of mentally as subjective experience. I say "may" here because we may be aware, or not, of this mental process. Not all mental processes are within awareness and they are not always accessible to awareness. We can call this *nonconscious★* mental processing. Much of the mind may not involve *conscious★* experience.

How can this be? When processes move above and below the plane, mental experience and neural firing occur. From a simple neuroscience perspective, we can state that consciousness seems to be correlated in time with activation of the prefrontal areas of the brain and connections of this activity with other distributed areas of the brain. The degree of complexity achieved in these widespread neural areas involves many regions besides the prefrontal ones that are coordinating and balancing the whole *system★*. This degree of complexity is directly related to states of integration and may also influence what we can become aware of, the ways we become conscious of something or not. When activity in other regions is not linked to prefrontal integrative functioning, we can suggest that a process arises—neurally and mentally—but we are not aware of it. For example, activation of the perceptual processing circuits (in the back of the brain, with the occipital area for vision, for example) that are not linked with the neural activity in the prefrontal region would explain how sensation and even perception may not have consciousness as a part of the layers of processing of incoming data from the outside (or bodily or relational) world. In other words, we can have perception without awareness.

Blindsight is one clinical example of just such a phenomenon in which a person is unaware of visual input but is in fact registering both the neural and the mental components of visual perception. A person with blindsight puts his hands up to block a ball from hitting his face, but he cannot "see" within awareness what is coming toward him. Mental processing regulates the flow of energy and information, and he enacts a behavior to prevent an injury. Others might suggest that this is simply the brain enacting a protective reaction, and we do not need to evoke the concept of "mind" to describe this phenomenon. And this raises our essential suggestion: The regulation of energy and information flow can occur without awareness and is still what we are defining as part of what the mind is. In a similar fashion, relationships can be shaped by our interactions without the awareness that we are engaging with others in a certain way. The emergent self-organizing process we are defining as an aspect of mind is actively at work without awareness. Even without this conscious aspect of experience, we can still see how the relational interactions give rise to mental experience that shapes those very interactions.

Another way of imagining this issue of the preponderance of nonconscious mental activities is to come back to the plane of possibility as a model for the way the mind and brain co-influence one another. We turn again to the central concept that energy manifests itself across time as shifts in probability that form a probability pattern, a trajectory or curve of alterations of probability across time. To emphasize the scientific foundations for this view we need to recall that this is the way physics and its study of quantum mechanics depict the nature of how energy changes across time. Here is a surprising hypothesis that emerges from listening carefully to direct reports from individuals experiencing the wheel of awareness practice and then attempting to correlate these accounts with the plane of possibility model of energy shifts and mental experience. Energy probability patterns that dip into the open plane of possibility are those that evoke the experience of awareness. I know this is an odd way of speaking about something so intimate as awareness. But receiving input from hundreds of people about the experience of the hub of the mind, of becoming aware of awareness itself (the equivalent, I suggest, of the open plane of possibility), makes this view not only appealing, but also empirically consistent with first-person data. So let's walk with this a bit on our journey and see how it works out.

This proposal suggests that awareness rests in the plane at zero probability/infinite possibility. When people from all over the world, from differing *cultures** and differing backgrounds and education, report focusing the hub on the hub itself, they describe this "wide as the sky," "deep as the ocean," "tranquil sense of clarity" that emerges with a sense of profound openness and even "infinite possibility." These are reports from those doing the wheel of awareness practice before they have ever seen the model of the plane of possibility. And yet when they describe the rim review, the reports are quite different and varied. The gist of these first-person reports is that the rim elements are filled with change and unfolding, not openness and stability. From these accounts we can suggest that mental processes that transform energy patterns arise as probability curves move above zero (the plane), taking shape initially as moods and modes and other ways in which energy transformations become biased as represented by plateaus. As the probability curve moves even higher, toward 100 percent, we then encounter mental activities of information processing that, at a peak, transform into a representation. That's our mapping of mental process onto the probability shifts modeled in the plane of possibility view.

Mental processes span a spectrum of probabilities from open possibility within awareness to increased probablity with modes and moods, to the movement toward certainty with activities and representations. These are depicted as the movement from plane to plateau to peak. This transformation of energy probability curves reveals the distribution of energy flow patterns from awareness to representation fundamental to information processing.

But how do we actually become aware of a mental process—how do we place into consciousness a mood or mode, an activity or representation? Taking on this view, we can suggest that one possibility is that some form of an oscillating process might exist whereby we dip into the plane and then go up into the plateaus or the peaks to become aware of these mental processes that arise as energy probability patterns transition beyond the plane. On the brain side, a forty-cycle per second (40 herz) process has been proposed to correlate with consciousness as neural firing patterns are gathered along a *thalamocortical* "sweeping" process that temporarily links activated elements. Our mental experience of that oscillation is to become aware of those linked elements. And so from the plane model, perhaps awareness (in the plane) somehow samples in an oscillating fashion elements above the plane (mental processes) as well as below the plane (neural processes) so that we become aware of them. Sometimes those above plane movements are not sampled in this oscillating way, and we have mental experience and neural firing without awareness. Perhaps being "slightly aware" of something is a minimal amount of oscillatory sampling and so we get a "vague sense" of something within our conscious experience but cannot clearly see it. At other times, we may become lost in identifying as the peak itself, aware but without a broader perspective on what is happening when we lose self-consciousness in the flow of an experience. This might be seen as clear awareness but without tapping into other elements of experience, such as a sense of self. Yet at still other times, we may just come to "rest" within awareness itself, as happens in the more advanced step of the wheel of awareness practice where one bends the spoke to return to the hub and experiences the commonly reported expansive sense of *awareness of awareness*.

The wide spectrum of subjective experience within awareness may reflect the changing ratios of plane-plateau-peak oscillations as awareness emanates from the open plane. How exactly the subjective sense of knowing within awareness actually happens, we don't know. But taking this possible initial view, that awareness emanates from the probability curve of open possibility, we can understand the experience of the wheel of awareness hub that people so frequently describe. We can also offer a description of ways of understanding the varied qualitative differences in states of being aware. The hub in the wheel is the parallel of the plane of possibility and we can have various ways of "being in the hub" or "being out on the rim." We can cultivate the mind by practicing *mindful awareness** in which we strengthen the hub of the mind itself. Mindful awareness may contain more grounded experience within the plane, within the hub of the mind. In contrast, we may enter states of being on *automatic pilot★* in which we may be aware, but without the larger *context★* of the self that is being in the experience. When done with intention, this may describe the experience of flow. But at other times, becoming "lost on the rim" is a time when we have become outraged or lost in a thought to the detriment of remaining in an activity with open *presence★*. Something about this shift in probabilities—from open (plane) to raised (plateau) to certainty (peak) seems to fit well with the mind and its capacity for awareness in our varied life experiences.

"Mental processes" is a term that can refer to both the first representational steps, from sensation to perception, and to the more stimulus-unbound forms of information processing—like thinking, feeling, and remembering—that we're calling "mental activities." A representation starts with stability but ultimately is really a verb, an active unfolding process itself, merging with "thinking" that can involve images, feelings, memories, and other aspects of our mental life. And so mental processes such as representations and activities blend with one another in an ongoing symphony that creates the music of the mind. These mental processes are manifestations of shifts in the probability patterns upward, toward 100% probability at a peak representation and less than 100% subpeak probability patterns for mental activities. Mental activities involve an active mechanism that alters probability patterns across time. This would be, for example, how you can have a thought about the Eiffel Tower, including its image in your mind's eye and the correlated neural firing in the occipital *cortex★* of your brain. Let's call these *"explicit mental processes★"* in that when we have them we may readily know their origins as part of mental life. We may or may not be aware of them all the time, but when we are in fact conscious of them, we know we are feeling or remembering or thinking or that we have a specific image in "our mind's eye." That is what "explicit" means—we know it to be what it is, a mental process of which we are now currently aware of its mental nature.

Yet some aspects of our mental life are not so readily known for what they are. We can call these "*implicit mental processes*★" in that even when we are aware of their effects, we don't know that these are emerging from some aspect of our mental life. An example of an implicit mental process would be a mood, a mode, a motivation, or an attitude. The effects of these mental processes can be within awareness or not, but often the impact of their actions, even when within awareness, is not experienced as coming from a part of our mental life. We just believe that this "is the way it is": that our motivation is good, our mood is reality, this way of perceiving reality is the reality, and our attitude is simply "common sense." Just as with *implicit memory*★ in its pure form, implicit mental processes affect our conscious experience, but we just don't have the sense or the knowledge that they are filters shaping our experience. We don't know, at least initially, that an implicit mood, motivation, stance, or other aspect of our state of mind is implicitly shaping our thinking, emotions, memory, perceptions, intention, reasoning, or other aspects of mental activities. This is what "implicit" means; we do not readily know it for what it is.

We can envision implicit mental processes as plateaus in our plane model of the mind. In the wheel metaphor, this would be seen as the inner layer of the rim that filters what we think and feel through the lens of our present state of mind or what we can call a "mode." A mode is the form of implicit processing that biases how explicit mental processes arise. As an example of modes, let's examine an overview of the difference between the *left mode* and *right mode* of processing information.

Although the issue of the *laterality* of brain anatomy and function has become somewhat controversial, there are important research data that support the following statements. The right side of the brain develops earlier, processes data more directly from the body and the *brainstem** and *limbic** areas, and has a dominance in sending and receiving *nonverbal signals**. In addition, the right side of the brain seems to be more active in the creation of a stress response, in making a map of the whole body, in storing *autobiographical memory**, and in making mindsight maps of me, you, and us. While the left side of the brain contributes to many of these processes as well, it does so in a less significant way and therefore we call each of these somatic, emotional, and autobiographical mental activities part of a right mode. It may be most helpful to think of the "mode"—left or right—as an implicit mental process that shapes our mental activities, or the explicit ways we perceive, think, feel, remember, reason, imagine, and interact in the world. In many ways, a mode shapes our way of being.

The left mode derives from and also influences the activity of the left side of the brain. This side is dominant for a number of mental processes that fortunately (for our memory systems) begin with the letter L. The left *hemisphere** is later to develop than the right, getting active in function and growth during the second year of life. It is linear in its processing, as opposed to the more holistic aspects of the right. It is logical in its deductions, seeking cause–effect relationships in the world as it uses *syllogistic reasoning* instead of the visuospatial processing dominant in the right mode. The left is linguistically oriented, imbued with the digital packets of linguistic language. And the left mode is considered to be more literal, and it loves to makes lists (like this one!). Specializing in factual memory (as opposed to the autobiographical memory of the right brain), the left mode tends to see the text whereas the right focuses on the context. The left likes the letter of the law within the lines, and the right sees the meaning between the lines.

In a given moment, both sides of the brain are often actively contributing to our mental experience and our neural firing patterns. Linking these two differentiated sides of the brain and modes of processing is common as integration is a natural push of our *complex systems*★ of brain, mind, and relationships too. Yet the anatomical differences between left and right can help us understand how energy and information flow on each side of the brain would set the stage for such differing modes of processing and the potential overemphasis of one mode over another. These modes can certainly be quite integrated, but they can also become isolated from one another. When one mode dominates over the other, we may become prone to rigid ways of thinking or to chaotic intrusions of emotion or memory. Living with only a dominance of one mode or the other limits our capacity for integration. *Chaos*★ and *rigidity*★ are manifestations of such impaired integration. And we can learn to see how implicit mental processes can dominate our explicit mental activities (thinking and feeling and perceiving and remembering) and can mold our representations (a specific thought, an emotion, a perception, an image). And with these insights we can then use the focus of attention to change how these implicit processes may be limiting our lives and blocking integration, creating a powerful way of freeing our minds and bringing health into our lives.

Modes shape how we think and feel as well as how we perceive and remember. A related implicit mental process is a stance, a mental attitude that also filters these explicit mental activities of thought and feeling. Another implicit mental process is motivation: a kind of mental priming that readies our whole system to respond in a certain fashion to achieve a certain "intended goal." Intention can be implicit or can sometimes become an explicit manifestation of implicit motivation as these mental processes set our attentional spotlight, bias how we interpret interactions, and directly shape our behavior (sometimes without our knowing). This is why we call these implicit mental processes and do not refer to them as nonconscious ones. The manifestations of motivation as intention can be within awareness; we just don't realize our own minds are biasing our experiences in this way. We can certainly, with effort in the moment and training in the long run, learn to make these implicit processes readily visible to us. Mindful awareness practice may be one such *mindsight** skill training practice that stabilizes how we come to see our own mental processes. With such refined perception, implicit processes become something we can detect and then can change to benefit our lives. The same is true with mood: This overall tone of our state of mind implicitly shapes all of our mental life, even if we are not aware of the origins of this shaping process. And with training, it becomes possible to detect a previously hidden mood and then alter its impact on our ways of feeling and thinking.

Mood, motivation, stance, and modes are all implicit mental processes that shape our subjective experience. The neural activity of these implicit processes is represented below the plane of possibility. Such implicit processes are revealed as plateaus of increased probability that bias which peaks will arise on the trajectory of probability from plateau to peak, in the movement from mental activity to representation. It is from these plateaus—of enhanced likelihood of neural firing (below the plane) and of mental subjective experience (above the plane)—that implicit processes continually shape our lives.

You may have noticed from your own direct first-person immersion in the wheel of awareness practice that it is more challenging to observe a plateau of mood or intention than the more readily perceived subpeaks of thinking or remembering or peaks of representations like thoughts or images. Implicit mental life is harder to see more directly than the explicit mental activities and representations. We can surmise from this common first-person finding that the explicit peaks of certainty are more dramatically contrasted to the open plane of possibility from which we are proposing that awareness arises.

Here is a next step of our basic proposal. Imagine the distribution of probability patterns from zero to 100 (this is rising up from the plane to a peak for mental experience). Now consider that the span between the plane and the flat surface of a plateau just above the plane is the mental zone within which implicit processes arise. It is hard to observe these more subtle implicit processes because their probability values are closest to zero. The larger the contrast, the more readily we can sense within awareness the mental process. As probabilities move in a spectrum of values, at some point we can graphically see that a peak arises from the plateau's surface. In this span is where a mental activity is found. This we're calling a "subpeak," because it is below a peak. Then once we are at the peak of 100% certainty, we have come to a representation. And so we can summarize this view in this way: Explicit mental processes are found in the plane diagram as peaks (representations) and subpeak intervals (mental activities). We can readily observe in awareness the mental nature of those probability patterns that are most distinct—most distant—from that of the plane where awareness arises.

In contrast, an implicit mental process, like a mode or mood or motivation, is found in the interval between the plane and the surface of the plateau. Let's call this span the "subplateau" for ease of reference. Because these subplateau probability values are closer to that of the zero value of the plane, it is harder to observe these directly within awareness or to know that these are mental processes that are shaping our subjective experiences and lives.

The plateaus and subplateaus fluidly shift toward and away from the plane and may be more challenging to perceive. In some ways, it is like asking a fish to describe the water in which he lives. Our implicit processes are the water in which we swim, the air in which we live. When energy probability patterns arise from the plane, they emerge in probability plateaus with a broad diversity (z-axis) and a range of various probabilities (y-axis). Yet as the spectrum of probability patterns moves upward, the cone begins to narrow as probabilities move toward certainties and the broader span of diversity of the plateau begins to become more confined, more like the constricted range of diversity found in peaks. This suggestion reminds us that there is actually a spectrum of probability values, zero to 100, and diversity ranges through which these energy patterns transition. While we have named one set of subplateau mental processes as implicit, there really is a natural continuum along this probability spectrum. For example, some "explicit thoughts" may loosen in their directness as they drop from the peak of 100% certainty of a representation ("I am thinking of the Eiffel Tower") to a lower level of a mental activity ("I have a vague sense of some structure, but I don't know exactly what it is"). If this probability distribution lowers enough and the diversity range widens, I might even say that I am having a "sense of Paris," a certain mood I am in, and we'd then call this an implicit mental process. That's all fine for our vocabulary so we can easily speak with one another about this wide spectrum of modes, activities, and representations, but the plane model reminds us that mental processes are actually distributed naturally along this wide spectrum of probability and diversity. There may be no artificial breaks between implicit and explicit or among motivation (subplateau), intention (somewhere between subplateau and subpeak), thinking (subpeak), and specific impulse to act or even enacted behavior (peak). The further away from the plane we go, up toward 100% probability, the easier it is for us to notice the "explicit" details of what is happening as a mental process. So we'll use this notion of implicit and explicit for ease of reference, but let's keep this continuity of values in the front of our minds. The lower the percentage along the probability spectrum, the more "implicit" the characteristics of the mental process and the more challenging it is to declare what exactly is going on. Embracing this spectrum of shifts feels right, and it accords with how the mind appears to actually be functioning.

All of these implicit and explicit processes shape the transformation of information as energy shifts and changes along the spectrum of probability pattern transitions. In the broadest sense, information processing includes emotion, *cognition*, *mental models*, memory, reasoning, decision making, moral imagination, and an infinite amount of other processes for which we have no names. Each mental process has its own inherent life, its own innate qualities that are sometimes derived from input from the physical world but even in that instance are part of mental life. For example, if I dream of freedom, I am having a real mental experience, but it is not limited to nor constricted by a physical origin. I may sense this as a dream image of breaking out of a prison, of flying in the clouds, of charting an unknown sea, but the theme of freedom is a concept, a representation of an idea: It is not those images of the physical world. Concepts and percepts reveal the wide range with which we create information from energy swirls within the mind. We can see mental processes as transformations of energy patterns that change the form of information, energy patterns that stand for something other than themselves. This is how energy, in certain patterns, becomes information in our mental experience.

Let's imagine the view that a set of neuronal firing patterns is associated with the thought about freedom. And given our plane model, we can rest comfortably with the primes of both neural firing and of mental activity as being irreducible aspects of this one reality of energy and information flow. Because this is potentially such a controversial issue, this is an important caveat to re-emphasize: Neural firing and subjective mental experience are not the same phenomena. They are two sides of one reality. We are not making them separate but are in fact revealing how they are intimately interconnected. In the nervous system, the movement of electrochemical energy flow transforms current firing patterns into ever-changing shifts in further firing. A neural representation, say, of "freedom," is an action item in the brain—it is filled with potential changes and shifts, some of which manifest as actualities emerging from these potentialities. Given that the skull-based brain is filled with 100 billion neurons and hundreds of trillions of synaptic *linkages*★ interconnecting all of these packets of energy and information flow, there is an estimated 10 to the millionth power number of possible on-off firing patterns that the brain can generate. When you add to this number (a number larger than the estimated atoms in the universe) the fact that the brain is continually changing in response to experience, then you can truly say that the number of possible firing patterns of the brain is nearly infinite. You could never in a lifetime try to experience each of the possible patterns! (This is one reason I can never understand why someone would say that he is bored with life—he should just try out some new patterns.)

We immerse ourselves in the proposal that mind is an emergent process arising from the flow of energy and information in our bodies (brain) and between ourselves and other people and the planet (relational). The regulatory aspect of mind is a *self-organizing*★ process. And what about our subjective experience of knowing within awareness? Perhaps this can also be seen as an emergent property of energy and information flow as well. If so, it may be that awareness arises from the open plane of possibility. This is where energy probability patterns are in the infinite state—zero probability, open possibility. And what of the "known" of our mental lives—our mental processes of perception, thinking, feeling, and memory? What this extensive discussion leads us to here is the suggestion that these mental processes are also emergent processes that are created when energy patterns move above (mental) or below (brain) the plane of open possibility. This fits with the role of mind as a regulatory, self-organizing process in that mental processes, as we have seen, transform information by regulating energy flow in the body and in our relationships. This model provides a number of helpful insights into the nature of our *primary experience*. It offers a researchable perspective (through first-person and scientific studies) that can be validated with further study. It also enables us to embrace the

broad spectrum of mental experience that ranges from awareness to mode, mood, and motivation (implicit processes), to
feeling, thinking, perceiving, and remembering (explicit mental activities), and to sensations, thoughts, perceptions, and
images (explicit representations). Even mental elements like
intention and "free will" may be seen as mental processes that
bridge the implicit and the explicit range of our mental lives.
While this is a coherent theoretical model inspired by first-
person experience and shaped by science that is useful in its
practical applications, you'll need to try out this proposal for
yourself and explore how seeing the mind as emerging from
and regulating energy shifts in probability fits or does not fit
with your own experience.

When we note that physicists ultimately state that "energy is
the capacity to do stuff" and that this capacity is measured in
ranges of probability—from certainty to infinite possibility—we
can see how our taking the step of seeing the mind in energy
and information terms is so useful and empowering to create
a *consilient** perspective on these issues. Mental processes happen in the "*space of the mind*," the prime of mental life, the reality of subjective experience. They have correlates in the brain
side, of course, as I've been discussing here. One prime does not
always lead the other, but both the neural and mental sides of
this one reality likely mutually influence one another in important ways that have profound implications for our understanding of mind. When we are on automatic, the brain may "drag
the mind around." And when we exert our free will with intention, the mind may be leading the brain's activity in new directions. Ultimately this discussion of mental activities as shifts in
energy probability patterns enables us to see how to strengthen
the mind with more specificity—and even how to shift the

functioning of the brain. Strengthening the mind empowers us to improve our lives.

IMPLICATIONS: WHAT DO MENTAL PROCESSES AND THEIR MODES, MOODS, ACTIVITIES, AND REPRESENTATIONS MEAN FOR OUR LIVES?

The mind is more than a process correlated to only neural functioning. Our mental experience also fundamentally arises from energy and information patterns that are shared with others and with our world. One of the profound implications of our exploration of the deep nature of mind is to expand our ways of understanding the power of relationships to support the health of our minds. When we view the mind as a self-organizing, emergent process that arises from both relationships and from the body, we're in a new and stronger position to address the question of what our mental processes actually are and how to optimize our mental well-being.

To illustrate how relationships shape the mind, let's imagine that you and I go for a walk along a park overlooking the ocean. Along our walk, we stop to watch some birds. As we lift our heads to the sky, I let the thought of freedom that arises in my experience go into the background, and my awareness becomes filled now with a feeling of *gratitude* about being alive and appreciative of our planet. I let this emerging sense of openness sift through my subjective experience. We continue our walk along the path in the park, chatting with each other about this or that. You tell me that you are concerned about a distant country's genocide, about the scourge of disease plaguing humanity in various nations, about the threat to our well-being, globally. I think about the freedom of the birds, the rights of others to have such a feeling in their lives, too. But the image fades away, and I pick up something from you that pulls me out of that peak, into a different plateau—a mood, a *state of mind**— something I can't quite articulate. It's what we are calling an implicit process, shaping my conscious experience but without declaring its mental nature. I am awash in something, but I don't really know what. Our energy patterns have dropped out of that peak of the birds in flight that we shared in *joint attention*, strengthening our connection, and now the explicit feeling of freedom is fading from the front of my mind.

We move in our conversation from the importance of global issues and I ask you about how you are doing, how you are in your personal life. Now you start speaking about a recent breakup you've had, and the plateau we are both in now has certainly shifted from the plateau that arose when we stopped to watch the birds and that which gave rise in me to a freedom peak. You have been feeling sad, rejected, and alone. Your mental activities at this moment now are a wash of transformations as you wrestle with past rejections, the wish that I'd be more understanding in the present, and your worries about your future. All of this is a flowing process, some in awareness, much of it not, and the energy patterns are not up to a peak, not right now, as they just float in implicit movements of mood as we walk along. You take in the view of more birds flying—in pairs—in the trees above and I notice that you are crying. I see that you've been watching two birds find a nest, and I can imagine, through mindsight, what you might be feeling. In my own neural side, I automatically make a mindsight map of you, and I can feel, inside of me, heaviness in my chest, a fullness in my throat. I feel your sense of despair and put my hand on your shoulder, and then I take your hand.

I do this naturally, perhaps driven by my right hemisphere's way of being connected to you and to your nonverbal signals in my right mode of being . . . but my *left* hemisphere knows, with its left mode way of being filled with facts, that studies have shown that holding the hand of someone with whom you are emotionally close reduces the pain of physical injury. Rejection in fact has been shown to activate the same *circuits*★ that register bodily pain; it actually hurts! So both my left and my right modes have "reasons" to back up the behavior of holding your hand.

That's the backstory. But in the moment I just hold your hand because I *implicitly know* that it can make you feel better, and this arises from a gut feeling of what to do, and emerging from my own past experience . . . nothing to do with science! (Perhaps this spontaneous response is primarily a right mode gesture. These gut sensations and *autobiographical*★ and relational memories have right hemisphere dominance.) So we go on walking. And depending on what I say, and what you share, the flow of energy that is *our* mental activity, not just "mine" or "yours," will give rise to peaks of representations within our integrated and shared experience that can help you or thwart you. We *resonate*★ with each other, mutually influencing each other's neural and mental realities as we connect with each other along our walk. Our togetherness will shape our mutual mental life and the pathway by which representations of your rejection will be transformed. The mind is not only embodied, but it is also truly relational. The whole of we is greater than the sum of our individual parts. We are embedded in each other and what arises is beyond two separate brains just interacting as isolated entities.

If I were your therapist, this experience could be therapeutically and intentionally used to create wider *windows of tolerance*★

for your ability to stay present, within awareness, with the feeling of rejection and even the feeling of hopelessness. These can become "just points on the rim" and instead of utilizing all sorts of *defensive* maneuvers to not be aware of those representations, you could simply rest in the hub of your mind, in the plane of possibility, and just let them unfold. In many ways, mental processes that are engaged to prevent us from simply "being with" whatever arises in awareness actually move us toward the chaos or rigidity that characterizes our own human suffering. When we pull away from pain, we actually make it worse. Moving toward a challenging feeling or situation helps us stay present. If integration is indeed the natural outcome of mental processing, then our job—within ourselves or in helping others—is to find a way to avoid the fearful or avoidant strategies we've employed in the past from being activated, again, in the present. *Tracking* where another person is in the moment, that is, *joining* with someone exactly where he or she is, helps to expand the window of tolerance and initiate the steps to bring *resolution* to painful nonintegrated processes in our lives.

And so you and I emerge from our imagined walk, here on the page, together. What were you thinking as we went down that stroll? What are those thoughts you had just now, really? Here is the wild idea: A thought is a realization of potentiality into actuality as energy shifts in probabilities across time. Let's review to be sure you and I are together on these fundamental issues. Energy is the "capacity to do stuff" and is measured in probabilities that range from certainty to infinite possibility. A mental process is the realization of a possibility into an actuality. A thought, as a mental activity, is the realization of a possibility into an actuality, in that moment. Mental processes arise from the plane of open possibility (this, as we've seen, is where—

unusual as this may seem—we are placing awareness) and can pass through the first layer of increased probability (implicit processes from plane to plateau in our model). These implicit processes are modes, moods, mental models, attitudes, and motivations. Our implicit plateaus of increased probability bias our peaks; they shape the nature of our second layer of explicit mental processes that are our active transformers of energy patterns and our "*instantiated*★ momentary certainties" of representations that span the range from plateau to peak. At the lower of these subpeak levels, we have our information processing activities of thinking, feeling, reasoning, and analyzing. When this fluid "thinking" rises further toward the peak of certainty, it coalesces as an instantiation of an actuality from the vast sea of possibility. We call this a representation and we experience this as a specific emotion, thought, image, memory, or perception.

You knew all of that already from our earlier discussion, so why did I explain it again? Inside of me, right now, I feel this vague sense of worry, a feeling of rejection, of being alone, misunderstood, isolated. Arising from these implicit processes is now a more specific pattern of explicit activity or a sequence of thoughts that feels something like the following. You won't like me anymore because after writing about the walk and considering what it would be like if you were in therapy with me as your therapist it will create a second motivation inside of you to reject me. The first motivation: All of this talk about probability patterns and movements away and toward the plane is just too much! Just make it simple and concrete, and stop being so abstract! Now, those specific thoughts feel like pebbles I can hold; they are representations that, now that I've shared them with you here, feel solid as a rock. They've crystallized with a certain stability, a certain solidity, that lasts just long enough for me to envision each thought as if it were truly stable and whole. I know what I am thinking, right now. I have a "certainty about what is in my mind" in this moment. I have a clear sense of the known within the knowing of awareness. But now the thoughts begin to fizzle, to shimmer a bit, coming in and out of my awareness. Images of being a high school kid, alone eating lunch, rise in my attentional spotlight. Probablity lowers, diversity increases, and the inner sense of what is going on becomes unstable, changing, unclear. Images of being in junior high school, hanging with the political kids who were for non-violent resolution to our international wars and who didn't fit in with the "cool crowd" or the "jock athletes," all fill my awareness. And inside (but where else would this be?) I feel a wash of sadness and a bit of hopelessness. Rising from this subpeak movement is a peak thought: I'll always be alone. Misunderstood. Rejected. And so I write this here, and rewrote the model there, in the hope beyond despair that I can connect with you, that you'll be resonating with me, that we will be together on this journey into the deep nature of mind.

And when I write this word "I," I feel energy flood into my awareness with a sense of vitality. But who am "I," really? And who in fact is actually asking? I look at the sun passing through the leaves of the trees outside my window, and a shiver passes through my arms and legs. I am this body; I am this connection to the trees. I feel alive, like there is hope, that perhaps all of this will be worthwhile, that we'll connect, that somehow this will all make sense. And I imagine that I am connected to you— that through this shared understanding we'll actually meet each other along this wild journey we call life.

Our mental experience rides along the waves of energy patterns that are shared between people and the planet and that pass through the mechanisms of the body. While we've seen the primes of neural and mental experience, where does this relational aspect of mental processing fit? Are relationships a prime? If we embrace the emergent property of complex systems as this self-organizing process that arises, in part, from energy flow patterns shared between people, then relationships are indeed a prime of mental experience. The sum is greater than the whole of its parts—and this emergent process of mind cannot be reduced to just one or the other by itself. Relationships contribute to this emergence as much as the embodied brain. And the sharing of energy and information flow of relationships gives rise to mental processes as much as these processes shape our relational sharing of this flow. Here, too, influences are mutual. On our imaginary walk, what you do and what I do are not happening in isolation. And how you feel and what I feel are not independent; instead they are co-constructed mental experiences. This is the *intersubjective* nature of our shared lives.

And what does it mean, then, to have shared awareness? Why is conscious experience so important, for example, in *psychotherapy*, family life, and *cultural evolution*? In our model, awareness somehow emerges from the open plane of possibility. And perhaps, as we've discussed, the rapid oscillation between the plane (awareness) and plateau/peak (mental process) is a way of describing the knowing (awareness) and the known (mental process). The shape of our personality over time and the architecture of our mind in the moment emerge from patterns of plateaus that bias which peaks will arise. Our plateaus and peaks are context-sensitive but are also shaped by our *temperament*★ and our experience. In this way, the plane (awareness) remains an open, receptive place along energy's continuum. Our sense of *self*★ is shaped by all of these paths from plane to plateau to peak. If we are not careful, we might confuse these patterns above the plane with the totality of who we are. When this happens, a person's identity becomes highly constricted, their mental activities can become repetitive, and life may lose its sense of adventure and freedom and vitality.

And so the application of these ideas of mental processes is that they are a fundamental part of our subjective lives but they have the risk of being misconstrued as restrictively defining who we are. If we get caught up in one implicit mode or another, left or right, we run the risk of seeing through an unintegrated lens of life, biasing our internal way of being and shaping how we connect with each other in families, schools, and communities. Finding a way to honor both the left and right modes, for example, is an intentional act of integration that can shape how culture unfolds. In relationships, we have the opportunity to embrace the fullness of our potentials in all modes of being. Without such an awakened stance, we run the risk of having educational and societal practices that may distance people from each other, creating an illusion of a totally separate self, a world full of "individuals and their individual minds" that do not support collaboration and connection. The mind is truly both embodied and relational, and we have the power in our relationships to support mental processes that are integrative and filled with vitality. This is the power of intention to create integration. Embracing this view of mental processes focuses our lens on how to increase the capacity to move into the plane of possibility, a common home we all share. And with this strengthening of the hub of our mind, awareness is strengthened and the freedom to change and to integrate our mental processes so that we can move flexibly from plane to plateau to peak and back again is cultivated. We are each unique in our plateaus and peaks; we find a common ground within the plane of possibility. What this means is that people can come to feel more at home with the openness that is the plane we all share and the place where we meet on our journeys through life. And as we move on this path together, we need to remind ourselves not only to care for one another and for those in need, but also to have fun, soak in the soaring of the birds, and be sure to take time to smell the roses!

MENTAL WELL-BEING AND
THE HEALTHY MIND PLATTER

CONCEPT: WHAT ARE THEY?

Within *interpersonal neurobiology*★, we see well-being emerging from the *process*★ of *integration*★ in which *differentiated*★ elements of a *system*★ are then *linked*★ to enable harmonious and adaptive functioning to unfold. **Mental well-being**★ involves a *healthy*★ *mind*★ that has a vibrant, engaged functioning of our *subjective experience*★, our *awareness*★, an array of *mental processes*★, and the core feature of the mind's *regulatory*★ functioning. This latter aspect of the mind is defined as an *embodied*★ and *relational*★ process that regulates the flow of *energy and information*★. As a *self-organizing*★, *emergent*★ process arising from both our *relationships*★ and our bodies, the mind can be seen as situated in these two important but differentiated aspects of our lives. In this way, a healthy mind depends on how we connect with others and our larger world as well as the *state*★ of our brain's functions within the larger interconnected body.

Identifying several key activities that promote integration in our *brain*★ and in our relationships, a colleague of mine (David Rock of the NeuroLeadership world) and I created a **healthy mind platter**★ as a visual reminder of what people could do each day to promote mental well-being. At the time, the United States Department of Agriculture (USDA) was releasing a new "food plate" as the suggested daily nutritional intake, so we released the mind platter as a parallel suggestion for how children, adolescents, and adults could approach the way they focused their *attention*★ and spent their time on a daily basis. Derived from science and placed in an easily remembered format (see Figure J), the healthy mind platter is now used in a range of educational programs to promote a daily intake of the essential "nutrients" to promote mental well-being.

The seven groupings or daily *mental activities*★ are each forms of "time" distributed around a platter. Here they are in brief:

1. Focus Time: Closely paying attention;
2. Play Time: Activities that are spontaneous, playful, and *creative*★;
3. Connecting Time: *Joining* with other people and with nature;
4. Physical Time: Moving the body, aerobically if possible;
5. *Time-In*★: Reflecting inwardly on sensations, images, feelings, and thoughts;
6. Down Time: The nongoal-directed focus of open attention; and
7. Sleep Time: Shhhhh . . . .

IMPLICATIONS: WHAT DO MENTAL WELL-BEING AND THE HEALTHY MIND PLATTER MEAN FOR OUR LIVES?

By taking a stance and defining at least a core aspect of the mind, we are in a position then to articulate the central role of integration in healthy mental functioning. This step enables us to see that systems have a natural push toward harmonious functioning. The system we are examining involves our bodies, our relationships, and the self-organizing process of mind that arises from them as energy and information flow is passed through the neural mechanisms of the body, shared in relationships, and regulated by the mind. We need to identify and then move away from processes that block the innate push to differentiate and link aspects of the system.

When such blockages occur, *chaos**, *rigidity**, or both, arise, the mind becomes dysregulated, and our bodies and relationships are not coordinated and balanced in their movement across time. Mental well-being is jeopardized and the system is no longer in a *FACES** movement that involves flexibility, adaptability, *coherence**, *energy**, and stability.

The healthy mind platter offers a reminder for a daily way to spend time and it is built from the science of health and identifies the regular ways we can focus attention to promote mental well-being. If individuals, families, schools, and communities were informed of this research-based set of daily mental nutrients, people could have the knowledge they need to at least *prime* their awareness that there is a practical strategy available to promote mental well-being. The next challenge, of course, is to see how these empirically supported suggestions can actually be applied regularly.

The healthy mind platter's seven "times" can be applied within a wide range of settings. In schools, the platter is useful as a wall hanging that enables a teacher to guide students through a range of activities—or reminders of ones (such as sleep)—on a routine basis. In clinical settings, the platter offers a form of prevention that outlines how to supplement direct engagement with the clinician with take-home reminders of the basic elements that support a healthy lifestyle for mental life. For parents, the platter serves as a guidepost for a child's day, reminding them how to structure a range of activities to "promote optimal brain matter." For organizational leaders, the platter offers them a way to connect with their staff around the mutually beneficial goal of reducing *stress★* and maintaining a healthy mental lifestyle. For *reflective practice★*, the healthy mind platter has embedded within it the research-proven finding that taking time-in as a form of *reflection★* inwardly is actually quite good for your mental, physical, and relational health! For the general population, having some practical guideline for promoting mental well-being is a welcome addition to the many competing stimuli that distract and overwhelm us in this modern age.

Here I'll make a few general comments about the application of each of these seven times outlined above.

1. Focus Time. When we focus on one thing at a time with interest and energy, we engage *circuits★* in the brain that enable neurochemical releases locally and globally to initiate *neuroplastic★* changes in the brain. Widespread acetylcholine release (likely from a region called the nucleus basalis during the close paying of attention) supports the activation of genes necessary to create the protein production and structural changes that underlie *memory★ encod-*

ing★ and learning. In addition, the localized activation of neuronal firing is associated with the release of brain-derived neurotrophic factor (BDNF), which supports gene activation and *synapse*★ formation among those *neurons*★ that are activated with attention. After they complete formal schooling, many individuals stop closely paying attention. This may be a risk factor for developing dementia, and engaging attention in a focused manner may actually be preventative and therefore good for our mental well-being! You don't have to take more tests after you are finished with school, but you do need to care about learning more and paying close attention!

2. Play Time. Being playful is rewarding and supports healthy neuroplastic growth. Part of this benefit may be from the sheer joy of spontaneously engaging in novel activities that capture attention and release chemicals that support brain growth. Playfulness is not the same as being engaged in formalized competitive sports that are rule-bound and filled with aggression. Instead, the emphasis is on new and creative forms of interacting with oneself, others, and the world. Imagination is given free reign, interactions are novel and spontaneous, and the outcomes are not predictable or constrained by goal-directed actions. Being playful is healthy because it frees us in our relationships to be able to collaborate without judgment. With playfulness our minds can become vulnerable and take risks as we push the envelope to go beyond our usual ways of being and of doing, and our brains can try out new combinations of firing patterns. These enriching states enable the mind's subjective inner life to have vitality and fun(!). They allow our awareness to explore new ways of knowing and exciting

and unpredictable things to be known. And such play time offers the regulatory aspect of the mind an opportunity to create higher degrees of integration with new levels of complexity to be achieved.

3. Connecting Time. Studies of health, longevity, happiness, and *wisdom*★ each point to one common major finding: positive relationships. When we connect with others, ideally in person if possible, we engage the fundamental social circuitry of the brain and create the relational reality of our "*self*★" as being defined not only by our synaptic firing patterns, but also by our social interconnectedness. Social connections shape the mind. When those connections are formed with a sense of *gratitude* and *generosity*, when we appreciate our relationships and bring *kindness*★ to them, we flourish. Kindness in many ways is how we honor and support one another's vulnerabilities. Another "g-word" is "*giving back*," offering to others something that helps to improve their lives. Studies repeatedly demonstrate that giving back to others (or what some prefer to call "gifting") actually promotes well-being in ourselves, and it improves life all around!

Another dimension of connecting time is how we relate to nature. Our "relational minds" are not just about our relationships with people, but they also include our relationship with the planet. When we take time to connect with nature, even in small ways throughout the day, we promote mental well-being. In an urban environment, we can take time to appreciate the clouds rolling by between walls of buildings. When we connect with kindess to the natural world around us, we place our mental lives in the larger *context*★ that we are not only part of a larger humanity, but we are a fundamental part of life on Earth. This overall approach of connecting time can be remembered as *"3g2p"*★ as we bring *g*enerosity, *g*ratitude, and an effort to *g*ive back in our connections with other *p*eople and the *p*lanet. Having this sense of belonging is essential for mental well-being.

4. Physical Time. Our bodies are more than just transport vehicles for our heads. Not only is *interoception*★ a crucial way for the awareness of interior signals from the body to inform our mental lives, but the active movement of the body itself is actually an activity that promotes healthy brain plasticity. If medically possible, physical time should include aerobic movement to optimize the neuroplastic benefits of this bodily motion. People in modern life are becoming too sedentary, reducing the benefits of long-term learning for students, and actually making adults medically vulnerable to illness. So getting up and moving is good for everyone! Some studies suggest that the positive benefits of aerobic exercise require that it be voluntary. And so the exciting challenge is how to creatively inspire—not force—people to get up and move. By placing physical time on the platter, our hope is that it becomes a natural part of daily life, like brushing your teeth or having a meal. We do these daily activities as a habit, and wouldn't it be fabulous to make daily exercise an automatic habit people choose to engage in?

5. Time-In. The external world is filled with compelling stimuli that capture our attention, sometimes in multitasking ways. The notion of time-in is inspired by the research findings that have demonstrated significant benefits when we take time to reflect inwardly, to focus attention on the array of internal mental activities such as sensations,

images, feelings, and thoughts, as we *SIFT** the internal world of the mind. Reflection on the internal world in a way that stabilizes attention and creates an open, *receptive state* has been shown in *mindful awareness** studies to promote a wide array of benefits, from improving immune function and gene regulation, to enhancing our capacity to regulate emotions and attention and to engage with others, and ourselves, with more *compassion** and kindness. It even creates a *left shift* in the brain that is associated with the ability to approach rather than withdraw from challenges. Time-in on a daily basis can support the continued growth of these roots of *resilience** and is an important part of a daily mental diet. Yoga, t'ai chi, walking *meditation*, and qigong are examples of mindfulness practices where the body is moving and may be especially appropriate for young people and others who may find sitting still somewhat challenging. But even for children and teens, it is rewarding to see that shorter times—5 to 10 minutes—of inward reflection are actually quite achievable. The *wheel of awareness** practice can be divided into shorter 5-minute segments than its 20-minute full application; awareness of the breath practice can be done at any interval, and even a few minutes a day would be a great way to start. Whether your body is moving or not, time-in is a workout for the brain, an essential training of the mind, and an activity that research has proven can strengthen *empathy** and our interpersonal relationships.

6. Down Time. As busy people in a busy world, we may find that there is always "something more to do" and an ever-present feeling of being overwhelmed. It is easy to feel compelled to always "do" rather than just "be." Down

time acknowledges the importance of time to just not do anything in particular, to just "chill out,"to relax, and to simply be. The benefits for the brain appear to be that we can "recharge" an always on-the-go neural system and, while we are awake, the brain can organize its *neural firings**, consolidate its learning, and enter a *default mode,* our resting state. The resting state's integrative functioning has been shown in research studies to be associated with well-being, so purposefully engaging some time to just "be" may allow these integrative circuits to recalibrate from all the doings that engage our attention all day long. Finding time to relax is essential to keep the mind healthy. And so in schools, at work, and at home, finding ways to have down time is an important part of our daily mental diet.

7. Sleep Time. Each of these "nutrients" on the platter supports the neuroplastic growth of the brain in ways that cultivate *neural integration**. Sleep time is the same: When we sleep, the brain literally integrates the learning from the day as it consolidates new experiences, old memories, and even random firing patterns into dreams and long-term learning. This is called memory *consolidation.* A lack of sufficient quality or duration of sleep can impair learning. This is a problem for sleep-deprived children and teens, and insufficient sleep challenges our ability to pay attention during the day. It also alters our sugar metabolism, making us prone to obesity. Sleep rests the body, enabling us to *repair** and recover from physical challenges of the prior day. For each of these reasons, sleep is good for us. Anyone who has been camping in nature knows that when the sun goes down, you start getting sleepy and you go to bed, and you then sleep far more than you usually do in an electri-

cally wired home. Add to this the digital distractions of life, and the sun going down loses all its *meaning**. But the sun comes up, and it's then time for school (or work) and away we go. Bleary-eyed, attention-challenged, memory consolidation-deficient, metabolically thrown off, we march on, day after day, without the sleep we need. Do I need to say more? Sleep time is crucial for mental well-being!

The healthy mind platter offers us a chance to work together to create the conditions for healthier minds. Naturally, there are many other important elements that influence mental health, such as nutrition (including the need for healthy sources of omega-3 fatty acids in the diet), socioeconomic conditions (and the importance of reducing poverty), and genetic and epigenetic factors (and their impact on the capacity to regulate stress). The suggested practices of the platter help the mind to intentionally focus attention to positively shape how the brain and our relationships function in more health-promoting ways. My hope is that with a universally acceptable and practical set of ways to focus our attention and spend our time, we can see how to apply these basic "times" to promote health and the integration from which it emerges. The great news is that integration creates a healthier physiology for our bodies. Integration promotes mental attributes of clarity, resilience, and happiness. And integration is at the heart of being kind to others and to ourselves. A key element in making these integration-promoting activities a reality in people's lives may be in making them part of the daily routine. Regular practice appears to be a crucial factor in research studies that show the positive impacts of learning new habits. How will *you* get your daily seven mental nutrients today?

38
38

UN-HEALTH AND DIS-EASE

CONCEPT: WHAT ARE THEY?

Interpersonal neurobiology★ views *health*★ as emerging within optimally *regulating*★ *systems*★ that are *integrated*★ as they coordinate and balance their many *differentiated*★ parts into a *linked*★ and functional whole. Health from this perspective is a systems *process*★, one that emerges, for example, as an individual is integrated both internally within the body *and* relationally within connections to other people and to the environment. We do not see individuals' health as separate from the health of the world around them. And the health—the integration—of an individual in turn can have integrative effects on the larger world.

In terms of the *mind*★ itself, the *triangle of well-being*★ reveals the perspective that health emerges as *energy and information flow*★ occurs through the *embodied*★ mechanism called the *brain*★ and through the sharing or exchange of what we call *relationships*★. While the mind has several aspects, including our core subjective personal experience, our various *mental activities*★ and the process of *awareness*★ (and its features of a sense of knowing and the known), there is also another feature. This is the aspect of the mind seen as an embodied and relational, *emergent**, *self-organizing** process that regulates the flow of energy and information. Regulation arises from the coordination and balance of that *flow**, enabling optimal functioning when the linkage of differentiated elements of the system occurs. For example, when an individual links the differentiated right and left *hemispheres**, the *domain of integration** called *bilateral** integration can be facilitated, and the optimal use of both *modes** of being and acting in the world is achieved. For a relationship, when two people honor each other's differences and promote a linkage via *compassionate**, respectful, *attuned communication**, then their integrative relationship thrives.

And so "health" is seen as an outcome of integration. This view is supported by important independent research findings that reveal how, whatever their cause (genes, toxins, chance, or experience), impairments to *neural integration** are associated with major impediments to mental well-being such as in the conditions of schizophrenia, autism, bipolar disorder, posttraumatic stress disorder, and the *developmental** *traumas** of *abuse** and *neglect**. These findings support the view that health and living with the adaptability and ease of well-being emerge from integration in our neural and relational lives. Likewise, "**un-health and dis-ease***" can be seen to arise from impediments to integration.

The *river of integration** is a visual metaphor that reveals the scientific perspective that as time moves forward, integrated systems flow in an optimal route that is flexible, adaptive, *coherent**, energized, and stable (see Figure K). This can be remembered with the acronym *FACES**. When integration is challenged, the system moves toward either bank of the river: *chaos** or *rigid-*

ity★. These are the two *states*★ that are out of integration. How is integration impaired? When a system cannot achieve differentiation and then linkage of its specialized components, the flow of that system is not integrated, elements are not coordinated and balanced, and the system's flow moves fully onto those banks of *chaos*★, *rigidity*★, or both.

Un-health and dis-ease are terms that refer to the state of a system—an individual or a set of interconnected individuals within a relationship, for example—that has a tendency to move toward chaos, rigidity, or both. So this does not get too cumbersome in the reading, let's just say that when a system is "integratively challenged" it is prone to rigidity or chaos (knowing that it can be one or the other, or both). Here is an exciting finding from systems science: There is a natural drive for *complex systems*★ to move toward integration, toward wholeness, toward health. A complex system is one that is open to influences from outside of itself and capable of chaotic behavior. Sounds familiar? So our lives, as complex systems, have a nautral inclination toward well-being. This view enables us to see each of our lives as potentially filled with health, but "stuff" gets in the way, and life can dish out any of a number of challenges to this natural inclination toward integration. Differentiation can be impaired, as in individuals with learning challenges or with difficulties with *social cognition*, such as autism. Or linkage can be difficult, as with those with bipolar disorder or with a history of trauma and neglect. Whatever the cause, impediments to differentiation or linkage result in impediments to integration. The result is a tendency toward chaos and rigidity. In formal psychiatric terms, these might be called mental disorders or diseases, but we can think of these as examples of un-health, dis-ease, and challenges to our natural drive toward integration and health.

IMPLICATIONS: WHAT DO UN-HEALTH AND DIS-EASE MEAN FOR OUR LIVES?

Much of the field of *mental health*★ is focused on addressing the disorders that plague people's lives. Shaped by the various categories of disorder, a clinician's compendium of work aims to alleviate symptoms and reduce the devastating effects of disorder. Yet little is done to actually focus on, or even define, mental health. I've asked over 100,000 mental health professionals around the world, face to face, if they'd ever been offered even one lecture defining the mind, and fewer than 5% say "yes." A similar statistic is true when this question focuses on mental health. What is going on in the field that this focus on disorder is so prevalent? Why isn't the field called "mental dysfunction?"

Here is one way to reconsider how the important work people do in the field of mental health can be reframed within the light of integration as being the core mechanism of health.

When one opens up the clinician's encyclopedia of psychiatric disorders, the *Diagnostic and Statistical Manual of Mental Disorders* (the *DSM*, published by the American Psychiatric Association in various modern versions over the last 30 years), one finds a fascinating pattern. Every symptom of every syndrome can be seen as an example of chaos, rigidity, or both. One important implication of this finding is that we can reframe the *DSM* as a work that is actually describing conditions with impediments to integration. As technology has developed, research is revealing that this proposal is backed up by empirical findings as mentioned above. Clinical conditions, such as the experientially induced developmental trauma of abuse and neglect, or schizophrenia, bipolar disorder, or autism, which are possibly caused by genetics or toxins, have impediments to the differentiation of localized regions or insufficient connections through integrative fibers of the brain.

And so I propose that the *DSM* may actually be a book that describes impediments to integration. The book itself never refers to integration, it does not refer to health and, by intention and design, it does not try to find connections among the broad array of conditions that it defines and describes. The *DSM* is a book of vocabulary and definitions, identifying clusters of syndromes and their symptoms that have been profoundly important in helping move the field of psychiatry and related clinical disciplines forward in our work. The *DSM* shapes much of a modern clinician's thinking in training and in practice, and it shapes how research projects are planned, executed, and interpreted. In many ways, this approach is a major force in shaping the ideas we have about disorder, about what we can think of as un-health and dis-ease.

The history of the *DSM* is illuminating for understanding the state of the art of the field of mental health and the implications for possibly reframing our field in *health* terms rather than with a focus on *disorder*. The developers of this influential text, some of whom were my teachers, wanted to make a set of descriptions of psychiatric disorders available to all clinicians so that we could have a common vocabulary when we spoke with one another. If someone in Tennessee was speaking with someone in Texas or in Turkey, and she used the term "depression," now, with the *DSM*, both people would know that they were referring to the same descriptive list of diagnostic criteria. This was and *is* a very important goal for how we speak with one another. To achieve this, the creators of the categories elected to have a nonconceptual foundation and instead to focus on observational findings, symptoms, and signs, which would be used to cluster individuals into professionally agreed-upon categories of disorder. This was a challenging and important task. Studies could then be further conducted, using these criteria, to understand the syndrome: its causes, manifestations, treatment, and outcome. This goal and its execution have been milestones in the advancement of the field of psychiatric care.

And now we are at a fascinating juncture in the field of the mind. The mental health field has no definition of the mind, let alone one for a healthy mind. The fields of psychiatry and psychology (two academic disciplines I love) do not have a definition of the mind. Even fields such as philosophy and branches of neuroscience do not have a definition of the mind. We also have a field of education that does not define the mind. And so without defining the mind, how can we define a healthy mind? And if we have not made an effort to define the mind and a healthy mind, how can clinicians help people strengthen and vitalize their minds? How can teachers help develop strong and healthy minds in schools?

This brings us to the implication of our discussion of unhealth and dis-ease. People are part of a larger world. The mind of a person is an emerging, *self-organizing** process that arises as energy and information passes through the embodied mechanism of the brain and as it is shared through patterns of communication within relationships. Yes, the mind is also a person's *subjective experience** and awareness, and it includes mental activities and *representations**, such as *emotions**, thoughts, *perceptions**, and memories. But by defining a core aspect of mind as regulatory we are then able to see how regulation can be strengthened. Regulation involves the monitoring and modifying of energy and information flow. When monitoring is challenged, the individual cannot see this flow (in body and in relationships) with clarity, depth, or detail. The result is potential impediments to well-being. Why? Because without seeing clearly, it is challenging to modify with strength and specificity . . . toward integration. Imagine driving a car with blindfolds on. That is what a mind without a stabilized monitoring capacity is like. You may not crash, but you are at risk of not regulating well and will be prone to an accident. And driving a car, moving the steering wheel, applying the accelerator and brakes when appropriate, enables you to modify the speed and direction of the car. The same is true for the mind: We modulate in a way that creates optimal levels of *arousal**, of being energized. Without enough *energy**, we are *hypoaroused* and not functioning optimally. Or we may *hyperaroused* when we have excess energy, or too much speed on the highway (see Figure N). Either condition is a form of dysfunctional arousal that can emerge without proper modulation.

And so a healthy mind is one that monitors energy and information flow with a stability, depth and clarity that enables it to then be able to modulate that flow with strength and specificity toward integration. Knowing this, we can actually offer specific practices to take a troubled mind, one at risk for un-health and dis-ease, and, with *intention** and practice, help cultivate a healthy and resilient mind. Whatever the cause of impaired integration, this approach enables us to take the important and empowering step to help people focus their *attention** to differentiate and link aspects of neural functioning and relational communication to strengthen their mental lives.

We can respectfully invite those in the field of mental health to consider these basic notions:

1. The lack of a framework of health is an understandable starting place we have had, but it now needs to be reconsidered. It is time to offer a working definition of mental health for the field of . . . mental health.

2. The lack of a framework connecting the various defined disorders to each other has left us with categories of dysfunction without an overarching foundation for understanding what dis-ease and un-health are fundamentally about.

3. Without a conceptualization of mental health, or of the mind, or of the role of the brain and relationships in shaping the developing mind over the life span, we are left without a way of approaching interventions that is comprehensive and health-focused.

4. We can in fact extend our conversation by offering a working definition of an aspect of mind as an embodied and relational process that regulates the flow of energy and information. And we can offer a working definition of health as integration.

5. When we envision emotion as shifts in integration, we can then see why "mental disorders" are often termed "emotional disorders." We can also see why "mental health" and "emotional health" are so often used interchangeably. Emotion is both a physiological and an interpersonal process, reflecting how the mind is both embodied and relational.

6. By defining the mind and mental health, we are in a new position to reframe our work in the fields of mental health, education, parenting, organizational leadership, and public policy. We can move our work in each of these areas toward a health model, we can create practices that promote well-

being and that do not just address symptom reduction, and we can support the growth of healthy minds, brains, and relationships as fundamental parts of our shared efforts.

7. Knowing that the mind can change relationships and the brain, we are empowered to use the focus of attention to promote integration in ways that can transform people's lives. This is a collective effort and one that links the best of neuroscience with the best of community. We can do this now, we can do this well, and we can do this together.

And so where do we go from here? Applying these ideas of interpersonal neurobiology out in the world is an exciting challenge. If we use each of the various efforts to help the mind develop, we may find these ideas about un-health and dis-ease galvanizing in different ways.

For parents, these take-home lessons about well-being empower you to find ways to promote integration in your family life. A first step to achieve this is to *make sense** of your own life. One of the most robust predictors of how your child will be attached to you is in the way you have come to sense and understand how your past childhood experiences have influenced your development as an adult. There are clear methodologies available to make sense of your past and using these can free you to become the parent you truly want to be. What happened to you as a child is not the key issue; rather, it is how you come to terms with what happened to you that matters most. You can also help your kids make sense of the events that happen in their lives. This is part of a larger science-informed strategy that helps you promote the integration of your children's mental lives as well as their brains and their relationships. When you promote integration, you help your child's mind develop with *resilience*★ and well-being. Nothing is a guarantee, but such integrative parenting prepares your child to have the integrative *circuitry*★ that is needed to live a full, *creative*★, and connected life.

For clinicians, this view of un-health and dis-ease changes how we can approach our clients, how we treat our patients, how we ourselves are present, fully, for the therapeutic relationship. As with parents, we should also start from "the inside out" as we make sense of our own lives and develop the *mindful*★ *presence*★ that effective therapy has been demonstrated to entail. I deeply believe, from my own practice as a clinician and as a mental health educator, and from reading the science, that mental health practitioners can change the field from the *bottom up*★. I've met too many senior clinicians and researchers who've privately said to me in essence, "I've spent my whole career not defining the mind or health, why should I change now?" that I am not so hopeful that change will come from a *top-down*★ manner, from the established teachers and leaders in the field. And if it ultimately does, that would be wonderful! But we don't have to wait. By reframing our field for how it is named— mental health, not mental disorder—we can claim our rightful place as integrationists working to bring together science and practical application. We can move beyond the important and essential first step of naming categories of disorder and expand our reach to include mental health and indeed what the mind is as fundamental steps in what we do with the field. We can allow each person to be seen as the unique, differentiated individual that he or she is and promote the integration in life that is his or her birthright. Health is a secular ethic that can be embraced by all. And when we see health as emerging from integration, here is the outcome: The external expression of integration is *kindness*★ and compassion. Having a health-as-integration focus enables us to sow the seeds of a kinder world.

For those who teach directly or do research in education, whether it is the earliest years, in kindergarten through twelfth grade, or college and graduate programs, we are in a crucial position to inspire youth to rewire their brains toward integrative health. Creative ways of using the *healthy mind platter*★ within the classroom can help structure daily activities that promote integration and well-being. When we realize that the mind, brain, and relationships are all interconnected, we come to see the power of our connections with one another to create integration. The relationship a teacher has with a student can be one of the most powerful inspirations she offers in order to guide a student's passions and direct his future choices. Recently I spoke with several professionals about what school experiences served as "turning points" in their life paths. Without exception, each person indicated a particular teacher and the relationship he or she had with that educator. When asked what it was that was so empowering, so life-transforming, the results were clear: The teacher saw the student for who he or she was. That way of being seen, of *feeling felt*, serves as a powerful way to become who we are and can inspire us for a lifetime. We are all *sentient* beings, individuals filled with an internal subjective reality unique to each of us. When others align with this internal sentience, we feel validated and seen. This is the power and possibility of the role of a teacher in students' lives.

For those in the field of *reflective practice*★, including the wide array of mindfulness approaches and social and emotional learning programs, teaching others to reflect upon the inner nature of the mind is a fundamental part of an *internal education*★ at the heart of well-being. Internal education promotes *mindsight*★

skills, the abilities to monitor the energy and information flow of the mind (within our bodies and within our relationships) with stability and then to modify that flow toward integration. Mindsight is the heart of *emotional and social intelligence*, and it is a *prefrontal*★ ability that is strengthened with reflective practice. In many ways, reflective practitioners are the teachers of our prefrontal functions. The *middle prefrontal functions*★ emerge with mindful practice; eight of nine of them have been found as outcomes of secure parent–child *attachment*★; and each is found in many *wisdom*★ traditions. For many mental health practitioners, this list of prefrontal functions is a "wish list" for the positive outcome of *psychotherapy*. We need to weave reflective internal skills throughout our educational and public settings in order to promote well-being.

For public policy and organizational leadership applications of these ideas about health and un–health, and ease and dis-ease, we can take the interpersonal neurobiology approach of *consilience*★, of finding the common findings across disciplines, and suggest that policymakers and leaders consider that their role might be also reframed as that of integrators. Rigorous scientific studies of our interconnectedness reveal that we have influences on one another that are often hidden. At the Center for Culture, Brain, and Development at UCLA, we find that societal practices shape synaptic connections. Public policy shapes the way a *culture evolves*. Imagine if those individuals involved in public policy formation and organizational leadership embraced the notion of integration as health and the ways in which our relationships with one another shape the brain toward an integrative state of compassion and kindness. Our communities and our companies would become centers of integration. What a world that might be! Science suggests it is possible to achieve;

the question is, are we ready to take the leadership role in facing that challenge and trying to create that change?

For each of us as citizens of our communities, our countries, our world, we have a wonderful challenge to bring integration into our lives. I say wonderful because it is literally a wonder-filled opportunity to connect with others, and ourselves, in a way that promotes creativity and compassion. As we cultivate the inner resources to *join* with others, we address the important need to heal un-health and dis-ease, to bring health and ease into the world. If we take on this challenge, what will result? Research suggests that when we *give back* to others in this way of trying to promote others' well-being, we are happier and healthier. Living a life with this kind of *generosity* of spirit, of open-heartedness, enables us to be *receptive* to others as well as to ourselves. In these complex lives we live, in this ever-more complex world, it can indeed be challenging to appreciate the small steps we can take. But living with *gratitude,* too, has been found to be conducive to our own well-being. And so the take-home question, the challenge we face, is can we live a life of generosity and gratitude, giving back to others and finding a way to promote integration in our individual and collective lives? This is the momentous question, a moment of opportunity, to reframe our lives toward promoting for each of us the health and the ease of well-being of an integrative individual and collective way of living.

MAKING SENSE OF TRAUMA
AND ITS RESOLUTION

CONCEPT: WHAT IS THIS?

The *mind*★ can be overwhelmed by experience such that it leads to temporary or long-term alterations in our *healthy*★ *relational*★ and neural functioning. When the negative impacts of a life-threatening or mind-disabling experience are long-lasting, when the psychological wounds of such an experience persist and do not heal well, we call this *unresolved*★ trauma. By **making sense of trauma and its resolution**★, we can directly address how to understand the impact of experience on the mind and how to bring care to those suffering from posttraumatic sequelae.

The capacity to adapt to our ongoing experience involves the response of our nervous and social *systems*★ to harness the *energy*★ and the *information*★ we need to respond to the immediate needs of a situation. At times those very mechanisms of adaptation, needed in the moment, can be sustained over long periods of time in ways that are no longer adaptive. For example, the secretion of *cortisol* in the short run in preparing to deal with *stress*★ is a necessary and useful response to mobilize physiological and neural energizing *processes*★ to cope with an acute stressor. However, if this corticosteroid remains elevated for prolonged periods of time, it can become no longer useful, even toxic to the *nervous system*★. For even longer periods following an unresolved trauma, *cortisol* levels may go from immediate rises and the subsequent prolonged elevation to a later depletion in cortisol and the inability to respond well to subsequent stressful events.

IMPLICATIONS: WHAT DO MAKING SENSE OF TRAUMA AND ITS RESOLUTION MEAN FOR OUR LIVES?

Determining the difference between having experienced intense negative events in contrast to an individual's lack of resolution of those experiences can be an important starting point in illuminating how to make sense of trauma. Whether the experiences were embedded in a one-time occurrence, a repeated set of events, or part of a *developmental*★ *context*★ of *attachment*★-related trauma such as *disorganized attachment*★, lack of resolution implies that the mind will have acquired lasting negative impacts on its functioning.

Studies suggest that for one-time events, the vast majority (more than 80%) of individuals will be able to cope with a stressful experience and in the long run not develop a posttraumatic disorder. Acute responses may include stress, *anxiety*, sleep disturbances, depression, and anger, but these can find a way toward resolution even without therapeutic interventions in many individuals. One way of understanding this perhaps surprising finding is that we have mechanisms of adaptation from millions of years of evolution that can deal with stress, "let it go," and move on to living a full and unencumbered life.

But for a significant minority of individuals, one-time over-whelming events may disrupt normal functioning in a persistent manner. An *interpersonal neurobiology*★ view of this finding is that the body's normal responses to stress are not released, prolong-ing acute reactions that then become chronically maintained stances of vigilance. *Implicit memory*★ may remain in its pure form, without integration by the hippocampus into a larger, explicit context. The *meaning*★-making process of the mind cannot fit the event into a larger *narrative*★ context. This may involve impediments to the prefrontal region's ability to "make sense" of how a past event *links*★ *coherently*★ with the present, thus also constraining the anticipated future. Individuals may feel frozen, confused, and locked in being passive historians, at best, rather than being the active and *creative*★ authors of their unfolding life stories. Interpersonally, the lack of co-construct-ing narratives within *relationships*★ that can provide both shared meaning making and ongoing social supports isolates the indi-vidual from fitting into a larger "we" that weaves the traumatic experience into a collective and healing life story. These are all examples of impaired *integration*★.

In developmental trauma, a young child growing within attachment relationships that may be the source of terror and isolation could have lasting impacts on how her coping mecha-nisms not only function in the moment, but how they grow in the long run. Studies suggest that, unfortunately, developmen-tal *abuse*★ and *neglect*★ can have negative impacts on the growth of those neural fibers that link widely separated areas to each other. Depending on the timing of the traumatic experiences, the particular fibers involved will vary: Those that are active in their development at the time are the most vulnerable to dis-ruption in their normal growth. These are the integrative fibers that coordinate and balance the nervous and social systems and are therefore *regulatory*★ circuits. These include the *prefrontal*★ area, the *hippocampus*★, and the *corpus callosum*.

In addition, studies have also revealed how the molecules regulating *gene expression* are altered in regions of the *brain*★ that are responsible for responding to stress. These *epigenetic*★ changes make the *hypothalamic-pituitary-adrenal (HPA) axis* unable to function as well in response to stressors, making the child even less adaptive to the usually ongoing dysfunctional relational world in which he or she continues to develop. Challenges to functioning well in school and with peer relationships will be manifestations of such developmental trauma. Studies of disor-ganized attachment also reveal that *dissociation*★ can develop as a response to repeated overwhelming events with *attachment fig-ures*★, *fragmenting the child's sense of self*, making relationships with others problematic, and disrupting the continuity of *conscious-ness*★ and adaptive *emotion regulation*★, especially in response to future challenging situations. This situation may make the use of *fight-flight-or-freeze* reactions as well as the more ancient *immobi-lization defense reactions* more likely to occur.

Less profound developmental impacts from less intense but still wounding experiences can exist and they can have persis-tent and important effects in a young child's life. Being repeat-edly told, for example, that "you are no good" or that "you'll never be happy" can have lasting negative sequelae on an indi-vidual's belief in himself. Even more subtle assaults on *attuned communication*★ over long periods of time can induce a *state*★ of *shame*★ that may have ongoing negative impacts on a child's sense of *self*★, behavior, and relationships with others through various developmental stages of life. These are sometimes called "small t" traumas in that they do not have the "big T" intensity of life threats that might activate the fight-flight-or-freeze response, or even the shut-down defenses of immobilization. Nevertheless, long-lasting negative impacts of overwhelming forms of interaction during the formative years of development can be seen as psychological wounds and considered as examples of unresolved trauma in need of intervention.

The process of integration helps us to see how interventions might be applied from the interpersonal neurobiology perspective in the resolution of trauma. One-time events, developmental trauma, or nonintegrated "small-t" trauma are examples of how an individual remains imprisoned by events in the past. A broad view of unresolved trauma can then be seen to involve a number of *domains of integration** depending on the timing and type of overwhelming experience. For example, dissociation is an illustration of impaired integration of consciousness. The internal disconnection individuals may have acquired as a means of adaptation may then remove them from readily accessing *autobiographical memory**, relational needs, and even the feelings of the body. Such an ongoing dissociative adaptation may be seen as an impairment to both *bilateral** and vertical integration.

The integration of *memory** links the *implicit** *encoding** of events together into their *explicit** forms. When *representations** of past events are available for experience within *awareness**, the prefrontal region can become involved in integrating these events into the larger past-present-future *mental time-travel* capacity of *self-knowing awareness*. This is the essence of narrative integration and how we come to *make sense** of our lives. We learn to use words to clarify confusion and make sense of madness. At the heart of these integrative interventions is the notion of "bring it on"—of reaching a state of fluidity in the *flow of energy and information*★ such that the system—neural and social—can embrace an ever-emerging free *flow*★ of whatever arises as time moves forward.

Meaning making in the brain can be seen to involve at least five facets of (a) associations, (b) beliefs, (c) *cognitions*, (d) developmental periods, and (e) emotional responses. While narrative word-based work is powerful and important, the *nonverbal*★ world of our shared communication and bodily experience is often an essential place to begin to make sense of our subjective lives. Interventions that work with bodily movement and sensation, focusing on the *kinesthetic* and the subjective feelings of the *sensorimotor* system, begin to get to the preverbal impacts of trauma on an individual's life. The *implicit knowing* that arises from overwhelming events can become the focus of work within awareness. Other *implicit mental processes*★, such as states of mind, mood, and motivation, can also be shaped by unresolved trauma and are an important focus of intervention. All of the associations, beliefs, and cognitions that arise can then be held within the spotlight of attention—even without words—such that this shared experience can enable memory *retrieval*★ to begin to become a form of memory modification. In other words, previously disabling representations of past events can be shared within therapeutic interventions and their disabling and constricting impact on the individual can begin to subside. Making sense harnesses all of our senses, from the input of the body to word-based thoughts, as we integrate meaning into our lives.

Developmental arrests in the form of impaired growth from the time of trauma onward can become the focus of skillful support within a *"zone of proximal development."* This is the term for the span of ability that bridges between what an individual can do without support (the bottom of the zone) to what she can do with support (the upper part of the zone). Working at this zone of proximal development allows the teacher, therapist, parent, and friend to provide the scaffolding needed for effective learning and growth.

Emotional responses can be seen through this lens as constrictions in the ability to stay integrated during the activation of representations from the memory of a past event. When *emotion*★ is seen as "shifts in integration," this dysfunctional emotional response makes sense: The individual loses integrative harmony at certain moments in which the context of an interaction is related to an unresolved trauma. Another way of viewing this pattern is that the person has a narrow *window of tolerance*★ for this particular trauma-related issue and bursts through this span of integrative functioning readily in unresolved conditions (see Figure M). Integrative interventions widen this window and allow the individual to learn new adaptive mechanisms to maintain healthy functioning in the face of whatever arises.

Whether the lack of resolution involves prolonged developmental assaults on security of attachment or difficulties handling one-time events, the notion of impaired integration helps us see how finding areas of *chaos*★ and *rigidity*★ in a person's life enables us to identify which domains of integration need to be the focus of intervention. The great news is that resolution is possible. We are just beginning to study how effective therapeutic relationships can produce the deep neural growth that may enable these impediments to integration to be reversed. Even if the early challenges to development cannot be directly undone, it may be quite realistic to expect that new *neuroplastic*★ growth in the integrative and regulatory areas of the brain may indeed be quite possible to achieve. We are even beginning to find in research studies how the focus of attention with *mindful awareness*★ can alter some of the epigenetic factors that regulate our genes' expression. Future studies will hopefully be able to demonstrate that theraputic interventions can even heal the possible epigenetic changes of trauma. And so finding ways to utilize these important applications that likely integrate our neural and social lives to help resolve trauma is a powerful and realistic direction for us to take in order to alleviate suffering for so many individuals.

40
40

THE MEANING OF
WELL-BEING

CONCEPT: WHAT IS IT?

What is *the meaning of well-being**? Concepts such as *health** and happiness come to mind, but what are these *states** truly about, and what do they really mean? Studies suggest that our health is a function of living with *energy** and vitality, of being fit and "in shape," of being adaptive and resilient. We can live to our fullest, fulfilling our potential, meeting challenges head-on, and finding purpose in our lives. When we are healthy, our bodies function well, our *relationships** thrive, and our *minds** are strong.

And happiness? A positive approach to psychology suggests that we can focus on our character strengths, finding ways to maximize these core capacities and live with a preponderance of positive emotions that "*broaden and build*" our inner strengths and our connections to others. Some might view happiness as being filled with the positive states of joy, elation, and *gratitude*. We could also look to studies of an experiential type of "flow" that suggest the use of this term for the moments of being immersed in an experience and letting go of self-consciousness and the subjective sense of a separation between oneself and an activity.

The Greeks had a term, *eudaemonia*, which addresses this fundamental question directly. In contrast to the hedonia perspective on what it means to be happy—with positive states of excitement, thrill, and energized joy and elation dominating one's life—a life of eudaemonia instead is filled with a sense of connection, purpose, and equanimity. Eudaemonic well-being is perhaps closest to how *interpersonal neurobiology*★ views *integration*★ as health. Integration involves the *linkage*★ of *differentiated*★ parts of a *system*★. When that system is the system in which we as humans grow and develop, where we live and emerge in our moment-to-moment lives, we can begin to see that the meaning of well-being has powerful implications for how to live our lives.

IMPLICATIONS: WHAT DOES THE MEANING OF WELL-BEING MEAN FOR OUR LIVES?

The "*meaning*★" of well-being in our lives draws on five fundamental aspects of the meaning of meaning: (a) associations, (b) beliefs, (c) *cognitions*, (d) *developmental*★ phases, and (e) emotions. When we look at the proposal that the underlying mechanism of health is integration, then these ABCDE's of well-being are illuminated. For example, the state of living with eudaemonia would enable the linkages (associations) that arise in our internal neural and interpersonal *relational*★ lives to cultivate differentiated states and then make associational linkages with others that create the harmony of integration in our lives. This is how we connect to each other and the world. This associational meaning also refers to the openness we have to receive anything that arises within the field of *awareness*★, to be open to whatever associations emerge as we move through life. This is a way of living that has "bring-it-on" as a theme: Whatever arises in my awareness is fair game and welcome in my conscious experience. As the poet Rumi suggests in his classic view of the mind as being like a guest house, we invite all states into our lives, realizing that even uncomfortable feelings and thoughts may be guests with special and illuminating gifts we cannot predict or control. Life is an unfolding *process*★ of continually taking on new associations and we are invited to live with that ease and openness of well-being.

The beliefs of an integrated life also embrace an openness to our potential to follow our dreams, to take on the challenges in life with humility and grace, to be grateful for what is, and to be ready to improve the lives we and others may find ourselves living. These are the beliefs of eudaemonia that give a sense of meaning—of finding purpose and value in what we do. These are the inner states of *intention*★ that bias our *perceptions*★ and our convictions in an optimistic yet realistic way, that move our behaviors toward a broaden-and-build stance of positive regard for ourselves and for others.

What are the cognitions of a life of well-being? *Cognition* is often used to signify how we think and how we reason and make decisions (the process that precedes—not much, at times—action). And integrative cognition is a way of differentiating *representations*★ of thought and then linking them in spontaneous and ever-emerging ways. In this view, we can see that the cognition of well-being gives birth to *creativity* and innovation, to giving freedom to the mind to imagine new ways of living, new ways of envisioning how the world could be beyond simply thinking about how the world is. This cognition of well-being invites us to transform the world of thought from a closed system of constrained considerations and analysis to an *open system* of possibility.

The developmental aspect of well-being means that the phases of growth through which we continually emerge are given a freedom of expansion as we traverse the journey of time in our lives. From the womb to the tomb, this path is filled with an array of potential blockages to integration. On the neural side of development, we can have toxins or other innate factors shut down the differentiation of our circuitry, ultimately limiting our capacity for *neural integration*★ as appears to be a possible situation in the emergence of autism with a diminishment in gamma waves in electrical and magnetic studies of the *brain*★ that reflect impairments to neural *synchrony*. The result is challenges in the capacity for *social cognition*, an intricate *information process*★ that depends on neural integration and enables an individual to become a part of a larger social network of connection and support. We may also have impediments to linkage that also impair integration: Individuals with bipolar disorder may have a genetic, inborn predisposition to have a diminished number of inhibitory fibers from the *prefrontal*★ region that link to, and coordinate and balance, the *subcortical*★ *amygdala*★. The result of this impairment to neural integration results in *dysregulation* and phases of dysfunction that challenge well-being. Experiential factors like *abuse*★ and *neglect*★ may inhibit the growth of the linking fibers of the brain (the *corpus callosum, hippocampus*★, and prefrontal regions) and also limit integration. Whatever the genetic vulnerabilities, toxic exposures, or experiential events in our lives, factors that inhibit integration also challenge well-being.

The emotional meaning of well-being brings us to the suggestion that *emotion*★ is a shift in integration. When this shifting is in the downward direction, we see a diminishment in differentiation, linkage, or both. The system has a tendency to become *chaotic*★ or *rigid*★ in its *flow*★, away from the central harmony of the flow of the *river of integration*★ (see Figure K). These states are what might be called the distressing emotions, the uncomfortable states of prolonged anger, sadness, or fear. Jealousy, *shame*★, and humiliation would also be the social and emotional sides of downward shifts in integration. We do not honor others and others do not honor and link to us. Our connection to the body—its sensations and movement—can also be downshifted as we feel disconnected and out of touch with our somatic selves. In contrast, well-being is associated with states of upward shifts in integration. Differentiation is enhanced and linkage cultivated in our *embodied*★ and our relational lives. Positive emotional states "broaden and build" our internal and interpersonal worlds. This brings us to the *triangle of well-being*★, which enables us to see how integration in the body and in our connections to others is the fundamental mechanism that creates a healthy mind.

Living a life of mental well-being is filled with the fluidity of integration: We are able to take on whatever arises with *resilience*★ and clarity. We welcome guests into the guesthouse of our ever-evolving life, embracing uncomfortable states and returning to baseline as they move in and out of our experiences. This is the basis of equanimity—of having the courage to be present with whatever is uncomfortable or comfortable—and coming to find an inner place of clarity and peace not in spite of life's challenges, but because of them.

Living a eudaemonic life of connection, purpose, and equanimity is not something that necessarily happens automatically. Research suggests what *wisdom*★ traditions have long proposed: We can, in fact, build happiness into our lives. Unlike a view that you are fated to have a certain limited degree of how "happy" you can be, the empowering view of being able to enhance well-being and happiness is bolstered by the science of *neuroplasticity*★, which reveals how experience can change the structure of the brain itself. Experience—what we do and how we are—includes how we focus our *attention*★. Attention drives the direction of *energy and information flow*★ through the embodied *nervous system*★ we call brain and through our connections with one another and our environment that we call *relationships*★.

How we focus attention shapes everything. When we shape our energy and information flow toward integration, the quality of our lives is enhanced. Relationships are a good example. Studies of happiness, health, longevity, and wisdom reveal that our relationships are the common factor underlying each of these positive aspects of a life of well-being. What do relationships do when they are respectful and *compassionate*★? Healthy relationships support a differentiated way we can be and then promote a linkage of ourselves to others and our planet. We can call this "*3g2p*"★ in that we bring gratitude for what we have in life, *generosity* of spirit that is the heart of *kindness*★ to ourselves and others, and an internal stance and external behavior focused on giving back to help improve the lives of other people and our planet.

This finding of 3g2p at the heart of health and well-being illuminates not only the centrality of integration, but also the promotion of a eudaemonic life. Living a life of connection emerges from generosity, gratitude, and *giving back*, or what some simply call "gifting" to others. This stance enables us to see how we move from "*me to we**" and live as more than "just me" to realizing deeply that "I am connected to you" and ultimately that "I am a part of we." Integration is not the same as fusion: Embracing the reality of we does not need to involve losing me.

One example of a prevalent misconception is that if "I am me" in this body, in this time called life, I had better get as many toys as possible, win as many points as possible, and accumulate as much stuff as possible before I die. These are the tangible signs of material acquisition that in modern times are sadly mistaken for the signs of accomplishment on the road to happiness. You have succeeded, this stance believes, if you have more stuff.

Yet we don't often see a hearse followed by a moving van. If you walk through a cemetery, the tombstones generally don't say, "Joe got a lot of stuff while he was here." Instead, they invariably say something about the relationships people had while they were alive and what those connections will mean to those who remain.

And these interpersonal connections are one side of the connection dimension of a eudaemonic life. We also have connections within our somatic selves—connections to these bodies that are our corporeal home for the century or so that we are given to walk this earth and breathe this air. Enjoying the body, keeping the body fit, and loving the energy of the body's vitality are all fundamental to our inner connections.

And on the mental side of our triangle (yes, we are exploring the connections of relationships, the *embodied brain*, and now our mind), we can experience the wide-open possibilities of our *subjective experience**. The *plane of possibility** model of the mind and brain suggests that we have a range of patterns of degrees of probability that the energy flow of mind rides

upon. This range moves from the certainty of particular *peaks**
and the probability of *plateaus** to the open plane of possibility.
And so we can propose that a life of well-being involves the
innate or learned capacity to freely move from plane to plateau to peak and back again to plane. This is the flexibility at
the heart of equanimity: We can freely take on whatever challenges that arise—internal or external—and embrace these as
the guests of the home of our mind. Achieving this emotional
equilibrium (read: integrative stability and balance) is natural
for some, but for most of us it can be learned and strengthened
with *reflective practice**.

And so in addition to building the quality of our relationships with people and the planet with the 3g's and keeping our
connections to our body filled with fitness and enjoyment, our
connected life can be enhanced by training the mind. How
do we do this? Simply put, we need to build our capacity for
integration by utilizing the focus of the mind's attention. This
mind-fitness program begins with the fundamental experience
of awareness—the integration of *consciousness**—at the heart of
every journey of transformation.

How do we integrate consciousness? Integration is the differentiation of elements of a system and then their systematic (no
pun intended) linkage. The *wheel of awareness** practice offers a
direct approach to differentiating the elements of consciousness from one another and then, step by step, linking them to
each other. First we differentiate the different elements of the
rim: external sensations (sight, hearing, olfaction, taste, touch),
interoception (the internal signals of the body from muscles,
bones, and viscera such as heart, lungs, and intestines), *mental activities** (emotions, thoughts, images, memories, attitudes,
beliefs, intentions), and our relationships (the sense of connec-

tion we can cultivate with other people and the planet). As we do this, we then experience the differentiation of the *hub* from the rim, as we distinguish the experience of the knowing within awareness (hub) from that which is known (rim).

It has been fascinating to receive the responses of the subjective sense of liberation that people feel when they experience this wheel practice and become more aware of awareness itself. One way of understanding this repeated response to the practice is through the lens of the plane of possibility: The hub (awareness) is the plane (of open possibility). The rim (that which we are aware of) is composed of the plateaus of increased probability (perhaps the inner-rim dimensions of the *implicit mental processes** of intentions, beliefs, attitudes, *modes**, and mood) and of the peaks of certainty (the outer-rim aspects of particular thoughts, images, feelings, or memories).

When we embrace fully the proposal that the mind is composed of at least three aspects—subjective experience, consciousness (the knowing and the known of *mental processes**), and a core *self-organizing** process that *regulates** energy and information flow—we come to a direct focus on what *mental health** means. Energy in scientific terms is the "capacity to do stuff," a set of unfolding potentials, an aspect of reality that, according to physics, moves from possibility to certainty. We measure energy flow as changes in these potentialities, as patterns of probability that move along this continuum, as probability distributions. And so if one aspect of the mind is indeed an embodied and relational process that regulates the flow of energy and information, we can take the natural step of seeing this self-organizing process as directly shaping these *probability patterns** across time. If life is stuck in repeated peaks, imprisoned by the limitations of fixed plateaus, then this is an inflexible life. The person is experiencing the *rigidity*★ bank outside the river of integration. If a life is filled with extremely broad peaks, with an activation of a wide array of thoughts and feelings and memories all at once, we are describing the profile of *chaos*★ within this perspective. Again, this is a nonintegrated state: a chaotic intrusion shutting off mental well-being.

A practice of training the mind to move probability patterns in a flexible and fluid manner, from plane to plateau to peak and back to plane, is the essence of equanimity. The wheel practice is an integrative training of the mind and is built from the interpersonal neurobiology view of integration as the heart of health. Other mind-training practices that promote integration are helpful applications as well and involve our taking *time-in*★ to reflect on the inner nature of the mental lives of ourselves and of others. Some time-in approaches would include the fundamental strategies of *mindful awareness practices*, such as breath awareness, which focus *attention on intention* and *awareness on awareness*. A daily time-in practice seems to be a powerful component of creating a healthy mind. Other aspects of shaping the mind toward health are included in a *healthy mind platter*★ that highlights seven essential "daily mental nutrients" that people of all ages can embrace.

Physical time reminds us that exercising the body, aerobically if medically possible, is helpful in promoting neural plasticity. Sleep time allows the brain to *consolidate* its learning from the day. Connecting with people and the planet (with the 3g2p approach) enhances our relationships. Focus time is when we have the close paying of attention that promotes neuroplasticity by altering the chemical milieu in the brain that enhances its capacity to grow and learn. Down time is the way we simply unwind and recharge the brain, and play time is time to be playful, to be spontaneously engaged in moment-to-moment experience in new and *creative** ways. And time-in, taking time to reflect inwardly on our sensations, images, feelings, and thoughts—to *SIFT** the mind—helps to promote the stimulation and growth of the integrative fibers of the brain.

Embracing the notion of the mind as being both embodied and relational permits us to see directly how mental well-being arises from our relational connections and the synaptic connections in our bodies. In these ways, mental well-being can be enhanced by training the mind with these practical strategies to increase the integrative nature of our connections both to others and the world and those connections within ourselves.

These connections give life a sense of meaning and purpose. The "meaning of well-being" involves each and every one of these meanings of meaning. When we move to an inner place of clarity in the plane of possibility, these internal connections of the ABCDE's of meaning in the brain create a life of emotional purpose. This emotional meaning signifies leading a life that moves toward ever-expanding senses of connection and ever-increasing levels of integration. It never stops; we are never done. This is the joy of an ever-*emerging** sense of being alive, of being connected within ourselves and with other people and the planet. Internally, integration means creating *COHERENCE**—being connected, open, harmonious, emergent (things arising fresh and new), *receptive*, engaged, noetic (a sense of deep knowing), compassionate, and *empathic**. Externally, integration means creating more connections of meaning with the world of nature and other individuals. We come to feel not only connected, but also deeply embedded as a part of a "we." This is how a life of well-being is truly embodied and embedded in our integrative journey through this extraordinary adventure we call life.

41
41

DOMAINS OF INTEGRATION

CONCEPT: WHAT ARE THEY?

Defining *mental health*★ as emerging from *integration*★ enables us to explore many aspects of life in which this *linkage*★ of *differentiated*★ elements can be promoted. Several **domains of integration**★ can be outlined that deal with different aspects of our lives and can be the focus of education, parenting, clinical intervention, organizational consultation, and personal growth. Naturally, any aspect of our lives in which elements can be differentiated and then linked could be defined as a "domain" and become the focus of our efforts to promote integration. And any aspect of our lives in which *chaos*★ and *rigidity*★ are interfering with adaptive, *healthy*★ functioning would reveal the "domain" that is in need of integrative intervention. And so we could have dozens of domains, or hundreds, depending on how we divide up reality and our lives. We could also take the alternative route, and simply have all of life be like one domain, and just see each instance as an opportunity to dive deeply into the world of integration. Whichever way you would choose to divide up the world of experience, the concept of domains in our lives that are in need of integration provides a framework for clinicians, educators, parents, consultants, and everyday citizens to focus their *attention*★ in ways that promote health.

Here, we'll divide the pie of human experience into nine domains. These areas of integration appear to be broad enough to be comprehensive, few enough to be readily remembered, and specific enough to be practical in their application in our lives. The essential idea is that chaos and rigidity alert you to an area of life—your *mind*★, your *brain*★, your *relationships*★—and let you know that this aspect of your living is not integrated. What this means is that differentiation may be blocked and aspects of this part of life are not specialized, not developed well. In addition, linkage between these differentiated aspects of this domain may be impaired, also resulting in impediments to integration. Once this assessment of the domain in need of attention is made, it then becomes possible to focus on promoting the missing differentiation and linkage to cultivate integration. This approach becomes a readily accessible way to assess a situation, strategically plan an intervention, and then implement the integrative work to bring health into one's own or others' lives.

IMPLICATIONS: WHAT DO THE DOMAINS OF INTEGRATION MEAN IN OUR LIVES?

When life becomes filled with chaos or rigidity, you know that integration is impaired. If your experience within a relationship, for example, is dominated by explosive anger or frustration, you can be sure that some aspect of differentiation between you and your partner is blocked, or some way in which the two of you are linked is not occurring. Without differentiation and then the linkage of those unique identities of the two of you, integration is not present and the flexibility and vitality of the relationship is compromised. Likewise, impaired integration can result in a deadened quality in the relationship, a boredom, inflexibility, or a loss of vitality. Whether it is in chaos or rigidity, the *system** of two people in a relationship moves to these banks outside the *river of integration** (see Figure K). What would we call this area of your life? We might suggest that this is a domain of interpersonal integration. Work would then be needed to promote differentiation, to honor differences, and even to take pleasure and pride in them. Then, the linkage of differentiated aspects of this domain—of two people in a relationship in this case—would take the form of *compassionate**, caring communication, with curiosity and concern, connecting the two of you together. This is the creation of interpersonal integration.

There are many areas of integration, but each of them has the following common feature. A certain aspect of life is capable of becoming chaotic or rigid. That "domain" can then be the focus of attentive change, fostering a diminishment in chaos and rigidity, and the *instantiation** of *states** of well-being that come with integration. The outcome of focusing integrative work on a given domain is a flexible, adaptive, *coherent**, energized, and stable (*FACES**) shift in the functioning of that area of life.

At least nine domains of integration can be identified and become the focus of a practical approach to promoting well-being at home, in school, in organizations, and in our communities (see Figure L). Here we'll briefly review each of these nine domains and highlight practical aspects of their applications in everyday life. You may find that these categories can collapse into fewer ones or expand into more. For many, these nine have served as useful and comprehensive ways to embrace the whole of integration and apply it in everyday living.

The integration of consciousness

Consciousness* involves the experience of knowing and the awareness* of the known. For example, we can become aware of a feeling in the foot. We "know" that our foot is resting on the floor. We feel the pressure of the sole of the foot on the wood panels beneath the foot, and we have the experience of being conscious (knowing) and sensing the input from the foot (the known). In parenting, education, and clinical work, being conscious of something, being aware, is a universally found mental experience that is necessary for learning and healthy *development* in many arenas in life. Choice emerges from consciousness.

When integration of consciousness is not present, individuals may be prone to identify thoughts and feelings as the whole of who they are. A feeling arises, and this *emotional*★ state becomes who the person is. Rather than "having a feeling," the individual becomes swept up by the feeling and lost in the power of its persuasion. Sometimes this *flow*★ is a useful way of getting lost in an activity, of *joining* fully, without reservation and perspective, and becoming interwoven with an action. This flow can be fabulous. But ideally we can choose flow, rather than it choosing us at an inappropriate time. So if the timing is right (reading a book, making love, losing oneself in a walk in the woods), being in the flow of an experience can be a highlight of life. If we become lost in the experience of anger, however, we can lose ourselves in the emotion without the discernment that this emotional state is just a temporary feeling, not the totality of who we are. Here the flow of anger has chosen us, and everyone loses. While *mindful awareness*★ permits flow to be a choice in our lives at appropriate times, being mindfully aware is not synonymous with flow. Likewise, the integration of consciousness permits us to be aware of these choices and to be clear about feelings and thoughts that arise as not being the totality of who we are. Integration of consciousness creates the fuller sense of identity and permits freedom to choose our immersions in the course of life.

The integration of consciousness involves differentiating at least two aspects of being aware from one another. One is to differentiate the various elements that can be known from each other: our first five senses, the sixth sense of the body, the seventh sense of *mental activities** such as thoughts and feelings and memories, and our eighth *relational sense** of our interconnectedness with others. We can also distinguish the experience of knowing (awareness itself) from the known (all of these *mental processes**—from sensation to *perception**, feeling to thinking). One way of effectively catalyzing the integration of consciousness is the *wheel of awareness** practice, which offers a direct exercise in differentiating each of these elements from one another and then linking them. The outcome for many who practice the wheel immersion is a significant change in their inner sense of equilibrium and their interpersonal sense of connection.

Other *mindful awareness practices** may also provide integration of consciousness changes because these exercises catalyze *awareness of awareness* and *attention to intention*. These practices strengthen the *prefrontal** fibers and their integrative functions in the body as a whole. Through a *process** of *internal attunement**, the observing *self** attunes to, or focuses attention in an open and *receptive* manner on, the experiencing self. This internal attunement creates and amplifies states of *neural integration** in the individual. Integration of consciousness is a useful starting place for anyone to begin the journey to strengthen the mind.

Bilateral integration

When the two sides of the *hemispheres** work well together, there is no need to intentionally try to promote *bilateral** integration—it is often already fully in place! This view is consistent with a modern neuroscience perspective that our two asymmetric sides of the *nervous system** usually coordinate and balance their functions. But given the anatomic separation and unique dominance of these "*modes**" of processing on either side of the brain, sometimes one side or the other can dominate in a person's ever-changing life. When our external environment, for example, pulls us to be analytic in our reasoning, cool in our calculating, certain in our opinions, there may be a preference to draw on what are called "*left mode*" processes that have the L's of being later to develop, linear in their sequencing, logical in their search for cause-effect relationships, linguistic in their preference for expression, and literal (as well as loving lists!). In contrast, the *right mode* is preferentially early in its development, holistic in its processing, visuospatial in its *representational** dominance, *nonverbal** in its expression, and filled with raw input from the *subcortical** limbic**, *brainstem**,* and bodily signals. In addition, the right mode is a key player in autobiographical data, has a map of the whole body, and is responsible for *stress** regulation**. Naturally, the two working together as a functional whole is the best way to go . . . unless it is better that you not feel what your body is telling you or that you should not understand logically what is happening around you. These are some of the many reasons why it may be adaptive, at least temporarily, for one mode or the other to retreat in activity and the other to dominate in awareness.

Bilateral integration utilizes both the left and right modes of processing as the two sides of the brain work collaboratively with each other. This form of integration also reveals how one mode may become dominant to the exclusion of the other in the experiences of everyday life. In other words, it is natural to have some times when one or the other mode is activated—this is simply how specialized functions operate. But when one mode is shutting down another (as in "I need to be certain and I can't stand living with ambiguity"), or another mode simply cannot stay within a *window of tolerance** for some feeling or *memory** ("I cannot be in touch with these memories; they are too painful!"), then bilateral integration may need to be a focus of intervention. The way this feels is that a person seems constricted in left mode dominance and is prone to outbursts and *dysregulation** of the chaotic sort in right mode dominance. The whole of this ebbs and flows, so these are not absolutes of behavior, but rather tendencies, sometimes present at certain moments and with the presence of certain people. The mind emerges in *context**! The wonderful aspect of this approach is that it is not a pathology or deficit perspective. Coming from the foundation of health and *resilience** as outcomes of integration, we simply look for the impediments to differentiation and linkage that are creating chaos and rigidity and then, like a laser beam, go directly to where this impediment is blocking the natural drive for the individual or family to be whole. This is an empowering approach that teaches while it integrates.

Vertical integration

Generally, our *cortex** enables a coordination and balance of a wide array of neural inputs from throughout itself and with the subcortical areas below it. This linkage of differentiated regions appears to be a neural correlate of the experience of consciousness. When we become aware of input from the body, the brainstem, and the limbic areas, we combine these subcortical signals with the vertically higher cortical regions to have this form of reflective awareness. This is vertical integration. Why would anyone not have such important access to the *wisdom*★ of the body, to the regulation and protection of the survival reflexes of the brainstem, and to the evaluative, emotional, and attachment-focused limbic processing? One reason is *attachment*★ history. If the relationships you may have had were not *attuned*★, the signals from your body may have never been seen by others, and, in fact, you may have felt overwhelmed by the unfulfilled needs emanating from the subcortical regions. Being aware of these signals, in this situation, would have put you beyond the boundaries of the window of tolerance. So to maintain functioning, impairing cortical access to subcortical signals can be a very important adaptation. In adulthood, however, such a disconnection can make people not be able to respond when others ask, "How do you feel?" Our nonverbal, nonrational, body-based subcortical signals form a crucial foundation for knowing what has *meaning*★ in our lives. Impairments to vertical integration often shut down the sense of vitality in life.

Promoting vertical integration involves cultivating awareness of the lower input from the body, brainstem, and limbic areas. This means exploring the way the muscles and bones feel as well as coming to sense the input from the hollow organs (the viscera) such as the intestines, the lungs, and the heart. Brainstem input is explored in the *no-yes procedure*, which activates our *survival reflexes*★ of *fight-flight-or-freeze* reactions. And limbic input involves our reactions of fear, feelings of distress at separation from loved ones, and longings for connection. Helping a person stay within the window of tolerance for holding these signals in the *space of mind* within awareness is the key to initiating vertical integration. With time and practice, a state of being barely tolerant of subcortical signals can transform into treasuring them for the wisdom that they bring about how we actually are feeling in the moment.

Memory integration

The natural flow of memory involves the integration of initial inputs of the various layers of *implicit memory** with each other to form the factual and autobiographical aspects of *explicit memory**. Implicit memory processes include perception, motor action, emotion, and bodily sensation. *Mental models*, or schema, are also a part of implicit processing, as is *priming*, or the readying of oneself for an experience. When memory integration occurs, the *hippocampus**, part of the limbic region, acts as a master puzzle-piece assembler to arrange the implicit pieces into coherent pictures of lived experience (oneself in an episode in time, called *episodic* or *autobiographical memory**) and facts about the world (called *semantic* knowledge). When integration is impaired, free-floating (nonintegrated), implicit puzzle pieces are not assembled into coherent factual and autobiographical *information**. Instead, an "implicit-only" memory, when *retrieved**, enters awareness without the sense that something is being recalled from the past. This lack of an *ecphoric sensation* makes the individual prone to naturally experience the retrieval of pure implicit memory as if it were emotion, bodily sensation, perceptual images, and behavioral impulses being generated anew in the here and now. In many ways, this blockage of the hippocampal process can explain much of posttraumatic stress and the nature of *flashbacks*.

Memory integration involves focusing a spotlight of attention on elements of implicit memory that have not yet been integrated. Attention engages the hippocampus, and this involvement can enable previously disconnected *representations** to become part of an integrated whole. Now this integrated memory is called "explicit" and, when retrieved, it has an ecphoric sensation—it feels like something is being recalled from a past experience. This is how we know that a factual or an autobiographical memory is coming from a past event and is not something happening as a new experience in the moment. As memory retrieval can modify the synaptic linkages among memory representations, this act of focusing attention on previously unassembled memory fragments can be seen as the transformative process that underlies memory integration.

Narrative integration

We are a story-telling species, and creating *narratives** with one another about what has happened to us in the past is a way we both interpersonally connect, and it is the way we *make sense** of our lives. We build upon lived experience that is *encoded** in implicit and in explicit memory, and then we shape a new process, one of having a narrator function that articulates what is happening and to whom it is happening. This narrator is an observing function of a "self," one that narrates its own unfolding. In this manner, narrative integration is how the capacity to observe the self over time permits us to make sense of our lives as we link the past, the present, and the anticipated future. This *mental time travel* permits us to transcend our present worries and plan for the future based on what we've learned from the past.

When narrative integration is impaired, a person has difficulty making sense of his life or the lives of others. There may be many reasons contributing to this difficulty, including *traumatic*★ experiences, overwhelming and dysregulated emotions making autobiographical *reflection*★ challenging, and other neurological origins such as a lack of neural capacity to *mentalize*★ and make *mindsight maps*★ of the self or of others. One way of describing a story is that it is the linear telling of a sequence of events. This telling involves the actions and the mental life of the individuals in the story. In many ways, a story addresses a conflict in need of resolution, a violation of expectations in need of explanation, or an experience that does not fit well with a set of beliefs about the self or others. Narrative integration likely involves our sense-making left hemispheric mode along with our right hemispheric specialization in bodily sensations, autobiographical memory, and mentalizing functions. When the left mode's drive to tell a story combines with the goods of the right mode, this bilateral collaboration likely involves an *interhemispheric resonance* that links these two sides to one another and contributes to the making-sense process at the heart of narrative integration and the creation of a coherent lifestory.

State integration

We all have states of mind that shape the inner architecture of our lives in many ways. Some of these states are transient, like when a particular *mood*★ or feeling washes over us briefly. Other states are more persistent, as in when we have learned a particular way of being, such as playing tennis or being serious at work. State integration involves honoring the differences across states in a form of inter-state integration. This is the way, for example, that we honor the need for solitude and the need for being social. We cannot meet those two states' needs at the same time;

we integrate them by honoring differences and promoting linkages via collaboration that enables each state to have its needs met across time. This integration may occur across a day, a week, or a month, but the idea is the same: We find a way to honor the multiplicity of our selves.

Intrastate integration involves enabling a given state to work well within itself. If I enjoy dancing but have not given myself permission to develop or maintain that skill, I may find that the passion for movement and music takes a backseat to more serious pursuits. I need to honor these feelings, allowing that part of myself to grow, develop, and continue to learn. This is how I differentiate a love of dance and nurture its internal *cohesion*★ in my life. The dancing state of mind can be honored and allowed to flourish. Many of us have aspects of our lives—of being playful, of being *creative*★, artistic, and spontaneous—that after childhood may have gone by the wayside. State integration reminds us of the importance of honoring each of these states and finding the ones that we treasure and nurturing their growth and *presence*★ in our lives. When we are fulfilled in this way, we fill ourselves with the vitality of integration.

Interpersonal integration

One state that is sometimes a challenge to create is that of a "we-state" of mind. Being a "we" entails integration in that we maintain our differentiated self while also resonating with another person. Integration is not about becoming homogeneous; it is about retaining the unique aspects of our many dimensions. Interpersonal integration enables us to focus on how we can become a part of we yet not lose our essence as me. Some challenges to this *relational*★ form of integration can stem from an attachment history where, as a young child, our unique essence was not honored and instead may have been ignored or intruded upon. If ignored, we may have had an *avoidant attachment*** and developing a premature autonomy likely enabled us to survive. "I can do this by myself" is a stance helpful in that situation early in life, but it can be impairing to a sense of belonging in the future as the child grows into a teen and then an adult. In contrast, if others were intrusive and pushed their own internal states onto my own, if I had an *ambivalent/resistant attachment***, I may get lost in not knowing who I am versus who you are. My boundaries are porous and I might not have yet found a way to be both myself and be connected in the setting of an anxious sense of self. Either of these forms of insecure attachment can lead to challenges to interpersonal integration.

The steps of making sense of one's early life history, as can be facilitated by way of the *Adult Attachment Interview,*** can help a person develop *earned secure attachment* and learn to become a healthy part of we. The key to this development, at any stage of life, is to move from either of the extremes of avoidance (with a shutting down of the need for attachment connections) or of ambivalence (with the escalation of the need for attachment). This movement can be initiated with self-reflection, but it often requires a loving connection with another person—someone in a close relationship or a professional trained to help promote security of attachment. Whether with a therapist or with a friend, the movement toward security is at the heart of becoming open to interpersonal integration. As relationships are the most important factor in studies of good health, longevity, happiness, and wisdom, finding a way to promote interpersonal integration may be an essential step in developing these positive aspects of living a full and rewarding life.

Temporal integration

Our human brain is capable of making maps of time. What this means is that we can make representations of the past, compare them to the present, and imagine the future. The upside of this ability is that we can reflect on and learn from the past in a proactive way, we can design mechanisms to deal with our environment as we anticipate seasonal shifts and our own changing needs, and we can make plans for the future. The downside of this temporal capacity, this ability to map out time, is that we can be haunted by the past in our worries, we can dread anticipated changes in our environment, and we can lose touch with the present as we become intensely focused on the future (or the past). Being human is not so easy. Sometimes we become human doings in order to deal with the existential issues that arise with these time-travel abilities. We busy ourselves in an effort to deal with three fundamental outcomes of temporal processes: (1) We long for certainty, but because we can map out time, we know that nothing is really certain; (2) we long for permanence, but we know that nothing will last forever as time moves ever forward; and (3) we long for immortality, but we come to know that we all must die one day. No matter how busy we try to be to distract ourselves from an awareness of these temporal realities, we are, in fact, left in a challenging position. Whether we develop a clinical condition, such as depression over these tensions, or obsessive-compulsive disorder as an attempt to create certainty in the face of an uncertain life, impediments to temporal integration are common and often disabling in our modern life.

When I was younger, I remember waking up early in the morning at times and wondering when these types of existential issues would ever "just go away." Then I came to realize that these issues are simply ever-present themes of what it means to be human, to be a human being, not just a human doing. So to embrace this being human, temporal integration faces these issues straight on—not through distraction, not through wishful thinking that they will all go away, not through denial. As a domain of integration, which are the elements here that are in need of being differentiated before they can become linked? These temporal dimensions are the three listed above—the longings for certainty, permanence, and immortality. So with temporal integration we come to understand that these existential longings are normal: They are part of our human condition. Next we look to the realities of uncertainty, transience, and mortality. We don't run from them; we look at them straight in the eye and say, "Come on in." Without the differentiation of these polar opposites of our longings versus actual realities, temporal integration is impaired. Some people at this stage might say, "Okay . . . so I'll just get rid of my longings and learn to accept reality." To this I answer, not really. Integration is embracing opposites, of holding in awareness the tension of seemingly contradictory things—thoughts, feelings, ideas, and these polar longings and realities. We don't need to rid ourselves of our longings . . . they are understandable and, in some ways, essential in bringing vitality to life. So we embrace them—as impossible as they are to achieve—because as longings they are feelings and hopes that are as real as these polar realities. But these feelings must come to exist within our lives side by side with a full embrace of the polar realities, held, respected, treasured. It is this embracing of what is—longings and realities all—that is at the heart of temporal integration's capacity to bring deep equanimity into our lives.

Transpirational integration

As individuals work on developing the eight domains of integration—consciousness, bilateral, vertical, memory, narrative, state, interpersonal, and temporal—a ninth form of "integration of integration" tends to emerge, often without planning, intention, or expectation. I didn't know what to call this domain, so I made up the term of "breathing across the domains" or "transpiration" (across-breathe). Transpirational integration entails an awareness of an expanded sense of self. Individuals working at this level of integration, for example, might feel impassioned to become involved in efforts to clean the polluted lake near their home, or they might feel an inner drive to help others in poorer neighborhoods or in developing countries. For some, this urge to *give back* is expressed not so much as "this will feel good" (which it inevitably does), but that it is the "right thing to do." As one person stated to me, "It's just that they [the people he was helping] are me." It is this sense of breathing across a skin-defined boundary of the self and creating a larger sense of identity that the notion of transpiration tries to capture.

Transpirational integration may emerge from the fascinating reality that our human brains are capable of making a mindsight map of "me" that uses the body as a boundary for where the "self" begins and ends. But why does a self need the skin to define its identity? Transpiration turns that question inside out, widening a sense of belonging to a larger whole while not losing a sense of personal or at least bodily identity. When we examine studies of happiness, health, longevity, and wisdom, this sense of being a part of an interconnected whole is in fact part of the achievement of those positive attributes. We widen our circles of concern and come to feel part of something "larger than ourselves." This sense of belonging not only feels good, but it is also good for you and others around you. Transpirational integration is the gift that keeps on giving.

42
42

FROM ME TO WE: SYNAPSE, SOCIETY, AND AN EXPANDED SELF

CONCEPT: WHAT IS THIS?

Who are we, really? And what does it mean when we say, "This is me"? What is the "this" that we call "the self"? And why are so many studies revealing that in our modern life people are feeling ever more isolated even though they are more digitally connected? How can we be "together" yet feel so alone? One way of understanding this is that a sense of a "self" is being created from our *cultural* ⋆ *contexts* ⋆ that in fact is being reinforced as individual, alone, isolated, disconnected, and encased in a body without real closeness with others. What is sorely lacking is a needed experience of belonging—of being a part of something much larger than what is defined by the body alone. Studies show that this isolated "me" is filled with *stress* ⋆ and despair, and it does not create happiness, *health* ⋆, or longevity. Other studies suggest that the more disparity a society has between the income levels of the poor and the wealthy, the more mental disorders, drug addiction, mistrust, and impaired medical health and longevity for all people living in that social environment. We are profoundly influenced by the cultural and economic settings in which we live. When we live with a sense of injustice, of mistrust and disconnection, all suffer. We can suggest that these conditions promote a sense of an isolated self, one lacking in a vital and trusting membership in a larger whole.

How do we **expand a sense of self from me to we***? How do we transform our sense of who we are?

The self is a fascinating subject of study, and an even more fascinating subject of experience. When we state that our mental life is composed of *subjective experience**, *awareness** with its sense of knowing and that which is known, and all the *mental activities** that arise as the known of our experiences (*emotions**, thoughts, memories, images, and the like), we come to realize the subjective experience of "self" is, in fact, a product of the *mind**. When we peer straight into the notion that the mind can be viewed as an *emergent process** that arises from and also *regulates** both *relational** and *embodied** patterns of *energy and information flow**, then we come to embrace the reality that our mental life is not simply defined by the body. So if that relational *flow** defines, in part, the mind—and if the mind is how we subjectively experience a sense of self—then it is natural to embrace the reality that the self is, in scientific fact, both an embodied and a relational process. The self is not limited to the body.

On the body side, if the *brain** has a proclivity to take in signals from the culture, from the media, and from family behavior and stories, each of which communicates the notion that a "self" lives and dies with the body, then naturally the brain's *synaptic shadows** of those experiences will create *narratives** and accompanying *mental models* that shape a sense of self as defined by and limited to the body. This openness of the brain to respond to experience is called *neuroplasticity**. As our interactions with the world unfold, culture—transmitted as patterns of communication within our larger society and within our families—shapes the environmental context in which the brain's very architecture is formed. This is not conjecture; rather it is simply how the brain develops over time. Culture shapes *synapse** formation and brain architecture. And so a "sense of self" that emerges within both embodied and relational *processes** can be doubly reinforced and a *re-entry** loop is created in which communities of individuals with similar synaptic shadows have communication patterns emanating from and reinforcing a cortical processing that contributes to a bodily defined sense of self. Albert Einstein called the outcome of this process an "optical delusion." Over time, such a mutually reinforcing set of patterns becomes fixed, beliefs become interpreted as realities, and future generations come to believe, and enact, the same perspectives, over and over again.

And so in modern times, despite our massive technological connectedness, this may be our challenge: We have to liberate a sense of self so that we honor both the embodied and the relational aspect of who we are. Put in another way: I am more than me. I am connected to you. And I am a part of we. This is how we transform from only me, to also we. This is how we move from me to we.

IMPLICATIONS: WHAT DO MOVING FROM ME TO WE AND AN EXPANDED SELF MEAN IN OUR LIVES?

By examining the nature of the stories and beliefs and neural underpinnings that define a sense of self, we open ourselves up to a crucial reality. Culture can reinforce a restricted view that the self is all about "this is mine and not yours" and "I am better than you, because you are different from me." On and on, we can see that a strictly bodily defined self carries with it various impactful risks. On a personal level, we can come to feel the despair of isolation, the longing for belonging that feels impossible to achieve. We are alone, together. Finding ways to expand a sense of self from me to we offers the hope of healing this isolation. In the outcome, people will be happier, healthier, and live with more *meaning*★ as they find a true sense of belonging and connection.

On the larger scale of our life as a human family on the planet, this sense of isolation as a separate, bodily defined self poses a grave risk: Life becomes about accumulating material items for "me" and "mine" and then protecting those items from "you" and "yours." The evolutionarily inherited tendencies embedded in our neural *circuits*★ to identify an "in group" and an "out group" are understandable. If you and I were from the same clan in Cave A, we'd protect each other and increase chances of our genes' survival. Even more, we'd cooperate with each other, be altruistic, and take care of one another. Survival goes to the most collaborative is actually what Darwin was saying in a deep way about the process of evolution. But let's be clear: When it comes to those people from Cave B, we are potentially in serious danger. We either need to conquer them and mate with them, or we need to be prepared to fight and destroy them. And as we "progressed" in our evolution, when we became able to grow and store food, to prepare for difficult times of famine and drought, then the stakes became even higher. We need our stuff or we will all die. Forget about those folks from Cave B; we need to care for our own. That's real community—we have membership to ensure our collective survival. But does that still work in an age of such massively interconnected caves?

The various studies of "mortality salience" in which people are exposed to even subliminal signs of threat lead to the finding that we treat with more *kindness*★ those similar to us (from our Cave A) and then treat with more hostility those not similar to us (from Cave B). Even brain-imaging studies reveal that if we see someone like us (from Cave A), our *middle prefrontal*★ circuits of *empathy*★ become activated. Yet when we see that same face but this time with *information*★ that suggests that this person is not similar to us, that same region shuts off its activity. We relate to those from *our* cave, and we become more hostile and disregarding of the humanity of those from the *other* caves.

And so we have neural propensities to make us-versus-them distinctions. Yet we share the same air, water, global resources, air traffic *systems*★, and Internet access, and we are all citizens of this large cave we call Earth. How can we say that if you are from the north corner of Earth I'll love you, but if you are from the south corner, watch out! We need to move forward from these neural propensities inherited from our constricted cave environment into a new way of sensing what the "self" is. If "me" refers also to those from "our cave," then the same issues about a bodily defined self can apply to a cave-defined self. Culture can reinforce a neural instantiation of a limited sense of self. The process of feeling more meaning and happier in life with an expanded sense of self may also go along with helping preserve the health of our planet if we can deal directly with these issues. But how can we move to this expanded sense of self?

Moving from "only me" to "also we" is tricky. We have modern culture reinforcing a loop of communication that the self lives in the body, that we are defined by our cave membership. We have millions of years of evolution driving our circuits to compare cave members to one another and to favor our mates and disregard the foreigners. And we have busy lives with massively interconnected communication methods in ways never before seen. With a click of a mouse you can see in real time revolutions and governments collapsing, nuclear meltdowns and massive oil spills, and the painful aftermath of earthquakes and tidal waves. We are being confronted with noncave members in ways that our neural circuitry has never evolved to handle. What are we to do?

It *is* possible to go beyond the impulses of our evolutionary circuits and to grow in a healthy way as a human culture even in the face of technical advances that have moved beyond our neural preparedness. But the way to do this, I'll suggest to you, is to return to our innermost sense of identity—our sense of what "self" really means. This is how we apply the lessons of our *interpersonal neurobiology*★ exploration to the understanding of who we are in the world.

Mind can shape culture. As our communication with one another changes, *cultural evolution* transforms the context in which children develop, adolescents challenge us, and adults structure the societies in which we live. Our planet's very health depends upon how our environment-changing human family takes seriously how our cave membership is defined. We are a collaborative bunch—but only for those we feel are members of the same cave club. Helping our planet may come from our intentionally shaping cultural evolution to support an expanded sense of self, to grow beyond an isolated and localized me, to transform our cloistered clan mentality and cultivate a truly collaborative and globalized we.

The challenge for all of us is in finding ways to embrace an individual, body-centered, and small-cave membership sense of self, while also expanding our circles of concern so that we realize that our extended relational self is real. "I" do live in this body, in my body. But "I" also live in my connections with others, and I also live in others. And these others are not just people similar to me. That's a great starting place, but it is not a place to end the expansion of cultural life. This is the hard part: to move into this sense of me as being more than me, but a part of we. And this we extends beyond what is familiar, beyond our cave mates, to embrace the larger whole of our human family.

It's funny, but because I don't have a background myself in this way of viewing the world, I can imagine a rational scientist thinking, this is really strange: "Dan has gone off the deep end." But let me try to be as clear as possible. I am not speaking metaphorically here, but from the reasoning of science. The self is not a body-limited process. Self is not just constrained by the body. Our sense of group membership does not have to be constrained by evolutionary circuits of us-versus-them thinking. These are ways of being on *automatic pilot** that do not have to imprison our lives. Our whole line of reasoning throughout interpersonal neurobiology is that our mental lives are both embodied and relational. And so the application of this science-informed view is for the following purpose. If threat creates a deepening neural divide that makes us favor Cave A members and hate Cave B folks, our planet is on a course to destruction. The caves are too big, our lines of communication now so interconnected, the communication too rapid, and the weapons too lethal. Beyond sticks and stones, beyond just the next hill, we've wrapped our self-unsophisticated brains around technologically sophisticated achievements that put us at grave risk. Okay, fine. And so what is the suggestion?

Awareness.

Big deal, you say. But hold on for a moment. Awareness is the *space of the mind* that enables us to pull out of automatic pilot. Awareness gives *cortical override* mechanisms a chance to inhibit the evolutionary impulses to hate those not like us. We've outlined here the fundamental steps that may make us neurally at risk for planetary destruction: too much stuff, not enough food and water, too many people, and too much tension. But awareness of these fundamental challenges holds the promise, perhaps the only possibility, that we *can* move from only me to also we in a way that makes collaboration as natural as breathing. Because we are collaborative creatures by evolution, hardwired with the potential to be coopertive and to help others, the issue is really expanding a sense of self and expanding a sense of identity, so that it is not limited to our old cave clan mentality. We can shape the pathway of cultural evolution toward collaboration with the collective intelligence of shared awareness. We share the same air, we share the same water, and we share this same home, our planet Earth. When we embrace the reality of this shared home, we come to realize that I am you, that we are in this together . . . literally, together. *We* are together.

43
43

INTERNAL EDUCATION

CONCEPT: WHAT IS IT?

Internal education★ is a didactic approach to learning about the *mind*★ and how it *develops* over the life span. By educating a person in this way, so that he or she acquires the knowledge, *awareness*★, and skills about the mind to promote the growth of *resilience*★, *reflection*★, and *relationships*★ (a new set of "*R's*" at the core of a curriculum), we can prepare children, adolescents, and adults to face the challenges of the modern world. But why an "internal" education? Isn't learning the way we've been learning good enough?

If you ask a simple question to educators across all the developmental ages of students, "what are you educating when you teach?" most teachers respond, "I am developing the mind of my student." And then the next question: "How many of you have had even one lecture that defined what the mind is?" The answer from more than 4,500 kindergarten through 12th-grade teachers is identical to that of the 100,000 *mental health*★ professionals I've surveyed: Two to five percent respond "yes." Now the reality is that even the fields of psychology, psychiatry, cognitive neuroscience, and philosophy of mind do not have a definition of the mind, though naturally they do have descriptions of *mental processes*★ such as our thinking and feeling, memory and reasoning. But as educators (and as clinicians), if we are the professionals who apply this knowledge in promoting the growth of the minds of our students (or of our clients and patients—or as parents of our children), wouldn't it be helpful to (a) specifically define what it actually is that we are trying to help develop and (b) then go directly to the source and help that entity, the mind—once defined—to grow well?

If you can see the practical logic of these questions, then the natural next layer of responses might go like this. What *is* a definition of mind? How can I use that definition to directly help my student (or client/patient/child) to develop a stronger, more resilient, more capable, more innovative, more *empathic*★, and more prepared mind? This is the exact approach of internal education: It is the way we educate the mind directly about the mind itself.

IMPLICATIONS: WHAT DOES INTERNAL EDUCATION MEAN FOR OUR LIVES?

In *interpersonal neurobiology*★ we've taken the *consilient*★ step of integrating a wide array of sciences into one common foundation for viewing the nature of reality, human development, and well-being. In this approach, we see the mind as being a term we use to describe a number of *processes*★. One is *subjective experience*★, the inner felt sense of the moment-to-moment unfolding of our inner lives. This is a *prime*★ of reality: an irreducible aspect of our experience that cannot be translated into other forms, such as "just an outcome of *brain*★ firing." Subjective experience is real, even though it cannot be easily quantified. Relationships that focus on, and honor the reality of, the subjective experience of the individuals involved are *healthy*★, *meaningful*★ relationships. So as a first starting place, internal education promotes the active exploration of first-person subjective experience. When we then try to express that internal personal experience outwardly and when we begin to attempt to communicate this inner reality to others, we are in an act of translation. This is helpful didactically, and it may even strengthen certain regulatory circuits in the brain itself, but we must realize that this second step becomes an important but distinct external report of an inner experience.

Next, we can say that the mind also has something called *consciousness*★. Consciousness, or the experience of being aware, has two aspects. One is the sense of knowing that emerges when you are aware of something. The other is that which is known. You may be aware right now of my putting the word GLOBE here in this sentence. You have your sense of *knowing* that GLOBE is here, now, and you have the *known* of what GLOBE means. The knowing and the known are different, but each is a part of consciousness.

Within the group of the known elements is also a set of processes we can call *mental activities*★. These are the familiar mental experiences of *emotions*★, thoughts, images, memories, perceptions, beliefs, *intentions*★, attitudes, hopes, dreams, longings, and the like. These are all fundamental to cognition and its role in *information processing*★. When we learn about the nature of our thinking itself, we call this a "meta-process," or in this case *metacognition*. Studies reveal, for example, that children who learn to reflect on the nature of their emotions with their parents have better skills for balancing their emotions. They are also better at understanding their own and others' emotions and how those feelings impact behavior and reasoning and even their perceptions of the world. When we discuss with children the inner nature of our mental lives, we use *reflective dialogues* to engage them in a focus on the inner world. Reflecting on the inner nature of one's own and others' mental lives is the basis of *emotional and social intelligence*. In turn, these important inner skills are correlated with improved academic performance.

When someone learns the skill of seeing the inner nature of the mind of the *self*★ or the other, in research fields we call this *mentalizing*★, mind-mindedness, psychological mindedness, or *theory of mind*. This ability to sense the *psyche*—which is often traditionally defined as the soul, the spirit, the intellect, or the mind—is at the heart of what it means to perceive the inner world. In practical terms, the concept of *mindsight*★ is helpful as it is seen as the core mechanism underlying social and emotional intelligence that enables someone to understand and actively shape the inner nature of mental life. We "see the mind" with neural *circuits*★ that embed *mindsight maps*★ of ourselves and of others, maps that help us see from another's point of view and create empathy as well as self-understanding. Beyond only perceiving the life of the mind, mindsight enables an individual to change the internal mental landscape and move it to more adaptive functioning, toward health. But how can a *perceptual*★ skill enable someone to change what he or she perceives? Turning to another core feature of mind will help us answer this question.

There is another fundamental aspect of the mind that can be defined as an *embodied*★ and *relational*★ process that *regulates*★ the *flow of energy and information*★. By taking the step of defining this core feature of mind, we are in a new position to form an internal education that teaches both perceptual and regulatory skills to children, adolescents, and adults in a range of educational settings. Mindsight is the capacity to see and to shape the mind. Applying these ideas in the curriculum opens the doors wide open to creating resilience as we cultivate stronger reflective and relational skills in students across the life span.

Let's take this definition of a core feature of the mind, part by part, to see how internal education would apply these ideas of mindsight in the classroom, consulting room, boardroom, or even the living room. I'll use the term "teacher" here, but keep in mind that guiding the *development*★ of the mind can be facilitated by teachers as well as by clinicians, organizational consultants, administrators, and parents. We are all potential teachers as we help each other's minds grow and develop. Here is the definition to work from: A core feature of the mind is an embodied and relational process that regulates the flow of energy and information. Here it is, step by step, in the reverse sequence:

1. Energy and information: *Energy*★ is "the capacity to do stuff" according to physicists. *Information*★ is a swirl of energy that has meaning and that has shared symbolic value. The word "water" is information. The letters w-a-t-e-r are not the liquid itself. While the liquid water itself has features, aspects, and qualities, plain water is, well, just water. It is not symbolic of something other than itself. This doesn't make it less; it just means that information is a symbol for something other than itself. How children find information in the energy we send them as teachers makes all the difference as to their ability to learn. Learning involves the scaffolding of information and the construc-

tion of a foundation of knowledge and skills. Without the ability to attend to what is being communicated, or to extract the information from the energy being sent, little lasting learning is likely to occur.

2. *Flow**: This change in energy and information over time means that the mind monitors and modifies changes over time. Nothing is static in the mind: Everything changes, and everything is a verb, an active dynamic process. Engaging a mind can be enhanced when teachers embrace this reality of mental experience and learn to become familiar with its natural characteristics. Embracing this flowing nature of mind can enrich a curriculum and bring curiosity and passion to the heart of the educational experience.

3. Regulation: Think of when you drive a car or ride a bicycle. When you regulate these vehicles you need to both see where you are going and to shape your direction and speed. You need to monitor and modify that which you are regulating. Fortunately, we can teach students directly how to monitor and modify energy and information flow. When teachers are themselves given the mindsight skills to monitor and modify energy and information flow in their own mental lives, then they are in a position to teach these skills to their students. This is how internal education directly develops the mind! But *where* is the mind that is being monitored and modified? Read on!

4. Process: The mind is a verb, not a noun. Process means that something is shaping the unfolding, or *state**, of something over time. Seeing the mind as a process that regulates energy and information flow empowers teachers to teach how to develop the mind as a skill. There is no fixed entity called "mind." The mind is not a stone, not a noun-

like unchanging object. As a process, the mind is open to the *context*★ in which it arises. The mind is a verb.

5. What is this process that we are calling the mind? In *complex systems*★, there is a fundamental property in which the interactions of elements of the system gives rise to a process called *self-organization*★. In other words, what emerges from the system is a process that regulates the flow of the system itself. In the case of the mind, we are stating that the mind is an *emergent*★, self-organizing process that regulates the flow of energy and information. To see how to improve this self-organizing process, we need to look at the origins from which it arises. Here we come to the mind's embodied and relational nature. This is the "where" of where this aspect of the mind resides.

6. Relational: Although we think of "my mind" as belonging to "me" and "your mind" as belonging to "you," the truth is that our mental life emerges, in part, from our communication with each other. This is the relational aspect of mind. A relationship is the sharing or exchanging of energy and information. And so when we teach people to monitor energy and information flow, part of *where* we look is toward our relationships. We focus *attention*★ directly on how we communicate with one another—how we share energy and information—in the form of both verbal (words) and *nonverbal*★ signals. Nonverbal communication includes eye contact, facial expressions, tone of voice, posture, gestures, timing, and the intensity of responses. These signals likely emanate from the *presymbolic representations* that enable us to be with and communicate from our direct, *primary experience*. When these signals are *attuned*★ to others, we come to *resonate*★ with other people. This

is how we promote interpersonal *integration**. As we learn to modify energy and information flow as it is exchanged (the relational side of mind), as we learn to enhance the art of connecting to one another, we can learn to promote stronger relationships by way of how we cultivate integration. Integration is seen as the core mechanism that creates resilence and health. *Integrative communication** honors differences between people, and it promotes *compassionate**, respectful communication as a way of *linking** two or more individuals. Cultivating integration in our communications with others is how we monitor and modify our relational minds toward well-being.

7. Embodied: In addition to riding along and regulating the waves of energy and information flow between ourselves and others (and our larger environment) within relationships, the mind also emanates from and regulates this flow in our bodies. The *nervous system** itself is composed of neural connections that are the mechanism of electrochemical energy flow throughout the body and within the skull. These brain mechanisms can be monitored and modified by the mind. For some, this may sound odd: Isn't the brain in charge of the show? Well, the causal influences among brain and mind—and relationships—are in all directions. Brain does shape mind, but mind does shape brain. And relationships are influenced by these two and influence them as well. These are three sides of one reality—the reality of energy and information flow and how it is shaped by bodily mechanisms (brain), shared in communication patterns (relationships), and regulated by an emergent self-organizing process (mind). And so we can use the process of awareness to intentionally focus on energy and information flow

through our bodily mechanisms, through the body proper and the layers of the skull-encased brain itself.

8. As with relational monitoring and modifying, embodied regulation entails moving the flow of energy and information toward integrative states to create resilience and well-being. What this means is that we honor differences and promote linkages—within the nervous system of the body and in our connections with one another. The "where" of the mind is both in our brains and in our relationships. And the "how" of a healthy mind is in integration. We can quite specifically focus on various *domains of integration*★ that offer an accessible foundation from which to explore the many ways of integrating the brain, including from side to side in *bilateral*★ integration, up and down in vertical integration, and then the integration of the various forms of *memory*★, *narrative*★, and *states*★. Across these domains, teachers can promote the health and resilience needed to build strong and vibrant minds in students of all ages.

Internal education invites teachers and students alike to use mindsight skill training to develop these capacities to monitor with more stability, depth, and clarity and then modify with more strength and specificity toward integration. Part of this approach is to use *time-in*★ as a *reflective practice*★ of looking inward to develop these crucial skills of seeing and shaping the mind. Time-in is an important part of a daily practice of the mind to build the mindsight skills at the heart of a resilient and compassionate mind. And internal education also can suggest a "daily mental diet" that uses research-established findings to suggest what a regular set of activities would be to support optimal brain growth and optimal relational health.

The *healthy mind platter** is an enjoyable and accessible visual image of how these daily mental nutrients can be introduced in various settings at home, in the classroom, or at work (see Figure J).

Time-in focuses the mind on its own internal and interpersonal workings, promoting integration of the brain and harnessing the power of awareness to strengthen the regulation of emotion and attention, and even enhance empathy and flexibility.

Focus time harnesses the power of the careful focus of attention to release chemicals that promote *neuroplastic** growth—how we change the brain in response to experience at the heart of memory and learning. Focusing on one process at a time and reducing multitasking and following through with an unfolding area of study can enhance long-term learning.

Play time reminds us that being spontaneous and exploring the world, engaging in novel experiences with delight and an open sense of discovery without a sense of right-or-wrong results, is an important way to activate the brain and promote innovation and *creative** learning.

Physical time reminds us to participate in physical activity, aerobically if medically possible. Studies suggest that this is not only good for our physical health and helps us feel better, but it also helps promote neuroplasticity and support learning.

Down time is when we have no agenda, no plans, and no goals we are trying to achieve. This is an important time to just let the brain rest, to recharge, and to find a way to "chill out" without accomplishing a prescribed task.

Sleep time is something in modern life that is usually insufficient. When we sleep, we integrate the brain and *consolidate* our learning from the day. Making the conscious effort to create the conditions that promote sleep, such as turning off the computer, lowering the lights, and getting oneself ready to transition out of being our wide-awake, digitally connected selves is important in making sleep time a reality.

Connecting time involves our connections to other people and our planet. Study after study suggests that these connections improve our health. I try to remember some of the key features of connecting time with the term *3g2p**: We come with *generosity* and kindness for others and ourselves, we *give back* to help the lives of others, and we find the *gratitude* for this gift of being alive. And we bring these 3 "g's" (generosity, giving back, gratitude) to our relationship with other people and the planet (the 2 "p's"). Connecting in these ways to people, ideally in person when possible, reminds us of our relationships to others. And as we spend more time appreciating nature, we are immersed in the reality that we are a part of our planet and that we all share this common home we call Earth.

Internal education can happen anywhere. It can be formalized in school settings to teach these important mindsight skills that are the foundation for social and emotional intelligence. It can be taught at home, giving children in families the opportunity to learn these important skills of reflection and having relationships that promote resilience. It can be a part of clinical work; clinicians can invite clients and patients to strengthen their minds no matter what initial condition brought them to seek help. And it can become a part of an organizational worldview; those in the workplace can embrace the reality that what makes a company or institution work well and thrive are the people and the relationships among them.

Together, we can make internal education a fundamental part of our *culture**. The quality of our lives will be enhanced and the future of our children's lives will be improved with these skills of the mind. And in the course of educating the mind about the mind, the world in which we live will be aided as we come to realize that we are in relationship not only with other people and with ourselves, but also with this precious planet we call home.

Figure A. The sphere of knowledge of interpersonal neurobiology. The surface of the sphere represents the pocket guide's entries, which serve as entryways into the interconnected network of knowledge in this field. Source: Wikipedia

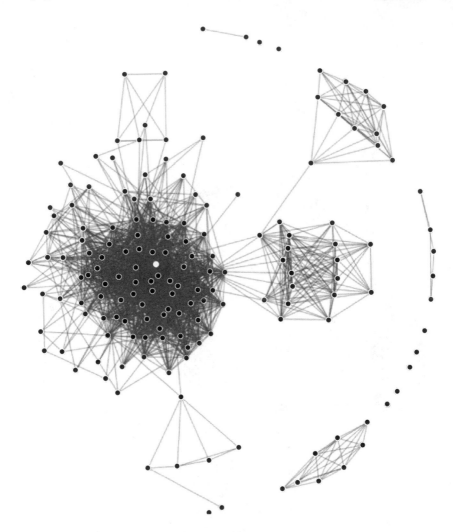

Figure B. A graphic illustration of how the pocket guide's entries serve both as entryways into the sphere of knowledge and as nodal points linking the different nodes of knowledge to one another as they form the conceptual infrastructure of interpersonal neurobiology. Within the sphere are also nodes that serve to bridge across different terms that are ideas, facts, and processes found as nodes within the nodal network section of this book and are defined, along with other important terms, in the annotated index. Source: Wikipedia, commons.wikimedia.org/wiki.File:Sna_large. png#filelinks.

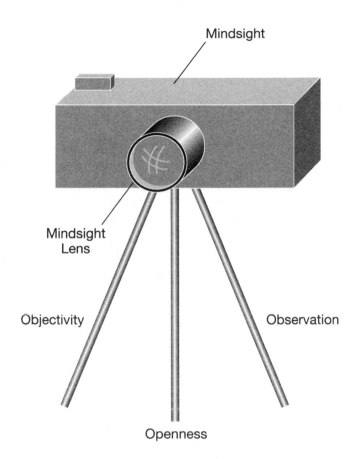

Figure C. The mindsight tripod. Openness, objectivity, and observation are the three processes that stabilize the mindsight lens in order to see and shape the inner world with clarity, depth, and power. With openness, we accept things as they are; with objectivity, we realize that what we are aware of is just one element of our experience and not the totality of our identity; with observation, we have a sense of ourselves as observers witnessing the unfolding of experience as it emerges moment by moment. Copyright © 2010 by Mind Your Brain, Inc. Used with permission by Daniel J. Siegel, M.D., from *Mindsight: The New Science of Personal Transformation* (2010).

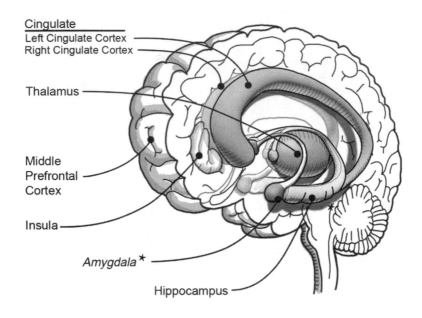

Figure D-1: The Middle Prefrontal Cortex. This diagram reveals the limbic region (cingulate, amygdala, hippocampus) and its relationship to the middle prefrontal cortex (which includes the anterior portion of the cingulate, the orbitofrontal cortex, the dorsal and ventral aspects of the medial prefrontal area, and the ventrolateral prefrontal cortex, which is considered by many to include the insula). Copyright © 2012 by Mind Your Brain, Inc. Used with permission by Daniel J. Siegel, M.D., from *The Developing Mind: How Relationships and the Brain Interact to Shape Who We Are* (2012).

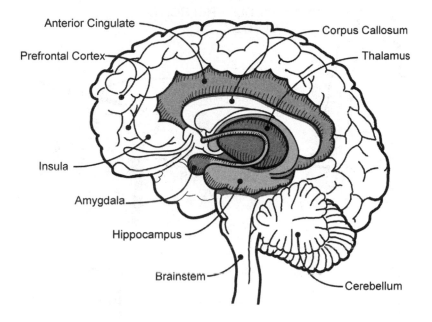

Figure D-2: The Brain. Midline view of the brain revealing the major regions, looking from the left side toward the right. The left limbic region (with the amygdala and hippocampus) is highlighted and its close proximity to the prefrontal and anterior cingulate areas is revealed. The corpus callosum connects the two hemispheres and the thalamus serves as the gateway of sensory input to the brain. Please see text for full descriptions of the functions of these various regions. Copyright © 2012 by Mind Your Brain, Inc. Used with permission by Daniel J. Siegel, M.D., from *The Developing Mind: How Relationships and the Brain Interact to Shape Who We Are* (2012).

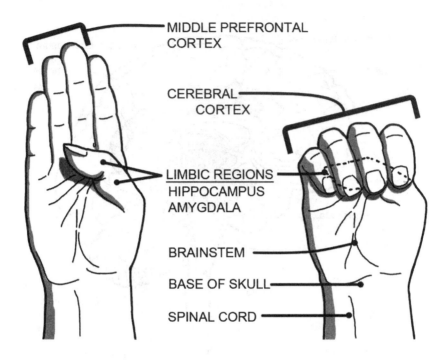

Figure D-3. The brain in the palm of the hand. This is a "handy model" that depicts the major regions of the brain: cerebral cortex in the fingers, limbic area in the thumb, and brainstem in the palm. The spinal cord is represented in the wrist. Please see text for explanation. Copyright © 2012 by Mind Your Brain, Inc. Used with permission by Daniel J. Siegel, M.D., from *The Developing Mind: How Relationships and the Brain Interact to Shape Who We Are* (2012).

Mind

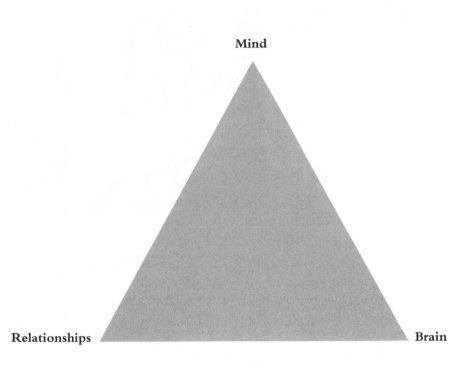

Relationships **Brain**

Figure E. The triangle of well-being. The harmony of integration is revealed as empathic relationships, a coherent mind, and an integrated brain. The brain is the mechanism of energy and information flow throughout the extended nervous system distributed throughout the entire body. Relationships are the sharing of energy and information flow. The mind is the embodied and relational process that regulates the flow of energy and information. Copyright © 2010 by Mind Your Brain, Inc. Used with permission by Daniel J. Siegel, M.D., from *Mindsight: The New Science of Personal Transformation* (2010).

Figure F. The Still-Face Experiment. These still photograph frames are moments of interaction during an experiment designed by Ed Tronick, Ph.D., which demonstrate how a young (4-month-old) infant needs attuned communication with her parent to regulate her own internal state. In F-1, frame A, we see the mother beginning to have a "still face" in which she shows none of the prior connecting signals with her infant. This reveals, from frames A to D, the infant moving from initial uncertainty to intensifying states of dysregulation, including losing postural control. In F-2, a similar sequence unfolds but with a more intense initial response and a complete turning away by frame D. The infant looks for a response and then looks away, tries again, and then looks fully away. A repair, not seen in these frames, quickly restores the communication between mother and baby and reestablishes the infant's equilibrium. Images used with permission from Ed Tronick, Ph.D.

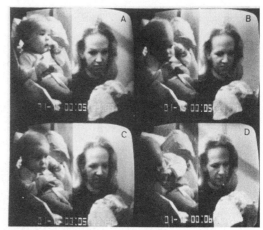

F-1

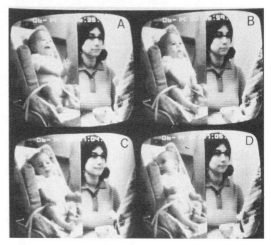

F-2

A Schematic of the Six-Layered Cortical Columns and the Bottom-Up and Top-Down Flow of Information

Layer	Top-Down	Top-Down Dominance	Top-Down
1	⇓	⬇⬇⬇	⇓
2	⇓	⬇⬇⬇	⇓
3	⇓	⬇⬇⬇	⇓
AWARENESS	⇨→⇨→	→⇨⇨⇨	⇨→→→→→
4	↑	↑	↑↑↑↑↑
5	↑	↑	↑↑↑↑↑
6	↑	↑	↑↑↑↑↑
	Bottom-Up	Bottom-Up	Bottom-Up Dominance

Figure G. A metaphoric map or schematic proposal of top-down and bottom-up processing and the six-layered cortical columns. The information from sensation flows "bottom-up" from the lower layers of the columns streaming from layers 6 to 5 to 4. Information from prior learning, called "top-down," streams from layers 1 to 2 to 3. Awareness is proposed to emerge by the commingling of these two streams. In the first condition, bottom-up and top-down are balanced, and the resultant awareness blends the two streams. In the second condition, top-down input is dominant and prior expectations and categorizations overshadow incoming sensory streams within awareness. In the third condition, sensory input in the here and now is dominant and awareness reflects a predominance of input from this sensory flow. Mindfulness may enable layers 3 and 4 to be disentangled by at first practicing enhancement of the bottom-up flow of present sensory experience. Used with permission. Copyright © 2010 by Mind Your Brain, Inc. Daniel J. Siegel, M.D., *The Mindful Therapist* (2010).

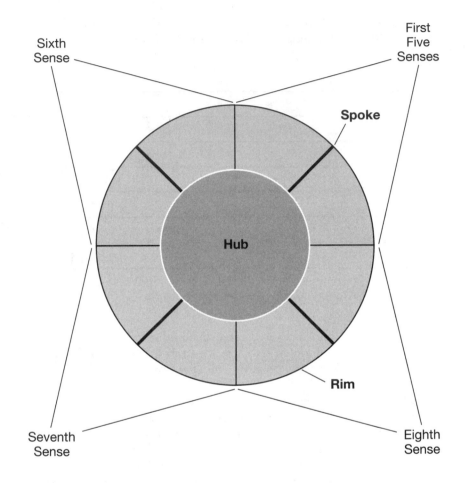

Figure H. The wheel of awareness. The hub represents the experience of knowing within awareness; the spokes are focused attention; the rim is the known of awareness including our sensations and other mental processes. The sectors of the rim are as follows: first five (outer world), sixth (body), seventh (mental activity), and eighth (relationships) senses. Used with permission. Copyright © 2007 by Mind Your Brain, Inc. Daniel J. Siegel, M.D., The Mindful Brain (2007).

Subjective Experience

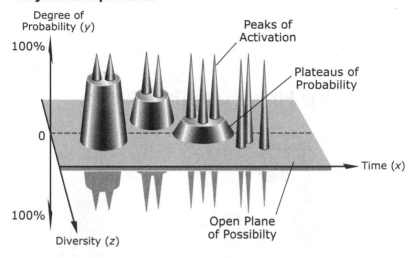

Neural Firing

Figure I. The plane of possibility. This is a visual metaphor for embracing several dimensions of human experience. (1) We can envision that our primes of neural firing (below the plane) and mental subjective experience (above the plane) reflect one another—and sometimes one leads the other, as the brain drives subjective experience or the focus of attention drives neural firing across time (represented on the x-axis). (2) Based on degrees of probability, the y-axis (vertically above and below the plane) graphs when open possibility exists in the plane (as in open mindful awareness), or certainty manifests at a peak of activation (a particular thought, feeling, memory—and their parallel in neural firing). (3) The diversity of mental experience or neural firing possible is symbolized along the z-axis (away and toward you out of the page) so that the wider the zone along this axis, the more variety of neural firing/mental experience is possible. The plane is wide open; the plateau is broad or narrow, but limited in its diversity; a peak of activation is singular in its array of mental experience or neural firing. (4) A peak represents a specific activation of mind or brain instantiated in that instant—activations that are committed to manifest as that particular activity in that moment of time. A plateau represents a state of mind or profile of neural firing that may have various shapes and degrees of height and broadness: Lower means less certainty of which firings might be possible and wider signifies more variety, a wider set of propensities; higher indicates a greater probability of firing of those options that are primed or made more likely to occur in that state or profile, and narrower indicates a more restricted set of choices of which peaks might arise from that particular plateau. The open plane of possibility reveals a zero probability that any particular peak or plateau will arise and thus represents an open state of mindful awareness and a receptive neural profile at that moment. Used with permission. Copyright © 2010 by Mind Your Brain, Inc. Daniel J. Siegel, M.D., *The Mindful Therapist* (2010).

The Healty Mind Platter

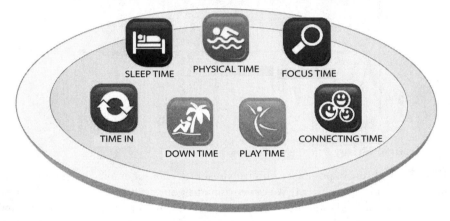

The Healthy Mind Platter, for Optimal Brain Matter

Figure J. The healthy mind platter. Created by Daniel J. Siegel, M.D., and David Rock. The platter reveals seven daily mental "nutrients" for optimizing mental well-being. See text and DrDanSiegel.com for full descriptions.

Figure K. The river of integration. This represents the movement of a
system across time. When the system is integrated, it is adaptive and harmonious in its functioning. When linkage of the differentiated elements
(integration) does not occur, then the system moves to rigidity, chaos, or
some combination of both. Used with permission. Copyright © 2010 by
Mind Your Brain, Inc. Daniel J. Siegel, M.D., *Mindsight: The New Science of
Personal Transformation* (2010).

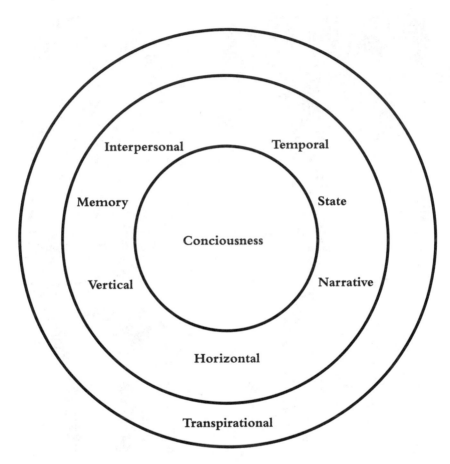

Figure L. The domains of integration. Used with permission. Copyright ©
2010 by Mind Your Brain, Inc. Daniel J. Siegel, M.D.

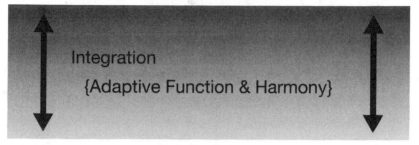

CHAOS

Integration
{Adaptive Function & Harmony}

RIGIDITY

Figure M. The window of tolerance. Our mental experience and our neural firing patterns for particular emotions or situations appear to have a span of tolerance in which we can function optimally. Within that span, within the window, we do well; outside the window, we push beyond tolerable levels of arousal and move to either chaos or rigidity and lose our adaptive and harmonious functioning. Used with permission. Copyright © 2010 by Mind Your Brain, Inc. Daniel J. Siegel, M.D., *The Mindful Therapist* (2010).

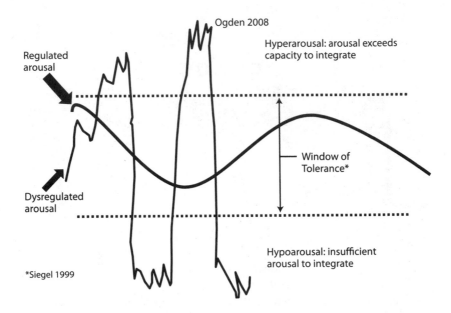

Figure N. The modulation model of Pat Ogden. This drawing reveals the movement of states of arousal into the dysregulated hyperaroused state (above) and the hypoaroused state (below) that are beyond the window of tolerance. Copyright © 2008, used with permission from Pat Ogden.

ANNOTATED INDEX
ANNOTATED INDEX

The following terms are used at various places in the text and are found in italicized letters the first time they are used in an entry. Some of these terms are "nodal points"—indicated with asterisks here and in the text—which means that they are key ideas, concepts, or processes that serve as points of connection for the various other terms found in the entries. These nodes create the foundation for an intricate sphere of knowledge that is the framework for this book. All nodal points are also listed, by themselves and without entry numbers and without definitions, in a separate nodal network following this index for ease of reference. The first time a nodal point is found in an entry—it is either in **bold★** when it is also an entry heading or it is simply designated with italicized letters followed by an asterisk (*like this*★). When a term is not a nodal point, it will simply be listed here without an asterisk and in the text itself it will be in *italics* only.

There are several nodal points of the network that are so dispersed throughout every entry that their page numbers are not listed here in the annotated index. These include terms such as *process*, *relationships*, *self*, *state*, and *system*. As with all nodes, it may be helpful to keep these terms in mind throughout the reading as you explore the ways these ideas interrelate with one another.

In addition to a brief description of the term and its meaning, here in this annotated index and in the nodal network the term is followed by an abbreviation in parentheses. This designates whether the primary origin and present use of the term is from the broad field of research (Res) disciplines across the wide range of sciences, or if it is predominantly derived from and used by various areas of application (App) such as clinical work, education, parenting, organizational consultation, or reflective practice. If the term originates in both areas or if it is commonly used with acceptance in both domains, then both the research and applications origins are included (Res/App). As time moves forward, there may be a consilient framework that becomes more commonly shared in which many more of these concepts and terms will hopefully become shared by both the activities of research and practical applications. These distinctions of Res and App are important to make here because not all terms are known, understood, or accepted by the other field of activity. The goal is to keep you well informed, so that you know when to skillfully use and integrate these important terms in your own work and how to communicate with others in the fields of academia and in practical applications with ease and respect for important but somewhat distinct areas of endeavor.

★ **Abuse (Res/App):** The mistreatment of one person by another. Abuse is an example of impaired integration in which differentiated needs of one individual are not honored and compassionate connections are not cultivated. Abuse can take many forms, including emotional, physical, sexual, and verbal. Pages: 8(7); 9(3); 16(3, 5); 38(2, 4); 39(3); 40(4)

Action potential (Res):   The process of the neuron in which charged particles, or ions, flow in and out of the membrane to create the equivalent of an electric flow down the long axonal length of the neuron.
Pages: 8(1, 2, 5); 28(3); 36(7)

Adolescence (Res):   The developmental period between childhood and adulthood that involves significant restructuring of relationships and the neural architecture of the brain.
Pages: 14(3); 18(3); 21(8)

* Adult Attachment Interview (AAI) (Res):   A research instrument that assesses individuals' recollections and how they have made sense of their own childhood experiences. The parents' AAI findings are the most robust predictor of how their children will be attached to them.
Pages: 18(5); 20(8); 21(6, 8, 9, 11, 12); 31(2); 34(4); 41(13)

Affect (Res):   The way an internal emotional state is externally revealed. Also called "affective expression."
Pages: 28(6); 32(2)

* Affect regulation (Res):   The mechanisms by which emotion and its expression are modulated. Allan Schore's regulation framework focuses on the importance of attachment relationships in shaping the important prefrontal circuitry involved in affect regulation early in life.
Pages: 14(3)

Alignment (App):   The process by which the internal state of one person is altered to reflect the internal state of another individual.
Pages: 20(3)

Allostatic load (Res): The result of the compounding of stressful experiences in a person's life.
Pages: 2(3)

⋆ Ambivalent or Resistant attachment (Res): The classification of attachment that arises from inconsistent and intrusive communication patterns from a caregiver. Also known as resistant attachment because of the ways the child behaves in the reunion stage of the Infant Strange Situation.
Pages: 20(9); 21(3, 4, 5, 9, 10, 13); 31(3); 32(12); 41(13)

⋆ Amygdala (Res): Part of the centrally located limbic regions of the brain. This almond-shaped cluster of neurons is involved in the appraisal of meaning, the processing of social signals, and the activation of emotion. Along with the orbitofrontal cortex and anterior cingulate, it plays a crucial role in coordinating perceptions of memory and behavior.
Pages: 7(2); 10(4, 6); 13(1, 3); 30(4); 32(10); 40(4); F(4, 5)

⋆ Anterior cingulate cortex (Res): A curved structure at the top of the limbic area/bottom of the prefrontal region that coordinates a number of processes, including the focus of attention, the linkage of thinking with feeling, the registration of bodily states such as pain, and the social representation of interactions, such as rejection.
Pages: 5(3); 6(4); 11(1, 2, 4); 13(2, 3); 19(4); 27(2); F(4, 5)

⋆ Anterior insula (Res): The front-most part of the insula cortex that serves as a ventrolateral prefrontal region and transfers information in a vertical fashion between the cortex and the subcortical regions, including the limbic areas and the body proper.
Pages: 11(2, 3)

Anterograde amnesia (Res): The process of not being able to encode information following the moment of an insult to the head or the psyche.
Pages: 15(5)

Anxiety (Res): An internal state of agitation that may be in response to present experience, to anticipating the future, or to reflecting on the past.
Pages: xxii; 19(1, 5); 20(9); 21(4); 39(2)

Anxious sense of self (App): The inner state of being without a coherent sense of identity, often fraught with a sense of anxiety or agitation without an internal clarity. May be found in individuals with a history of ambivalent/resistant attachment in childhood or of preoccupied attachment in adulthood.
Pages: 21(3); 41(13)

Apoptosis (Res): The diminution or pruning of synaptic connections in the absence of stimulating experience. Also called *parcellation*.
Pages: 9(2)

Appraisal and arousal (Res): The second phase of an emotional response, following initial orientation of attention and preceding the creation of categorical emotion. Appraisal involves the evaluation of the meaning of an event and the accompanying shifts in arousal states in various areas of the brain and body proper.
Pages: 3(3); 13(3); 14(6); 32(1, 8)

★ Arousal (Res/App): The degree of activation of a system, sometimes called a state of arousal. Regulation of the degree of activation, of arousal, of various circuits in the brain is funda-

mental to the process of self-regulation. States can be described as hyperarousal, hypoarousal, and dysregulated arousal.
Pages: 3(3); 11(1); 12(1); 32(1, 8, 12); 33(1); 38(7); F(15, 16)

* Attachment (Res):   An inborn system within mammals that has evolved in ways that influence and organize motivational, emotional, and memory processes with respect to significant caregiving figures. The attachment system motivates an infant to seek proximity to parents (and other primary caregivers) in order to be soothed and protected from harm. Studied by Harry Harlow in primates and later by various developmental researchers in humans, attachment figures are the few individuals with whom a child is attached and with whom they seek connection and communication when in distress.
Pages: xxxviii; 3(3); 6(5); 9(5); 10(4); 13(3, 4); 14(3); 19(4); 20(1–11), 21(1–13); 22(3, 4); 23(1); 25(3, 4); 27(6); 28(13); 32(12); 34(4); 38(12); 39(2, 3, 7); 41(8, 13)

* Attachment classifications (Res):   These are the categories of a child's relationship with a caregiver (not a feature of the child!) (i.e., the child's behavior in response to separation from a particular attachment figure after separation, based on the Infant Strange Situation) or a state of mind of the adult (e.g., based on the Adult Attachment Interview). These categories of attachment fall into four general groupings (child's relationship with the attachment figure/adult's present state of mind):   secure/ autonomous-free, avoidant/dismissive, ambivalent-resistant/ preoccupied, and disorganized/unresolved trauma or grief-disoriented. Attachment categories for children are based on relationships and are not an aspect of the child per se. Attachment

theory suggests that classifications are not fixed and can change over the life span.
Pages: 20(6); 21(1–13); 31(3)

★ Attachment figure (Res): One of the few individuals in a child's, adolescent's, or adult's life who was or is turned to as a source of comfort during times of distress. For a child, attachment figures are often parents and can be other adults as well as older children who offer contingent communication in which the child's internal world is seen, made sense of, and responded to in a timely and effective manner.
Pages: 20(3, 4, 6); 21(3–5, 7); 24(3, 6); 39(4)

★ Attachment theory (Res): Originally postulated by Mary Ainsworth and John Bowlby, it is the conceptual framework that views early relationships between parent and child as highly influential on the child's development of an internal working model of security that is changeable throughout the life span but can have lasting impacts on interpersonal and emotional functioning.
Pages: 20(1, 2, 4)

★ Attention (Res): The process that regulates the flow of information. Attention can be within awareness, which is called "focal attention," or it can be without awareness as "nonfocal attention." We can aim the focus of attention, sustain attention, and shift attention, all as a part of executive functions.
Pages: xxxv; 3(2, 3, 5, 6); 5(1, 3); 6(2, 4, 6); 7(1, 2); 8(8–10); 9(2–5); 10(2, 4); 11(2); 12(4); 13(3); 14(4, 5); 15(7, 10); 16(7); 17(5); 18(2); 20(11); 21(11); 22(2–4); 23(2, 4); 25(1–7); 26(2, 3); 27(4); 28(15);

29(5); 30(2, 4); 32(8); 34(5); 36(7, 17, 26, 35, 39); 37(2–5, 7–10); 38(7, 9); 39(6, 8); 40(6, 8, 10); 41(2, 5, 10); 43(7, 10); F(10, 11)

Attention to intention (App): The focus of attention on one's intentional states that is a common aspect of mindful awareness practices.
Pages: 3(5); 7(1, 2, 4); 14(5); 25(1, 2, 5); 40(10); 41(5)

Attractor states (Res): Reinforced patterns or activated states of mind that are fairly stable in specific conditions or contexts. These states "attract" particular ways of behaving or patterns that neurons fire that then reinforce their own creation. Attractor states are a way that a system organizes itself and achieves stability in the moment.
Pages: 35(1, 2)

★ Attunement/Attuned communication (Res): A quality of integrative relationships in which differences are respected and compassionate connections are cultivated. It also refers to the ways in which internal emotional and bodily states are the focus of attention and are "attuned to," such that they become "seen" by the adult within infant-caregiver relations or between two individuals in interpersonal interactions.
Pages: 6(4–6); 15(3); 20(3, 10); 21(6, 9); 23(1–5); 25(3–5); 27(2); 28(8, 13); 32(12); 34(1, 3, 4, 6); 38(2); 39(4); 41(5, 8); 43(7); F(8)

★ Autobiographical memory (Res): The memory of oneself at some point or points in time. This is a form of explicit memory. Single events are encoded in episodic memory, or the memory for an episode of oneself in time. Autobiographical memory is a phrase sometimes designating the larger clusters of many episodes of experience.
Pages: 13(1, 3); 15(6); 30(3, 6); 36(25, 36); 39(5); 41(9, 10)

★ Automatic pilot (Res/App): A way of being that is driven by a state of mind that is devoid of active reflection and that often involves top-down processing. It is reflected in reactive and enduring patterns of thought and bodily posture and movement, in which the past is shaping present perceptual biases, emotional responses, and behavioral output.
Pages: 3(6); 10(7); 12(3, 4); 13(4); 24(5); 29(4, 6); 36(23); 42(7, 8)

Autonoesis/Autonoetic consciousness (Res): Self-knowing awareness, associated with episodic and autobiographical memory and connected to "mental time travel"—the linkage of past, present, and anticipated future.
Pages: 19(6); 23(3); 27(2)

Autonomic nervous system (ANS) (Res): Extends from the head down into the body and it regulates heart rate, respiration and other bodily functions. A basic view of the ANS is that it is made of several branches, including a sympathetic "accelerator" and a parasympathetic "brake" as well as portions of the vagal nerve with its various layers. The autonomic nervous system provides bidirectional neural communication between our visceral organs and our brainstem.
Pages: 15(2); 27(2)

★ Avoidant attachment (Res): The classification of attachment in which a child's relationship with a caregiver is characterized by the caregiver's generally not attuning to the internal state of the child. In the Infant Strange Situation, the child avoids the return of the attachment figure.
Pages: 20(9); 21(3–5, 7, 8); 31(3); 32(12); 41(13)

★ Awakened mind (App): A state of awareness that is not on automatic pilot and can use the power of intention to drive attention to shape the firing of neurons in new and helpful ways. A state of clarity and focus that make choice and change possible.

Pages: 3(5); 12(4); 13(5); 29(6); 36(41)

* **Awareness (Res/App):** The mental experience of consciousness. Awareness involves a sense of knowing and often includes that which is known. There may be many "streams of awareness" that involve at least four aspects: sensation, observation, concept, and nonconceptual knowing.

Pages: xxiii, xxxvii; 1(1–4, 9, 11); 3(5, 6); 5(1–5); 6(1); 7(1–3, 5); 9(4); 10(7); 11(2, 5); 12(3, 4); 13(4, 5); 14(4, 6); 17(5); 19(3); 22(1); 23(3); 24(3–5); 26(1–4); 28(7, 9, 10, 12, 14, 15, 17); 29(1); 30(4–7); 31(4, 6); 36(2, 4–9, 11, 14, 18–24, 27–29, 32, 35, 37, 39–41); 37(1, 3, 5, 7); 38(1, 6); 39(6); 40(3, 8); 41(4, 5, 8, 9, 14, 15); 42(8); 43(1, 10); F(9, 10)

Awareness of awareness (App): The process of being conscious of the process of being conscious. A differentiation of the knowing from the known helps focus on the sense of knowing at the heart of awareness. Focusing attention on awareness itself is a part of the wheel of awareness practice in its more advanced stages.

Pages: 25(1, 5); 26(7); 28(15); 36(22); 40(9, 10); 41(5)

Axon (Res): The long length of a neuron that extends from the cell body out to make synaptic connections with other neurons.

Pages: 8(1, 2, 5)

Basal ganglia (Res): Beneath the outer cortex, this is a set or cluster of neurons that is thought to mediate rule-guided behavior.

Pages: 7(2)

Behavioral system (Res): Neural circuits that interconnect to drive behavior, such as the attachment system, the affili-
ative system, and the resource-allocation system. These systems
have evolved over hundreds of millions of years and have innate
features that shape human behavior. Overlaps with emotional
operating systems, because "emotion" can be seen to "evoke
motion."
Pages: 13(3)

★ **Bilateral (Res):**   Referring to both the left and right sides,
or the two hemispheres, of the skull-enclosed part of the brain.
Pages: 38(2); 39(5); 41(6, 7, 11, 16); 43(9)

★ **Bottom-up (Res/App):**   This term has several uses. The
two most common are (1) processes that arise from anatomically lower areas (such as the body proper, the brainstem, and
the limbic areas) and then influence higher regions (the cortex); and (2) processes that are as direct and instantaneous as is
neurally possible, such as sensation, as opposed to "top-down"
processes, which would refer to processes influenced by prior
experience, such as memory and perception.
Pages: 5(3); 13(5); 17(3–5); 18(3); 25(6); 38(10); F(9)

★ **Brain (Res/App):**   In this book, this term indicates the
extended nervous system distributed throughout the entire
body that is intimately interwoven with the physiology and
movements of the body as a whole. It is a term referring to the
embodied neural *mechanism* that shapes the flow of energy and
information. Often the term is used to signify only the skull-
encased portion of the nervous system, a "head-brain," but in
this book the term is used in this broader, whole-body mean-

ing. The neural net processors around the heart and the gut, for example, are part of this larger notion of "brain" and could be called the "heart-brain" and the "gut-brain."

Pages: 1(3); 2(4); 3(1, 3); 4(1); 5(2); 6(3); 7(2); 8(1); 9(1); 10(1); 11(1); 12(2, 3); 13(1); 14(1, 2); 15(1, 9); 16(1); 17(3); 18(3); 19(1); 20(4); 21(3); 22(2); 25(2, 3); 26(2); 27(1); 28(1); 29(4); 30(2); 33(3); 35(1); 36(6); 37(2); 38(1); 40(6); 41(2, 6); 42(1); 43(3); F(4–7)

★ **Brain in the palm of your hand (App):**   A visual model of the brain created by folding the thumb into the palm and placing the fingers over the thumb.

Pages: 3(3); 10(1–4); 12(3); 15(8); F(6)

★ **Brainstem (Res):**   A lower brain structure, deep within the skull. It mediates states of arousal and alertness and regulates the physiologic state of the body (temperature, respiration, heart rate). It also houses the clusters of neurons that activate the fight/flight/freeze survival reactions, which are part of our brainstem reflexes.

Pages: 3(3, 4); 5(3); 6(4); 10(2–6); 11(1); 12(1–3); 13(1, 2, 4, 5); 14(1, 2, 6); 15(5, 6); 16(7); 19(3, 7); 21(4); 23(2, 3); 27(2); 36(25); 41(6, 8); F(6)

Broaden and build (Res):   Barbara Fredrickson's idea in positive psychology that our positive emotions enhance our inner strengths and build our connections to others and ourselves.

Pages: 40(1, 3, 5)

★ **Caregiving/caregiver (Res/App):**   An individual who attends to the needs of another. Healthy development may involve the growth of the individual from primarily receiving

care to being able to both receive and to give care to others. Attachment figures are caregivers and these terms are often used synonymously, but in everyday life not all caregivers are attachment figures in the mind of a child or others receiving care.
Pages: 13(3, 4); 15(3); 20(1–7, 10); 21(1, 3, 4, 5, 7, 9, 10); 22(3); 24(3); 31(3); 34(1)

Catecholamines (Res): A form of molecule (adrenaline and noradrenaline) that serves as a neurotransmitter and neuromodulator as well as a hormone carried through the bloodstream.
Pages: 7(3); 30(4)

Categorical affects (Res): The external expression of categorical emotions. Sometimes also used for the internal experience of a categorical emotion.
Pages: 32(2); 43(3)

Categorical emotions (Res): The third stage of an emotional response that follows initial orientation and appraisal-arousal. As these initial stages become elaborated and differentiated, examples of the categorical emotions that arise include sadness, anger, fear, disgust, surprise, joy, and shame. See also *Primary emotions* and *Emotion.*
Pages: 32(2, 8)

Cell membrane (Res): The protein/lipid layer surrounding the cell. For the nervous system, the cell membrane functions to transfer electrochemical energy flow in the form of an action potential (ions flowing in and out of the membrane) and a chemical release via neurotransmitters at the far end of the axon.
Pages: 8(1, 2)

Cerebellum (Res):   A portion of the brain at the back of the skull that plays an important role in integrating bodily information along with emotional and cognitive processing.
Pages: 12(1)

★ Chaos (Res):   Defined in various ways, but generally refers to the highly unpredictable, random nature of movement of a system. Complex systems are defined by their capacity to enter chaotic states.
Pages: 1(6); 4(4–5); 7(2, 5); 15(9, 10); 16(2–7); 17(1, 2, 6); 32(5, 10–12); 33(1–5); 34(2); 36(26, 37); 37(3); 38(2–4); 39(7); 40(10); 41(1–3, 7); F(13, 15)

Childhood amnesia (Res):   A normal part of human development in which access to explicit memory is unavailable for a period of time in early childhood. Two phases have been described that likely relate to genetically encoded neural maturation patterns: (1) a first phase before the age of about 18 months in which the child does not encode explicit memory and (2) a second phase after the age of 3 to 7 in which explicit memory is available at that time, but after 7 years or so there is a difficulty of accessing previously available explicit recollections.
Pages: 21(8)

★ Circuit/Circuitry (Res):   Interconnected neurons that are linked by genetics and experience and that carry out specific functions such as perception or action.
Pages: 3(5); 7(3); 8(5, 7, 9); 9(4); 10(3); 13(2, 3); 14(3, 5); 15(7, 8); 16(7); 17(4, 5); 18(2); 19(1, 2, 4, 6, 7); 20(10); 21(4, 10); 22(1); 23(1–3); 24(2, 6); 25(2, 4, 6); 28(16); 32(2); 33(2, 3); 34(1, 2, 5, 6); 36(18, 36); 37(4, 6, 9); 38(10); 39(4); 40(4); 42(4, 6, 7); 43(3, 4)

Central nervous system (CNS) (Res):   The components

of the nervous system, such as the skull part of the brain, that interconnect with the peripheral nervous system that is spread throughout the body.
Pages: 2(3); 3(1)

★ **COAL (App):**   An acronym standing for a state of mind that is "curious, open, accepting, and loving"; this is the essence of being mindful.
Pages: 14(5); 25(5, 6)

Co-construction (Res):   The way in which two or more people mutually contribute to the creation of something, such as a narrative that makes sense of an experience.
Pages: 5(5)

Cognition (Res):   A general term referring to the activities of the mind such as thinking and reasoning that are sometimes artificially separated from "emotional" processes.
Pages: 32(7); 36(30); 38(3); 39(6); 40(2–4); 43(3)

Cognitive science (Res):   An interdisciplinary field that includes a range of academic studies that examine cognitive processes. Research areas include computer science, psychology, and cognitive neuroscience, a branch of the field of neurobiology that focuses on mental activities, such as thinking, reasoning, and memory.
Pages: xx; 28(3)

★ **Coherence/Coherent (Res):**   The fluid and adaptive flow of integrated elements across time. Coherence is created across states of mind as a form of diachronic (across time) integration.

Pages: 4(4); 15(10); 16(3, 5); 17(1, 6); 20(8); 21(6, 7, 13); 31(6); 32(6, 8); 34(1, 5); 36(3); 37(3); 38(2); 40(11); 41(3); F(7)

* COHERENCE (App):   An acronym for the characteristics of a coherent flow of human systems. A scientifically derived view of coherence reveals that its qualities spell the word with *c*onnection, *o*penness, *h*armony, *e*ngagement, *r*eceptivity, *e*mergence (things arising in new and spontaneous ways), *n*oesis (a sense of nonconceptual knowing), *c*ompassion, and *e*mpathy. Pages: 16(5)

* Coherent narrative (Res):   The term from the Adult Attachment Interview research that suggests an individual has made sense of his or her life history and its impact on present functioning. A coherent narrative in a parent is the most robust predictor of a child's attachment to that parent. Coherence analysis utilizes Grice's Maxims to help assess the coherence of the AAI. Pages: 20(8); 21(6, 9, 7, 13); 31(1, 4, 6, 7); 32(5); 39(3); 41(11)

* Cohesion (Res/App):   The quality of elements sticking together. Cohesion exists within a given state of mind as a form of synchronic (in-the-moment) integration. Cohesive states of mind can be highly functional and responsive to the environment, but if they are excessively rigid and not flexible across time, they can lead to dysfunctional reactions. Cohesion unites feelings, thoughts, bodily movements, and interactive tendencies. Pages: xxiv; 28(13); 41(12)

* Compassion (Res/App):   A term with several meanings including "feeling with" another person, sensing another's pain, and even the enacting of behaviors to help reduce the suffering of others (as in an act of compassion). There is also a universal (nondirected) compassion, or a sense of care and concern toward the world of living beings. Compassion can also be toward the self, "self-compassion," and includes qualities of kindness, acceptance, feeling a part of a larger human journey, and letting go of judgments about the self.

Pages: xi; 1(10); 2(3, 5); 3(2, 5); 4(4); 5(4); 6(2, 7); 8(6); 10(1, 7); 11(3); 12(3); 16(2, 5); 18(1); 19(3); 22(2); 24(1, 5); 25(5–7); 28(2, 13); 31(6); 32(5); 33(5); 34(1); 37(8); 38(2, 11, 12, 13); 40(6); 41(3); 43(8, 9)

* Complex system (Res): A collection of elements that (a) is open to influences from outside of itself, (b) changes in a nonlinear way such that small inputs lead to large and unpredictable long-term changes, and (c) is capable of entering chaotic states. Complex systems can be influenced by an emergent, self-organizing process that recursively shapes the flow of the system as it changes across time.

Pages: 1(6, 9); 14(4); 15(2, 9, 10); 16(2–4); 27(6); 28(1, 2); 29(3); 32(4); 34(2, 5); 35(1); 36(26, 40); 38(3); 43(7)

Complexity theory/Chaos theory (Res): Mathematical views of how systems function across time with the properties of self-organization and emergence. A complex system is defined as an open, nonlinear, chaos-capable system.

Pages: 16(4); 34(2)

Concept/Conceptual (or Categorical) representations (Res): Prelinguistic representations that symbolize the mind's creation of ideas, such as notions about the mind itself. They have no direct correlates in the external, three-dimensional world and in this way are more abstract than perceptions of objects. Notions of freedom or of compassion would be examples. See *Representations*.

Connectionist theory (Res): A mathematical view that examines the parallel distributed properties (PDP) of a system and how the impact of these interconnections influences the flow of information. See *Parallel distributed processing*.

★ **Consciousness (Res):** The subjective experience of being aware. It has at least two dimensions: access to information, and the phenomenal or subjective personal quality of an experience. Another way of viewing consciousness is that it has the sense of knowing and that which is known. See also *Awareness*.
Pages: 1(2, 3, 10); 5(2, 3); 7(1); 14(4); 19(6); 21(11); 22(5); 24(4); 26(1–3, 5); 28(9, 11); 29(1); 30(3); 36(18, 19, 21, 22); 39(4, 5); 40(8); 41(4–6, 16); 43(3)

★ **Consilience/Consilient (Res):** The discovery of common findings among independent disciplines (E. O. Wilson, *Consilience*, 1998). Consilience is the intellectual approach to the field of interpersonal neurobiology.
Pages: xiii; 1(5); 9(1); 21(7); 27(1–6); 28(1, 4, 5, 16); 29(3); 30(7); 32(3, 4, 7, 10, 12); 34(5); 36(33); 38(12); 43(2)

Consolidation (Res): The process by which encoded memories are integrated into cortical representations for long-term storage and are then free from dependence on the hippocampus for retrieval. May be a fundamental outcome of dreaming and sleep. Sometimes called "cortical consolidation."
Pages: 37(9, 10)

Constraints (Res): Factors that are modified by complex systems as they balance continuity and flexibility. Constraints are

tex, or neomammalian cortex, this is the outer region of the cerebral hemispheres. It consists of highly folded layers, usually about six cells deep, filled with "cortical columns" of highly linked neuronal clusters. The clusters' communications with other columnar areas allow for more and more complex functions to emerge. The neocortex mediates information-processing functions such as perceiving, thinking, and reasoning.
Pages: 3(3, 4); 5(3, 4); 6(4); 7(2); 9(4); 10(2–6); 11(1–3); 12(3); 13(2–5); 14(1–6); 15(1); 18(3); 19(3); 21(6); 23(3); 25(3); 27(2, 6); 32(10); 34(2); 41(7); F(4, 6)

Cortical columns (Res):   The often six-cell-deep columns of neurons that form the basic microarchitecture of the neocortex.
Pages: 17(3); F(9)

Cortical override (App):   The capacity of the cortex, especially via the prefrontal region, to coordinate and balance the input from the subcortical regions, often inhibiting impulse and emotional dysregulation.
Pages: 3(4); 12(3); 42(8)

Cortisol (Res):   Sometimes known as the "stress hormone," this corticosteroid is released during stress to alter metabolism in an adaptive manner. Prolonged stress may disrupt the functioning of the HPA axis, which regulates cortisol secretion, by way of direct neural impairment and alteration of the regulation of genes that control this important way an individual adapts to ongoing life events.
Pages: 2(3); 7(3); 30(4); 39(1, 2)

★ **Creative (Res/App):**   A way of being in which life

emerges in new and fresh combinations of inner experience and outer explorations.

Pages: xxxviii; 4(5); 14(4); 17(2, 4, 5, 7); 18(2); 22(2); 37(2, 5, 7); 38(10); 43(10)

Cultural evolution (Res/App):   The way culture changes over time, influencing the mind across generations. Cultural evolution is a major force shaping how the brain has developed in modern times, surpassing genetic aspects of evolution.

Pages: 2(5); 5(2); 36(40); 42(6–8)

* Culture (Res):   The social environment in which an individual lives. Culture shapes the context in which energy and information are shared among people by way of patterns of interactions, rituals of behavior, communicative symbols, and structural aspects of the environment.

Pages: 2(4); 5(2); 6(5); 14(3); 19(4); 20(2); 22(2); 26(7); 27(5); 31(2); 32(2, 11); 36(41); 38(12); 42(3–6)

Default mode (Res):   The resting state of brain function that is present when an individual is given no task to perform. The circuits involved in the default mode link widely separated regions to one another, and are hence integrative circuits.

Pages: 15(7, 8); 16(3); 32(10); 37(9)

Defenses (App):   Reactions of the mind to reduce states of dysfunction. Defenses are often automatic (enacted without conscious intention), can be learned and become traits of a person's personality, and can also have evolutionary origins as "animal defenses," such as the dorsal dive.

Pages: 12(2); 19(4); 24(5); 31(5); 36(37); 39(4, 5)

relationship attachment in which there is no organized strategy to the return of the parent in the Infant Strange Situation. Thought to be associated with parental frightening, frightened, or in other ways terrifying behaviors that induce a "biological paradox" in the child in that one set of survival circuits drives the child to move away from the source of terror while the other attachment circuit motivates the child to seek comfort and protection from the attachment figure. This is the go-away/go-toward response to a terrifying individual that leads to an internal sense of fragmentation and the developmental outcome of dissociation. Mary Main and Erik Hesse and colleagues were instrumental in identifying and illuminating the nature of disorganized attachment.
Pages: 20(7); 21(4, 5, 10–13); 31(3); 32(12); 39(2, 4)

Display rules (Res):   The learned ways of regulating the expression of emotion in a culture or a family.
Pages: 11(4)

★ Dissociation/Dis-association (Res):   The process by which usually associated processes are dis-associated or compartmentalized from one another. Clinical dissociation can result in blocked access to memory and emotions, bodily numbness, or impairments to the continuity of consciousness across states of mind (this was first described by Jean Charcot in the 19th century).
Pages: 21(5, 11); 32(12); 39(4, 5)

Divided attention (Res):   The splitting of attention in which one stream is in focal, conscious attention and encodes both explicit and implicit memory while a second nonfocal stream registers elements of the experience only into implicit

memory storage. Nonfocal attention involves the regulation of information flow (attention) but not within awareness, and therefore it is thought to not activate the hippocampus needed for explicit memory encoding.
Pages: 7(3, 4); 10(2); 26(2); 30(4); 37(8)

DNA (Res): Deoxyribonucleic acid, the basic form of molecule that makes up our genetic material. DNA makes up our chromosomes and is twisted into a double helix spiral within the nucleus of the cells of the body.
Pages: 8(4)

* Domains of integration (App): Specific areas of an individual's life that can be the focus of intervention to promote well-being in the brain, relationships, and mind. Domains of integration include consciousness, bilateral, vertical, memory, narrative, state, interpersonal, temporal, and transpirational.
Pages: xxix; 2(5); 4(6); 15(10); 16(7); 26(1); 32(12); 38(2); 39(5, 7); 41(1–17); 43(9); F(14)

Dorsal (Res): Refers to the back as opposed to the front.
Pages: 12(2); F(4)

Dorsal dive (App): Refers to the activation of the dorsal branch of the primitive vagal nerve in which blood pressure and heart rate both drop when a sense of helplessness arises and a flaccid freeze or feigned death response is engaged. Can lead to fainting.
Pages: 12(2)

Dorsal branch of the vagal nerve (Res): The unmyelinated branch of the vagal nerve that is part of the parasympathetic system with major functions of regulating organs below

our diaphragm (e.g., the intestines for digestion). Also involved in the primitive "shut-down" response and fainting.
Pages: 12(2)

Dorsolateral prefrontal cortex (Res): Also known as the lateral prefrontal cortex, this region is thought to be a primary center for focal, conscious attention because it links to activities in other regions of the brain.
Pages: 5(4)

Dualism (Res): A term used to designate how the mental aspect of reality is separate, or in a "dual reality," from the bodily aspect of reality.
Pages: 4(3)

Dyad (Res): A pair of individuals. Dyadic regulation is the way the interaction between two people regulates the internal state of the individuals, as with an infant and attachment figure.
Pages: 2(3, 4); 32(11, 12)

Dyadic regulation (Res): The regulation of internal states of arousal or affect by means of attuned communication that helps modify the internal state of one or both individuals in a pair.
Pages: 15(3); 20(3)

★ **Dysregulation (Res):** The inability to attain proper coordination and balance within a system (body, mind, group), leading to excessive arousal or insufficient arousal that are both outside a window of tolerance. Dysregulation is an outcome of impaired integration.
Pages: 2(4); 7(4); 20(3); 40(4); 41(7, 11); F(8)

Earned secure attachment (Res):   The present state of mind of attachment that is secure despite having had a history of challenging attachment relationships early in life. "Earned" aspects of security are often learned from new relationships and from reflection that makes sense of one's own life history.
Pages: 41(13)

Ecphoric sensation (App):   A feeling that a recalled memory is accurate whether or not it is. Ecphoric sensations give the signal that something is coming from the past. Déjà vu may be an example of a neurologically activated ecphoric sensation in the absence of accurate recall.
Pages: 30(3, 4, 6); 41(9, 10)

Ecphory (Res):   The process of reactivating explicit memory when there is a match between retrieval cue and memory representation.
Pages: 30(3)

Elaboration of arousal (App):   Brain processes that assess whether a stimulus is "good" or "bad" and that determine whether an organism should move toward or away from the stimulus, and whether action or no action should be taken.
Pages: 32(1, 2, 8)

★ Embodied (App):   Of the body.
Pages: xxv; 43(8) and throughout text.

Embodied brain (App):   A perhaps redundant phrase that is intended to remind us that the "brain" is in fact thoroughly interconnected with the body as a whole, by way, for example, of the peripheral and autonomic nervous systems, the endocrine and immune systems, and signals from the physiological processes of the whole body.

Pages: xxv; 1(9); 2(4); 4(6, 7); 8(2, 3, 4, 9); 22(4); 27(4); 28(2, 5, 12–14); 34(3); 36(8, 11, 40); 38(1, 6); 40(6, 7); 43(8)

⋆ Emergence or emergent/Emergent process or property (Res): An ongoing process arising from the interactions of a complex system's basic parts. Emergence is a property of certain systems that makes the whole greater than the sum of its parts.

Pages: 1(1, 3–7, 9); 4(1, 2, 3, 7); 16(2, 5, 8); 17(2, 3, 6, 7); 18(3); 24(4); 28(9, 10, 12, 15, 16); 29(2, 5, 6); 31(6); 32(4); 34(3); 36(3, 10, 12, 19, 32, 34, 40); 37(1); 38(2); 42(2); 43(7, 8)

⋆ Emotion (Res): Changes in the state of integration. Within the brain, emotion links various systems together to form a state of mind. It also serves to connect one mind to another. Emotional processing prepares the brain and the rest of the body for action, to "evoke motion." See also *Primary emotions* and *Categorical emotions*.

Pages: xxxiv; 1(3); 2(4); 3(3); 7(2); 10(4); 11(2); 12(1); 13(2, 3); 16(8); 17(2); 19(3); 20(3); 21(7); 23(3); 24(2); 25(3); 26(2); 29(5); 30(2, 4, 5); 32(1–12); 33(3–5); 34(5); 35(3, 4); 36(1, 5, 30); 38(6, 8); 39(7); 40(1, 2, 5, 11); 41(4); 42(2); 43(3); F(15)

⋆ Emotion regulation (Res): Research on emotion often reveals that emotion as a process is, in fact, fundamentally regulatory and so this term may be somewhat redundant. Seeing emotion as a "shift in integration" helps us see how regulation is fundamental to what "emotion is," given that integration is a core mechanism of regulation. Areas of the brain involved in

emotion regulation are integrative, and they link widely separate regions with one another. See *Affect regulation*.
Pages: 2(4); 6(3, 4); 11(2); 13(2); 14(3); 21(11); 25(2, 3); 32(1, 11); 37(8); 38(6); 39(4); 43(10)

Emotional and social intelligence (Res): Mental skills that enable an individual to understand the impact of emotion on behavior and thinking, to regulate emotions and behavior, to understand the importance of emotions in others, and to understand social interactions and engage in adaptive ways with others in social situations. A capacity to envision and shape the mind, to have mindsight, is thought to be at the root of emotional and social intelligence.
Pages: 6(4); 11(2, 4); 20(10); 22(3, 4); 38(12); 43(4, 11)

Emotional balance (Res): The movement of an individual's internal and interpersonal lives such that the states of arousal attain enough intensity so that life has meaning, but not too much arousal for life to become chaotic or too little arousal for life to become rigid and depleted. Emotional balance is one of the outcomes of middle prefrontal integration.
Pages: 3(4); 6(3, 4); 10(6); 20(5); 27(2); 40(8)

Emotional communication (Res): The sharing of internal affective states, with words but often more directly through the nonverbal signals of eye contact, facial expression, tone of voice, gestures, posture, and timing and intensity of response. Beyond simply the communication of categorical emotion, the alignment of states inherent in emotional communication is a fundamental mechanism of this form of interpersonal connection.
Pages: 18(2)

Emotional operating system (Res): An assembly of evolutionarily and functionally linked circuits that mediates particular affective states, such as anger, sadness/separation distress, and fear.
Pages: 13(3)

Empathic joy (App): The positive feeling of taking joy in the joy of others, in feeling pleasure in their pleasure, and feeling pride for their accomplishments. Feeling good about another's well-being.
Pages: 18(2); 40(11)

★ **Empathy (Res):** A term with many definitions. Empathy is described as the ability to see the world through another's person's perspective (cognitive empathy) and to feel another person's feelings (emotional empathy). One can imagine what it is like to be another person (empathic imagination) and also to put oneself in another's shoes (empathic identification). These various definitions of empathy can overlap with the use of the term *compassion*, but they generally are more about understanding and perspective than about being driven to help another reduce suffering.
Pages: xxxvii; 2(3); 3(4); 6(2, 4, 6); 10(3, 5); 11(3); 19(3, 6, 7); 22(3); 23(3); 25(3, 6, 7); 27(2–3); 31(6); 34(6); 36(14); 37(8); 42(5); 43(4, 10)

★ **Encoding (Res):** The process by which neural activation during experience alters synaptic strengths.
Pages: 5(4); 7(2–4); 10(4); 13(1–3); 15(5); 21(8); 29(4); 30(2–7); 31(3, 4); 39(5); 41(10)

★ **Energy (Res):** A term from physics that means the "capacity to do something." Energy comes in various forms, such as

kinetic, thermal, nuclear, electrical, and chemical. The nervous system functions by way of the flow of electrochemical energy.
Pages: xxii; 1(1, 6–10); 2(1); 4(2); 8(2); 10(4); 11(1); 15(2); 19(1); 23(4); 28(2–5, 8, 10, 11); 29(2); 34(1); 36(2, 31–33, 37); 37(3); 38(7); 39(1); 40(9); 43(5, 6)

* Energy and information flow (App):   The movement across time of energy and the swirls of energy that have symbolic value, that stand for something other than the pattern of energy flow alone. Energy and information can flow within the body (an embodied mechanism) and are transferred between people in relationships (sharing). The mind can be viewed as an emergent process that arises in the form of self-experience (subjectivity) and self-organization (regulation) as energy and information flow within and between people.
Pages: xxvi; 1(1–11); 2(1); 3(1); 4(1); 5(3); 7(1); 8(6); 9(3); 10(1); 11(1, 2); 12(2); 14(3); 15(3, 4); 16(1); 18(1); 19(4); 20(6); 21(11); 22(1); 23(1); 24(4); 27(4); 28(1–17); 29(2); 30(7); 32(4); 33(2); 34(1, 3); 36(3, 4, 10); 37(1); 38(1); 39(6); 40(6); 42(2); 43(2, 5–8), F(7)

Engram (Res):   The initial impact of an experience on the brain; the encoding of a new memory.
Pages: 30(6)

* Epigenesis (Res):   The process in which experience alters the regulation of gene expression by way of changing the various molecules (histones and methyl groups) on the chromosome.
Pages: 8(5–7); 14(3)

Episodic memory (Res):   The encoding, storage, and retrieval of a sense of self as experienced in one specific episode of time. See also *Autobiographical memory*, which is sometimes

considered to be composed of searchable collections of episodic memories.
Pages: 13(1); 30(3, 6); 41(9)

Eudaemonia (Res):   The ancient Greek term for a life of well-being that has connection, meaning, and equanimity.
Pages: 40(2–3)

★ Executive functions (Res):   The key functions attributed to the prefrontal regions; these include the regulation of attention, emotion, memory, behavioral response, and planning.
Pages: 6(4); 14(4); 20(10); 25(2, 3); 28(16)

Experience–dependent (Res):   The form of neural growth in which novel experience induces the activation of genes to create the proteins that result in new synapse formation or synapse strengthening.
Pages: 8(3)

Experience–expectant (Res):   The form of neural growth in which synapses grow based on genetic information and the maintenance of these synapses relies on the exposure of the organism to "expected" stimuli, such as light, sound, or caregiving. The lack of such stimuli leads to the loss of these genetically established connections.
Pages: 8(3)

★ Explicit memory (Res):   During memory recall, this layer of memory is coupled with an internal sensation of remembering. There are two forms: semantic (factual) and episodic (with repeated episodes being called autobiographical). The encoding or deposition of explicit memory requires focal, conscious attention. Without focal attention, or with the excessive release of the stress hormone cortisol, items are not encoded explicitly but are encoded implicitly.

Pages: 5(4); 7(2, 4); 13(1, 3); 15(4–6); 30(2–6); 34(6); 36(24); 39(5); 41(9, 10)

★ **Explicit mental processes (App):**   Energy and information flow patterns that are manifest in ways that, when in awareness, are sensed as part of mental experience directly. These include the explicit mental activities of thought, emotion, memory and perception, and the related experience of explicit mental representations. They are actually on a continuum with implicit mental processes, such as mood, mode, and intention, which are lower on the probability curves in the plane of possibility.

Pages: 1(2); 36(23–30, 33, 38)

★ **FACES (App):**   An acronym for the movement of an integrated system with the qualities of being flexible, adaptive, coherent, energized, and stable.

Pages: 15(10); 16(3, 7); 17(1, 5); 32(5, 6); 34(1); 37(3); 38(2); 41(3)

Fear modulation (Res):   The regulation of fear that may involve inhibitory fibers from the middle prefrontal regions downward to the fear-processing limbic amygdala.

Pages: 6(4); 27(2)

Feeling felt (App):   A fundamental sensation for when another person senses accurately what one is feeling inside of oneself.

Pages: 19(6); 23(1); 38(11)

Fight-flight-freeze (Res):   The basic survival set of reactions mediated by the brainstem in response to threats and associated with increased sympathetic tone. A complex defense system, it

integrates motor actions with increases in sympathetic activation to generate the necessary energy to respond to a threat, including the tensing of muscles in the freeze reaction (often a preparation for subsequent fleeing).
Pages: 3(3); 10(3); 11(1); 12(1, 2); 14(6); 18(4, 5); 24(6); 39(4, 5); 41(8)

Flashback (Res):   The experience during a recollection of a traumatic event that one is reexperiencing portions or the whole of that event without a sense that something is coming from the past. May be explained by the notion of implicit-only activations that lack an ecphoric sensation when not integrated as explicit memory representations.
Pages: 30(5); 41(9)

Flashbulb memory (Res):   The clear recollection of a commonly experienced event shared by many individuals. The "flashbulb" designation refers to the notion that a camera flashed at a collective moment in time can became an important engram within a group of individuals. Reveals the relational nature of our memory systems.
Pages: 13(2)

Flexibility of response (App):   See also *Response flexibility*.
Pages: 6(4); 23(3); 27(2); 33(1–5); 43(10)

★ Flow (Res):   The change or movement of something across time. Also, the term "flow" refers to the state of being immersed in an activity and losing one's sense of self-consciousness as the boundaries of self and activity become permeable and one gets lost in an experience.
Found throughout the text.

Focal attention (Res):   Attention with awareness.
Pages: 7(1–5); 13(3); 15(7); 26(3); 28(15); 30(2, 4)

Fragmented sense of self (App):   An internal sense of discontinuity and rupture. Found in disorganized attachment and the experience of dissociation. May also be present in unresolved trauma and grief.
Pages: 21(5); 21(11, 13); 39(4)

Frontal lobes (Res):   The front of the cerebral cortex, sometimes called the "associational cortex" in that it makes linkages among widely interconnected processes fundamental to higher thinking and planning.
Pages: 10(4–5); 14(3)

Frontal release (Res):   The process of shutting down the frontal areas of the cortex, especially the prefrontal regions, that then permits lower areas to act without inhibition.
Pages: 3(4)

Generosity (App):   A positive attitude of kindness, abundance, and openheartedness.
Pages: 37(6, 7); 38(13); 40(6); 43(11)

Genetic expression/Expression of genes (Res):   The process by which information on the chromosome, contained in a gene, is transcribed into RNA and then translated into proteins by the ribosome such that changes in anatomic structure can be created. For the nervous system, gene expression leads to synaptic growth. Epigenetic factors regulate gene expression.
Pages: 2(3–4); 8(4, 6–8); 9(2); 14(3); 16(7); 20(4); 39(4, 8)

Giving back (gifting or giving back) (App): A behavior of reaching out to others and extending help in the service of bringing positive change into their lives.
Pages: 37(6); 38(13); 40(6); 43(11)

Glial cells (Res): As fundamental cells of the nervous system, including oligodendrocytes and astrocytes, these cells number in the trillions, are generally smaller than neurons, and carry out a number of functions. Though we say that they "support" neurons through myelin production and regulating blood flow, science is just beginning to discover the many ways glial cells may influence energy and information flow through the nervous system.
Pages: 8(4, 5, 6)

Gratitude (Res/App): An attitude of appreciation and thankfulness for others, for ourselves, and for life.
Pages: 17(7); 32(5); 36(3, 4); 37(6, 7); 38(13); 40(6); 43(11)

★ Hand model of the brain (App): See *Brain in the palm of your hand.*

★ Health (App): A state of optimal regulation and adaptive functioning of body, mind, and relationships. Good health emerges from integration.
Found throughout the text.

★ Healthy mind platter (App): A visual image depicting daily mental activities that promote optimal mental health.
Pages: 8(9, 10); 25(4, 7); 36(15); 37(1–10); 38(11); 40(10); 43(10); F(12)

Hebb's Law (Res): Based on the proposals of Donald Hebb, this notion considers that the firing of neurons at one time will increase the likelihood of their firing together in the future.

Sometimes paraphrased as "neurons that fire together, wire together." It parallels Freud's Law of Association.
Pages: 9(2)

* **Hemispheres (Res):**   Refers to the left and right sides, or "half-spheres," of the brain, especially the neocortex. The left hemisphere develops later, and it specializes in ways of being and perceiving that involve linear, linguistic, logical (cause-effect relationship seeking, syllogistic reasoning), literal, and list-making characteristics (notice all the "l"-based words!). In contrast, the ways of being and perceiving that the right hemisphere dominates in are early development, holisticness, nonverbal reactions, visuospatial imagery, metaphoric meaning, context sensing, stress-response mediation, autobiographical memory and reflection, and an integrated map of the whole body. Both hemispheres tend to work together, but these differentiated dominances help the whole, when linked, to achieve more complex functions.
Pages: 9(4); 11(3, 4); 14(6); 15(6, 7); 17(4); 21(9); 36(25, 36); 38(2, 6); 41(6); F(5)

Hijacking (App):   A term used with states in which lower regions become aroused in a nonfunctional way that leads to the shutting down of higher cortical functions. Sometimes called "emotional," "amygdala," or "bottom-up" hijacking. See also *Low road*.
Pages: 10(6)

* **Hippocampus (Res):**   Located in the central part of the brain, this seahorse-shaped structure is a part of the medial temporal lobe limbic area. The hippocampus plays a central role in flexible forms of memory, in the recall of facts and autobiographical details. It gives the brain a sense of the self in space

and in time, regulates the order of perceptual categorizations, and links mental representations to emotional appraisal centers.
Pages: 6(4); 7(2, 3); 10(4); 13(1, 3); 15(4–7); 30(2–4, 6); 39(3, 4); 40(4); 41(9, 10); F(4)

Hypothalamic-pituitary-adrenocortical (HPA) axis (Res): This system responds to stress and its function over time and can be adversely affected by trauma.
Pages: 2(3); 39(4)

Hypothalamus (Res): Located in the lower region of the brain, near the pituitary, it is responsible for physiological homeostasis as a master hormone regulator.
Pages: 11(1); 13(2)

Immobilization defense reactions (Res): An alternative to the fight-flight-freeze response, this second, very ancient, defense system is associated with behavioral shut down, fainting, and feigning death. Activated in response to life threats and unavoidable harm, this system may be a central mechanism in dissociative reactions to trauma and appears to depend on the physiological consequences of activation of the unmyelinated dorsal vagus nerve.
Pages: 12(2); 39(4, 5)

Implicit knowing (App): The sense of the meaning of an experience in the present or in the past within memory that is "known" without words but is within conscious experience. Implicit is not the same as nonconscious but rather has the sense of an innate, preverbal knowing that is timeless in that it lacks a sense of the origins from which the knowing has arisen. Implicit knowing lacks an ecphoric sensation and can be a part

of the retrieval of implicit memory, or it can be an ongoing meaning-making process in the present.
Pages: 1(2); 39(6)

★ **Implicit memory (Res):**   Involves parts of the brain that do not require conscious, focal attention during encoding or retrieval. Perceptions, emotions, bodily sensations, and behavioral response patterns are all examples of implicit layers of processing. Mental models (schema or generalizations of repeated experiences) and priming (getting ready to respond) are basic components. Implicit memory in its nonintegrated form lacks a sense that something is being recalled from the past.
Pages: 7(2–4); 13(3); 15(4–6); 30(2–4, 6); 31(4); 36(24); 39(3, 5); 41(9, 10)

★ **Implicit mental processes (App):**   Mental activities, such as moods, intentions, stances, and modes, that shape our perceptions, feelings, thinking, and memory without a sense of these influences having origins within the mind. Are on a continuum with explicit mental processes.
Pages: 1(2); 35(4); 36(24–30, 33, 38); 39(6); 40(9)

Infant Strange Situation (Res):   The research measure of an infant's attachment to his or her caregiver that determines the child–parent relationship category of attachment; originally formulated by Mary Ainsworth. The assessment measures the infant's behavior upon reunion with the attachment figure following a brief set of separations.
Pages: 21(5, 7, 9–11)

★ **Information (Res/App):**   Patterns of energy that carry meaning and "stand for" or symbolize something other than the energy itself. Information is itself a verb in that it gives rise to

further processing in cascades of associations and linked meanings that emerge over time.
Found throughout the text.

★ **Information processing (Res):** A transformation of energy flow patterns that alters, reorganizes, and interconnects its symbolic value and emerging meaning over time. Aspects include selecting, sorting, segmenting, shifting, grouping, categorizing, comparing, contrasting, coalescing, transfiguring, labeling, associating, and recombining.
Pages: 5(2); 8(3); 17(4); 28(4); 32(7); 35(4); 36(4, 16, 21, 23, 31, 38); 43(3)

★ **Insight (App):** An inner sense of knowing. Specifically used as one of the middle prefrontal functions that involves self-knowing awareness, or autonoetic consciousness, which links the remembered past with the lived present and the imagined future.
Pages: 3(2, 4); 6(4); 10(3, 5); 12(2,3); 18(4); 19(2); 20(5); 21(7); 22(3); 27(2); 28(2); 30(4); 36(14, 26, 32)

Instantiation (Res): The activation of a process.
Pages: 36(38); 41(3); 42(5)

★ **Insula (Res):** A structure in the middle prefrontal cortex that links bodily processes to higher cortical areas. Information from the body moves up the spinal cord's Lamina I and the vagal nerve and reaches the brainstem and then the insula. First the dorsal, then the anterior insula seem to be involved in the process of interoception (awareness of internal bodily sensations). Its direct link to other middle prefrontal areas, such as the anterior cingulate, by way of spindle cells has been associated with forms of self-awareness.
Pages: 6(4); 11(2–4); 19(3, 6, 7); 23(2, 3); F(4)

* Integration (Res/App): In general, the linkage of differentiated elements. The mind's process of linking differentiated parts (distinct modes of information processing) into a functional whole is postulated to be the fundamental mechanism of health. Without integration, chaos or rigidity ensue. Integration is both a process (a verb) and a structural dimension (a noun) and can be examined, for example, in the functional and anatomic studies of the nervous system.
Found throughout the text.

* Integrative communication (App): When individuals are honored for their differences and become linked through respectful and compassionate communication.
Pages: 1(10); 2(5); 3(4); 4(4); 18(1–6); 19(2, 6); 20(10); 21(9, 12); 27(3); 28(16); 34(1, 4, 6); 43(8)

* Intention (Res): A mental state that primes the brain to function in a certain way. Intention is a stance or readiness of an individual to carry out certain goal-directed actions. Intention creates patterns of behavior in predictable sequences that are then detected by another individual (by way of a postulated mirror neuron and superior temporal sulcus system) to create a map of "the other's intention" inside of the self.
Pages: xxiii; 1(1); 3(2, 5); 6(2, 3, 6); 7(1, 2, 4); 9(4); 12(4); 14(4, 5); 15(7); 17(2); 19(2, 3); 20(3); 23(5); 24(5); 25(1, 2, 5, 6, 7); 26(3); 27(5); 28(12, 17); 29(6, 9); 30(6); 35(1, 2, 4); 36(1, 3, 7, 11, 23, 27, 28, 30, 33, 36, 41); 38(5, 7); 39(6); 40(3, 9, 10); 41(5); 43(3, 8)

Interactive repair (Res/App): The process by which two or more individuals communicate following a rupture in their connection in order to reestablish the integrative nature of their relationship.
Pages: 20(3)

models and expectations for future interactions. These "working models" are open to potential change throughout the life span.
Pages: 20(2, 3); 21(2, 3)

★ Interoception (Res): The perception of the interior of the body, our "sixth sense," including signals emerging from Lamina I of the spinal cord that derive from muscles, bones, and viscera (heart, lungs, intestines) of the torso of the body. May precede the ability to know what we are feeling, to become aware of shifts in internal bodily states that influence our affective arousal. This awareness seems to involve action of the right anterior insula in the prefrontal cortex and is correlated with the capacity for empathy for the feelings of others.
Pages: 11(2, 4, 5); 19(6); 23(3); 25(7); 26(2); 28(10); 36(14); 37(7); 40(8)

★ Interpersonal attunement (Res/App): The way one person attunes in an open and empathic way to the internal state of another.
Pages: 6(5, 6); 21(6); 23(1, 2, 5); 25(3, 5); 34(1–4)

★ Interpersonal neurobiology (IPNB) (App): A consilient field that embraces all branches of science as it seeks the common, universal findings across independent ways of knowing in order to expand our understanding of the mind and well-being. Sometimes abbreviated as IPNB, this field explores the ways in which relationships and the brain interact to shape our mental lives. IPNB is meant to convey the embracing of everything in life from society (interpersonal) to synapses (neurobiology).
Found throughout the text.

Interpersonal resonance (App): The way two or more

minds align their states and become mutually influenced by one another.

Pages: 19(6, 7); 23(1–3); 28(13); 34(4)

Intersubjectivity (App): The shared experience created in the joining of two or more minds, revealing how the whole is greater than the sum of its parts. Intersubjective experience cannot be reduced to simply two subjectivities being added together; this is an example of interpersonal resonance.

Pages: 23(1)

Intraregional/Interregional integration (Res): The linkage of components within a region (intra-) or between regions (inter-) of the brain. In the left hemisphere of the brain, for example, vertical integration among interconnected cortical columns within the same region allows for a detailed assessment of a single mode of representation (for example, when a perceptual representation matches a linguistic category in the production of carefully defined words).

Pages: 17(4)

* Intuition (App): A term that denotes the nonlogical knowing that emerges from the processing of the body, especially the parallel distributed processors of the neural networks in the heart and intestines that send their signals upward, through the insula, to regions of the middle prefrontal cortex.

Pages: 1(2); 3(5); 6(4); 11(4); 27(3)

Invariant representations (App): Mental models, or schema, that summarize repeated experience and form a top-down filter of present-moment sensations that bias perception based on aspects of memory.

Pages: 30(2)

Join (App): To become part of a larger whole.
Pages: 15(9, 10); 18(2); 19(5, 7); 23(1, 3, 5); 36(37); 37(2); 38(13); 41(4)

Joint attention (Res): The shared focus of attention on an object or idea by two or more individuals.
Pages: 18(2); 36(35)

* Kindness (App): The visible, natural outcome of integration. Positive regard for others, compassionate intention, and acts of extending oneself in the service of others are all manifestations of the differentiation and linkage of selves within a larger "we" at the heart of being kind. Involves honoring and supporting the vulnerability of others and the self.
Pages: 1(10); 6(4, 5); 25(4–6); 27(5); 28(2); 34(6); 37(6, 8); 38(11, 12); 40(6); 42(5); 43(11)

Kinesthetic (Res): A process involving the feeling of movement.
Pages: 28(2); 39(6)

* Lamina I (Res): A layer of the spinal cord that carries data from the body upward to the skull-encased brain.
Pages: 10(6); 11(1–5); 23(3)

Laterality (Res): The finding that many functions are predominant on one side or the other of the brain.
Pages: 10(7); 14(6); 36(25)

Law of Association (App): Sigmund Freud's proposal that simultaneously experienced events will become associated with each other in memory, published prior to Donald Hebb's similar postulate that stated the notion of "neurons that fire together, wire together."
Pages: 9(2)

Left mode (App):   An implicit mental process that is shaped by the neural functioning of the left side of the brain and includes a dominance in linear, linguistic, and logical processes. See also *Right mode.*
Pages: 36(24–26, 36, 41); 37(8); 38(2); 41(6, 7, 11)

Left shift (Res):   The finding from affective neuroscience research and especially the work of Richard Davidson that mindfulness meditation is associated with an increase in the baseline electrical activity of the left frontal region of the brain. The left shift has been interpreted as indicating an enhanced "approach" state in which challenging stimuli are held within awareness versus a right dominant frontal activity that is associated with withdrawal.
Pages: 22(3); 25(3); 37(8)

* Limbic regions (Res):   Located in the central part of the brain called the medial temporal lobe, these areas include the amygdala and hippocampus, which coordinate input from the higher cortical regions, with streams of input from the lower brainstem and the body proper. Limbic structures integrate a wide range of mental processes such as appraisal of meaning, processing of social signals, and the activation of emotion. The limbic area evolved during our mammalian evolution and is thought to be essential for attachment.
Pages: 3(3, 4); 5(3); 6(4); 7(2); 9(5); 10(2, 3, 6); 11(1); 12(1); 13(1–5); 14(1, 2, 6); 18(4); 19(3, 7); 23(2, 3); 27(2); 30(2); 32(10); 36(25); 41(6, 8, 9); F(4, 5, 6)

Linguistic representations (Res):   The way the brain encodes information about sensations, perceptions, concepts, and categories within socially shared language.
Pages: 11(4)

★ Linkage (Res):   The connection of separate components to each other. Linkage can be both functional and structural and can involve the exchange of energy and information.

Pages: xxxii, xxxvii; 1(10); 2(5); 3(2, 5); 4(3, 6); 5(4); 7(2); 8(2, 4, 6); 10(3); 11(2); 13(4); 14(2); 15(5, 6, 9, 10); 16(1, 7, 8); 18(1, 2); 19(5, 6, 8); 20(3); 25(3); 26(1); 27(1, 2, 3, 6); 28(16); 32(4, 5, 7, 10, 11, 12); 33(5); 34(1, 4, 5); 35(2, 3); 36(31); 38(2, 3); 40(2, 4, 5, 6, 8); 41(1, 2, 3, 7, 10, 12); 43(9); F(13)

Long-term potentiation (LTP) (Res):   Refers to a way that the firing of neurons strengthens their synaptic connections to one another and increases the probability the pattern will be repeated. This is one process by which experience leads to structural changes in the linkages among neurons during the encoding of events into long-term memory.

Pages: 7(2)

Lost in familiar places (App):   A propensity of the mind to recursively seek out situations that are filled with patterns of energy and information flow that resemble past environments. When such situations are echoes of a nonideal past, this becomes a process that can create a self-fulfilling prophecy, reinforcing old ways of being and "creating one's own worst nightmare."

Pages: 17(6); 19(5); 31(5); 33(3); 35(2)

Low road (App):   The state of "flipping one's lid" so that the integrative middle prefrontal functions become temporarily disabled and chaos and rigidity may ensue. The terms "emotional hijack" and "amygdala hijack" refer to a similar process whereby lower limbic and brainstem areas flood higher ones and take over functioning of the individual in a dysfunctional manner.

Pages: 3(4, 5); 10(6, 7); 17(6)

★ **Making sense (App):** A process of sorting through memory, here-and-now experience, and imagination such that we create a coherent picture of the essence of what is occurring in our lives. Making sense can be seen as an integrative process, linking past, present, and potential future in a way that enables these elements of thought, feeling, memory, and imagination to situate us in a social world of experience.
Pages: 22(3); 31(1, 4, 6, 7); 39(1–8); 41(11, 13)

★ **Me to we (App):** A phrase denoting the need to move a sense of identity from being dominantly centered on the self as limited to the boundaries of the body to an expanded self-identity that also includes the sense of being a member of a larger whole.
Pages: 40(7); 42(1–8)

★ **Meaning/Meaningful (App):** A term with multiple "meanings" that refers to a range of important mental dimensions of our lives such as the significance of an event, the outcome and consequence of an experience, making sense and understanding something, and the truth of something. The meaning of something in the brain can be recalled with the mnemonic ABCDE: the various associations, beliefs, cognitions, developmental phases, and emotions that arise in relationship to a stimulus.
Pages: 1(3, 4, 8); 2(1–3); 3(3); 6(7); 10(4); 13(3,4); 14(6); 15(8); 19(1,8); 20(2,3); 28(3); 31(2,4); 32(4–7, 11); 36 (4, 26); 37(10); 39(3, 6); 40(1–11); 41(8); 42(4,5); 43(3,5)

Meditation (Res): A practice of focusing attention in various ways that strengthens the mind. There are numerous forms of meditation.
Pages: 6(2); 8(8); 25(1); 26(5); 37(8)

* Memory (Res): The way past events affect future function; the probability that a particular neural network pattern will be activated in the future. See also *Implicit memory* and *Explicit memory*.
Pages: 1(1,2); 3(3); 5(4); 7(2–4); 9(1,5); 10(4, 5); 13(1–3); 14(6); 15(7); 17(3, 4); 18(5); 21(8, 10, 11); 24(3, 7); 28(12); 29(4, 9); 30(1–7); 31(1, 3, 6); 32(5); 34(6); 35(3); 36(2, 4–6, 24–26, 30, 32, 38); 37(4, 9); 39(5–7); 41(7, 9–11); 43(9); F(14)

* Mental activity (Res/App): The dynamic processes that are a part of the fundamental descriptions of our mental lives and shape how information is transformed. These include emotion/feeling, thinking, perception, planning, meaning-making, and memory encoding, storage and retrieval. Mental activities also involve imagery, beliefs, hopes, dreams, attitudes, intentions, and desires. A mental activity may be distinguished from the process of being aware, of the subjective sense of knowing within consciousness. A mental activity also can generate a mental representation. Some mental activities can be described as explicit in that we readily know that they are impacting us. Other mental activities, such as attitudes and intentions, may be described as implicit mental processes in that we may not realize that a mental process is influencing us in the moment.
Pages: 28(6, 10, 14); 29(6, 9); 30(7); 36(2–4, 8, 12, 17, 18, 27, 29, 30, 31, 36, 37); 37(7); F(10)

* Mental health (Res/App): A term denoting both a state of well-being of the mind and a field of study and clinical practice. In practice, the absence of symptoms or of meeting criteria for a mental disorder is sometimes used as the default position for describing what mental health is, given that an accepted definition of this state is generally not clearly offered in many

branches of this important field of study and practice. In interpersonal neurobiology, mental health is viewed as emerging from integration in the brain/body and in relationships. The mind as a self-organizing, emergent, embodied, and relational process moves the system toward integration and a sense of resilience, harmony, and vitality. See *COHERENCE* and the *Middle prefrontal cortex.*
Pages: 1(4); 4(4); 6(5); 16(6); 22(4); 25(4); 27(3); 29(10); 32(10); 36(15); 38(4, 5, 8, 10); 40(9); 41(1); 43(1)

Mental model (Res):   A generalization of repeated experiences; also known as a schema.
Pages: 6(1); 20(3, 8); 21(2, 9); 30(2, 3); 31(4); 36(30, 31, 38); 41(9); 42(3)

★ **Mental processes (App):**   The whole of our mental lives that includes subjective experience, awareness, mental activities, modes of information processing, and representations.
Found throughout the text.

Mental space (App):   The openness to possibilities enabling a pause before acting on a thought, behavioral impulse, or emotional reaction. If the mind is seen as a self-organizing, emergent process of energy and information flow, then "mental space" refers, literally, to the distribution of probabilities that are embedded within the full range of possible energy patterns. Mental space, then, is the opening of probabilities in a movement toward the plane of possibility, a shift that overlaps with the metaphor of the hub of the wheel of awareness. See also *Space of mind.*
Pages: 13(5); 33(2); 36(4, 8)

Mental time travel (Res):   A term coined by Endel Tulving to designate the capacity to link the remembered past, present

experiences, and the anticipated future. This is also known as autonoetic consciousness, or self-knowing awareness.
Pages: 10(5); 39(5); 41(10, 14)

★ **Mentalize/mentalization (Res):**   The ability to understand other people's minds as a form of metacognition. It is also related to theory of mind, mind-mindedness, mind-perception, psychological mindedness, reflective function, and aspects of mindsight.
Pages: 2(3); 21(6, 13); 22(3, 4); 34(4, 5); 36(16); 41(11); 43(4)

Metacognition (Res):   I never met a cognition I didn't like. This is a form of "thinking about thinking" that starts developing in the early years of life, and it includes learning about the distinction between actual reality and the appearance of reality ("the appearance-reality distinction"); the fact that feelings influence thinking and behavior (part of "emotional intelligence"); how knowing what you believe and perceive and what I believe or perceive may both have validity but be different ("representational diversity"); and how what one knows at this moment may change in the future ("representational change").
Pages: 43(3)

★ **Middle prefrontal cortex (App):**   Consists of medial and ventral prefrontal, orbitofrontal, and anterior cingulate cortices. The neural circuits in this interconnected set of regions function to integrate the processing of social information, autobiographical consciousness, the evaluation of meaning, the activation of arousal, bodily response, and higher cognitive processing. Nine middle prefrontal functions include body regulation, attuned communication, emotional balance, fear modulation, flexibility of response, insight, empathy, morality, and intuition. These are the outcome of mindfulness meditation practice. Also, the first eight are outcomes of secure attachment relationships.

Pages: 3(4); 6(4, 5); 10(3, 5, 6); 11(1, 2, 3, 5); 13(3); 14(5); 19(3, 4, 7); 20(10); 21(6); 23(3); 25(3); 26(75); 27(1–7); 33(2, 3); 34(2, 5); 38(12); 42(5); F(4)

★ **Mind (Res/App)**:   Includes at least three fundamental aspects: personal subjective experience, consciousness with a sense of knowing and that which is known, and a regulatory function that is an emergent, self-organizing process of the extended nervous system and relationships. In this way, a core aspect of mind is defined as an embodied and relational process that *regulates* the flow of energy and information.

Found throughout the text.

★ **Mindful awareness/Mindful (Res)**:   Awareness of present-moment experience, with intention and purpose, without grasping on to judgments. Traits of being mindful are having an open stance toward oneself and others, emotional equanimity, and the ability to describe the inner world of the mind.

Pages: 6(1–7); 7(4); 11(4); 13(5); 14(5); 17(3–5); 18(5); 19(6); 21(6); 22(3, 4); 23(2); 24(7); 27(6); 36(22, 23); 37(8); 39(8); 41(4, 5); F(11)

★ **Mindful awareness practice (App)**:   A skill-building training that focuses attention on intention and the cultivation of awareness of awareness. Repeated and regular practice has been shown to strengthen the ability to regulate emotion and attention, improve empathy and insight, promote healthy immune functioning, move the electrical activity of the brain toward a "left shift" of approaching challenging situations, and increase the activity and growth of regulatory and integrative regions of the brain. Examples of mindful awareness practices

include mindfulness meditation, centering prayer, yoga, and tai chi chuan.
Pages: 25(1–7); 27(7); 36(27); 40(10); 41(5)

* Mindsight (App): The ability to perceive the internal world of the self and others, not just to observe behavior; to have a perception of the inner world of minds. It is the way we not only sense but also shape energy and information flow within the triangle of the mind, brain, and relationships. Mindsight is the ability to monitor energy and information flow in the body and in relationships and then to modify that flow toward integration.
Pages: 2(3); 10(5); 21(6, 13); 22(1–5); 23(1); 24(6); 27(7); 34(4–6); 36(27, 35); 38(11, 12); 43(4–6, 9, 11); F(3)

* Mindsight maps (App): Creating representations of the mind by the mind. Three such mindsight maps are of "me" (insight), "you" (empathy), and "we" (morality and a sense of belonging to a larger whole).
Pages: 10(5); 14(4); 27(2, 3); 36(14, 15, 25, 35); 41(11, 16); 43(4)

Mirror neurons (Res): A set of neurons that is distributed in various regions of the brain and that has both motor and perceptual functions. Mirror neurons become activated at the perception of behaviors of others with predictable sequences that enable related areas (the superior temporal sulcus) to create maps of another's intentional state. Mirror neurons then enable both behavioral imitation and internal simulation of the other. The proposed mechanism of mirror neurons is supported by a number of investigations but some scientists feel it is not substantiated yet.
Pages: 11(3); 19(2, 3, 6, 7); 23(2, 3)

* Mode/modality (App): An organizational process of the brain that links similar representation modules into a mode, such as those involving visual perception to form the visual mode. Modes or modalities can themselves be coordinated to form a "system," such as a cross-modality perception linking vision with hearing. A related term is *module*, a set of neural circuits carrying a certain type of (usually localized) information and using a similar form of neural signal or code. Modules can be linked together to form a mode; modes come together to form a system. *Mode* can also be used to signify an implicit mental process, such as the left mode or the right mode, that shapes our mental activities.
Pages: 5(2); 15(7, 8); 16(3); 32(10); 36(2, 3, 11, 24–26, 36); 37(9); 41(6, 7, 11)

* Mood (Res/App): The general tone of emotions across time that creates a bias in the system toward certain categorical affects. Mood shapes the interpretation of perceptual processing and gives a "slant" to thinking, self-reflection, and recollections.
Pages: 1(2); 24(1); 25(3); 26(3); 28(6, 12); 29(7–9); 30(6); 32(2); 35(3); 36(2, 3, 11, 24, 27, 35); 39(6); 41(11)

* Morality (Res/App): The capacity to imagine, reason, and enact behaviors on behalf of a larger social good. It may require the ability of an individual to make a mindsight map of "we."
Pages: 3(4); 6(2, 4); 10(3, 5); 27(3)

Mutual regulation (App): The bilateral influence of two people upon each other's coordination and balance of internal states.
Pages: 15(3)

Myelin (Res): The fatty sheath created by glial cells that insulates the long axonal lengths of neurons such that the speed of

neuronal firing is increased by 100 and the resting or refractory period is decreased by 30 times. The result of practice, myelin thus increases the effective communication among interconnected neurons by 3,000 times, creating the enhanced functioning necessary for skill building.
Pages: 8(5, 6); 14(2, 3)

Myelinogenesis (Res):   The creation by glial cells of the myelin sheath around interconnected neurons.
Pages: 8(5)

Name it to tame it (App):   The finding that placing a linguistic label on an internal or external process can help calm the mind and stabilize attention so that one can perceive with more clarity into the nature of an experience.
Pages: 21(13)

★ Narrative (Res):   The linear telling of a sequence of events. Narratives entail a focus on action and on the mental states of the individuals of the story, including the self or narrator.
Pages: 5(4); 9(4); 14(3, 5); 15(6); 17(6); 20(8); 21(6–11, 13); 30(3); 31(1–7); 32(5); 39(3, 5, 6); 41(10–11); 42(3); 43(9); F(14)

★ Neglect (Res):   The lack of care-taking of a child's emotional, social, and physical needs, which results in significant impairment in the growth of the child's brain.
Pages: 4(5); 8(7); 9(3); 16(3, 5); 38(2); 39(3); 40(4)

Neocortex (Res):   See *Cortex.*

★ Nervous system (Res):   The entire set of interconnected neural cells, including neurons and glia, that extends throughout the whole body and that function, in part, by the electrochemical energy flow across the distributed system. Immune, cardiovascular, gastrointestinal, and endocrine systems as well as social interactions directly influence its functions. Includes the skull-based brain as part of the central nervous system as well as the peripheral and autonomic nervous systems.

Pages: xxi, 1(5); 2(3); 3(1–3); 4(1); 5(3); 8(6); 9(3); 14(6); 15(2, 7); 16(6); 18(5); 19(7); 20(6); 21(10); 22(2); 23(1); 27(2, 4); 28(2); 32(1); 34(1); 36(14, 31); 39(2); 40(6); 41(6); 43(8); F(7)

Neural correlates (Res): Neural firing patterns associated in time with some process, such as thinking or consciousness.

Pages: 5(3); 26(7); 36(5, 18); 41(8)

★ Neural firing (Res): The activation of neurons involves the flow of energy in the form of electrical movement of ions in and out of the neural membrane and chemical transformations as neurotransmitter release and receptor engagement at the synapse. Neural firing can lead to subsequent activation or inhibition of the downstream neurons. See *Action potential.*

Pages: xxii, 1(8); 3(5); 7(5); 8(1, 3–5); 9(1–53); 10(4, 6); 14(4–5); 15(3, 4); 17(3); 21(2); 28(8); 29(1, 4, 5–6, 7); 30(1); 34(2); 35(2); 36(6, 7, 9–15, 18, 20, 24, 26, 27, 31); 37(9); F(11, 15)

★ Neural integration (Res/App): Linkage of differentiated neurons within the brain. It results in optimal self-regulation with balance and coordination of disparate regions into a functional whole.

Pages: 3(4); 4(5); 6(5); 15(6); 20(11); 27(3); 34(3); 37(9); 38(2); 40(4); 41(5)

★ Neural map (Res): A pattern of neural firing that represents something, such as a memory, bodily sensation, or perception.

Pages: 10(4, 6); 14(1); 19(2, 3)

Neural net profile (Res):   The recruitment of various activated neuronal circuits into a localized process such as a memory representation or more globally into a state of mind.
Pages: 35(1)

Neural network (Res):   A set of interconnected neurons.
Pages: 11(4)

Neural pathways (Res):   The functional linkage of neural circuits.
Pages: 7(4); 14(3)

Neurobiology of we (App):   The neural underpinnings of how an individual can experience the sense of joining that moves "me" to "we."
Pages: 19(1–8)

Neurogenesis (Res):   The production of new neurons from neural stem cells that can occur in certain regions such as the hippocampus of the brain across the life span.
Pages: 8(5–6); 14(2)

★ Neuron (Res):   A basic type of cell in the nervous system. It is composed of a cell body, receiving ends called dendrites, and a long axon that reaches out to other neurons at a synaptic linkage.
Pages: 1(8); 3(5); 7(2, 5); 8(1–6, 10); 9(1–5); 10(4); 11(2); 12(1); 14(2–4, 6, 7, 10); 15(1); 16(7); 17(4); 28(2–3, 8); 29(1); 30(1, 2); 32(2); 35(2); 36(31)

★ Neurons that fire together, wire together (Res):   A commonly used saying that refers to the way in which simul-

taneously activated neurons will become more likely to fire together in the future because of the synaptic linkages created during this event. See *Law of Association*; *Hebb's Law*.
Pages: 3(5); 7(5); 9(1–5); 16(7)

* Neuroplasticity (Res): The overall process with which brain connections are changed by experience, including the way we pay attention.
Pages: 3(5); 4(5); 6(4); 8(1–10); 9(3, 4, 5); 14(2); 36(7); 40(6, 10); 42(3); 43(10)

Neurotransmitters (Res): Chemicals released at the ends of neurons that diffuse across the synapse and activate the downstream neurons' receptors.
Pages: 8(2); 15(1); 20(6); 28(3)

No state (App): This is the state of mind often created, at least initially, in response to hearing "no" repeated several times; For many, this is a reactive state of mind that can engage various aspects of the fight-flight-freeze response.
Pages: 18(4, 5)

Noesis (Res): A way of knowing that can include semantic knowledge as well as nonconceptual knowing; it is the sense we have of knowing about the world and about ourselves.
Pages: 31(6)

* Nonconscious (App): Processes that are not a part of awareness or conscious experience in the moment.
Pages: 7(1); 19(5); 24(2); 30(4); 36(18, 19, 27)

Nonjudgmental awareness (Res): The state of being aware

without being swept up by prior expectations, which is at the heart of mindful awareness and likely a parental trait with secure attachment.
Pages: 6(1, 2)

Nonlinear dynamical systems (Res):   Complex systems (ones that are open and capable of chaotic behavior) that have three major features: self-organizing properties; nonlinearity (meaning that small initial inputs can lead to large and unpredictable long-term outcomes); and emergent patterns with recursive characteristics.
Pages: 16(2)

★ **Nonverbal (Res/App)**:   The nonlinguistic signals that include eye contact, facial expressions, tone of voice, posture, gestures, and the timing and intensity of response. Primarily sent and received by the right hemisphere of the brain.
Pages: 2(2); 10(6); 11(3); 13(4); 19(3, 6); 32(1); 36(25, 26, 36); 39(6); 41(6, 8); 43(7)

No-yes procedure (App):   The simple activity of saying "no" harshly several times (seven is good), then pausing and stating "yes" in a pleasant, soothing tone several times. This procedure provides an experiential immersion within our different states of mind in that it evokes a reactive state for no and a receptive state for yes.
Pages: 18(4–5); 41(8)

Open systems (Res):   A cluster of entities that have a functional linkage (a system) that is influenced by factors outside of the system.
Pages: 16(2, 5); 18(5); 38(3); 40(4)

Orbitofrontal cortex (Res):   A part of the prefrontal cortex

just behind the eyes, this important region is molded by relational experience and interacts with other aspects of the middle
prefrontal cortex in shaping attachment and self-awareness.
Pages: 6(4); 13(3); 27(2); F(4)

Parallel distributed processing (PDP) (Res):   The ability of a system such as the spider-web-like constructed brain to
simultaneously process different types of stimuli across different
neural networks in a rapid and highly complex manner. PDP
processors, animate or inanimate, can learn from experience.
Pages: 15(3); 35(1)

Parasympathetic nervous system (Res):   One of two
branches of the autonomic nervous system. The parasympathetic
branch is inhibitory and de-arousing, producing, for example,
decreases in heart rate, respiration, and alertness. Involves aspects
of the vagal nerve. See also *Sympathetic nervous system*.
Pages: 15(2)

Parcellation (Res):   The pruning of synaptic connections.
Also called *apoptosis*.
Pages: 9(2)

★ **Peak (App):**   In the plane of possibility, a peak is the
visual depiction of 100% certainty, as in a particular thought or
memory.
Pages: 29(8–10); 30(1, 5–7); 33(3–4); 36(8, 11, 16–18, 21–23, 27–30,
35, 38–41); 40(8, 9, 10); F(11)

★ **Perception (Res):**   The process by which external stimuli
are received and organized within representations of ongoing
experience. Can occur without consciousness but has impacts
on internal meaning and external behaviors.

Pages: 7(2); 11(3); 13(1, 3); 14(3); 17(3); 19(2); 28(6); 29(9); 30(2); 36(2, 5, 9, 13, 14, 19); 38(6); 40(3); 41(5, 9); 43(4)

Perceptual representations (Res): A percept represents a constructed bit of information created from the synthesis of present sensory experience with past memory and generalizations contained in experientially derived mental models. It is the essence of top-down processing in that what we perceive is shaped by what we have experienced in the past.
Pages: 36(16)

★ Plane of possibility (App):   The visual depiction of energy and information flow patterns that are in the zero probability (infinite possibility) phase of energy shifts. The plane can be directly experienced in the hub of the wheel of awareness practice. Arising from the open plane are plateaus of increased probability and peaks of particular activations that represent, respectively, moods or intentions and other mental activities such as emotions, images, memories, or thoughts.
Pages: xxix; 26(7); 28(12, 14); 29(1–11); 30(1, 5, 6); 36(8, 16, 18, 19, 20, 22, 27, 28, 37); 40(7, 11); F(11)

★ Plateau (App):   In the plane of possibility, the plateau is a visual depiction of increased probability as energy flows.
Pages: 29(7–10); 30(1, 5–7); 33(3, 4); 36(8, 11, 21, 23, 24, 27, 28, 29, 35, 38, 40–42); 40(7–11); F(11)

Polyvagal theory (Res):   A theory posited by Stephen Porges in which humans have an autonomic nervous system consisting of three circuits: a sympathetic nervous system and a parasympathetic nervous system that contains two vagal circuits. The three circuits respond in a hierarchical manner based on their phylogenetic (evolutionary) emergence. The newest circuit is uniquely mammalian and mediated by a myelinated vagal circuit linking the neural regulation of the face and heart to form an integrated social engagement system. The social engagement system inhibits the older circuits that evolved to provide the neural platforms for defense strategies in more primitive species. The social engagement system, by dampening defense systems and the "stress" response, is associated with a receptive state that enables the individual to efficiently and enjoyably interact with others. The sympathetic nervous system supports defense strategies associated with reactive behaviors of fight-flight-or-freeze. The phylogenetically oldest circuit is mediated by an unmyelinated ancient vagal circuit associated with shut-down behaviors, dissociative experiences, and fainting. "Neuroception" is the process posited by this theory that suggests that we continually evaluate, without awareness, the context of a situation for its inherent threats to survival and match the body's physiological state with social engagement, fight-flight-freeze, or shut-down behaviors.

Pages: 12(2)

* **Prefrontal cortex (Res):** Central to the process of creating meaning and emotion and enabling a flexibility of response, it sits at the interface between lower regions (brainstem and limbic areas) receiving input from the body and higher regions (the cortex) involved in integrating information. It includes the dorsolateral prefrontal cortex, ventral areas such as the insula, and medial structures such as the orbitofrontal cortex, the ventromedial prefrontal cortex, and, in some views, the anterior cingulate cortex.

Pages: 3(3, 4); 5(4); 9(4); 10(5, 6); 13(3); 14(1–2); 18(3); 27(6); 32(10)

⋆ Preoccupied attachment (Res): The adult state of mind with respect to attachment associated with a child's having an ambivalent/resistant attachment and characterized in the Adult Attachment Interview as being filled with intrusions from leftover issues from the past.

Pages: 21(9–10, 13); 31(3)

⋆ Presence (App): A way of being open, receptive, and ever emerging in our states of being as we connect with others and with our inner world.

Pages: 2(1); 17(2, 3, 4, 6); 18(3); 20(5); 24(5); 36(23); 38(10); 41(12)

Presymbolic representation (App): A neural net profile of activation from sensory input that is "as close to the input" as possible with a minimum of top-down influences from prior experience. See *Sensory representation*.

Pages: 43(7)

Presynaptic/Postsynaptic (Res): Refers to the position of neurons in their synaptic linkage either before or after the synapse.

Pages: 8(2)

Primary emotions (App): The shifts in brain state that result from the initial orientation and elaborated appraisal and arousal processes. Primary emotions are the beginning of how the mind creates meaning. They are not to be confused with categorical, or basic, emotions. See also *Emotion*; *Categorical emotions*.

Pages: 32(2)

Primary experience (App): The direct felt sensation before conceptualization and words and before top-down influences of the past shape perception.

Pages: 23(4, 5); 24(3); 25(6); 36(32); 43(7)

★ **Prime (App):** An irreducible aspect of something. Heads and tails (and the edge) are primes of a coin. Similarly, subjective mental experience can be considered a prime in that it cannot be reduced into neural firing. Neural activity, with ions flowing and neurotransmitters being released, is not the same as our mental lives of subjective experience and awareness. These two aspects of reality—brain and mind—are certainly related, but they are not equivalent.

Pages: 4(3); 28(7–9, 13–15); 29(1); 32(3); 36(6, 10, 11, 13, 31, 33, 40); 43(2); F(11)

Prime/Primed/Priming (Res): Making ready, making more likely.

Pages: xxxvi; 7(2); 19(3); 20(11); 30(1, 2, 4); 33(3, 4); 36(27); 37(3); 41(9)

★ **Probability patterns (App):** The distribution of shifts in probability that energy flow makes as it moves from openness (infinite possibility, zero probability) to probability (enhanced likelihood) to certainty (100% probability). These probability patterns are represented in the model of the plane of possibility and describe how the self-organizing aspect of mind can shape energy flow within the body and within relationships; the patterns are reflected in this model within both subjective experience (above the plane) and in neural firing patterns (below the plane).

Pages: 16(2); 28(10–12,); 29(1, 2, 6–10); 30(6, 7); 36(10, 12, 13, 17, 20, 21, 23, 28, 29, 32, 33); 40(7, 9, 10); F (11)

Procedural memory (Res): A form of implicit memory for motor behaviors.
Pages: 30(3)

★ **Process (Res):** An action or set of actions that alters the state or condition of something. Virtually everything related to mind is a process.
Found throughout the text.

Prosody (Res): Variations in vocal tone in contrast to speaking in an invariable or monotonic way. Includes rhythm, intonation, pitch, inflection, volume, tempo, resonance, intensity, and cadence (crescendos and decrescendos).
Pages: 19(6)

Prospective memory (Res): How the mind attempts to anticipate the future on the basis of what has occurred in the past. This can also be called "memory for the future."
Pages: 10(5)

Proximity seeking (Res): Behaviors engaged in order to get close (physically, mentally) to another person to enhance a sense of feeling connected, secure, and safe. Attachment relationships are based on healthy proximity seeking, especially during times of distress, to soothe and comfort states of uncomfortable arousal. Proximity seeking allows for dyadic regulation of affect.
Pages: 20(3); 21(5, 9)

Psyche (App): A dictionary definition includes the synonyms of soul, spirit, intellect, and mind.
Pages: 43(4)

Psychopathology (Res): A term referring to disturbances of the psyche or the mind.
Pages: 16(5); 27(1); 34(2)

Psychotherapy (Res): The relational process by which the mind is the focus of clinical intervention.
Pages: 3(6); 5(3); 9(3, 4); 10(1); 22(2); 26(5); 29(1, 4); 30(5); 31(5); 34(2); 36(40); 38(12)

R's of education (App): Beyond the first three R's of reading, 'riting, and 'rithmetic, educational programs can embrace a new three R's of reflection, relationships, and resilience. Cultivating these three basic aspects of looking inward, supporting the importance of relationships with other people and the planet, and honing the emotional skills of being resilient are each a part of an internal education.
Pages: 9(4); 22(5); 23(4); 27(6); 43(1)

Reactive state (App): The state of fight-flight-or-freeze in which an individual is reacting with a sense of threat and is no longer receptive and open to input from others in a flexible way.
Pages: 12(2); 18(4); 19(2); 20(6); 21(4); 24(5, 6)

Receptive state (App): The state of being open in a flexible way to input from outside of oneself, as opposed to being in a reactive state.
Pages: 16(5); 17(3); 18(4, 5); 23(1, 2); 24(1); 28(13); 33(5); 36(8, 40); 37(8); 38(13); 40(11); 41(5); F(11)

Receptor (Res): The area of the postsynaptic neuronal membrane that receives the neurotransmitter released by the

presynaptic cell, leading to the activation or deactivation of the ensuing action potential.
Pages: 8(2); 28(3); 36(13, 14)

Recruitment (Res):   A process that temporarily links distinct, differentiated elements into a functional whole. Emotions recruit distributed neuronal clusters to fire together within a cohesive state in the moment.
Pages: 35(1–2)

★ **Recursive (Res):**   The quality by which processes feedback on themselves to reinforce their own patterns of activation.
Pages: 1(6, 9); 17(6); 19(5); 28(15); 29(5)

★ **Reentry (Res)**:   A process by which positive feedback loops reinforce the initial patterns of activity, as in neural firing in the brain or in communication patterns within relationships. Reentry recursively stabilizes a neuronal firing pattern in that moment and allows for the subjective awareness of the processing to become a part of conscious experience. Reentry also occurs in interpersonal relationships as it reinforces patterns of functional, or dysfunctional, communication—the sharing of energy and information flow—as they become embedded in interactional habits within a family.
Pages: 29(6)

★ **Reflection (App):**   Focusing attention on the inner mental experience of self or others. Sensing the inner states of mind of another alters our own inner state. Therefore, looking toward our own inner world serves as the source of empathy for others' mental experience. Hence, reflection is both an inner and interpersonal gateway to insight, compassion, and empathy.
Pages: 6(5); 9(4, 5); 15(8); 18(5); 21(2, 7, 9, 12); 22(4); 23(4); 25(6); 27(6); 28(7); 31(5); 37(4, 8); 41(11); 43(1, 11)

this is a sensory mechanism with which we sense our connection to others or entities outside of our bodily defined self. The first five senses bring in the outside world (sight, hearing, smell, taste, touch); the sixth sense is our interoception with which we sense the inner states of the body (muscles, bones, viscera like the heart, lungs, and intestines); a "seventh sense" with which we sense our mental activities; and this eighth sense.
Pages: 18(6); 26(3, 7); 41(5)

* **Relationships (Res/App):**   The patterns of interaction between two or more people that involve the sharing of energy and information flow. Can also more generally involve the patterns of interaction between two or more entities. Donald Winnicott's notion that a baby only exists in relationship to the mother highlighted the concept of a "good enough parent."
Found throughout the text.

* **Remembering (Res):**   In brain terms, the construction of a new neural net profile with features of the old engram and elements of memory from other experiences as well as influences from the present state of mind. The subjective mental experience of recollection can involve explicit ways of remembering the past with a sense of awareness of something coming from memory, or it can be implicit and influence feelings, thoughts and behaviors without a sense of something coming from the past.
Pages: 1(2); 8(3); 13(1); 16(1); 30(1); 36(4, 9, 16, 17, 23, 26, 28, 33)

* **Repair (Res/App):**   Establishing integrative communication after a rupture.
Pages: 3(5); 10(7); 20(2, 3); 24(1–7); 33(5); 37(9); F(8)

* **Representations (Res):**   This term can be used for neural representations (neural net profiles that symbolize something)
or for mental representations (the subjective experience of the
known within awareness). Patterns of neural firing that correlate
in time with mental symbols; a way of symbolizing various types
of information about outer and inner worlds. Different types of
representation are processed in different parts of the brain.
Pages: 2(1); 7(2); 10(4); 19(3); 20(3, 8); 21(2); 30(3); 36(1–6, 8, 9,
11–18, 21, 23, 26, 28, 31, 34, 36, 38); 38(6); 39(5, 6, 7); 40(3); 41(6,
10, 14); 43(7)

* **Resilience (Res):**   The quality of being able to effectively
adapt to stressors.
Pages: 6(3, 6); 9(3, 4); 20(11); 21(7); 22(3, 4); 23(4); 27(6); 37(8, 10);
38(10); 40(5); 41(7); 43(1, 5, 9, 11)

* **Resonance (Res/App):**   The mutual influence of interacting systems on each other that allows two or more entities to
become a part of one functional whole.
Pages: 19(3, 6, 7); 23(1, 3); 28(13); 34(4)

* **Resonance circuits (App):**   Interconnected neural
regions that enable a person to tune in to others and align his
or her internal states with those of another person. The resonance circuits include the mirror neuron system and superior
temporal sulcus that detect predictable sequences and map
intention; the insula that brings information down from the
cortex to the limbic areas; and the brainstem, and the body
proper, including the viscera and muscular responses. Then
these lower inputs arise through the Lamina I of the spinal
cord and the vagus nerve to reach to the anterior insula, anterior cingulate, and then to other areas of the middle prefrontal

cortex (especially medial prefrontal and possibly orbitofrontal areas) where mindsight maps of "me," "you," and "we" are constructed.
Pages: 19(6, 7); 23(2, 3)

★ **Response flexibility (App)**:   The ability to respond flexibly and creatively to new or changing conditions instead of responding automatically and reflexively. Mediated by the middle prefrontal cortex, it allows the individual to pause and put a space between impulse and action.
Pages: 27(2); 33(1–5)

Responsive (Res):   The behavior of a parent with sensitivity that promotes secure attachment.
Pages: 20(2); 34(4)

Reticular activating system (RAS) (Res):   A traditional neuroscience term signifying a collection of brainstem nuclei (clusters of neurons) that has input into the cortex and influences "states of arousal" or wakefulness and that in contemporary ways is considered as influencing degrees of activation in regions of the brain involved in attention and cognition.
Pages: 12(1)

★ **Retrieval (Res)**:   The process of reactivating a neural firing pattern that is similar to, but never identical with, the engram first encoded during an experience.
Pages: 7(2); 15(5); 30(2–7); 31(3); 39(6); 41(9, 10)

Retrograde amnesia (Res):   An inability to access memories that were laid down before a traumatic incident.
Pages: 15(5)

Right mode (App): An implicit mental process that is shaped by a dominance of the neural activity of the right side of the brain and which includes holistic, nonverbal, visuo-spatial, autobiographical, mindsight map-making, subcortical input with an integrated map of the whole body. Also see *Left mode*.

Pages: 36(24, 25, 36, 41); 41(6, 7, 11)

* Rigidity (App): Inflexible states that are completely predictable and unchanging.

Pages: 4(4, 5, 6); 7(5); 15(9, 10); 16(3–7); 17(1, 2); 32(5, 10–12); 33(1–5); 36(26, 37); 37(3); 38(3); 39(7); 40(10); 41(1–3, 7); F(13, 15)

* River of integration (App): A visual metaphor for the central stream of integration that is harmony and a FACES flow of being flexible, adaptive, coherent, energized, and stable. The two banks outside this flow are of chaos and of rigidity.

Pages: 4(5); 16(3); 17(1–7); 33(2); 38(2); 40(5, 10); 41(3); F(13)

* Rupture (Res/App): The disruption of attuned, integrative communication between two people. Successful reparation of ruptures can build coping skills and establish internal resources for adaptive functioning.

Pages: 3(4); 10(7); 20(3); 24(1–7); 33(5)

* Secure attachment (Res): The relationship a child has with a sensitive, attuned caregiver. Also used to signify an adult's state of mind with respect to attachment in which there is a coherent narrative that makes sense of the past.

Pages: 6(5); 20(3, 5, 11); 21(6); 22(3, 4); 23(1); 25(4); 27(6); 32(12); 34(4); 41(13)

Secure base (Res): The sense an individual has that an attachment figure will be a reliable source of security and safety.
Pages: 20(3)

★ **Self (Res/App):** A term signifying an internal sense of identity, sometimes including one's body, personality, or membership in relationships or groups. There are many "selves" of a healthy individual. The self is often seen as a singular noun, whereas it may be better considered as a "plural verb." Includes functions of the self, such as a somatic, linguistic, emotional, reflective, and social self.
Found throughout the text.

★ **Self-awareness (App):** Conscious access to aspects of the experience in the moment and autobiographical memories. See *Autonoesis/Autonoetic consciousness.*
Pages: 11(2, 4); 19(4, 6); 25(7)

Self is a plural verb (App): The self can be seen as an ever-emerging process that arises in connection to many elements, including our relationships with others. "Self-identity" through this lens views the bodily defined, skin-bounded sense of self as only one aspect of what the whole self entails.
Pages: 15(8)

Self-knowing awareness (App): See *Self-awareness*; *Insight*; and *Autonoesis/Autonoetic consciousness.*
Pages: 19(6); 23(3); 27(2); 39(5)

★ **Self-organizing/Self-organization (Res):** An emergent process of a complex system that shapes its unfolding across time. This is a fundamental property of complex systems that arises from the interaction of elements of the system, not something that is programmed into the system's functioning. Self-organization moves the system to "maximize complexity," which can be viewed as arising from the linkage of differentiated aspects of a system. Self-organization toward integration is experienced as harmony and coherence: It is the flexible, adaptive, coherent, energized, and stable (FACES) movement of the system across time.

Pages: 1(1, 4, 6, 7, 9, 10); 4(2); 16 (3, 4); 22(5); 24(4); 28(12); 29(3); 32(4); 36(19, 32, 40); 37(1, 3); 38(6); 40(9); 43(7)

★ **Self-regulation (Res):** Processes that maintain the functioning of the individual in optimal ways.

Pages: 8(8); 16(5, 6); 20(7, 10, 11); 25(3); 28(16); 34(1–6)

Self-states or specialized selves (App): Repeatedly activated states of mind that, over time, become specialized, goal-directed sets of cohesive functional units. Human development is filled with the growth of multiple self-states, such as those with the need to be social and those requiring solitude. A healthy life is filled with a multiplicity of selves.

Pages: 25(4); 25(4); 35(1); 41(7)

Semantic memory (Res): A form of explicit memory dealing with facts.

Pages: 13(1); 41(9)

Sensitivity (Res): Term used in attachment research to denote the tendency of a parent to attune, make sense, and respond to the internal world of the child as he or she communicates through signals that may be nonverbal or verbal.

Pages: 20(2); 34(4)

Sensorimotor (App):   The integration of the sensory and motor systems of the body.
Pages: 39(6)

Sentience (App):   The experience of feeling; the capacity to sense; having a subjective core of sensation.
Pages: 38(11, 12)

★ Shame (Res/App):   A state of mind filled with a sense of the self as being defective. The physiology of shame can create heaviness in the chest, nausea in the belly, and the avoidance of eye contact with others. One view of the developmental origins of shame posits that when in need of attunement during states of heightened arousal—such as in joy or in distress—the lack of attuned response from others can induce the physiological state of shame and its accompanying cognitions of the self being "damaged goods."
Pages: 3(5); 24(2–6); 31(6); 32(2, 8); 39(4); 40(5)

★SIFT (App): An acronym that stands for sensation, image, feeling, and thought. An accessible term that helps people to remember to reflect on their inner mental lives by "SIFTing" the mind with an inward focus of attention.
Pages: 25(2); 37(8); 40(11)

★ SNAG (App):   Stands for "stimulate neuronal activation and growth." An acronym for how focused attention can intentionally alter synaptic connections in the brain.
Pages: 7(5); 9(1–5); 16(7); 25(5)

Social brain (Res/App):   The term used to designate aspects of the brain that are directly involved in social interactions or to the notion that the brain as a whole is the social organ of the body.
Pages: 19(7)

Social cognition (Res): The mechanisms by which social interactions are processed by perception, thought, and behavioral interaction. Deficits in social cognition result in difficulties understanding the meaning of social processes, including challenges to interpreting and sending subtle forms of nonverbal communication and seeing from another's point of view.
Pages: 13(2); 38(3); 40(4)

Social engagement system (Res): A set of circuits in the brain that includes the ventral vagal nerve, which activates receptive interactive behaviors to connect with other people.
Pages: 18(5)

Social neuroscience (Res): A subdivision of the field of neurobiology or neuroscience, which in turn is a division of the field of biology, that is focused on the ways in which a neural function is a substrate for and correlated with social interactions. This field is not the same as interpersonal neurobiology, which is a consilient approach that embraces all fields of science and finds the universal principles across the often-independent divisions of knowledge and offers this synthesis for practical application in a broad range of activities to cultivate understanding and well-being.
Pages: 27(1)

Social referencing (Res): Looking to the facial expressions and other nonverbal aspects of another, such as a parent, to determine how to feel and respond. Joint referencing, in contrast, is the mutual attention to a third object that arises, for example, when you point your finger at something and other people know you are indicating for them to look not at your finger, but at the object of interest. Both joint attention and social referencing

imply an awareness or sense that another person has an internal state, a mind filled with intention, attention, and feelings that are important and something to focus attention upon.
Pages: 18(2)

Social reward system (Res): A basic motivational drive to make contact with other individuals in a meaningful manner that activates the dopamine system and rewards the behavior.
Pages: 18(2)

Social synapse (App): Louis Cozolino's term for the ways in which our social connectedness harnesses the evolutionarily constructed social brain to form information transfer across our relationships. Social synapse is to communication between individuals as neurotransmitter release following an action potential is to neurons across the synapse. Both involve energy and information sharing: electrochemical energy for the neural synapse and light/kinetic (sight, hearing through the motion of air molecules, and the physical contact of touch) for our social synapse.
Pages: 18(2)

Somatic maps (Res): Representations in the brain of the physiological state of the rest of the body. A secondary somatic map is formed by the anterior insula from primary maps in the dorsal insula and allows us to not only be aware of the body's signals, but to pause and reflect on the body's input (interoception) and then do something to intentionally modify it. Antonio Damasio focuses on the ways in which these maps influence prefrontal functions and our emotional experience.
Pages: 19(3)

Space of mind/Spacious mind (App): The condition of the mind in which there is a pause before action, a "reflec-

tive space" in which inner processing can precede outwardly directed action. The "space" referred to here is a probability space, a function of the modulation of energy flow that moves mental life away from immediate action in certainty to an open "plane of possibility." See also *Mental space.*
Pages: 13(5); 24(6); 26(3–4); 41(9)

Speechless terror (App): Bessel van der Kolk's term for the loss of speech during a trauma or a flashback in posttraumatic stress disorder; this may reflect a shutting down of Broca's speech area.
Pages: 30(5)

★ **State (Res):** A temporary condition or assembly of activated elements such as neural firing patterns.
Found throughout the text.

State-dependent (Res): The process by which the context—internal and external—influences the functioning of a particular process.
Pages: 30(6)

★ **State of mind (Res/App):** An overall way in which mental processes, such as emotions, thought patterns, memories, and behavioral planning, are brought together into a functional and cohesive whole. A state of mind is shaped by the total pattern of activations in the brain at a particular moment. A state of mind coordinates activity in the moment and it creates a pattern of brain activation that can become more likely in the future. States of mind allow the brain to achieve cohesion in functioning.
Pages: 6(2); 16(1); 20(8); 21(8–10); 24(2, 4, 6); 28(12); 29(7–9); 31(6); 32(1, 2, 8); 33(2, 4); 35(1–5); 36(4, 24, 27, 35); 41(12); F(11)

State of mind with respect to attachment (Res): The phrase used for the present stance an adult takes toward attach-

ment experiences. In the dismissing state of mind, for example, there is a minimization of the importance of relationships.
Pages: 20(8); 21(8, 9)

Still-Face Experiment (Res): Ed Tronick's procedure whereby an infant at about 4 months of age is interacting with her caregiver and then, with a signal from the experimenter, the caregiver stops giving contingent, attuned communication. The baby becomes agitated, makes bids for reestablishing their prior connection, and then may withdraw into self-stimulating efforts to self-regulate. This paradigm painfully and powerfully reveals how the infant's state of being is profoundly dependent upon responsive signals from the caregiver in order to maintain equilibrium. Repair of this disruption is followed by a return of the baby's equilibrium. (See Figure F.)
Pages: 15(3); 20(3); 24(5); F(8)

★ **Storage (Res):** The alteration of a probability of firing of neural net profiles of activation in response to experience following encoding of memory.
Pages: 5(4); 30(2, 6, 7)

★ **Stress (Res):** The internal or external conditions that push the state of an individual away from equilibrium. Some stress is "eustress" and promotes optimal functioning, such as mild anxiety before an exam that can elevate performance. Other stress is harmful because it creates a negative impact on the individual's well-being. Cortisol is the hormone released in response to stress. Stress has been studied by a wide array of researchers, including Hans Selye and Robert Sapolsky.
Pages: 2(3, 4); 8(7); 9(2); 20(4, 6); 30(4); 36(25); 37(4); 39(2–4); 41(6); 42(1)

* **Subcortical (Res):**   Refers to neural regions below the cortex, including the limbic areas and the brainstem in the skull portion of the nervous system, and sometimes also the neural processing of regions in the body proper.
Pages: 3(4); 10(2, 6, 7); 11(3); 12(3); 13(2–5); 14(5, 6); 15(6); 19(3, 7); 23(2, 3); 40(4); 41(7–9)

* **Subjective experience (Res/App):**   The personal sensation of lived experience. This inner sentience is one component of mind; two other components are the sense of knowing within awareness and the self-organizing regulatory aspect of mind.
Pages: xxii–xxiv; 1(1–4, 9, 10); 5(3); 23(5); 24(4); 25(4); 26(8); 27(1); 28(7, 9, 14, 15, 17); 29(1); 31(2); 32(2, 3); 36(2, 6, 7, 10, 12–15, 18); 37(1); 38(6); 40(7, 9); 42(2); 43(2, 3); F(11)

Syllogistic reasoning (Res):   A form of information processing that seeks cause–effect relationships in logical reasoning; it is dominant in the left hemisphere's functioning.
Pages: 23(4); 36(25)

Sympathetic nervous system (Res):   One of two major branches of the autonomic nervous system. The sympathetic system excites and arouses, producing, for example, increases in heart rate, respiration, sweating, and states of alertness. See also *Parasympathetic nervous system*.
Pages: 15(2)

* **Synapse (Res)**:   The linkage between two neurons. The synapse is often a small space between the end of a neuron's axons or dendrites through which neurons communicate with each other by way of the release of neurotransmitters from

the presynaptic neuron and their reception by the receptors embedded in the membrane of the postsynaptic neuron.
Pages: 8(2, 5); 9(2); 14(2); 15(1); 18(2); 28(3); 37(5); 42(3)

* **Synaptic shadows (App):**   The effects of prior learning on present experience. This is the way the past, embedded in our learning-induced synaptic connections, casts shadows or influences shaped by our earlier experiences and that directly impact how we perceive, feel, and think in the present and even how we anticipate, plan, and create the future. These shadows are neither bad nor good; they are simply the "top-down" way that the past shapes present and future.
Pages: 9(4); 14(5); 18(5); 19(2, 5, 7); 21(8, 10, 12); 33(3); 42(3)

Synaptogenesis (Res):   The process by which new synapses are formed. Also may refer to the strengthening of previously existing synapses as a part of synaptic molding.
Pages: 8(5); 14(2)

Synchrony (Res):   The alignment of the functions of two or more differentiated elements of a system. Neural synchrony, for example, is revealed in gamma waves on an EEG that reflect the linkage of differentiated regions of the brain.
Pages: 40(4)

* **System (Res):**   A collection of functionally linked components. *Systems*—in the brain and body, and in our relationships with other people and the planet—are fundamental to mental experience.
Found throughout the text.

* **Temperament (Res):**   The innate, inborn propensities of an individual that are a part of the nervous system's tendencies

of response. Genes play an important role in the determination of temperament.
Pages: 15(9); 20(1, 5, 6, 11); 21(9); 36(40)

Thalamocortical circuit (Res): The interconnections between the thalamus and the neocortex.
Pages: 23(2); 36 (21)

Thalamus (Res): Sits atop the brainstem. It serves as a gateway for incoming sensory information and has extensive connections to other brain regions including the neocortex. Activity of the thalamocortical circuit may be a central process for the mediation of conscious experience.
Pages: 23(2); F(5)

Theory of mind (Res): The ability, developed during the first year of life, to detect that another person has a mind with a focus of attention, an intention, and an emotional state. The theory of mind is a component of the larger capacity of reflective functioning. The right prefrontal cortex plays a central role in mediating this fundamental process that is central to mentalization and mindsight.
Pages: 2(3); 43(4)

★ 3g2p (App): A term signifying how we can bring "three g's to two p's": We bring the generosity of kindness to ourselves and others, a gratitude for life, and an intention and actions focused on giving back in order to help improve the lives of other people and our planet.
Pages: 37(7); 40(6, 10); 43(11)

★ Time-in (App): A term signifying the practice of reflecting inwardly on sensations, images, feelings, and thoughts.

Time-in practices include those that develop mindful awareness and neural integration. One of several "daily mental activities" for well-being.
Pages: 6(6, 7); 8(9); 9(4, 5); 11(4); 13(5); 14(5); 17(6); 18(5); 22(4, 5); 23(1, 5); 25(1–7); 26(7); 27(6); 37(2, 4, 7); 40(10, 11); 43(9, 10); F(12)

★ **Top-down (Res/App):**   This term has several uses. The two most common are (1) processes that arise from anatomically higher areas (such as the cortex) and then influence lower regions (such as the body, the brainstem, and the limbic areas) and (2) processes that are influenced by prior experience, such as memory and perception, as opposed to the direct and instantaneous "bottom-up" processes, such as sensation.
Pages: 5(3, 4); 13(5); 17(3–5, 7); 25(6); 29(4); 30(2); F(9)

Track (App):   Paying close attention to the moment-by-moment experience of another person or of oneself.
Pages: 1(6); 36(37)

Trait (Res):   An enduring characteristic of an individual, influencing patterns of internal reaction or external response. A trait may refer to an inborn aspect of neural firing, such as temperament.
Pages: 6(2, 3); 25(6)

★ **Trauma (Res/App):**   An overwhelming experience that has potential negative impacts on an individual in the moment and in the future. Trauma often refers to an experience that is beyond the capacity for an individual to adapt effectively, and it can result in posttraumatic stress disorder in some situations.
Pages: xxxiv; 4(5); 7(2, 4); 8(7); 20(6); 21(11–13); 26(6); 30(4–6); 31(3); 39(1–8); 41(11)

★ Triangle of human experience/well-being (App): A visual metaphor for three aspects of one reality of human life. The three points of the triangle represent unique facets of energy and information flow: Mind is regulation; relationships are sharing; brain is the embodied mechanism of the flow.
Pages: 4(3); 6(7); 8(2); 15(10); 19(4); 28(12); 29(7); 32(6); 34(3); 36(8); F(7)

Tripod (App): The supportive structure of the metaphoric mindsight camera that enables us to see energy and information flow in the body and in relationship with more clarity, depth, detail, and stability. The three legs of the tripod include openness, objectivity, and observation.
Pages: 1(10); F(3)

Triune brain (Res): Paul MacLean's term for the three major evolutionarily defined sectors of the brain: the old reptilian brainstem, the old mammalian limbic brain, and the new mammalian neocortex. Lower areas develop first, and lower regions "bootstrap" functions derived from the lower areas so that the whole of these three parts are integrated in normal functioning.
Pages: 3(3)

★ Unresolved (Res/App): Refers to that state of lack of resolution of trauma or loss, as in the Unresolved/disoriented Adult Attachment Interview category in which the individual reveals lack of resolution in the disorientation of the narrative emerging in discussion of these issues.
Pages: 21(11–13); 31(3); 39(1, 2, 5–7)

Vagus/Vagal nerve (Res): The tenth cranial nerve that includes an ancient unmyelinated dorsal branch involved in the

shut-down response to life threats or unavoidable harm and a more modern ventral vagus involved in the social engagement system. The two branches of the vagal nerve originate in two brainstem nuclei: the ancient dorsal from the dorsal motor nucleus and the more modern ventral branch from the nucleus ambiguus.
Pages: 10(3, 6); 11(1, 4); 12(2); 23(3)

Ventral (Res):   Refers to the belly side as opposed to the dorsal side (the back).
Pages: 6(4); 27(2); F(4)

Vitality affects (Res/App):   The external expressions of primary emotional states.
Pages: 32(2)

★ **Wheel of awareness (App):**   A visual metaphor of the mind that is also a time-in practice to promote neural integration. The outer rim of the wheel represents that which is the object of attention, such as sight and sound, bodily sensations, emotions and thoughts, and a sense of connectedness to people and things outside of the bodily self. The hub represents the experience of being aware. (This reflective practice can be found at www.drdansiegel.com.)
Pages: xxix; 13(5); 18(6); 23(5); 24(7); 26(1–8); 27(4); 29(1, 7, 9, 10); 30(6); 36(14, 20, 22, 28); 37(8); 40(8); 41(5); F(10)

★ **Window of tolerance (App):**   A span of tolerable levels of arousal in which internal or external stimuli can be processed in a flexible and adaptive manner. Outside of the window for this particular state, the individual moves toward chaos or toward rigidity of response.
Pages: 33(1, 2, 4); 35(3); 36(37); 39(7); 41(7–9); F(15, 16)

★ Wisdom (Res/App): A deep clarity of knowing that has been associated with individuals who have the traits of being focused on the well-being of others and having the capacity to reflect on the inner lives of others and of themselves with kindness.
Pages: 4(6); 6(5); 10(3); 11(4); 25(4); 26(7); 27(3–5), 28(2); 31(2); 32(11); 34(6); 37(6); 38(12); 40(6); 41(8, 9, 16)

Working memory (Res): Holding something in the "front of the mind" for a brief period of time so that the item can be the focus of attention and then be sorted and altered to further information processing.
Pages: 5(4)

Yes state (App): The state of mind created when hearing "yes" repeated several times. This is an open, receptive state of mind that correlates with a relaxed body and an activation of the social engagement system.
Pages: 18(4–5); 24(6); 41(8)

Zone of proximal development (Res/App): A term from the work of Lev Vygotsky that indicates the span between what an individual can accomplish without help (the bottom of the zone) and what he or she can do with assistance from a supportive other, such as a teacher, parent, or therapist.
Pages: 39(6–7)

NODAL NETWORK